The History of the PRC (1949–1976)

The History of the PRC (1949–1976)

The China Quarterly Special Issues
New Series, No. 7

Edited by

JULIA STRAUSS

CAMBRIDGE
UNIVERSITY PRESS

CAMBRIDGE UNIVERSITY PRESS
Cambridge, New York, Melbourne, Madrid, Cape Town Singapore, São Paulo

Cambridge University Press
The Edinburgh Building, Cambridge CB2 8RU, UK

www.cambridge.org
Information on this title: www.cambridge.org/9780521696968

First published 2006 (*China Quarterly* 188 December 2006)
This edition 2007

Printed in the United Kingdom by The Charlesworth Group, Wakefield, UK

A catalogue record for this publication is available from the British Library

ISBN 978-0-521-69696-9 paperback

Contents

Cover illustration:
The Proclamation of the PRC, Beijing, 1 October 1949.
Photograph by Hou Bo.
Reproduced with the kind permission of *China Features*.

Notes on Contributors

ROBERT ASH is professor of economics with special reference to China and Taiwan in the department of economics and the Centre for Financial and Management Studies, and director of the Taiwan studies programme, at the School of Oriental and African Studies, University of London.

DAVID BACHMAN is a professor in and associate director of the Henry M. Jackson School of International Studies at the University of Washington (Seattle, WA). He is currently researching the history of the defence industries in China.

WILLIAM C. KIRBY is the Geisinger professor of history, director of the Fairbank Center for East Asian Research, and former Dean of the Faculty of Arts and Sciences at Harvard University. His work studies China's modern development in its international context. His recent, edited books include: *Realms of Freedom in Modern China* (Stanford University Press, 2004); *The Normalization of US–China Relations: An International History* (with Gong Li and Robert Ross) (Harvard University Asia Center, 2006); and *China and the World: Internationalization, Internalization, Externalization* (with Mechthild Leutner, Dayong Niu and Wen-hsin Yeh) (Hebei People's Press, 2006).

RODERICK MACFARQUHAR is the Leroy B. Williams professor of history and political science at Harvard University. *Mao's Last Revolution*, co-authored with Michael Schoenhals, was published by Harvard's Belknap Press earlier this year.

PAUL G. PICKOWICZ is distinguished professor of history and Chinese Studies at the University of California, San Diego. Most recently he is co-author of *Revolution Resistance and Reform in Village China* (Yale University Press, 2005), co-editor of *The Chinese Cultural Revolution as History* (Stanford University Press, 2006), and co-editor of *From Underground to Independent: Alternative Film Culture in Contemporary China* (Rowman and Littlefield, 2006). He is currently Distinguished Visiting Scholar at the Contemporary China Studies Programme, University of Oxford.

STEVE SMITH is professor of history at the University of Essex. His most recent book is *Like Cattle and Horses: Labor and Nationalism in Shanghai, 1895–1927* (Duke University Press, 2002).

JULIA STRAUSS is senior lecturer in Chinese politics at the Department of Politics and International Studies, SOAS. Her research interests include: the evolution of the 20th century Chinese state; the interaction between culture and institutions; comparative public administration, politics in Taiwan, and the implementation of environmental regulation in the PRC. She is the editor of *The China Quarterly*.

ANDREW WALDER is professor of sociology at Stanford University and the editor (with Joseph Esherick and Paul Pickowicz) of *The Chinese Cultural Revolution as History* (Stanford University Press, 2006).

WANG ZHENG is an associate professor of women's studies, and associate research scientist of the Institute for Research on Women and Gender at

© The China Quarterly, 2006   doi: 10.1017/S0305741006000877

University of Michigan. Her publications concern feminism in China, both in terms of its historical development and its contemporary activism, and changing gender discourses in China's socioeconomic, political and cultural transformations of the past century. She is the author of *Women in the Chinese Enlightenment: Oral and Textual Histories* (University of California Press, 1999) Her recent research deals with gender in Maoist urban reorganization.

SUSANNE WEIGELIN-SCHWIEDRZIK is professor for Chinese studies at the Department for East Asian Studies of the University of Vienna. She has published on 20th-century Chinese history and historiography.

Acknowledgement

Most of the articles in this volume were first presented at a workshop on the history of the People's Republic of China held at the School of Oriental and African Studies on 7–8 October 2005. The workshop owed its success to the engagement of its participants: in addition to the contributors here, Michael Schoenhals, Vivienne Shue and Elisabeth Croll all added immeasurably to the discussions. Daniel Koldyk served ably as rapporteur. Rowan Pease and Raphaël Jacquet did a wonderful job of making the administrative end of the workshop run smoothly. The SOAS Research Committee and the British Academy are owed huge thanks; without their generosity in funding, the workshop could not have taken place. Since these pieces were originally presented they have undergone several rounds of revision in preparation for publication. Our external reviewers' comments helped enormously in bringing intellectual coherence to the volume as a whole, and in terms of the final production Raphaël Jacquet must again be thanked for keeping us all on track and on time.

Introduction: In Search of PRC History

Julia Strauss

In a perhaps apocryphal exchange in 1972, when Henry Kissinger asked Zhou Enlai what he thought the outcome of the French revolution had been, Zhou responded that it was too early to say. This remark has taken on a life of its own precisely because it rings so true. The big, messy, contested phenomena that are revolutions inspire passionate reactions – both for and against – and each generation has a strong tendency to filter its perception of a given revolution through the political, social and epistemological concerns of its own time. This offers both paradox and opportunity. At present, the great political-social revolutions are largely out of favour. Their animating grand ideologies, teleological imperatives, frank human rights abuses and consequent historical narratives have become historically and epistemologically at least suspect if not downright discredited in a post-Cold War world of globalization and market triumphalism. However, now is an enormously vibrant time for the study of the history of the People's Republic of China (PRC) in its phase of active revolution between 1949 and 1976. In addition to the collection here, there are two other edited volumes on PRC history that have either recently been published or are due to be published in the near future.[1]

While political scientists were intensely interested in the revolutionary PRC when revolutionary Maoism was an ongoing concern in the 1950s, 1960s and 1970s, historians have only relatively recently begun to work on the PRC. One of the pioneering pieces to "cross the divide of 1949" was William Kirby's 1990 article on continuity and change in the ethos of technocrats at mid-century. Since then further historical work has confirmed the suggestions made then: that there were substantial continuities between the Nationalist and Communist eras, and the revolutionary divide of 1949 was much less of the sharp break than had always been assumed by the rhetoric of both Right and Left. In realms as different as the technocratic developmental project, the origins and evolution of the *danwei* (单位, work unit), industrial policy, worker's rights and notions of the family, historians and political scientists have implicitly confirmed de Tocqueville's working hypothesis: that the revolution does indeed complete the work of the old regime.[2] The past ten years have seen the publication of monographs on PRC history dealing with such topics as the

---

1. Joseph Esherick, Paul Pickowicz and Andrew Walder (eds.). *China's Cultural Revolution as History* (Stanford: Stanford University Press, 2006) and Paul Pickowicz and Jeremy Brown (eds.), *Dilemmas of Victory: The Early Years of the People's Republic of China* (Cambridge, MA: Harvard University Press, 2007).
2. A partial bibliography would consist of William Kirby, "Continuity and change in modern China: economic planning on the Mainland and on Taiwan," *The Australian Journal of Chinese Affairs*, No. 24 (1990), Susan Glosser, *Chinese Visions of Family and State, 1915–1953* (Berkeley: University of California Press, 2003), Xiaobo Lü and Elizabeth Perry, *Danwei:The Changing Chinese Workplace in Comparative Perspective*

© The China Quarterly, 2006   doi: 10.1017/S0305741006000464

political biography of a leading cultural cadre (1997), interaction of state and society over the revolutionary family (2000), and the communist takeover of urban areas in Jiangnan (2003).[3] The trickle of articles on PRC history that began in the 1990s has become a thriving sub-field in its own right, covering the regime's classification and categorization of intellectuals, the revolutionizing of the cultural artifacts of dance, museums and parades, and reconsidering a huge range of topics particular to the Cultural Revolution. Much more in the way of monographs based on this research can be expected in the near future.[4] Finally, a group of historians in the PRC itself have begun, however tentatively and carefully, to explore post-1949 topics on social and political history, including sensitive political campaigns such as the Campaign to Suppress Revolutionaries and the "Little" Leap of 1960.[5]

Depoliticization, Sources and Internationalization

Why, then, is there at present such an outpouring of work on the history of the PRC? There are three interlocking factors that have made possible this contemporary resurgence of interest in the history of the People's Republic: depoliticization, the increasing availability of sources and internationalization. Of these, a general process of depoliticization both inside and outside China is by far the most important. In the words of Esherick, Pickowicz and Walder, "history ... is now so far into the past that it is no longer burdened by the

---

footnote continued

(Armonk: M.E. Sharpe, 1997), and Mark Frazier, *The Making of the Chinese Industrial Workplace: State, Revolution and Labor Management* (New York: Cambridge University Press, 2002).

3. Neil Diamant, *Revolutionizing the Family: Politics, Love and Divorce in Urban and Rural China, 1949–1960* (Berkeley: University of California Press, 2000), Timothy Cheek, *Propaganda and Culture in Mao's China: Deng Tuo and the Intelligentsia* (Oxford: Oxford University Press, 1997), and James Gao, *The Communist Takeover of Hangzhou; The Transformation of City and Cadre 1949–1954* (Honolulu: University of Hawai'i Press, 2004).

4. Eddy U, "The making of *zhishifenzi*: the critical impact of registration of unemployed intellectuals in the early PRC," *The China Quarterly*, No. 173 (2003), Chang Tai-hung, "The dance of revolution: *yangge* in Beijing in the early 1950s," *The China Quarterly*, No. 181 (March 2005) and "Mao's parades: state spectacles in China in the 1950s," *The China Quarterly*, forthcoming, and Joel Andreas, "Institutionalized rebellion: governing Tsinghua University during the late years of the Chinese Cultural Revolution," *The China Journal*, No. 55 (2006).

5. Some of the more notable examples include Yang Kuisong, "Mao Zedong and the *zhenfan* campaign," *The China Quarterly*, forthcoming, Gao Hua, *Shenfen yu chayi zhongguo shehui zhengzhi fenceng 1949–1965 nian* (*Status and Difference: China's Political Stratification, 1949–1965*) (Xianggang yatai yanjiusuo, 2004), Gao Hua and Huang Jun, "Jiangsu's urban people's communes in the 1960s 'Great Leap Forward' movement," http://www.coldwarchina.com/zwxz/zgxg/gh/001636.html, and Zhang Jishun, "Shanghai nongli jiceng zhengzhi dongyuan yu guojia shehui yitihua zouxiang" ("Shanghai neighbourhood grassroots political mobilization and tendencies towards national integration") *Zhongguo shehui kexue* No. 2 (2004).

demand for relevance to the country's current evolution."[6] In the West, the Cold War inescapably framed both the first and second generations of scholarship on the revolutionary PRC in the 1950s and 1960s. Scholarship was part of a wider set of political concerns that needed to explain the mysterious and directly inaccessible revolutionary experiment that was such an important part of the intensifying Cold War, and this was reflected in the informal division of 20th-century China between different disciplines: the People's Republic was felt to be the proper concern of political scientists and sociologists, while the less politically relevant Republican period was ceded to historians; deposed regimes having little in the way of contemporary political relevance (other than the perennial question of how to deal with the Republic of China on Taiwan).

The first, second and third generations of literature on the PRC, a substantial part of it published in *The China Quarterly*, were of course not monolithic. Each generation had its own internal divisions between Right and Left, between those sympathetic or hostile to the revolution. The availability of sources also made for different generational foci. The first generation of scholarship in the 1950s and early 1960s tended to focus on the big structures of the Leninist system (often under the rubric of "totalitarianism") and Mao; the second generation in the mid-1960s to late 1970s was profoundly influenced by the unexpected outbreak of the Cultural Revolution and, on the whole, began to turn to society-centred explanations, often on the basis of émigré interviews and Red Guard publications. And as direct research access to China itself became increasingly possible, much of the third generation in the 1980s concentrated on questions of "contemporary relevance" and pre-1949 historical interest as less sensitive Republican era archives began to open.[7]

But irrespective of these differences, considering the PRC as *history* was not on the menu of choice in Western scholarship until a de facto depoliticization of the revolutionary era in the PRC was well under way. Within China itself, the Chinese Communist Party's stranglehold on understandings of the revolution and its own history was so inextricably bound up with regime legitimacy and contemporary politics that until well into the 1990s, critically minded Chinese historians could barely touch on the preceding Republican period, much less the post-1949 era. But irrelevance for contemporary politics

6. Esherick, Pickowicz and Walder, *The Chinese Cultural Revolution as History*, p. 16.
7. A proper evaluation of the first and second generations of scholarship on the People's Republic of China would easily be the topic of a self-standing essay. But for a few key examples of each see Richard Walker, *China Under Communism: The First Five Years* (New Haven: Yale University Press, 1955), Franz Schurmann, *Ideology and Organization in Communist China* (1st ed.) (Berkeley: University of California Press, 1966), Hong Yung Lee, *The Politics of the Chinese Cultural Revolution: A Case Study* (Berkeley: University of California Press, 1978), and Gordon Bennett and Ronald Montaperto, *Red Guard: The Political Biography of Tai Hsiao-ai* (New York: Doubleday, 1972).

makes for great opportunity for history, and now Western scholars, Chinese scholars and those who are able to shuttle between the two worlds of scholarship are able to engage increasingly in a type of historical work that was simply unimaginable ten or fifteen years ago.

Part of the background to this general process of depoliticization has been a result of the simple passage of time and consequent generational change as the passions that animated much of the Cold War (both pro and anti revolution) began to fade, and a younger generation of scholars came to maturity. But more has had to do with changes in China itself. As the Chinese Communist Party (CCP) moved out of its intense preoccupation with continuous revolution and mass mobilization and into a kind of developmentalist and softer form of authoritarianism in the 1980s, the bulk of scholarship on contemporary China has moved on with it to consider a very different set of contemporary questions on economic reform, inequality, corruption, representation, state capacity and the long-term viability of the Party, leaving the field of 1949 to 1976 open to historians and historically minded social scientists.

The raw materials of historical inquiry are down to sources, and the relative depoliticization from the mid-1980s onwards has led to a veritable explosion of sources relevant to the 1949 to 1976 period. Human and archival sources have been extant for quite some time, and since the early to mid-1990s it has become possible to get increasing access to both. With any number of reverses and hiccups, the general trend since then has been towards greater openness of archives, notably at the municipal level in Shanghai, Chongqing and Beijing, but also including some provincial and even county-level archives. Some material on the 1950s and 1960s began to be available to researchers as early as the mid-1990s, and on the whole access has widened in the intervening decade. The early to mid-1990s also saw an enormous increase in the volume of official and semi-official publications, from the decision taken in the late 1980s that each and every county would produce a gazetteer (*xianzhi* 县志) to the compilation of municipal and provincial gazetteers (*shengzhi* 省志, *shizhi* 市志) – often specialized by government function such as communications, education, interior, culture, industry, post, agriculture and so on. These official compilations include material on local geography, important events and government restructuring broken down by time period. Many provinces, counties and municipalities have also published collections on organizational history (*zuzhishi ziliao* 组织史资料), which detail by time period the restructurings, amalgamations and official incumbents of the highest positions in Party, state, military and mass organizations. Official chronologies (*dashi ji* 大事记) and statistical compilations whose data runs start with the 1950s are common. Since the early 1990s, the CCP has also published important compilations of documents – notably the *Selection of Important Documents Since the Establishment of the People's Republic* (*Jianguo yilai zhongyao wenxian xuanbian* 建国以来

重要文献选编), which now runs to 20 volumes – and more document-ary collections are in the process of being issued. Historical biographies of important figures feature prominently on the shelves of any major bookshop in China, and as a matter of sheer generational transition, the official memoir literature (*wenshi ziliao* 文史资料) that used to be focused on the Republican period now includes subject matter on post-1949 topics and commemorative events.

Oral history is also very fruitful, as many of those who lived through the events of 1949 to 1976 have become willing to talk about their experiences in an increasingly unguarded manner. In addition to the usual suspects in the usual places – cadres and intellectuals in the big cities of the east – it is now possible to interview people such as village cadres and peasants on topics (such as the post-Great Leap famine) and in places (such as rural Henan) that would have been largely if not completely taboo only a short time ago.[8]

Internationalization is the third factor to shape ongoing work in PRC history. The current relative political relaxation and the removal of earlier travel restrictions mean that Chinese scholars are now beginning to be able to investigate even sensitive areas of PRC history, such as the Campaign to Suppress Counter-revolutionaries, land reform and the post Leap readjustment. Dissemination through international projects like the Cold War history network at East China Normal University, seminars at universities in Hong Kong, workshops in China, Hong Kong and Taiwan, and teaching and fellowship exchanges is now routine. Chinese and Western scholars regularly interact directly in workshops and conferences in a variety of venues, as well as indirectly through translated works.

The potential volume of materials to be explored and particular subjects to be illuminated for the 1949–76 era in PRC history is vast, and raises more questions than can be answered in a single volume. Rather than focus on a particular time frame in the history of the People's Republic, offer a particular kind of approach or concentrate on similar units of analysis, the articles included in this collection have been deliberately chosen for their eclecticism. The pieces presented here encompass a range of different kinds of historical inquiry, and consider historical units of analysis as large as the socialist world economy or as small as the individual. Nor are the articles focused on a particular sub-period or event in the history of the PRC; in considering the entirety of the 1949–76 period fair game, we begin to

---

8. For examples, see Ralph Thaxton, "Corruption, coercion, and the loss of core entitlements under the people's commune: revisiting the causality of deprivation, starvation, and death in Mao's Great Leap Forward famine, with special reference to Da Fo village," paper presented to international conference "As China meets the world," 17–19 May 2004, and Felix Wemheuer, "Steinnudeln: Ländliche Erinnerungen und stattliche Vergangensheitsbewältigung der 'Großen Sprung' Hungersnot in der chinesischen Provinz Henan," PhD dissertation, University of Vienna, 2006.

question much of what is normally taken for granted in the conventional periodization within the Mao era.

The volume is bookended with macroscopic perspectives on contemporary Chinese history. It opens with William Kirby's assessment of revolutionary China's deep involvement with the external world, particularly the ways in which the politics and economy of the international socialist world of the 1950s and 1960s intertwined, and reminds us that the establishment of the basic institutions of the socialist economy is unimaginable outside the framing of the international socialism of the time, exemplified through Stalinism. It closes with Susanne Weigelin-Schwiedrzik's charting of Chinese historiography on the Cultural Revolution and Roderick MacFarquhar's postscript, which reviews the early days of *The China Quarterly* and the wider state of the field in the 1960s as a way of assessing what scholars did and did not get right at the time.

The middle articles consider a variety of topics over the course of the revolutionary People's Republic. The 1950s are represented by the articles by Julia Strauss on regime consolidation and the establishment of socialism from 1949 to 1956, and Wang Zheng on the Party's sudden reversal of its commitment to gender equality in favour of a more conservative policy of "thriftily, diligently build the country, and thriftily, diligently manage the family" in 1957. The 1950s and 1960s are bridged by David Bachman's institutional consideration of continuity and change in courts, elite politics and military preparedness, and Steve Smith's look at the nexus between the revolutionary state and rural society in contestation over pilgrimages to sites of healing "holy water." Robert Ash's piece focuses on the rural dimensions of economic policy, and lays out, in quite horrifying detail, the ways in which the revolutionary ideology of rapid economic growth disproportionately exacted huge costs on rural areas. Andrew Walder focuses on the detail of high factionalism at Beijing University in the early years of the Cultural Revolution, and Paul Pickowicz explores the relationship of the CCP to its mid-ranking artists and intellectuals by exploring the career of one filmmaker desperate for acceptance and validation.

At the most obvious level, many of these articles confirm what has already been suggested by earlier generations of scholarship. The young PRC's basic ethos and institutions *were* inextricably bound up with international socialism in general and Stalinism in particular. The early mass campaigns of the 1950s *were* in fact a form of terror. Individual intellectuals *did* routinely come to enormous grief in the sharp and sudden reverses of policy line from the top. The onset post-Leap famine in 1959 *did* lead to mass starvation and an appalling excess of expected deaths. The early to mid-1960s *was* a period of profound militarization for state and society. And the Party cadres of the new revolutionary state *did* fear, with some reason, that their degree of hegemonic control over rural society was much less assured than their didactic public pronouncements presumed.

But in more subtle ways, the degree of detail and texture made possible by the combination of new sources and new perspectives in these pieces does not merely confirm what has been known or guessed for the past 50 years of scholarship on the PRC. This collection of articles begins a process of implicitly questioning some old assumptions and at least tentatively asking new questions about periodization, ideology, possibilities for individual agency and where, in aggregate, fresher perspectives on PRC history may be heading. We include very different kinds of topics and approaches, whose units of inquiry range from problems of writing history itself (Weigelin-Schwiedrzik), China's place in the socialist world economy (Kirby), the deconstruction of a particular change in Party line towards women's work in 1957 (Wang), and the life history of a relatively unknown filmmaker trying to make his way under the Maoist system (Pickowicz). But the particular details uncovered in these works reveal surprising commonalities, despite differences in subject, scale and time period.

Questioning Conventional Periodization

Many of these articles either implicitly or explicitly question conventionally accepted periodizations. The ways in which particular years have been trumpeted and grouped serve as a kind of narrative shorthand – a first rough cut at fitting events into a larger flow of meaning – that until now has been heavily influenced by the PRC's official periodization of its own history, with 1949, 1957–58, 1966 and 1976 standing out as the temporal junctures of major changes. The years of regime consolidation and the establishment of the key institutions of socialism (1949–56) are conventionally seen as times of success and popular enthusiasm for New China; the launching of the Anti-Rightist Campaign in 1957 and the subsequent turn to the left in 1958 heralded the Great Leap Forward, economic crash, famine and subsequent economic readjustment; and the 1966–76 Cultural Revolution decade another surge of utopian leftism, disaster and mass disillusionment.[9]

The most important month and year for PRC history must of course be October 1949: when New China officially came into being, Mao announced at Tiananmen that China had finally "stood up," and official discourse proclaimed virtually everything to have come before of which it disapproved as "feudal." The presumptive sharp break between the feudal and reactionary and the progressive and

9. This rough periodization is offered in the Chinese Communist Party's own resolution of 1981 *On Some Questions Regarding the History of the Party since the Founding of the PRC*, and is repeated in most standard works; notably Maurice Meiser, *Mao's China and After* (2nd ed.) (New York: Free Press, 1986), Jack Gray, *Rebellions and Revolution: China from the 1800s to 2000* (2nd ed.) (Oxford: Oxford University Press, 2002), Frederick Teiwes, *Politics and Purges* (2nd ed.) (Armonk & London: M.E. Sharpe, 1993), and Kenneth Lieberthal, *Governing China: From Revolution through Reform* (2nd ed.) (New York: Norton, 2004).

enlightened in 1949, the progress made by the new regime in implementing its key programmes, and the positive support of the majority of the population in the early to mid-1950s remain grounding sources of legitimacy for the People's Republic. And yet, the Strauss article confirms that there was substantial continuity in state agenda and methods of policy implementation from the Nationalist period, and that the years of regime consolidation and the establishment of socialism represented neither "golden age" nor necessary precursor to disaster. It finds that the revolutionary regime's chosen method of pushing major initiatives through both the bureaucracy and society by a process of campaign mobilization and public accusation sessions worked very well – if bloodily – when the targeted "enemies" were clearly visible, and the basic goal of the state was to draw on an assumed widespread pulic support in overcoming the resistance of key social groups and establishing the state's basic institutions of coercion and state planning. These strategies were already working much less well as early as the mid-1950s: once campaigns moved into the narrower spatial confines of the work unit, many of the rank and file masses resolutely refused to be "stirred up," as it was in no one's interest other than a minority of designated activists to be too forthcoming in a period of campaign mobilization. The eventual radicalization and obsession with counter-revolution and ever-expanding categories of "enemies" from the mid-1950s on (that in turn foreshadowed even worse in the Cultural Revolution) were part of the very campaign mobilization that so successfully consolidated the regime and its basic institutions earlier in the decade, and the regime was reluctant – and perhaps unable – to renounce a strategy that was such an important component of its earlier successes both before and after 1949.

Bachman's piece on 1958–65 calls conventional periodization into question in not one but three ways, by sidestepping the Cultural Revolution entirely and asking the reader to imagine what might have happened had there been no Cultural Revolution. His work charts three different aspects of trends under way between 1958 and 1966: the sheer number of legal cases processed over the course of the 1950s and early 1960s, elite generational change, and an analysis of preparations for war in general and the establishment of the Third Front defence industry in particular. Bachman finds a series of surprises: there was both continuity and change, but not in the places that one would have expected. Despite the highly politicized environment of the late 1950s (and again during the Cultural Revolution), there was substantial institutionalization in the matter of judicial cases; irrespective of the Cultural Revolution purges, the senior leadership of the CCP and the People's Liberation Army was on the cusp of a major generational change in any case as a result of illness and retirement, and perhaps most importantly, the entire period was pervaded by deep concerns about defence and the high priority given to transforming an already highly militarized economy into a pure war one. Bachman finds that the antecedents to the Third Front policy of rapidly creating a military industrial complex for defence in China's impoverished interior were varied: from the Republican period, from the mid-1950s, and from Mao's own uncontested dominance in this arena even after the Great Leap, with the establishment of defence mobilization production lines among civilian industry. The obsession with defence made for enormous distortions in both the economy and China's overall prioritization of resources, and in ways that cut across both conventional period-izations and understandings of Mao's position in Chinese elite politics and decision-making in the years before the Cultural Revolution.

Other articles show that when one looks in different places, standard periodizations seem to be even more permeable. Kirby finds that the international economic exchanges between China and other socialist countries were largely uninfluenced by the high politics and tensions within international socialism in the late 1950s and early 1960s – trade continued as before despite the Sino-Soviet split. Looking at state-society relations at very local levels in the country-side, Smith sees evidence of similar upsurges in "holy water" incidents in periods as different as 1953–54 (the establishment of socialism), 1957 (turn to the left) and 1963–64 (economic stabilization in the countryside). Wang finds that 1957 – a year that marked the prosecution of rightists and generally signalled a turn to the left – was exactly the point at which elite politics resulted in an infinitely more conservative Party line towards gender issues. And in what is arguably the most important metric of all – grain consumption for rural China's vast population – Ash's systemic analysis of the entirety of the Mao era shows how materially irrelevant standard period-izations were for the majority of the population in the revolutionary PRC. Despite the economic recovery in the aftermath of the Great Leap Forward, it wasn't until the final years of the Cultural Revolution that peasants' level of food consumption began to approach that of the early 1950s.

Agendas of the Revolutionary State: International and Domestic Dimensions of Ideology and Implementation

The agendas of any state at any time are invariably multiple, shifting and in tension with each other. Politics, personalities, expedience and the crisis of the moment typically frame how some agendas subordinate others and in these respects "New China" was no exception. But the young People's Republic of China came into being at a particularly ideologically charged time as far as the wider international and security environment was concerned, and it was led by a group of revolutionaries committed to international socialism at a time when the Cold War was in fact quite "hot." Within a year of the establishment of the PRC, the US Seventh Fleet was patrolling the Taiwan Straits and UN forces were advancing towards China's border with Korea. The leadership of the CCP had strong ideological affinity with the Soviet Union and the world of internationalist socialism led by the Soviet Union, as well as even stronger practical and security reasons for aligning with that side of the Cold War; nothing less than China's survival was at stake. Thus the revolutionary PRC possessed any number of different key agendas. Some, like reintegrating the unitary state and ensuring China's security, were directly inherited from the preceding Republican era and inherent to the modernizing Chinese state. Others, like establishing the key institutions of socialism, the planned economy and collectivization, reflected its ideological commitments and strategic alignment to the international socialist camp. Still others, such as the stamping out of practices now known as "feudalism," were a combination of the two. And all were played out in an objective environment of resource shortages and serious worry about national security.

These articles all at least touch on the question of how the varied agendas of the revolutionary state were filtered through ideology, but some deal with these issues more explicitly than others. Kirby's piece on China's internationalization and participation in an attempted socialist world economy reminds us how deeply important it was to the Chinese leadership to be part of something beyond China's borders – in this case, the progressive international socialist world. He details how from the beginning, the CCP was explicitly internationalist in orientation; indeed without the Soviet Union there could have been no Chinese Communist Party and no People's Republic of China. Until the late 1950s, the PRC was the Soviet Union's most faithful ally and actively and enthusiastically set to emulating the key features of High Stalinism: the absolute rule of the Communist Party, the emergence of the cult of personality, and a planned state economy with priority given to heavy industry and defence. It also meant China's participation in an international socialist economy based on bilateral relations and agreements for preferential trade and development. Kirby lays out the ways in which this socialist world economy was beset with structural weaknesses, but suggests that there were any number of ways in which China actually gained through preferential trade, as the recipient in what we now call intellectual property, so that routine bilateral economic exchanges continued well after the time when political tensions tore the Sino-Soviet alliance apart in the late 1950s.

Robert Ash's work focuses on the domestic dimensions of the agricultural economy, but here too the implicit model of the Soviet Union under Stalin looms large in the analysis. The priority goal of rapid industrialization required a real and financial surplus from the agricultural sector, which in turn was realized through "unprecedented control over the labour force and agricultural output." Ash's analysis of not only grain extraction from above but real levels of peasant consumption from below from 1953 to 1976 shows, as few statistical tables can, just how vigorously the execution of the PRC's key agenda of crash industrialization via a planned economy squeezed the peasantry. Not only were state procurements on the whole higher than they had been under the first severe collectivization drive in the Soviet Union, per capita grain production was considerably lower. For most of the Mao period, grain production roughly kept pace with China's population – but only just – and Ash is able to make estimates suggesting that in aggregate the caloric intake of the rural population did not meet basic energy requirements for the majority of the Mao years, most disastrously so during the aftermath of the Great Leap, but by no means only at that time.

The Smith piece is concerned with another of the revolutionary regime's key agendas: the part of the revolution's modernizing project geared to the destruction of "feudal practices." At various points throughout the 1950s and early 1960s, rumours of the discovery of "holy water" would prompt spontaneous rural pilgrimages to these sites. For the state, the combination of "feudal superstition," its simple lack of control of the movement of individuals and its fear that the "holy water" incidents were linked to proscribed sectarian activity made this phenomenon a source of concern and anxiety, and it sought to repress the incidents – with only mixed success – through a process of isolation, education and ridicule. As Smith reminds us, the suppression of "holy water" pilgrimages (and perhaps "feudal superstition" more generally) was a matter given lower priority than other activities (like grain requisition), and as a result local cadres at least some of the time could either shield those they sympathized with in the search for holy water, or engage in taking it themselves. Destroying feudal practices relating to popular religion was, it seemed, virtually impossible: feudalism could and did go underground for lengthy periods of time, only to re-emerge elsewhere at a later date when control was relaxed.

How Individuals Coped: Dilemmas of Creative Accommodation

The highly ideologically charged unitary state that was established in 1949 demanded a great deal from its citizens in terms of commitment and compliance, and had few scruples about coercing its citizens in direct and indirect ways. But the regime's own anxiety about the holy water incidents and the reliability of its own rural cadres in stamping out feudal superstition attest to the truism that even an all-encompassing, politically driven regime could not absolutely control everything at all levels of society. Until now little has been known about how individuals coped with the enormous changes set in train by the revolutionary regime, but new sources, including seemingly unlikely ones in the archives, are now beginning to open at least small windows on these processes. Some individuals found that the very politicization of the revolution provided for opportunities for engagement as well as constraints to be borne. The choices may not have been pleasant or palatable, but from the highest

ranks of the elite decision makers in the CCP to the peasant woman
dispensing holy water, or to the ways in which protagonists lined up
with different factions within Beida (北大) and other universities in
Beijing in the early years of the Cultural Revolution, these articles
illustrate how individuals had agency and some room for manoeuvre
in pursuing their interests in a kind of creative accommodation with
the new state and its representatives.

Wang's piece brings together a number of themes: the dominance of
masculine power within the CCP (and therefore the state) despite the
Party's ostensible commitment to gender equality, the precariousness
of *any* extant political slogan or establishment organization in a
period of campaign leftism, and the ways in which even the highest
ranking women in the CCP relied on their informal connections with
sympathetic males of sufficient stature to broker deals on their behalf.
Wang's work in the Shanghai archives resolves a minor question in
gender history: why on earth did the All China Women's Federation,
whose entire purpose was to fight for gender equality under socialism,
abruptly turn away from its goal of women's liberation in 1957 to
embrace the socially conservative slogan "diligently, thriftily build the
country, and diligently, thriftily manage the family"? Wang shows
that far from being a socially conservative slogan designed to repress
women, this was a compromise formula, astutely brokered by none
other than Deng Xiaoping, almost certainly after receiving informal
representation from Deng Yingchao (邓颖超), the highest ranking
woman in the CCP at the time. While the All China Women's
Federation had as one of its main goals gender equality (and had
cannily parlayed Party support for this goal to overcome the
resistance of male cadres), in the suddenly highly politicized
environment of the Anti-Rightist Campaign it was no longer
acceptable to discuss China's problems openly, including ones related
to gender, for fear of being deemed a "rightist." This in turn presented
huge problems for an organization whose popularity at the grassroots
and very organizational raison d'être was predicated on the pursuit of
gender equality when it needed to produce a politically acceptable
report to open its Third National Conference in September 1957. The
very mention of gender equality was politically unacceptable, and
furthermore the balance of opinion near the top of the political system
in the Secretariat was extraordinarily hostile: since gender inequality
was a problem of capitalism, any mention of it would only be
ideologically confusing; it would be better to turn the Women's
Federation into an arm of the Party for general work or even do away
with it altogether. Wang describes how the quiet intervention of Deng
Xiaoping in brokering an acceptable compromise placated the
majority critics who would have been only too happy to do away
with the Women's Federation, preserved the organization and its
focus on women, and wrapped itself in the legitimating mantle of
Mao's own words for good measure. In Wang's piece we see how
creative accommodation can work at the highest elite levels of politics:

through the use of informal channels on the part of those without viable formal standing, and the political and rhetorical agility of those willing to represent those interests.

Smith's article on "holy water" incidents offers several examples of how individuals attempted to accommodate the revolutionary state while preserving practices of local value, turning the rhetoric of the state and its key legitimating symbols and agenda of welfare provision back on itself. Peasants seeking holy water justified their actions in terms of lack of access to health care, and spirit mediums cannily gave priority to members of the PLA and local martyrs. Rural communities were able at least intermittently to resist the stamping out of their cherished "feudal practices," and proved equally capable of combining old attachments to popular religion with new rhetorics to appeal to the power of the revolutionary state.

Walder's depiction of the factional struggles at Beijing University implicitly sees some degree of agency as well; the key factions at Beijing University were not distinguished by policy or status differences, rather they revolved around denunciation of those who either held or attempted to consolidate power. Nie Yuanzi (聂元梓) made her career in denouncing extant power holders at Beida and then the leader of the work team sent in to oversee the campaign, but found herself in a vulnerable position when she attempted to consolidate her own power base. Informal relations and personal contacts were as important to the hardening of factions in 1966–68 as they were to the resolution of the dilemma of the Women's Federation leadership in 1957; Walder shows clearly that from beginning to end, political actors exogenous to Beijing University were deeply implicated in the factionalism through a combination of personal links and political alliances to those within the university.

Pickowicz's exploration of the largely unsuccessful life and times of Zheng Junli (郑君里), a mid-ranking filmmaker, illustrates how difficult it was for intellectuals to negotiate accommodation with a regime in which political winds shifted so dramatically. Pickowicz describes Zheng's "complicated" background, eagerness to serve the new regime and make films, the repeated ups and downs of his post-1949 career, and his almost slavish willingness to reorient and accommodate to prevailing political power. After a critical savaging in 1951 for being bourgeois, Zheng made a thorough self criticism and henceforth was extremely careful to err only on the "left," even to the point of actively supporting the Anti-Rightist campaign in 1957. Reward for political loyalty eventually came with the opportunity to direct a big budget historical drama about the Opium War, *Lin Zexu* (林则徐). Zheng's timing was unlucky, as shortly after *Lin Zexu* opened to popular acclaim and positive reviews it was severely criticized by historians and film critics in the general atmosphere of post-Leap retrenchment. From there Zheng's career went downhill with a series of awful films, denied opportunities and his own persecution and death in prison in the early years of the Cultural

Revolution. Zheng Junli was himself only modestly protected in terms of political connections, and he operated in a highly exposed artistic field; filmmaking requires big budgets, relatively long time horizons from script development to viewing the final product, and cannot be as easily hidden as most realms of cultural production. Yet his attempts to be accepted, validated, and given status and professional opportunities by the Party (and the lengths he was willing to go to get his best chance) must have been replicated many times by any number of cultural intellectuals in the revolutionary PRC.

Creative accommodation – whether successful or unsuccessful – has many facets. Those shown in these articles include brokerage, the use of informal personal connections, and the deliberate adoption of new political rhetorics to enable individuals to make claims on new forms of authority and power. Wherever we hear the voices or see the actions of individuals – either through the recounting of the travails of the mid-level cultural producer/filmmaker who desperately tried to ingratiate himself with the Party, the peasant woman spirit medium who treated the favoured under the new regime first but also dared to point out that the people's hospital cost money but the water given by the gods was free, or the Party cadre at Beijing University who saw opportunity in the early stages of the Cultural Revolution and sought external support before denouncing a power holder – individuals had choices to make and did make them. The more nimble, better connected and flexible were, in any number of circumstances, able to engage with the revolutionary state in surprising ways.

Master Narratives and Alternative Histories: In Search of the History of the People's Republic of China

In different ways, these articles all reflect Weigelin-Schwiedrzik's proposition that the CCP has lost hegemonic control over the history of the PRC, while as yet nothing convincing has arisen to replace it. Weigelin-Schwiedrzik concentrates on the distinction between cultural and communicative forms of memory – the former defined by sacred texts and the latter by the personal living memories that can reach roughly three generations back. She illustrates the ways in which the CCP's efforts to finesse its own legitimacy after the Cultural Revolution has resulted in the breakdown of a straightforward teleological narrative of class struggle and victory, while neither the state nor significant "carrier groups" in society have thus far succeeded in (re)imposing an agreed on, baseline narrative; what exists at present is at best "fragmented memory."

While the CCP's loss of hegemonic control over the history of the PRC may well be problematic for a history-conscious state profoundly aware of its problems with legitimacy, the dissolution of a coherent master narrative has begun to open up space in which to construct potential alternatives from a variety of viewpoints. The view from Beijing is certainly different from that of rural Anhui; the peasant in search of holy water and decent health care has a different perspective from that of the cadre launching a campaign to suppress "feudal superstition." A wider range of sources makes for a more rounded picture of the same experience: macroeconomic data on rural grain consumption in combination with the stories of individual peasants recounted to the oral historian can bring much better nuance and understanding to the question of what life in the countryside was like under socialism in the early 1960s. And how individuals reacted within the constraints of the highly ideologically charged times in which they lived not only made the political personal, but (as Walder reveals) the personal was made political as well.

This collection represents an early attempt to reconsider the history of the revolutionary People's Republic between 1949 and 1976 in the light of periodization and narrative, how a range of state agendas was understood and implemented, and how individuals exercised agency in what room for manoeuvre they had. The articles question standard periodizations, and instead see more long-term processes that cross over the standard dividing lines of 1949, 1958 and 1966. Virtually all describe the existence of multiple, competing and ideologically charged agendas whose execution led to any number of unintended outcomes for individuals and the state itself, and some show quite surprising levels of agency as individuals sought to reach accommodation with a revolutionary regime that was remaking state, economy and society. But any volume at such an early stage in the re-assessment of the history of the PRC can only scratch at the surface. At present we can only suggest that in the short term what remains of the old master narrative is likely to be further eroded as work on the 1950s and 1960s is undertaken by Chinese historians. There are numerous other substantive topics that merit (re)consideration: the People's Liberation Army and civil-military relations more generally, the growth of the CCP, the cultural institutions of state, the ways in which nationally mandated campaigns were subject to regional and local variations in implementation, and assessing questions of the ultimate responsibility for both the costs and the accomplishments of the revolutionary experiment – to name but a few. We are still very much in search of PRC history, and hope that others will pick up where this volume concludes.

China's Internationalization in the Early People's Republic: Dreams of a Socialist World Economy

William C. Kirby

ABSTRACT   The People's Republic of China, like the Chinese Communist Party that ruled it, was from its conception internationalist in premise and in promise. The PRC in its formative years would be Moscow's most faithful and self-sacrificing ally, a distinction earned in blood in Korea and by the fact that, unlike the East European "people's democracies," the PRC's allegiance was not bought at gunpoint. This article researches one of the most ambitious international undertakings of that era: the effort to plan the development of half the world and to create a socialist world economy stretching from Berlin to Canton. What was China's role in this undertaking, and how did it shape the early PRC? How did this socialist world economy work (or not work)? How successfully internationalist was a project negotiated by sovereign (and Stalinist) states? Why did Mao Zedong ultimately destroy it, and with it, the dream of communist internationalism?

A defining characteristic of modern China is its incorporation into global systems. Whether one speaks of military, political, economic or cultural trends, China became an ever-greater participant in international currents over the course of the 20th century. In recent years there has been a great deal of study of the challenges posed by China's seemingly recent "emergence," but very little scholarly appreciation of longer-term processes of China's internationalization.

The longer term, it is true, is much longer than the history of the People's Republic or even of the entire modern period. Historians of longer *durées* – such as John Schrecker in his stimulating reinterpretation of the broad narrative of Chinese history on the basis of Chinese historical categories, or R. Bin Wong, in his *China Transformed* – deal in different ways with the challenge of looking at Chinese history apart from or (in Wong's case) in addition to the categories of analysis that have dominated the study of China since larger-scale contact with the West began in the late 18th and early 19th centuries.[1]

Historians of China in earlier periods have recently endeavoured to recover the international or, more accurately, the global dimensions of Chinese history, undoing myths (Western and Chinese) of stubborn isolationism. Joanna Waley-Cohen's excellent synthesis of this work, in her book the *Sextants of Beijing: Global Currents in Chinese*

---

1. See John E. Schrecker, *The Chinese Revolution in Historical Perspective* (New York: Praeger, 1991); R. Bin Wong, *China Transformed: Historical Change and the Limits of European Experience* (Ithaca: Cornell University Press, 1997).

© The China Quarterly, 2006   doi: 10.1017/S0305741006000476

History, recovers China's active participation in networks of international exchange that "stretched from Syria in the west to Japan in the east and from Korea in the north to Indonesia in the south, and which, by the 16th century, included Europe and the New World." In the process she deals with China's transformation by, and of, both religious waves (such as Buddhism) and global trading patterns (as with Latin American silver).[2] Well before this new wave of scholarship, the work of Morris Rossabi and others had already done much to refine the textbook conception of an immutable Sinocentrism in the working of traditional China's relations with its neighbours.

Historians of more recent times have long discussed the comparative role of forces external and internal to China in the shaping of its modern history. They have done so in debates that sometimes echo those many decades ago in Europe, which argued either for a *Primat der Außenpolitik* as the motive force of a nation's history or alternatively for the primacy of domestic politics even in the setting of foreign policy.[3] Yet the study of modern China in the West has never been burdened by a focus on foreign policy – and the actions of foreign policy elites – to the exclusion of other factors. John Fairbank shaped the question of a Chinese "response" to the West without writing a straightforward diplomatic history and without over-simplifying the complex and contradictory set of actors that comprised "the West."[4]

In Fairbank's professional youth, the study of modern China's foreign relations was at the centre of modern historical studies of China, both in the West and in China, where his teacher, Professor T. F. Tsiang (Jiang Tingfu 蔣挺黻), set the standard in the writing of modern international history.[5] Diplomatic history in particular exemplified the best of Chinese historiography,[6] and this tradition has been well maintained.[7] Yet this is a field in Chinese studies that stagnated in the West from the 1960s on. In recent decades the study of China's international relations has been overshadowed, in both

2. Joanna Waley-Cohen, *The Sextants of Beijing: Global Currents in Chinese History* (New York: W. W. Norton & Co., 1999).

3. See Eckart Kehr, *Der Primat der Innenpolitik. Gesammelte Aufsätze zur preussisch-deutschen Sozialgeschichte im 19. und 20. Jahrhundert* (ed. and intro. Hans-Ulrich Wehler) (Berlin: de Gruyter, 1965).

4. John K. Fairbank, *Trade and Diplomacy on the China Coast* (Cambridge, MA: Harvard University Press, 1953).

5. Jiang Tingfu, *Zhongguo jindai shi* (*Modern Chinese History*) (Changsha: Shangwu, 1938), and *Jindai Zhongguo waijiao shi ziliao jiyao* (*Materials of Modern Chinese Diplomatic History*) (Shanghai: Shangwu, 1931).

6. See for example Zhang Zhongfu, *Zhonghua minguo waijiaoshi* (*Diplomatic History of the Republic of China*) (Beiping: Beiping daxue chubanzu, 1936; Chongqing: Zhengzhong shuju, 1943).

7. Wu Dongzhi (ed.), *Zhongguo waijiaoshi: Zhonghua minguo shiqi, 1911–1949* (*History of China's Foreign Relations: The Period of the Republic of China, 1911–1949*) (Zhengzhou: Henan renmin chubanshe, 1990); and especially Shi Yuanhua, *Zhonghua minguo waijiaoshi* (*Diplomatic History of the Republic of China*) (Shanghai: Shanghai renmin chubanshe, 1994).

quantity and quality, by work on Chinese social and cultural history. Unlike the leading works in those fields, most of the standard monographs on China's foreign relations were written before the opening of Republican-era archives in the People's Republic of China (PRC) and on Taiwan. Thus there exists no standard work in the West on the international political relations of 20th-century China that makes extensive use of Chinese and foreign diplomatic archives. The realms of economic and cultural relations similarly lack an integrated treatment.[8] The present Western-language literature on China's foreign relations is heavily weighted towards the foreign policy of the contemporary PRC government, and even here there are but few works that offers a synthetic and historical overview.[9] The best study of China's foreign relations in all their dimensions, for historical and contemporary times – Jürgen Osterhammel's *China und the Weltgesellschaft* – has no English-language translation, and so its readership is unfortunately restricted.[10] And while many have studied the conflicts that have emerged over time in China's foreign political relations, few have focused on patterns of interaction, interpenetration and co-operation across national boundaries that have proved at least as important.[11]

Yet the history of the PRC is simply incomprehensible without a strongly international perspective. Its ruling party, the Chinese Communist Party (CCP), was the creation of a foreign power, and it began its rule of the country under foreign protection. The early PRC was a leading actor in a global revolutionary movement as well as in a military-political-economic alliance that stretched from Berlin to Canton. Internally, its system of government was self-consciously modelled on that of its foreign allies. And the lives of its 600 million subjects would be changed by the application of imported models of social, political and even cultural revolution. At best, the lines between things international, global or external on the one hand, and things "Chinese" on the other hand, became in many realms nearly impossible to draw. In order to study this era of China's international history, we cannot separate the internal from the external; rather, we should aim to examine processes of internationalization at home and abroad.

This is not to suggest that international influences were imposed upon China in this period. If PRC foreign policy evinced a tension

8. For an extended review of these issues and the literature see William Kirby, "The internationalization of China," *The China Quarterly*, No. 150 (1997), pp. 433–458.

9. See Thomas W. Robinson and David Shambaugh (eds.), *Chinese Foreign Policy: Theory and Practice* (Oxford: Clarendon Press, 1994); and John W. Garver, *Foreign Relations of the People's Republic of China* (Engelwood Cliffs, NJ: Prentice-Hall, 1993).

10. Jürgen Osterhammel, *China und die Weltgesellschaft. Vom 18. Jahrhundert bis in unsere Zeit* (München: C.H. Beck, 1989).

11. One unpublished exception can be found in the papers of the ACLS/SSRC Conference on Patterns of Cooperation in Modern China's Foreign Relations, Wintergreen, Virginia, 1987.

between communist internationalism and Chinese national interest, policies were nevertheless set by Chinese leaders whose own careers had been at once internationalist and nationalist. Within China, it was not the imposition, but the *internalization* of international cultural practices, be these of political activity, economic organization, legal and prison systems or whatever, caused at least as much by "agency" on the part of Chinese actors as by international "influence." How else, for example, can we understand the durability of certain strands of Western political thought in China, not the least important of which is Leninism, which to this day allows the People's Republic to survive as the world's last significant communist state? As suggested below, a Chinese leader's political worldview – itself as much international as "Chinese" – would go far towards determining the fate of the early PRC's most important international relationship.

Although both the internal and the external aspects of Chinese foreign relations require dealing with transnational and intercultural interactions – cultural, economic or political – I prefer the term "internationalization" to (for example) "globalization" for a very simple reason. States and governments matter, critically, to the private as well as the public dimensions of Chinese foreign relations in the 20th century, which took place in settings that were inescapably inter-*national*, across recognized (albeit sometimes disputed) national frontiers. And states and governments mediated, regulated and registered an ever-growing percentage of the activities of non-state actors.

A single essay cannot hope to address all these issues in the history of the early People's Republic. This article focuses on a topic in which all dimensions of China's international relations come into play in one measure or another: China's role in the socialist world economy during the 1950s and early 1960s. As most recent work on Sino-Soviet relations has focused primarily on external political relations,[12] it should be useful to explore the multiple, and ultimately political, dimensions of China's international economic relations, the alternative directions of which were stated starkly by Nikita Khrushchev in 1959[13]:

If we want to speak of the future, it seems to me that the further development of the socialist countries will in all probability proceed along lines of reinforcing a

---

12. This gap in our scholarship has now begun to be addressed in a series of conferences on China's internationalization led by a consortium of research centres: the Sinological Institute of the Free University Berlin; the History Department at Peking University; the Institute for East Asian Studies at the University of California, Berkeley; and the Fairbank Center at Harvard. For an excellent example of recent scholarship that looks at multiple patterns of interaction across borders see Mechthild Leutner and Klaus Mühlhahn (eds.), *Deutsch-chinesische Beziehungen im 19. Jahrhundert. Mission und Wirtschaft in interkultureller Perspektive* (Münster: Lit, 2001).

13. Quoted in *Pravda*, 27 March 1959, cited in Michael Kaser, *Comecon: Integration Problems of the Planned Economies*, 2nd ed. (London: Oxford University Press, 1967), p. 201.

single world system of the socialist economy. One after another the economic barriers which separated our countries under capitalism will disappear .... Not a single sovereign socialist state is able to shut itself up within its own frontiers and rely exclusively upon its own potential, or its own wealth. If the contrary were true, we would not be communist internationalists, but national-socialists.

The International Inheritance of the People's Republic of China

If the Kuomintang regime that ruled the Chinese mainland from 1927 to 1949 styled itself in English as "Nationalist," the CCP was, from its conception, internationalist in premise and in promise. Its founding, as the Chinese historian Xiang Qing (向青) has written, "was a direct consequence of Comintern intervention to establish a Chinese branch of the Communist International."[14] Its revolution, Mao Zedong would admit in a frank and difficult exchange with Soviet Ambassador Pavel Iudin in 1958, "could not have succeeded without the October Revolution."[15] Its proudest offspring, the new PRC, would bear an indelible Soviet birthmark.

When Mao Zedong declared that the Chinese people had finally "stood up" with the establishment of the People's Republic of China on 1 October 1949, he made it clear that they would not stand alone but would stand by the Soviet Union and its allies.[16] Stalin and Mao may often have been "uncertain partners,"[17] but the PRC in its formative years would be Moscow's most faithful and self-sacrificing ally, a distinction earned in blood in Korea and by the fact that, unlike the Eastern European "people's democracies," the PRC's allegiance was not bought at gunpoint.

Michael Sheng has argued that the CCP that took power was in a fundamental sense not "nationalist," as it lacked a core conception of a "Chinese nation" defined principally by borders, ethnicity or

14. Xiang Qing, "Zhongguo gongchandang chuangli" ("The founding of the Chinese Communist Party"), *Zhonggong dangshi yanjiu lunwen xuan* (*Selected Essays on CCP Party History*), Vol. 1, p. 296, cited in Arif Dirlik, *The Origins of Chinese Communism* (New York: Oxford University Press,1989), p. 192. The opening and now partial publication of the Comintern archives in Moscow demonstrates anew how CCP history is inextricably entwined with that of the Soviet Union. See Mechthild Leutner *et al.* (eds.), *Die Komintern und die national-revolutionäre Bewegung in China: Dokumente, Band 1: 1920–1925*, hrsg. von dem Russischen Zentrum für Archivierung und Erforschung von Dokumenten zur neuesten Geschichte, dem Ostasiatischen Seminar der FU Berlin und dem Institut für den Fernen Osten der Russischen Akademie der Wissenschaften (Paderborn: Schöningh, 1996; Band 2: 1926–27, Teil 1 und 2, 1999). The best general study of CCP relations with Moscow is now Yang Kuisong, *Zhonggong yu Mosike de guanxi, 1920–1960* (*The Chinese Communists and Moscow, 1920–1960*) (Taibei: Dongda, 1997).
15. Record of conversation, Mao Zedong and Soviet Ambassador to Beijing Pavel Iudin, 22 July 1958, reprinted in Odd Arne Westad (ed.), *Brothers in Arms: The Rise and Fall of the Sino-Soviet Alliance, 1945–1963* (Washington DC: Woodrow Wilson Press; and Stanford: Stanford University Press, 1998), p. 349.
16. Mao Tse-tung, *Selected Works*, Vol. 5 (Peking: Foreign Languages Press, 1977), p. 17.
17. Sergei N. Goncharov, John W. Lewis, and Xue Litai. *Uncertain Partners: Stalin, Mao and the Korean War* (Stanford: Stanford University Press, 1993).

language. It drew lines instead along class boundaries, limited "the people" to those on whose loyalty it could count, and placed the party-state on a higher moral plane than the nation-state. Thus despite its nationalist rhetoric, the CCP, "born pro-Soviet," could support the interests of the "proletarian state" of the USSR over the interests of the Chinese Republic, which the CCP sought to destroy.[18] As later events would show, this was an internationalism that could go beyond fealty to the Soviet founder to something more properly described, as Chen Jian has suggested, as universalism.[19]

In economics as in politics, it was never the aim of the PRC leadership to build "socialism in one country." That phrase summed up the model of Stalinist autarky when the Soviet Union survived "capitalist encirclement" as the world's only communist country during the inter-war years. By late 1949, however, the socialist world stretched from Berlin to Canton, and included one-third of the world's population. The PRC would not have to build socialism alone: the "fraternal partnership with the states of the socialist community, and, above all, with the Soviet Union [would] quicken the movement of the Chinese people on the road to socialism."[20]

The great Sino-Soviet exchange that ensued in the 1950s was, then, part of a larger web of co-operative relationships with all the "brother countries" of the socialist bloc. China was now a member of what Stalin called "two parallel world markets ... confronting one another."[21] The subject of limited Western academic interest in the 1950s,[22] the "socialist world economy" has not been the topic of serious historical inquiry since. In the case of China, perhaps this is because, as Lowell Dittmer has noted, much of Western scholarship on Sino-Soviet relations during the PRC era has studied the conflicts between the two communist powers, not their co-operation.[23] This is true also of post-1960s Chinese writing on the relationship,[24] though not, by and large, of Soviet histories and reminiscences on the 1950s,

18. Michael M. Sheng, *Battling Western Imperialism: Mao, Stalin, and the United States* (Princeton: Princeton University Press, 1997), pp. 187–191.

19. See Jian Chen, *China's Road to the Korean War* (New York: Columbia University Press, 1994).

20. V. I. Glunin, *Sotsialisticheskaia revoliutsiia v Kitae* (Moscow: Izdatel'stvo Sotsial'no-ekonomicheskoi literatury, 1960), p. 56.

21. Joseph Stalin, *Economic Problems of Socialism in the USSR* (New York: International Publishers, 1952), p. 26.

22. Exceptions are Kaser, *Comecon* and Frederic L. Pryor, *The Communist Foreign Trade System* (Cambridge, MA: MIT Press, 1963); Nicolas Spulber, "The Soviet-bloc foreign trade system," and Raymond F. Mikesell and Donald A. Wells, "State trading in the Sino-Soviet bloc," both in *Law and Contemporary Problems*, Vol. 24 (1959), pp. 420–434 and 435–453.

23. Lowell Dittmer, *Sino-Soviet Normalization and Its International Implications, 1945–1990* (Seattle & London: University of Washington Press, 1992), p. 10.

24. For example, Wu Xiuquan, *Zai Waijiaobu banian de jingli: 1950.1–1958.10* (*Eight Years in the Foreign Ministry: January 1950 to October 1958*) (Beijing: Shijie zhishi chubanshe, 1983), pp. 1–34. Perhaps the least politicized account of Sino-Soviet co-operation remains *Liunian lai Zhong Su youhao hezuo gonggu yu fazhan* (*The Stability and Development of Friendly Co-operation between China and the Soviet Union*

which have tended to stress the collaborative dimensions of Sino-Soviet relations.[25]

At present it is not possible to write the definitive history of China's role in the socialist world economy: the opening of Chinese party, state and firm archives that relate to the topic still lag well behind those of comparable Soviet and East European institutions. Yet material exists in China and elsewhere sufficient to open a discussion of several questions. How *did* this socialist world economy work (or not work)? To what degree was it genuinely "internationalist," even as it was negotiated by formally sovereign states? Here we can speak only of the Chinese experience. To investigate it, it makes sense to start with the foundations of Sino-Soviet relations before 1949; then to recount the organization of the socialist economic world as constituted in the 1950s; then briefly to assess the terms of trade between China and its socialist "brothers" and the broader impact of socialist economic internationalism on the PRC; and finally to try to explain the sudden end to the most self-consciously international age of Chinese economic development.

Viewing the wreckage of international communism at the beginning of the 21st century, it is easy to dismiss the effort to create an alternative world economy as doomed. Fail it did. Yet it was an ambitious and complicated undertaking that had a profound impact on China's economic development in ways that are visible still.

Soviet Models Before 1949

Before one could speak, after 1945, of a "socialist world," the Soviet Union alone was the model – in China as around the world – of communist economic development. Its belief in the "scientific" planning of an economy and the state ownership of industry, and its obsession with heavy industrial and military development as the keys to state power, would be shared by Nationalist and Communist regimes alike in China, and would make economic co-operation, when it came, all the easier. By 1949, a shadow of a "Soviet model" of state-led industrialization was already evident in Chinese industrial policy. The same could be said for foreign trade. By 1938, state industrial and military imports were almost entirely financed through a series of

---

footnote continued

in the Past Six Years) (*Guangzhou, 1955*). *A recent and balanced set of essays may be found in* Zhanhou Zhong Su guanxi zouxiang (1945–1960) (Trends in Post-war Chinese-Soviet Relations, 1945–1960) (*Beijing: Shehui kexue wenxian chubanshe, 1997*).

25. For example, O. B. Borisov and B. T. Koloskov, *Sovetsko-kitayskie otnoshenia, 1945–1980*, 3rd ed. (Moscow: Mysl', 1980). Borisov is a pseudonym for O. B. Rakhmanin; Koloskov is a pseudonym for S. Kulik. Both worked in the Central Committee of the CPSU, Rakhmanin being in charge of China policy. A more recent and (in political assessments) evenhanded account is Iu. M. Galenovich, *"Belye piatna" i "Bolevye tochki" v istorii sovetsko-kitaiskikh otnoshenii* (Moscow: Institut Dal'nego Vostoka RAN, 1992), Vol. 2 (1949–1991).

revolving barter/credit arrangements by which industrial and military goods and services advanced in credit were repaid in Chinese raw materials. Under these arrangements the Soviet Union and China reached three major credit agreements in 1938–39, assisting China's war effort during years when Western aid was minimal and foreshadowing the trading patterns of the 1950s.[26]

There were other, more difficult, precedents from the pre-1949 period. A series of Sino-Soviet economic enterprises in China's north-west and north-eastern border areas were less examples of bilateral co-operation than of old-fashioned imperialism, Soviet-style. In theory joint ventures, these were as a rule Soviet-managed facilities on Chinese soil. (It may be worth noting that in organizational terms, these enterprises were ancestors of the Soviet stock companies set up in the eastern zone of Germany in 1946, in part as a means of gaining reparations.[27]) Two examples of projects that formally came under joint Soviet-Nationalist government management were the Chinese Eastern Railway and the Dushan (独山) (Xinjiang) oil field: the former was the subject of the 1929 Sino-Soviet war, and was later sold to the Japanese over Nanjing's protests; the latter was initially, like most Sino-Soviet ventures, made directly with a Chinese provincial government, and became a joint venture at the national level only after first being seized by the Nationalist regime at a low point in Sino-Soviet ties in 1943.[28] This pattern continued after the Second World War. The 1946 Soviet proposal for the placing of all Manchurian heavy industry under joint Sino-Soviet management was, according to the chief Soviet negotiator (in response to Chinese suggestions that joint management made economic sense in only a few industries), "not an economic question, but above all a political question," reflecting the Soviet Union's *de facto* political and military power in that part of China.[29]

A second, unpleasant, precedent was in the legal status of Soviet citizens in China. The famous Karakhan Manifesto of July 1919 "to the Chinese nation," which stated the terms on which the Soviet state

26. Second Historical Archives, Nanjing, file 28 (2) 389, documents on the National Resources Commission and related payments to the Soviet Union through 1946. The two best sources on Sino-Soviet relations of this period remain He Jun, "Lun 1929–1939 nian de Zhong Su guanxi" ("Sino-Soviet relations, 1929–39"), dissertation, Nanjing University, 1986; and John W. Garver, *Chinese-Soviet Relations, 1937–1945: The Diplomacy of Chinese Nationalism* (Oxford: Oxford University Press, 1988).

27. Norman M. Naimark, *The Russians in Germany: A History of the Soviet Zone of Occupation, 1945–1949* (Cambridge, MA: Harvard University Press, 1995), pp. 189–190.

28. Sun Yueqi, "Kangzhan shiqijian liangci chu Xinjiang jilue" ("Record of two visits to Xinjiang during the war of resistance"), *Wenshi ziliao (Literary and Historical Materials)*, No. 84 (1982), pp. 135–149.

29. Sun Yueqi, "Huiyi wo yu Jiang Jieshi jiechu liangsanshi" ("Two or three items about my dealings with Chiang Kai-shek"), *Wenshi ziliao*, No. 84 (1982), p. 133. Or we may take as an example the case of the Sino-Soviet Aviation Company (Zhong Su hangkong gongsi), organized on the basis of an agreement in 1939 and extended by the Nationalists for five years in 1949: see *Minguo dang'an (Republican Archives)*, No. 1 (1995), pp. 31–42.

was prepared to renounce imperialism and its entitlements in China, made generous promises that were never fulfilled. For the Soviet Union was the only power *not* to relinquish its extra-territorial privileges in China. Stalin personally informed Liu Shaoqi (刘少奇) that any Soviet personnel in China would be "subject to Soviet jurisdiction. ... The Chinese side has no [legal] authority over [them]."[30] In one guise or another, all Soviet citizens would be under extra-territorial jurisdiction at least until 1960.[31]

Still, by 1950, there were strong reasons to explore a Sino-Soviet alliance that went beyond ideological affinity or strategic partnership. In economic development in general and industrial development in particular, the Sino-Soviet relationship of the 1950s harkened back to Sun Yat-sen's grand plan to develop "the vast resources of China ... internationally under a socialistic scheme, for the good of the world in general and the Chinese people in particular."[32] In economic relations, Sino-Soviet co-operation seemed less a revolutionary break than a logical progression from the nationalizations of industry and foreign trade of the Nationalist government, the growing power of state planning bureaucracies, and the series of Sino-Soviet agreements for joint industrial ventures and barter-credit exchanges.[33] In short, seeds for what Deborah Kaple has called "modern China's Stalinist roots"[34] were in the ground well before 1949.

Transitions to High Stalinism

When one adds to the above narrative the victory of the CCP in the Chinese Civil War, it is no surprise that the PRC entered into such a close alliance – economic as well as otherwise – with what was now officially called the "elder Soviet brother."[35] The alliance of 1950 built

30. Shi Zhe, *Zai lishi juren shenbian* (*Alongside the Giants of History*) (Beijing: Zhongyang wenxian chubanshe, 1991), pp. 446–47, cited in Shu Guang Zhang, "Sino-Soviet economic cooperation," in Westad, *Brothers in Arms*, p. 199.

31. Extra-territorial rights were indeed relinquished for White Russians in China. But with the Soviet nationalization of all facets of foreign relations – economic and cultural as well as political and military – there were no "private" activities for Soviet citizens in China, who were under the authority of the Soviet Embassy and therefore, the USSR claimed, were entitled to diplomatic immunity. This was made more explicit in a series of agreements with Chinese governments, including one of the secret protocols of the 1950 Treaty of Friendship, Alliance and Mutual Assistance which went further to claim that any criminal activity of Soviet citizens in China would be dealt with by Soviet, not Chinese, courts. On the latter point see Goncharov *et al.*, *Uncertain Partners*, p. 125.

32. Sun Yat-sen, *The International Development of China* (New York & London: Putnam, 1922), preface, p. v.

33. See for example Second Historical Archives, Nanjing, file 28 (2) 3644, documents on the Sino-Soviet barter agreements of January 1945 and January 1946. See documents on the Sino-Soviet Aviation Company Agreement of 1949 (supplementary to the agreement of 1939) in *Minguo dang'an*, No. 1 (1995), pp. 31–42.

34. Deborah A. Kaple, *Dream of a Red Factory: The Legacy of High Stalinism in China* (New York: Oxford University Press, 1994), p. 3.

35. Marie-Luise Näth, "East European Sinologists remember the first 15 years of the PRC: a balance sheet," in Marie-Luise Näth (ed.), *Communist China in Retrospect* (Frankfurt a.M: Peter Lang, 1995), p. 189.

upon the Nationalist experience but was – to cite Michael Sheng again – even more fundamentally "a logical extension of the history of CCP–Moscow relations in the decades prior to the proclamation of the PRC in 1949."[36]

Domestically, for much of its first decade, the People's Republic was a more attentive student of Soviet models in state-building – in the construction of its political, legal, educational and cultural infrastructures – than the CCP ever had been of Comintern approaches to revolution.[37] In the PRC's domestic political arrangements, for example, Soviet models were omnipresent. Mao and his colleagues followed, sometimes against Mao's own initial judgements, Stalin's suggestions that the PRC needed a "coalition government" as an initial façade for party dictatorship; it needed elections to the Political Consultative Conference; and ultimately it had to have (and would have, in 1954) a constitution modelled largely on the USSR's "Stalin constitution" of 1936. As Stalin put it in 1952: "If you do not have a constitution and if the Political Consultative Conference is not elected, enemies can charge that you have seized power by force."[38] (!) Lowell Dittmer has concluded:

The post-revolutionary political apparatus superimposed following liberation was essentially identical to the Soviet structure upon which it was patterned. The elites who led these revolutions shared the same general ideological outlooks as well as the specific objective of modernization without the putative inequities of capitalism. They fully expected their developmental paths to converge in the course of socialist modernization and the eventual realization of socialism.[39]

In so doing China was entering a broader, young community of socialist states, each of which was similarly emulating the Soviet Union in this, its most exaggerated phase of "high Stalinism." "Stalinism," as Ben Fowkes has written, "meant, first and foremost, uniformity."[40] This meant, everywhere in the Soviet sphere, the absolute rule of the communist party, the oligarchic rule of its Politburo, and, inevitably, the emergence of a dominant personality, a

36. Sheng, *Battling Western Imperialism*, p. 186. For an excellent analysis see Steven M. Goldstein, "Nationalism and internationalism: Sino-Soviet relations," in Robinson and Shambaugh, *Chinese Foreign Policy*, pp. 224–265. See also Niu Jun, *Cong Yan'an zouxiang shijie* (*From Yanan to the World*) (Fuzhou: Fujian renmin chubanshe, 1992). On the fundamental conflicts between the CCP and the United States see also Zi Zhongyun, *Meiguo dui Hua zhengce de yuanqi he fazhan* (*Origins and Development of US Policy towards China*) (Chongqing: Chongqing chubanshe, 1987).

37. See the transcript from the Soviet archives of Mao Zedong's conversation with Pavel Iudin, the Soviet Ambassador to China, on 31 March 1956, on the question of the Comintern's and Stalin's China policy, in *Far Eastern Affairs*, No. 4–5 (1994), pp. 132–144. Regarding models for state-building, Deborah Kaple argues that the adoption of a "high Stalinist" model gave the CCP even more power in society than the CPSU had. See Kaple, *Dream of a Red Factory*.

38. See Shi Zhe, *Zai lishi juren shenbian*, p. 408.

39. Lowell Dittmer, "Socialist reform and Sino-Soviet convergence," in Richard Baum (ed.), *Reform and Reaction in Post-Mao China: The Road to Tiananmen* (New York & London: Routledge, 1991), p. 19.

40. Ben Fowkes, *The Rise and Fall of Communism in Eastern Europe*, 2nd ed. (London: Macmillan, 1995), p. 52.

"little Stalin." It meant, too, the growth of public security organs, complete economic control by the state, and economic development giving highest priority to heavy industry and armaments. Despite the slogan of "specific roads to socialism" that had been proclaimed in Eastern Europe since 1946, the pressure to imitate the Soviet Union in nearly every respect became compelling in 1947–48 with the economic division of Europe between those in and those out of the American Marshall Plan, the political consolidation of communist rule, and the denunciation of "Titoist" alternatives to Stalinism. Throughout Eastern Europe, the establishment of command economies rushed forward, with the nationalization of industries, the collectivization of agriculture and the destruction of private commerce. As states extended their control of national economies, central planning commissions on the Soviet model followed everywhere, as did national economic plans that copied the Soviet plans of the 1930s. To co-ordinate all this in Europe was the task of the Council for Mutual Economic Assistance, or Comecon, established in January 1949. From its birth it pressured its participant economies to limit trade with the capitalist states and to strengthen the economic integration of the socialist camp.[41]

China's incorporation into this system began at several levels even before the establishment of the PRC. In early 1949 a small army of Chinese and Soviet officials began the process of formal tutelage: on Stalin's theory of the state; on policy towards nationalities; on the tax system of the USSR; on the role of party cells in factories and ministries; and so on.[42] In the winter of 1950, while Mao was negotiating the terms of the alliance with Stalin, Chen Boda (陈伯达) was visiting the Supreme Party School, the prototype for Beijing's Central Party School (*Zhongyang dangxiao* 中央党校); a Soviet labour union delegation was touring China; and a commission of Soviet urban planners was preparing to leave for Shanghai, with the aim of turning it into a modern, socialist metropolis.[43] Exchanges of teachers and farm animals followed in the spring. By the autumn, members of the Chinese Central Committee were having their suits made in Moscow.[44]

41. *Ibid.* pp. 52–65; Kaser, *Comecon*, pp. 9–41; Scott Parrish, "The Marshall Plan, Soviet-American relations, and the division of Europe," in Norman Naimark and Leonid Gibianskii (eds.), *The Establishment of Communist Regimes in Eastern Europe, 1944–1949* (Boulder: Westview Press, 1997), pp. 267–290, esp. 284–87.

42. RTsKhIDNI (Russian Centre for the Protection and Study of Documents on Recent History), Moscow, archive of the Central Committee of the Communist Party of the Soviet Union (CPSU CC), External Political Commission, fond 17/opis 137, Vol. 405, files on Sino-Soviet study commissions, lecture tours, etc., 1949–50.

43. RtsKhIDNI, Moscow, External Political Commission of the CPSU CC, 17/137, Vol. 406, report to Malenkov of 15 February 1950 on Chen Boda; Vol. 405, report of 1 June 1950 on the three-month tour of labour union delegates to China (20 December 1949 to 10 April 1950); Vol. 405, report of M. Abramov, vice-chair of Moscow City Executive Council on the delegation of city planners to Shanghai and other cities, 7 February 1950.

44. RtsKhIDNI, Moscow, External Political Commission of the CPSU CC, 17/137, Vol. 405, report to Molotov of 27 May 1950 on the sending of teaching teams to China; Vol. 406, report of 7 June 1950 on the export of Soviet horses to China; Vol.

In economic matters, CCP–Soviet economic co-operation had begun even earlier with an "unofficial" 1946 trade agreement between the USSR and the communist-held territories of the north-east. By May 1947 a permanent apparatus of Soviet foreign trade and transport organizations had been created in northern Manchuria. Soviet specialists then consulted on long-term plans for Manchuria's reconstruction, while also providing significant, immediate aid to the CCP war effort.[45] As defined by Zhang Wentian (张闻天), the "north-east model"[46] of economic development that emerged by 1948 followed both inherited Nationalist practice and Soviet advice in stressing the rapid growth of defence and heavy industries according to state plan. Thereafter large volumes of material were translated from the Russian on the practice of the "high Stalinist" Fourth Five-Year Plan (1946–50).[47] In July 1951, with Soviet advice, the concept of nationwide planning was reintroduced with the PRC's first annual economic plan. By the end of 1951 the state sector accounted for 80 per cent of heavy industry, 100 per cent of oil production, 98 per cent of iron and steel production, 82 per cent of machine-tool building, 76 per cent of electrical power and 70 per cent of the cotton textile industry.[48]

Mao Zedong's desire to transplant the Soviet experience to China sooner rather than later appears to have outpaced that of some of his comrades. For him, as for Stalin, the public commitment to "new democracy," with promises of a coalition government and a mixed economy lasting 15 years or more, was not much more than a useful slogan. Yet some senior CCP leaders – Liu Shaoqi (刘少奇), Chen Yun (陈云), Deng Zihui (邓子恢) and Bo Yibo (薄一波) – believed in

---

footnote continued

406, report to Suslov of 2 September 1950 requesting 51 Western-style suits for Chinese comrades. (The request was granted.)

45. This was negotiated by Gao Gang in Moscow: see the account and trade statistics in Borisov and Koloskov, *Sovetsko-kitayskie otnoshenia*, p. 30. On Soviet developmental advice before 1949 see *ibid.* pp. 31–38, and, particularly, details of the 1946 "unofficial" (because Moscow still recognized the Nationalist government) trade agreement in the memoir of M. I. Sladkovskii, *Znakomstvo s Kitaem i kitaitsami* (Moscow: Mysl', 1984), pp. 324–29. The participation of Soviet advisors in the Chinese Civil War began in 1946 when 100 Soviet engineers were sent to northern Manchuria to restore the rail links with the USSR. In 1948 Soviet engineers repaired over 100 bridges and 100 miles of track that had been destroyed by the Nationalist military. See S. A. Voevodin *et al.*, *Sotsial'no-ekonomicheskii stroy i ekonomicheskaia politika KNR* (Moscow: Majka, 1978), p. 82. For his oversight of railway repair and his aid to Lin Biao, Sladkovskii was given an Order of Lenin in Moscow in December 1948: see Sladkovskii, *Znakomstvo s Kitaem I kitaitsami*, p. 353. For a political and military perspective on CCP-Soviet co-operation in Manchuria after 1945 see Michael M. Sheng, "Mao, Stalin, and the struggle in Manchuria, 1945–46: nationalism or internationalism?" paper presented to the Conference on New Evidence on the Cold War in Asia, Hong Kong, 1996.

46. See Hua-Yu Li, *Mao and the Economic Stalinization of China, 1948–1953* (Lanham: Rowman & Littlefield, 2006), ch. 2.

47. Kaple, *Dream of a Red Factory*, pp. viii, 11–18.

48. Borisov and Koloskov, *Sovetsko-kitayskie otnosheniia*, p. 52.

it enough to promote an economy that would tolerate capitalism in a manner "specifically Chinese in form," promoting policies which, when carried much further decades later, would be called market socialism.[49] But Mao decided early to take China on a clearly Stalinist path, though he would implement it fully only upon the end of the Korean War with his new "general line for socialist transition" of October 1953. (It seems that Mao had already made this decision in 1950, and would admit in 1958 that he had kept it a secret for tactical reasons.[50]) Hua-Yu Li has noted that Mao was "committed to a Stalinist approach"[51] in all its aspects; this would be evident in his economic programme after 1953, which was inspired above all by his reading, back in the 1930s, of Stalin's famous *Short Course*, which was a history of the CPSU and the stages of Soviet economic development. Mao's "general line" plagiarized Stalin's of 1929, a sign of both respect and submission by a junior partner in global communism.[52]

China and the Socialist World Economy

The new world economy that China now joined had great ambitions and serious structural weaknesses. A Soviet article of 1961 described its ideal condition[53]:

The continuous growth of production in all socialist countries ensures a constant expansion of their trade. The world socialist market does not have the problem of sale for each individual country and for the world socialist system of economy as a whole. Difficulties in sale may arise only temporarily for individual items and are easily surmounted. Nor does the world socialist market ever experience crises or stagnation, characteristic of the foreign trade of the capitalist countries .... The state economic plans of the Soviet Union and People's Democracies incorporate plans for foreign trade, realized under trade agreements between the socialist

49. The short-lived era of "New Democracy" and the "Chinese NEP" of the early 1950s needs much more research. For an excellent inquiry based on Soviet archives see Arlen Meliksetov, "'New Democracy' and China's search for socio-economic development routes (1949–53)," *Far Eastern Affairs*, No. 1 (1996), pp. 75–92. The quotation is from the resolution of the Second Plenary Meeting of the Seventh Central Committee of the CCP (March 1949), and refers to the prospects for capitalism in a socialist China: "The existence and development of capitalism in China, the existence and development of free trade and competition, are not as limitless and unbridled as in capitalist countries, nor are they as limited and cramped as in newly democratic countries of Eastern Europe; they are specifically Chinese in form." Meliksetov, "New Democracy," p. 77.

50. Shi Zhongquan, *Mao Zedong de jianxin kaituo* (*Mao Zedong's Hard, Pioneering Road*) (Beijing: Zhonggong dangshi ziliao chubanshe, 1990), p. 132, cited in Hua-Yu Li, *Mao and the Economic Stalinization*, p. 2.

51. Hua-Yu Li, *Mao and the Economic Stalinization*, p. 1.

52. *Ibid.* p. 170. On the centrality of Mao's decisions in ending New Democracy see Meliksetov, "New Democracy," pp. 75–92, esp. pp. 82–83; Bo Yibo, *Ruogan zhongda juece yu shijian de huigu* (*A Review of Some Important Policies and Events*), Vol. 1, 1949–56 (Beijing: Zhonggong zhongyang dangxiao chubanshe, 1991), pp. 234–242.

53. A. Dudinskii, "Some features of the development of the world socialist market," *Voprosy Ekonomiki*, No. 2 (1961), translated in *Problems of Economics*, Vol. 4, No. 5 (1961), p. 58.

countries .... In contrast to the anarchy and unpredictable conjunctural fluctuation inherent in the foreign trade of the capitalist countries, trade in the world socialist market develops in conformity with the requirements of the planned economy of the socialist-camp countries, and serves as a major instrument in the co-ordination of their economic plans.

Apart from the fact that the economic history of the socialist bloc would hardly be devoid of crises in the 1950s – the chronic malaise of Soviet agriculture and the catastrophic collapse of China's agriculture at the end of the decade, among them – the socialist world had several built-in disadvantages. First, it consisted primarily of the less affluent and more war-damaged countries of Eurasia. The economic division of the world disrupted previous patterns of trade with more advanced Western economies. Thus the two major trade blocs in the post-war period enjoyed more similar levels of development within each and would be more "horizontally" integrated than the more vertically integrated trading patterns of the pre-war decades. Secondly, the use of trade to integrate centrally planned economies was particularly difficult in an environment in which domestic prices were insulated from international markets and the currencies effectively non-transferable or non-convertible one with another, not to mention with the "hard" currencies of the West. Thirdly, the political economy of Stalinism that emphasized absolute party control and centralized economic planning in a national setting meant that socialist economic co-operation began, and for the most part remained, set in a series of bilateral agreements, without an integrated, multilateral vision of the bloc as an economic whole. Only with Stalin's death would there emerge efforts to promote specialization and trade within the bloc.[54] Fourthly, as the economic reorientation of the late 1940s diminished trade with the capitalist countries and redirected it to socialist comrades, the international divisions of labour achieved in pre-war markets could not easily be replicated in socialist ones. Indeed, with every socialist country operating five- (or more) year plans, with each plan "cast in precisely the same pattern,"[55] there were new disincentives to trade. With each member emphasizing heavy industry at the expense of consumer goods and agriculture, the original bias in the Soviet model towards autarky could only be reinforced; hence

54. Khrushchev would remark as late as 1957: "We said long ago that a better co-operation should be established between our countries. It is impossible to develop everything everywhere simultaneously." Cited in Kaser, *Comecon*, pp. 64–65. See also Spulber, "The Soviet bloc foreign trade system"; Mikesell and Wells, "State trading in the Sino-Soviet bloc"; I. Oleinki, "Forms of international division of labor in the socialist camp," *Problems of Economics*, Vol. 4, No. 6 (1961), pp. 56–63. On the weaknesses of socialist international integration, particularly in the Stalin years, see Charles Gati, *The Bloc that Failed: Soviet–East European Relations in Transition* (Bloomington & Indianapolis: Indiana University Press, 1990), p. 20. Most optimistically see M. I. Sladkovski, *Semiletka i ekonomicheskoe sotrudnichestvo stran sotsialisticheskogo lageria* (Moscow: Institut Mezhdunarodnykh Otnoshenii, 1959).

55. Kaser, *Comecon*, p. 17.

the building of huge iron and steel complexes in East Germany, Poland, Czechoslovakia, Hungary, Bulgaria and Romania, not to mention the Soviet Union and China.[56] The great expansion of steel (Stalin's *nom-de-guerre*, after all) and munitions production in the socialist bloc may have made strategic sense with the onset of the Korean War in 1950, but this drives home the point that the fundamental basis of international socialist economic co-operation was, first and last, political.[57]

For all its limitations, the international socialist economy was a foundation of China's economic development in the first decade of the PRC and almost completely defined its international economic relations. Trade agreements were reached with the USSR, Czechoslovakia and the GDR in 1950; Poland, Hungary and North Korea in 1951; Romania and Bulgaria in 1952; Mongolia in 1953; and Albania and North Vietnam in 1954.[58] Although China never became a formal member of Comecon, it attended its standing commissions (organized by commodity), and the structure of its trade agreements with Comecon members was virtually identical to those between Comecon members.

After the adoption of Mao's new "general line" and the beginning of the PRC's First Five-Year Plan in 1953, China's trade with the Soviet bloc expanded enormously.[59] In industrial relations the broad outlines of this co-operation as it developed over the rest of the 1950s are well known: the construction of over 200 industrial projects, mostly as "turnkey" (that is, fully finished) installations which became the core of the communist state industrial sector; the transfer of thousands of industrial designs; and the visits of perhaps 10,000 Soviet and East European specialists to China and of over 50,000 Chinese engineers, trainees and students to the Soviet Union and its European allies. Millions of Soviet books were imported and thousands of them were translated. Soviet aid in particular was

56. See Pryor, *The Communist Foreign Trade System*, p. 25.

57. In Eastern Europe, excess engineering capacity became a major problem in the 1950s. A Hungarian observer wrote: "The various countries created ... whole industries parallel to each other turning out products in excess supply and unsaleable at a time when other goods were everywhere unavailable." T. Kiss, *A szocialista orszagok gazdasagi egyuttmukodese* (Budapest, 1961), p. 110, quoted in Kaser, *Comecon*, p. 20.

58. For Chinese documents on the negotiation of Sino-Soviet economic relations in 1950–52, see *Jianguo yilai zhongyao wenxian xuanbian* (*Selected Important Documents Since the Establishment of the Country*) (Beijing: Zhongyang wenxian chubanshe, 1991–), for example, Vol. 1, p. 95, Telegram from Mao Zedong to CCP Central Committee concerning Zhou Enlai's visit to the Soviet Union for negotiations, 2–3 January 1950; *ibid.* p. 98, Liu Shaoqi's report to Mao Zedong concerning Sino-Soviet metals and oil companies in Xinjiang, 2 January 1950; Vol. 2, p. 7, Zhou Enlai's instructions concerning important problems in employing Soviet experts in construction and design, 7 January 1951; Vol. 3, p. 340, Sino-Soviet report on negotiations between the USSR and the PRC, 15 September 1952.

59. Bilateral trade increased by over 25% in 1953 compared with 1952. Borisov and Koloskov, *Sovetsko-kitayskie otnoshenia*, p. 65.

simply massive, and, although it was not free, it was given on better terms than could then have been found from any other source – even if China had (as it clearly did not) alternative sources for credit, advice and investment.[60] For the Soviet Union, itself still a net importer of capital goods in 1954, industrial exports to China competed with domestic demand and East European markets for the same goods.[61]

While Chinese foreign trade officials noted that prices of certain commodities differed from those on the world market, overall and over many years the financial calculations of Sino-Soviet trade were deemed "reasonable and fair."[62] This is despite the fact that China, in importing capital goods only from the Eastern bloc, was in a "seller's market" and normally would have been forced to be a "price-taker." Soviet prices to China of certain commodities were higher than those of the same goods when exported to the West,[63] but as Feng-hwa Mah has shown, barter ratios for Soviet industrial equipment were "clearly to China's advantage as far as its industrial programme" was concerned. Where else in the world could China get five tons of steel products for one ton of frozen pork? Or a steel-pipe factory for 10,000 tons of tobacco?[64] Moreover, there is little evidence that Moscow used its bargaining power to a comprehensive economic advantage.[65] For example, Soviet technical assistance was never measured according to world market equivalents. Indeed, the concept of intellectual property was so alien to the Soviet bloc that scientific-technical documentation, including blueprints, was provided without direct compensation, as noted in the Sino-Soviet economic agreement of 15 May 1953. China was charged for the physical machinery, but the technology was basically free. For its part, the Chinese government was contracted to reimburse Moscow for only 50 per cent of the estimated costs of Soviet technical advisors in China. And if the international value of the ruble was overstated in Sino-Soviet agreements, given the very low interest rates of Soviet credits (never more than 2 per cent per annum), there can be little doubt that China fared very well indeed under the

60. See the excellent summary of Soviet aid in Dittmer, *Sino-Soviet Normalization*, pp. 17–25. The capital goods and military-related imports that comprised the bulk of China's imports from the Soviet Union were prohibited for the West as exports to China under the strategic trade regime of the US.

61. Alexander Eckstein, "Moscow–Peking axis: the economic pattern," in Howard L. Boorman *et al.*, *Moscow-Peking Axis: Strengths and Strains* (New York: Harper, 1957), pp. 82–83.

62. Feng-hwa Mah, "The terms of Sino-Soviet trade," *The China Quarterly*, No. 17 (1964), p. 175. As Mah argues elsewhere, prices are not everything: "For China, the availability of a ready market for its exports, the existence of a reliable (at least in the 1950's) supplier of the type of producer goods it needed, the availability of Soviet credit arrangements, and the convenience of conducting foreign trade between two planned economies may be considered more important than favorable prices." Feng-hwa Mah, "Foreign trade," in Alexander Eckstein *et al.* (eds.), *Economic Trends in Communist China* (Chicago: Aldine, 1968), p. 721.

63. Feng-hwa Mah, "The terms of Sino-Soviet trade," pp. 188–191.

64. Feng-hwa Mah, "Foreign trade," p. 724.

65. Eckstein, "Moscow-Peking axis," p. 88.

terms of a Sino-Soviet exchange in which each became the leading trading partner of the other.[66]

Bureaucratically, the creation of what Khrushchev imagined as "a single world system of socialist economy"[67] started with the negotiation of a set of bilateral commercial treaties, which defined the framework of trade and included provisions for most-favoured-nation treatment. Bilateral trade agreements of varying duration were then negotiated. Finally, specific contracts were signed between the foreign trade corporations of the governments, specifying quantities, prices and delivery dates of individual products. For multilateral transactions – rare at first but gradually facilitated by a "one price" rule for goods traded within the bloc – the Soviet State Bank served as the clearing house after 1957.[68] These ongoing negotiations brought together on a regular basis communist elites from East Berlin to Beijing who had the challenging task of co-ordinating their international economic obligations with their national economic plans. Just as domestic five-year plans were subject to periodic (usually annual) adjustment, so too the multi-year co-operative agreements between China and its Eastern bloc partners were in fact renegotiated on an annual basis to bring them more in line with the realities of production in a given year.

The documents of China's annual negotiations with the Soviet Union and the German Democratic Republic are now available to researchers.[69] These extraordinarily tedious materials give the historian new respect for the breadth of knowledge and attention to detail required of the diplomatic and trade representatives within the Eastern bloc: for it was no easy thing to plan the economy of

66. L. V. Filatov, *Ekonomicheskaia otsenka nauchno-tekhnicheskoi pomoshchi sovetskogo soiuza Kitaiu, 1949–1966* (Moscow: Nauka, 1980), pp. 11–12; L. Filatov, "Cost assessment of Soviet-Chinese scientific and technical cooperation," *Far Eastern Affairs*, No. 2 (1990), pp. 111–17; L. Nikolayev and Y. Mikhailov, "China's foreign economic policy," *International Affairs*, Vol. 9 (1973), p. 45. These rosy accounts are not fundamentally challenged in the published Chinese documentation. See Meng Xianzhang (ed.), *Zhong Su maoyi shi ziliao* (*Materials on the History of Sino-Soviet Trade*) (Beijing: Zhongguo duiwai jingji maoyi chubanshe, 1991). For a sober and positive assessment of Soviet technicians in development work see Waldemar A. Nielsen and Soran S. Hodjera, "Sino-Soviet bloc technical assistance – another bilateral approach," *Annals of the American Academy of Political and Social Science*, Vol. 323 (May 1959), pp. 40–49. China may have enjoyed better terms in its bilateral trade with the Soviet Union than did the East European countries in their trade with Moscow. See Horst Menderhausen, "The terms of Sino-satellite trade, 1955–1959," Rand Corporation Memorandum no. RM-2507-1-PR, prepared for the US Air Force (March 1962).

67. Speech of 7 March 1959, quoted in Sladkovski, *Semiletka i ekonomicheskoe sotrudnichestvo*, p. 32.

68. Spulber, "The Soviet bloc foreign trade system," pp. 424–25. Spulber notes (p. 427) that according to a rule against price discrimination in 1951, each socialist country was to charge any other the same price for the same goods, taking into account only differences in transportation costs.

69. In Moscow, in the Russian State Archive of the Economy (RGAE); in Germany in the Bundesarchiv, Potsdam, and in the Stiftung Archiv der Parteien und Massenorganisationen der DDR im Bundesarchiv, in Berlin (hereafter Stiftung Archiv).

one-third of mankind. These were, almost without exception, exacting negotiations, particularly on the pricing of goods in rubles,[70] which frequently had to be settled at the highest level. Zhou Enlai (周恩来) was the arbiter of China's soybean exports to the GDR in 1957–58.[71]

Yet in the 1950s these negotiations were also marked, much more often than not, by a sense of solidarity. The concept of "brother countries" was taken seriously, and the broader cause of building socialism appears to have been a factor facilitating compromise. The annual negotiations were thus frequently a means of adjusting commitments to take into account the difficulties of one or both parties.[72] In urgent cases, supplementary agreements were signed, as in 1953 when, in the wake of anti-communist riots in East Berlin, the PRC sent 50 million rubles worth of emergency foodstuffs to the tottering GDR. As Zhou Enlai wrote to his German counterpart, Otto Grotewohl, in a private letter: "In consideration of the friendship between the Chinese and German peoples and in order to overcome the current difficulties into which the American imperialists and the West German bandits have brought the German people, we see our assistance to the German people as our duty and as an honour."[73] There was no pretending, in short, that the idea of a socialist world economy was exclusively, or even primarily, economic in origin. It was, according to a Soviet study of the PRC in 1959, "trade of a consistently socialist type, which is organically inherent to a rapid tempo of development ... [by] socialist states which are united together by having the same type of socio-economic, political, and ideological bases and by having a unity of interests and goals."[74] As for the precise means of calculating economic value in socialist trade, the principle of "comradely mutual assistance" determined the use of "one or another variant of [financial] calculation among socialist states," according to a Soviet study of Sino-Soviet scientific and technical exchange.[75] In other words, if politics was in alignment, the economics would take care of itself.

China's incorporation into the socialist world economy had its distinctive tensions and problems. Not a few were of China's making: in attempting a First Five-Year Plan more Stalinist than the Soviet First Five-Year Plan; or in following Soviet examples too slavishly, for example in the sciences, where Lysenkoism controlled the field of

70. Galenovich, "*Belye piatna*," pp. 30ff.

71. Stiftung Archiv, Berlin, IV 2/610, v. 179, "Vermerk über die Besprechung beim Gen. Min. Präs. Tschou En-lai mit der Regierungsdelegation der DDR," 10 October 1957.

72. This would be true also in the realm of scientific and technological exchange: see for example RGAE, Moscow, 9480/1735, files on the Sino-Soviet scientific and technological agreement of 5 February 1958, based on the agreement of 12 October 1954.

73. Stiftung Archiv, Berlin, Nachlaß Grotewohl, Bd. 477, letter, Zhou Enlai to Otto Grotewohl, 11 August 1953.

74. Yu. N. Kapelinskiy *et al.*, *Razvitie ekonomiki i vneshneekonomicheskikh sviazei Kitaiskoi Narodnoi Respubliki* (Moscow: Vneshtorgizdat, 1959), p. 427.

75. Filatov *et al.*, *Ekonomicheskaia otsenka*, p. 87.

genetics even longer than in the Soviet Union[76]; or in architecture, where the great exhibition centres in Beijing and Shanghai remain pointed reminders of Stalinist taste. The most problematic exchanges with the Soviet Union were two that never happened. The Soviet Union first agreed and then cancelled its offer to provide technical assistance sufficient to develop nuclear weapons. A more bizarre source of tension was Khrushchev's proposal, during his first visit to China in 1954, that China send a million workers to Siberia to assist in the economic development of the Russian Far East. Mao Zedong then offered to send *ten* million. In the end, 200,000 went for temporary work.[77] At the same time, the several hundred thousand (mostly "White") Russians living in China since the Russian Civil War of 1917–21 were being repatriated to the Soviet Union in three stages.[78] Socialist brothers, it appears, did not need to reside in close proximity. This was true in the case of Soviet specialists in China who normally lived and ate in hotels separate from the Chinese units to which they were assigned. Inevitably too there were tensions between groups and individuals at the local level, more commonly, it seems, between Soviet advisors and Chinese than between East Europeans and Chinese.[79]

Perhaps the greatest impediment to co-operation between Stalinist regimes was the Stalinist political system itself, which institutionalized secrecy, suspicion and paranoia at every level. The memoirs of Mikhail A. Klochko, a Soviet scientist who served twice in China, in 1958 and 1960, depict all levels of Soviet and Chinese government – from the Soviet Embassy to the Chinese Academy of Sciences – as the leading obstacles to Sino-Soviet co-operation. Yet at the same time former Soviet advisors and their Chinese hosts would ultimately judge the advisory effort positively.[80]

The broader cultural dimensions of the relationship are contradictory because there was, in the Stalinist systems of both the USSR

76. See L. A. Schneider, "Learning from Russia: Lysenkoism and the fate of genetics in China, 1950–1986," in M. Goldman and D. Simon (eds.), *Science and Technology in Post-Mao China* (Cambridge, MA: Harvard University Press, 1989), pp. 45–65.

77. M. I. Sladkovskii, *Istoriia torgovo-ekonomicheskikh otnoshenii SSSR s Kitaem (1917–1974)* (Moscow: Nauka, 1974), p. 216, puts the proposal as emanating from Mao. The more recent work by Galenovich, "*Belye piatna*," p. 50, makes Khrushchev the author, and says that Mao was offended by the notion of China being a source of cheap labour for the USSR. Both accounts give evidence of a Soviet fear of Chinese designs on Siberia through Han settlement.

78. L. V. Zandanova, *Repatriatsiia grazhdan iz Kitaia v SSSR v 1947–1960 godakh* (Irkutsk: Irkutskii gosudarstvennyi universitet, 1996), pp. 183–204.

79. For a sharp, internal critique of boorish, overbearing behaviour on the part of some Soviet specialists in China see RGAE, Moscow, 9480/1724, report of M. Kudinova of 13 November 1958. Such behaviour may have been endemic in Sino-Soviet joint stock companies in Xinjiang: see G. Ganshin and T. Zazerskaya, "Pitfalls along the path of 'brotherly friendship' (a look at the history of Soviet–Chinese relations)," *Far Eastern Affairs*, No. 6 (1994), pp. 63–70.

80. Mikhail A. Klochko, *Soviet Scientist in Red China* (New York: Praeger, 1964). For a discussion of later memoirs and of the Soviet advisory experience in general see Deborah A. Kaple, "Soviet advisers in China in the 1950s," in Westad, *Brothers in Arms*, pp. 141–164.

and the PRC, no purely "private" dimension to cultural relations. (Not until December 1956 did the first group of 21 Chinese tourists, travelling at their own expense, visit the Soviet Union; and even then they were on a state-organized tour.[81]) To promote a "shared socialist culture" was the job of governments, and more specifically of the Society for Chinese–Soviet Friendship, which by 1959 had opened branches in 23 Chinese provinces and cities. Through its auspices nine million Chinese listened, with varying degrees of attentiveness, to 18,516 lectures and speeches between 1955 and 1959. Sixty-one million Chinese visited 27,500 photo exhibits. Yet of the 756 Soviet books translated by the Society, of which over 100 million volumes were published, how many were actually read, and by whom? Can one speak of an enduring impact of the 747 Soviet films shown in China and the 102 Chinese films shown in Russia? How did Russian audiences react to the many new translations of Lu Xun's (鲁迅) work?[82] In terms of the economic exchange, the most important cultural question is probably this: what was the longer-term impact of the technical and educational exchanges between the two communist powers? Why, as of 1962, of the 551 leading scientific personnel in the Chinese Academy of Sciences, were only six known to have been trained in the Soviet Union?

We do not know the answers to these questions, but it seems far-fetched to attribute the fall of Sino-Soviet economic co-operation to the cultural realm, however broadly conceived.[83] Certainly in economic terms this was, to borrow Steven Goldstein's phrase, "the alliance that worked."[84] For all the serious limitations to the economic exchange, there were no overriding economic, technological, or cultural reasons to call an end to a complex of international relationships that – whatever else they accomplished – had helped the PRC to succeed where the Nationalists had only begun: in building the capacity to be a significant military-industrial power.

Conclusion: The Primacy of Politics

From the perspective of 1950, it would have been difficult to imagine that Chinese co-operation with the Soviet Union and its allies – which made sense in some form for *any* Chinese government – would founder so quickly, never to be revived. The Sino-Soviet

81. New China News Agency report of 23 December 1956, in *Survey of the Chinese Mainland Press*, No. 1442 (1957), p. 41.

82. The statistics are from A. I. Arnoldov and G. M. Hovak, *Kul'tura narodnogo Kitaia* (Moscow: Izd.Akademii Nauk SSR, 1959), pp. 138–140. On political translations see Wei-shung Chang, "The impact of Soviet dialectical materialism on China through translations," *Studies in Soviet Thought*, Vol. 11, No. 3 (1971), pp. 208–211. On the occasional outcry against Soviet films in China see Galenovich, "*Belye piatna*," pp. 38–39.

83. For an interesting argument that emphasizes the "cultural" factor see Zhang Shuguang, "The collapse of Sino-Soviet economic cooperation," presented to the Conference on New Evidence on the Cold War in Asia, Hong Kong, 1996.

84. Goldstein, "Nationalism and internationalism," p. 232.

alliance was in some sense pre-ordained by the tutelary role of the USSR in international communism in general and over the Chinese Communist Party in particular. It began with grand dreams and clear blueprints, not just for "red factories" but for the path to the Stalinist society outlined in the famous *Short Course*.

That is one conclusion: that no alliance could have withstood the expectations that accompanied Sino-Soviet partnership, not just for security and economic development but for the path to a shared, indeed universal utopia. More concretely, since the entire system of the socialist world economy was founded on the presumption of shared political, ideological and military needs in the creation and defence of international communism, if the socialist political world became disputatious then everything else was thrown into uncertainty. In this world, far removed from that which Marx and Engels had imagined, politics was not the superstructural representation of economic forces; it was just the reverse.

One can read in the archives of China's economic relations with the Eastern bloc and never know of the tensions that would tear the bloc apart in the late 1950s and early 1960s. This is because there were no economic contradictions compelling enough to lead to a breakdown of co-operation. Even after the Great Leap Forward and the Sino-Soviet split, bilateral agreements, albeit of ever-lesser value, continued to be signed between China and other socialist nations and honoured into the 1960s and beyond.

The tensions ultimately emerged in politics, above all in Mao Zedong's growing pretensions to ideological originality, indeed to be the successor of Stalin as the leader of international communism, in a manner that challenged the concept of "scientific" planning, undermined a founding assumption of the alliance (Soviet leadership), and led China into economic chaos and international isolation. If one needs proof that Mao remained an "internationalist" (or better, a universalist) even as he broke with the USSR, it is in the triumph of his politics and ideology over China's national interests in the late 1950s and early 1960s, when he would place at risk the very existence of the Chinese nation and people to maintain his own conception of the Chinese and world revolution (and, certainly, his singular position in both). Yet beyond destroying the solidarity of the socialist economic world, Mao gave a death blow to communism as an international movement. As Khrushchev had predicted, in the place of the dream of communist internationalism would come, at best, a series of national socialisms.

The moment of no return came on 16 July 1960, when the Soviet Union notified Beijing that its experts would be withdrawn from China. Perhaps it was this decision that Khrushchev recalled when he spoke frankly in June 1964: "Many of us communists at first thought that in relations between socialist countries there ought not, in principle, to be a single hitch. But life has proved to be more complicated and contradictory than ideological conjectures."[85]

---

85. *Pravda*, 13 June 1964, cited in Kaser, *Comecon*, p. 221.

Morality, Coercion and State Building by Campaign in the Early PRC: Regime Consolidation and After, 1949–1956*

Julia Strauss

ABSTRACT The early to mid-1950s are conventionally viewed as a time when China broke sharply with the past and experienced a "golden age" of successful policy implementation and widespread support from the population. This article shows that the period should be seen as neither "golden age" nor precursor for disaster. Rather it should be seen as a period when the Chinese Communist Party's key mechanisms of state reintegration and instruction of the population – the political campaign and "stirring up" via public accusation sessions – were widely disseminated throughout China, with variable results. The campaigns for land reform and the suppression of counter-revolutionaries show that levels of coercion and violence were extremely high in the early 1950s, and the campaign to clean out revolutionaries in 1955 and after suggests some of the limits of mobilizational campaigns.

The establishment and evolution of the revolutionary People's Republic of China (PRC) has generated a substantial literature, much of it within the covers of this journal. As there is now access to sources that could only be dreamed about even ten years ago, that literature is on the verge of an important deepening of our understanding of this important stage in the Chinese revolution. And yet, despite this wealth of historical material, current views on the history of the PRC are inescapably coloured by teleology. From the vantage point of 2006, we *know* that the revolutionary experiment resulted in human, economic and ecological disasters, ending with the waning of the revolutionary impulse by the late 1970s. While this provides a useful and necessary corrective to earlier generations of scholarship, it risks reading later catastrophe back into earlier time periods, when no such outcome was discernible as even possible, much less likely. Nowhere is this more true than in reconsidering the history of the early PRC in its years of regime consolidation and the establishment of socialism (1949–56).

Earlier scholarship and the historiography of the Chinese Communist Party (CCP) itself concur that in its first years in power, the young PRC did an impressive job with regime consolidation. It

* The research for this article was generously supported by grants from the British Academy (International Exchange Scheme with the Shanghai Academy of Social Science), the SOAS Research Committee and the Fulbright Foundation. I owe particular thanks to Elizabeth Perry, R. Bin Wong and Vivienne Shue for their careful readings of earlier drafts. It goes without saying that any errors and omissions remain my own.

managed to implement key programmes, from currency stabilization to land reform, to the socialization of industry and enterprise, and an unbelievably rapid collectivization that was pushed through without the kinds of resistance and liquidations that had occurred in the Soviet Union. It managed if not to erase then at least to attenuate the shame of military weakness and foreign influence by fighting the world's then only superpower to a standstill in Korea only a year after coming to power. It made a reasonable showing in the non-aligned movement at Bandung. At least in comparison to what came later, during these years "New China" enjoyed the positive support of a large cross section of the population, enough that a generation, in urban areas at least, looked back to the early to mid-1950s as a veritable golden age; a time when the rhetoric of Chairman Mao actually was reflected by reality: China had finally "stood up."[1]

Little reconciles this earlier view with what we now know was to come *after* the years of regime consolidation and the establishment of socialism: the viciousness of the purges, the economic stagnation, the increasingly radical campaigns – one resulting in widespread famine and excess deaths of anywhere from 18 million to 40 million, the other in ten years of protracted trauma, purges, campaigns within campaigns, destruction of higher education and disillusionment of an entire generation of the educated. Given the subsequent history of the PRC, it is difficult for understandings of regime consolidation and the establishment of socialism to be as positively tilted as they were when the Cambridge History of the PRC was written, and scholarship in the past ten years has begun to reflect this. Pieces in edited volumes have begun to question directly whether the early to mid-1950s was really such a "golden age" after all, and are now focusing on the complexity, messiness and contingency of much of what transpired for both individuals and the coalescing state in the early stages of regime consolidation.[2] Other work considers such topics as bottom-up strike waves in response to the socialization of industry in Shanghai in 1956, the extremity of the tensions and resentments among middle-school teachers that smouldered from the earliest establishment of the educational system, a more critical view of such basic elements of the socialist system as the *hukou* (户口) registration, and a planned economy that discriminated heavily against the countryside."[3] A

---

1. For the best compilation of this view, see the essays in John K. Fairbank and Roderick MacFarquhar (eds.), *The Cambridge History of China, Vol. 14, The People's Republic, Part 1: The Emergence of Revolutionary China*, particularly Frederick Teiwes, "Establishment and consolidation of the new regime," pp. 51–143, and *Vol. 15*, "Urban life in the People's Republic of China," pp. 682–742.

2. See in particular Paul Pickowicz and Jeremy Brown (eds.), *Dilemmas of Victory: The Early Years of the People's Republic of China* (Cambridge, MA: Harvard University Press, forthcoming, 2007).

3. See Elizabeth Perry, "Shanghai's strike wave of 1957," *The China Quarterly*, No. 137 (1994), Eddy U, "Leninist reforms, workplace cleavages, and teachers in the Chinese Cultural Revolution," *Comparative Studies in Society and History*, Vol. 47, No. 1, pp. 106–133.

newly emerging generation of scholarship in the PRC has also begun
tentatively to re-evaluate key campaigns of the early 1950s, and as
these scholars, with even better access to archival materials and
interviews, themselves begin to delve into the history of the early
PRC, it is likely that even more critical views will be substantiated.[4]

This article attempts to bridge these two basic views by positioning
early PRC history (from 1949 to 1956 – the years of regime
consolidation and the establishment of socialism) in a wider context
of the evolution of the 20th-century Chinese state, whose agenda was
to complete the long-standing project to reintegrate the state vertically
in a form recognizably "modern," strong and revolutionary.
Modernity and strength were pursued on both domestic and
international fronts. The state's domestic agenda revolved around
promoting industrial growth, wiping out social and normative
practices deemed backward and "feudal," and constructing legitimacy
for the state; its international agenda played out in the realm of
ensuring its own security, and the pursuit of international status and
respect, notably in the international socialist movement. The pursuit
of all these agendas first required a strong state – one that could
simultaneously reintegrate a vast empire after years of fragmentation
and warfare, and pursue a range of developmentalist and revolutionary programmes for action. In outlining the broad trajectory of
domestic state reintegration in the early to mid-1950s, I make three
arguments: first, there was substantial continuity across the divide of
1949 as the young PRC managed to implement many of the state
building projects first aspired to by the departed Kuomintang (国民
党, KMT) regime; secondly, its chosen manner of implementation was
through simultaneously launching state building initiatives and
mobilizational campaigns (*qunzhong yundong* 群众运动); and thirdly,
its success in both state building and campaigns resulted from a
distinctive blend of coercion and normative appeals it applied to both
the implementing agents of the state (cadres) and society at large,
buttressed throughout by a didactive self-confidence in its own moral
rightness, unique vision and claims to transform past injustices while
leading China into the future.

Little of this is at substantive odds with more critical recent
assessments of the PRC. "New China" *was* highly coercive, it *did*
create a de facto caste system of status that led to systematic

4. Gao Hua, *Shenfen he chayi: 1949–1965 nian Zhongguo shehui de zhengzhi
fenceng* (*Status and Difference: Political Stratification in China, 1949–1965*) (Hong
Kong: Hong Kong Institute of Asia Pacific Studies, 2004); Yang Kuisong, "Xin
Zhongguo gonggu chengshi zhengquan de zuichu changshi – yu Shanghai 'suofan'
yundong zhongxin de lishi kaocha" ("The first attempt to consolidate political power
in cities: a historical analysis of the 'suofan' movement in Shanghai"), online paper at
www.coldwarchina.com, and Zhang Jishun, "Shanghai linong jiceng zhengzhi
dongyuan yu guojia shehui yitihua zouxiang" ("Shanghai neighbourhood grassroots
political mobilization and tendencies toward national integration"), *Zhongguo shehui
kexue* (*Chinese Social Sciences*), Vol. 146, No. 2, pp. 178–188.

discrimination and high levels of tension between city and countryside and within work units, and ideologically driven campaigns *did* ultimately exhaust and terrorize the population at large. However, work that turns a critical eye on such different social sectors as school teachers, intellectuals and workers may sidestep a larger question of the whole: the regime's own goals in the context of an even larger, century-long project of state (re)integration. The regime's early successes on its own terms were real, and merit (re)consideration in the light of increasingly available sources. The successful regime consolidation of the revolutionary PRC owed much to its inheritance from the KMT and its own superiority in definitively "out-generalling" the KMT military in the civil war and crushing all meaningful military resistance. The overwhelming and unexpectedly quick military victory created the necessary, but still insufficient, conditions for the establishment of a state strong enough to implement a wide range of revolutionary policies, and fundamentally remake the basic institutions of government and society. This article elaborates the mechanics by which the "sufficient" conditions for the revolutionary transformation of society were implemented: the CCP's particular mix of coercion and engaging the emotions with positive moral appeals, its frequent and successful application of campaigns to push through new policies, and its absolute confidence in its own moral correctness despite logical contradictions in the way its ideologically driven categories made sense of reality. In so doing, New China frequently reneged on its own promises, and it proved repeatedly willing to inflict substantial collateral damage on those unlucky enough to be on the wrong side of shifting definitions of "the enemy." The early to mid-1950s was not a "golden age." But nor did it necessarily contain the seeds of its own destruction.

Institutional and Ideational Legacies from the Republican Period

The issues the young PRC faced were indeed severe. When set in its own time and juxtaposed against its immediate predecessor, its accomplishments were impressive. The revolutionary regime was ideologically driven, and its ideology had to be brought into line with a daunting range of "objective" problems, starting with hyper-inflation and a ruined economy, a high population to arable land ratio, a mistrustful population and weak roots in the broad swathes of the central and southern parts of the country, and the economic, social and political legacy of a generation of unrelenting civil war and foreign invasion.

The PRC built on the institutional and ideational legacy of the KMT. Like all revolutionary regimes, its rhetoric drew a sharp line between it and the immediately preceding (and now de-legitimated) *ancien régime*. But in fact the PRC was a revolutionary regime that substantially conformed to de Tocqueville's key reflection on the French revolution: the revolution quite literally completed the work of the old regime, with "a central authority with powers stricter, wider, and more absolute."[5] When one looks closely at what was *done* in a macro sense rather than what was said, there was substantial extension of not only the CCP's own pre-1949 traditions and legacies of class struggle and mass line, but those of the now-vilified KMT. The KMT's weaker, looser version of party-state was the first to attempt to educate a citizenry in a modern *zhengdang* (政党) culture, the first to launch a society-wide urban movement (the New Life Movement), the first deliberately to pair moral incentives with the structural, technocratic and "scientific," the first to be heavily militarized in terms of both the rhetoric and models used, and the first to adopt a widely statist takeover and nationalization of industry.[6] Some of the reasons for this lie in a shared agenda of vertically reintegrating the state along "modern" lines. Others are a result of institutional and temporal conditions: a legacy of revolution and tutelage based on the Leninist party-state (*yi dang zhiguo* 以党治国), and subjection to the same relentless militarization of the Republican period – a militarization that only intensified over the course of the 1940s. Like the CCP, the KMT made serious attempts to partify the state bureaucracy from the late 1930s on, carried out extra-bureaucratic attempts to mix technical training and ideological education for state agents, and liberally used military metaphors and imagery at the core of state ideology.[7] Many of the features associated with the People's Republic of China were first attempted under the Nationalist regime, but with only variable and limited successes that were eventually undercut by a combination of poor military strategizing and a complete loss of control over the economy during the 1940s.

Not only were there substantial continuities in the basic agenda of the state, but many of the strategies to implement that agenda were carried across the divide of 1949, albeit in a much stronger form than their pre-1949 variants. For both Nationalists and Communists, almost all solutions to problems of economy, industry and defence

5. Alexis de Tocqueville, *The Old Regime and the French Revolution* (trans. Stuart Gilbert) (Gloucester: Peter Smith, 1978), part 3, ch. 8, "How, given the facts set forth in previous chapters the Revolution was a foregone conclusion," p. 209.

6. Henrietta Harrison, *The Making of the Republican Citizen: Political Ceremonies and Symbols in China, 1911–1928* (Oxford & New York: Oxford University Press, 2000),William Kirby, "Continuity and change in modern China: economic planning on the mainland and on Taiwan, 1943–1958," *Australian Journal of Chinese Affairs*, No. 24 (1990), pp. 121–141, Mark W. Frazier, *The Making of the Chinese Industrial Workplace: State, Revolution and Labor Management* (Cambridge: Cambridge University Press, 2002), chs. 2–3 (pp. 23–91).

7. Julia Strauss, "Strategies of Guomindang institution building: rhetoric and implementation in wartime *Xunlian*," chapter in Terry Bodenhorn (ed.), *Defining Modernity: Guomindang Rhetorics of a New China, 1920–1980* (Chicago: University of Michigan Press, 2002), pp. 195–222. See also Elizabeth Perry, *Patrolling the Revolution: Worker Militias, Citizenship, and the Modern Chinese State* (Lanham: Rowman and Littlefield, 2006), ch. 3 "China's first Leninist party-state, 1927–1949" and ch. 4 "China's second Leninist party-state, 1949–1965," for the Kuomintang antecedents to workers' militias.

were conceived of in statist terms; a vertically integrated unitary state of education and moral indoctrination for the untutored population was presumed to be a part of the answer to most questions, and even a hint of any federal solution completely inconceivable. The PRC was of course not identical in organization, programmes or ethos to the outgoing KMT. It had three extraordinary advantages that the KMT never possessed: the dominant military control over the vast territory of China that made it possible to impose coercive measures against "enemies" and stir up or dampen down popular participation; an ideology of class struggle that did not hesitate to suppress those deemed recalcitrant or blocking the revolutionary cause; and most distinctively the self-confidence and willingness to call upon mass mobilization in support of its policies.

Rethinking Campaigns: State Building by Institutionalization and Mobilization

The young PRC's chosen strategy of regime consolidation and establishing socialism was through, first, establishing and strengthening the coercive and infrastructural capacities of the party-state, and, secondly, launching political campaigns of mobilization. Scholars working on the contemporary period have begun to differentiate between Mao and post-Mao types of campaigns, with a "classic" Mao-era version that involved high degrees of mass mobilization, and a post-Mao variant in which campaigns devoid of any mass mobilizational element are launched by the leadership to focus the state bureaucracy on enforcement of previously existing rules and laws. But most of what has been written on the Maoist period stresses the importance of campaigns of mass mobilization while very little attention is paid to other sorts of campaigns.[8]

Since archives have begun to open and access to original documents written by and for the bureaucracy in the 1950s has increased, it is now possible to distinguish analytically between not two but as many as four different types of campaigns in the years before the Eighth Party Congress. The first was the kind that, like its post Mao variant, focused the attention of the bureaucracy in a particular policy area with the ultimate "target" the mobilization of the commitments and focus of the bureaucracy itself. The big pushes to register the population, construct granaries and train politically reliable police forces of the early 1950s, and the 1955 nationalization of private

8. For the clearest articulation of Mao and post-Mao types of campaigns, see Melanie Manion, *Corruption by Design: Building Clean Government in China and Hong Kong* (Cambridge, MA: Harvard University Press, 2004), ch. 5, "Anticorruption campaigns as enforcement mechanisms," esp. pp. 156–163 and 168–172). Charles Cell offers a typology of campaigns that includes the lesser known ones in *Revolution at Work: Mobilization Campaigns in China* (New York: Academic Press, 1977), but does not go much beyond typology. See also Gordon Bennett, *Yundong: Mass Campaigns in Chinese Communist Leadership* (Berkeley: Institute of East Asian Studies, 1976).

enterprise are the most obvious examples of this type of bureaucratic campaign. They concentrated on a particular problem of governance or society, but did not particularly attempt either to mobilize social support or to change the behaviour of relevant social groups. The second was the frequent, more limited type of campaign that was implemented through the bureaucracy to achieve some combination of behavioural change and positive normative commitments of a relatively restricted social or occupational group. The best examples of this were the early campaigns to wipe out prostitution and opium addiction, the thought reform campaign of 1953 aimed at intellectuals, and those directed at raising productivity in particular industries that took place throughout the 1950s. The third type of campaign involved both the bureaucracy and the citizenry more generally in effecting transformation of both the environment and behaviour, often in the realm of public health and hygiene, exemplified by tree planting and irrigation campaigns, and the campaigns against schistosomiasis and the "Four Pests."[9] Finally there were what we think of (and what the PRC itself continues to identify as) the "classic" and important political campaigns of the early PRC, the great mass *qunzhong yundong* that took place from 1950 to 1953: the Aid Korea/Resist America campaign of autumn 1950, the Campaign to Suppress Counter-revolutionaries of 1951, the Three-Antis and Five-Antis campaigns of 1952–53, and the land reform campaign, which took place at various times in different parts of the country, but was everywhere completed by the end of 1952. These highly visible and well publicized campaigns were characterized by the bureaucracy mobilizing very large segments of both rural and urban populations to gain popular support and high degrees of mass participation in favour of state-determined policies and outcomes. In the early to mid-1950s, the practical distinction between campaigns of bureaucratic intensification and campaigns of partial or mass mobilization was in practice much less clear than it became in the post-Mao era. Each had as its first target the mobilization and intensification of urgency within the bureaucratic institutions of state, but three of them went beyond the state itself as state agents pushed hard for a measurable degree of change in normative commitments and/or behaviour from either targeted social groups or society at large.

Although we are used to thinking of this most visibly public form of mass campaign as something particular to the Chinese Communist Party, in 1949 there were two other producers of campaigns or campaign-like behaviour to which the CCP could refer; the

9. See Joshua Horn, *Away With All Pests: An English Surgeon in China* (London: Paul Hamlyn, 1969), especially ch. 10, "Death to the snails! The fight against schistosomiasis," pp. 94–106, David M. Lampton, *The Politics of Medicine in China: The Policy Process, 1949–1977* (Boulder: Westview Press 1977), and Judith Shapiro, *Mao's War Against Nature: Politics and the Environment in Revolutionary China* (Cambridge: Cambridge University Press, 2001).

pre-existing Nationalist regime in China and Stalinism in the Soviet Union. *Yundong* (运动), state-led instruction in changes in behavioural norms with a limited version of mass mobilization, was recognizably part of the *zhengdang* (政党) political culture of the Nanjing Decade (1927–37), with the notoriously unsuccessful New Life Movement as its best example.[10] Like the wider state-building agenda of vertical reintegration and expansion of state power inherited from the KMT, the CCP extended and expanded a key vehicle first attempted, albeit unsuccessfully, by its immediate predecessor, in an ultimately much stronger and effective form. And while different in other respects, Stalinism's Stakhanovite movement resulted in processes that had close analogies in most of the mass campaigns of the early PRC: the singling out of a minority of enemies (variously called "wreckers," counter-revolutionaries, landlords, or corrupt bureaucrats or businessmen) as a way of mobilizing the majority in favour of intensive pushes for party-state determined policies.[11] Campaigns of mobilization – be they of the general population, specific target groups or the bureaucracy itself – had precedents in the Republican period and referents elsewhere in the contemporary Leninist world, to say nothing of the CCP's own experiences with mass mobilizational techniques in urban areas in the 1920s and the countryside in the 1930s and 1940s.[12]

What was so distinctive about the CCP's implementation of campaigns was neither its reliance on its categories of class struggle for the identification of enemies (as in the Soviet Union under Stalin) nor its belief in its own educative morality and ability to set the terms of individual self-cultivation for the individual to transform himself through a process of small-group study and self-criticism (as for the KMT in the 1940s and 1950s), but the CCP's genuine desire for popular participation, and its unusual degree of confidence that with proper education, the ultimate support of a broad cross-section of both rural and urban society for its policies would be present. Campaigns mobilized individuals in support of regime-determined goals, but they also coerced in subtle and indirect ways. The campaign mentality of activating collective emotions and heightening awareness

10. Arif Dirlik, "The ideological foundations of the New Life Movement: a study in counterrevolution," *Journal of Asian Studies*, Vol. 34, No. 4 (1975), pp. 945–980. The New Life Movement ran aground on its desire simultaneously to foster mass mobilization while keeping it within strict, state-determined limits.

11. Hiroaki Kuromiya, *Stalin's Industrial Revolution* (Cambridge: Cambridge University Press, 1988), pp. 31–35 on campaign purges and pp. 195–99 on radical worker mobilization.

12. The literature on these topics is vast, but for relatively recent treatments of the former, see S.A. Smith, *Like Cattle and Horses: Nationalism and Labor in Shanghai* (Durham: Duke University Press, 2002), For the latter, the classic general treatment remains Mark Selden's *China in Revolution: The Yenan Way Revisited* (Armonk: M.E. Sharpe, 1995). See also Odoric Wou, *Mobilizing the Masses: Building Revolution in Henan* (Stanford: Stanford University Press, 1994) and Yung-fa Chen, *Making Revolution: The Communist Movement in Eastern and Central China, 1937–1945* (Berkeley & Los Angeles: University of California Press, 1986).

made it a formidable tool for conformity (and driving alternative, critical opinions underground); campaigns also created an environment in which it was relatively easy to establish and/or strengthen the regular, "normal" institutions of police and security committees.[13] Through the vehicle of the campaign, the CCP was both willing and able to mobilize tactically both the regular bureaucracy and the population at large to isolate putative "enemies," overcome resistance in order to push through key programmes, establish the more workaday institutions of state coercion *and* draw out a widespread support for the regime that was simply assumed to be there.

In so doing, the party-state at the centre and the provincial, municipal and local cadres on whom it relied for implementation throughout the country relied on a distinctive blend of constantly shifting tactics: paternalism alternated with coercion, and populism with monocratic control.[14] Earlier generations of political scientists have long understood the revolutionary PRC in terms of its internal contradictions: the simultaneously articulated trends towards institutionalization and campaign mobilization and voluntarism that were at the very least in tension with each other.[15] Similarly, historians such as Maurice Meisner have long grappled with what many see as Maoism's inherent contradiction: simultaneously desiring popular mobilization and the people taking charge of their own revolution, and the need to guarantee the monocratic party-state's own desired outcomes through a process of heavy-handed control.[16]

While these tensions certainly existed in the later years of the revolutionary PRC, the coexistence of such logically incompatible phenomena as institutionalization with extraordinary mobilization, paternalism with terror, populist participation with party-state control, and all of the above with a larger revolutionary state's processes of regime consolidation and the establishment of the basic institutions of socialism, was not the "problem" that it became later. On the contrary, until at least 1953, campaigns cleared the ground for institutionalization by weeding out enemies and instructing the population in new norms of political culture and acceptable behaviour, paternalism rhetorically geared to the many made terror easier to implement against the few, and, when appropriately "stirred

13. On the skilled way in which the Communists engaged in "emotion work," see Elizabeth Perry, "Moving the masses: emotion work in the Chinese Revolution," *Mobilization*, Vol. 7, No. 2 (2002), pp. 111–128.

14. Elsewhere, I describe this dynamic as "paternalist terror"; see Julia Strauss, "Paternalist terror: the campaign to suppress counterrevolutionaries and regime consolidation in the People's Republic of China, 1950–1952," *Comparative Studies in Society and History*, Vol. 44, No. 1 (2002), pp. 80–105.

15. Lowell Dittmer, *Liu Shao-chi and the Chinese Cultural Revolution: the Politics of Mass Criticism* (Berkeley & Los Angeles: University of California Press, 1974), pp. 3–4, 185–186, 211.

16. Maurice Meisner, *Mao's China (and After): A History of the People's Republic* (New York: Free Press, 1977 and 1999), in 1977, pp. 385–86.

up," the masses did usually, although not uniformly, produce the kinds of results that the party-state wanted.

Morality, Coercion and State Expansion: Land Reform and the Campaign to Suppress Counter-revolutionaries

In 1951, the CCP launched two important political campaigns of mass mobilization, which taken together were aimed at mobilizing both rural and urban populations against a small minority of designated "enemies." These campaigns were not only "effective" in terms of accomplishing their key goals of land redistribution and identification and prosecution of enemies of the state. They were also an "efficient" means of implementing different things at once. They communicated the key elements of the leadership's particular ethos of class struggle as well as the economic, social and political categories by which class struggle was understood; transferred significant resources to key groups upon which it relied for support while physically destroying social and economic status groups who could block state initiatives for remaking the countryside; mobilized the majority of both urban and rural China into active support for, and complicity in, regime violence against those designated as internal enemies; and created a political atmosphere in which it was possible to begin the process of expanding the presence of the state at increasingly local levels.

Land reform in the countryside and the Campaign to Suppress Counter-revolutionaries in urban areas were undertaken at roughly the same time for those areas outside north and north-east China that had not already undergone land reform, and in central and south China they were concurrent and deliberately overlapping in the suburban borderlands between city and countryside. Both were geared at eliminating groups the regime considered to be key political, social and economic competitors: landlords in the countryside, ex-KMT military and party personnel with high rank; and a much larger range of assorted social undesirables such as bandits, local bullies, the leaders of counter-revolutionary religious sects and low level hoodlums hanging out on the streets. Both campaigns went directly to the population at large – the masses of both city and countryside – to elicit popular support for the regime's policies of mass transfer of property and crackdown on suspected political undesirables through the heavily stage-managed spectacle of accusation meetings (*kongsu hui* 控诉会) against individuals designated as enemies. Both used high degrees of state-sanctioned violence, with millions executed. And they left in their wake a much augmented state presence, in terms of expanded numbers of cadres and direct state organization of ever smaller units of society. They were both predicated on domestic components of the regime's internal state-building agenda: mobilizing support from society and stiffening the resolve of state cadres, and drastically expanding the coercive capacity of both the regular bureaucracy and new state organizations.

The first thing that stands out about the Campaign to Suppress Counter-revolutionaries and land reform is the contrast between their harshness in terms of rhetoric, implementation and sheer physical violence, and the tentative, careful and conciliatory way in which the CCP took over the big cities of the south and reassured the country at large upon coming to power in 1949. Depending on which set of incomplete statistics one refers to, the casualties incurred in these two campaigns probably ranged between a low estimate of one million and a high estimate of upwards of five million either sentenced to death by the state or spontaneously killed in the highly emotionally charged atmosphere of public accusation meetings.[17] The violence of these campaigns was inseparable from a wider regional context of deepening Cold War and China's involvement in the Korean War, and indeed the formal dates of the Campaign to Suppress Counter-revolutionaries are almost identical to the dates of China's open involvement in the Korean War. But their intent and main outcomes were domestic, signalling to a range of domestic constituencies (cadres in the bureaucracy itself, the social base from which the basic-level cadres of the state were to be recruited, unaligned social groups in city and countryside, and the campaign's designated "enemies" and their sympathizers) that conciliation was over and that the revolutionary regime meant business. Never again did the regime launch such united and deliberate campaigns to exterminate targeted social groups. Nor did it feel it needed to. Later target groups of mass campaigns such as entrepreneurs (the Five-Anti's), "corrupt" bureaucrats (the Three Anti's), intellectuals (the Thought Reform Campaign, the Anti-Hu Feng Campaign and even the vicious Anti-Rightist campaign) were

17. There are only rough estimates and inconsistent numbers on the total numbers executed and killed during these two campaigns. Frederick Teiwes suggests a lower-end estimate of between 200,000 and 800,000 (Teiwes, "Establishment and consolidation of the new regime," n. 24), while Jurgen Domes offers a figure of "no less than 5,000,000" in *The Internal Politics of China 1949–1972* (New York: Praeger 1973), p. 38, and Richard Walker's highly critical *China Under Communism; The First Five Years* (London: Allen and Unwin, 1956) p. 137, offers a "conservative" figure of 1,500,000. The official numbers on the Campaign to Suppress Counter-revolutionaries vary between 700,000 and two million. Domes cites two figures: the lower end of 800,000 executed was released at the Eighth Party Congress in September 1956, but a work report released by Bo Yibo in 1952 referred to a much larger number of 2,000,000, *The Internal Politics of China*, p. 52. Statistics were collected, but inconsistently, and categories of classification were at best ambiguous. In peri-urban areas and the countryside, counter-revolutionaries and landlords were often lumped together (and so would have been reported to different sub-bureaucracies). However, on the whole the bureaucratic incentives were likely to lead to under-counting rather than over-counting. Landlords who died of injuries inflicted by crowds in the course of accusation meetings were often not recorded as executed, because this reflected badly on the local cadres' control of the situation. There was also substantial variation in how vigorously the campaigns were executed in different regions. The Jiangnan seems to have been relatively mild, and the still unsecured rural south-west very harsh: here upwards of another million "bandits" were "suppressed," variably classified as bandits or counter-revolutionaries.

subject to mass criticism, thought reform, internal exile, loss of position and lengthy jail sentences, but were rarely, if ever, executed. The severity of these two campaigns of regime consolidation reflected the leadership's surprising degree of self-confidence in the inherent moral "rightness" of hitting hard at "enemies," its need to mobilize the lower reaches of the bureaucracy to implement such violence, and its absolute certainty that with proper instruction and organization, the support of the "masses" was a foregone conclusion, even when there were objective grounds for having doubts.

For example, when land reform was implemented between 1950 and 1952 in the country at large, there was a fundamental problem with the leadership's conceptualization of this very important part of the revolution as both "scientific" and morally and materially necessary. The Marxian system of economic classification by which rural society in China was understood had been developed in the particular context of north China. Here, despite questions about where particular individuals in a village stood, the standard categories of landlord, rich peasant, middle peasant and poor peasant and the idea of exploiting classes were comprehensible and broadly applicable.[18] When the CCP implemented land reform in the more commercialized and commo-dified countryside of the lower Yangtze region, it found that these received categories simply did not apply at all. A majority of the working rural population only engaged in agricultural production part time if at all, most males aspired to work in factories and many succeeded in so doing, absentee landlords were the rule and indeed in many cases had to be brought back to the countryside to be struggled against, and even small producers with low incomes frequently rented out all or part of their landholdings. The more commercialized and impersonal economic relations of the Jiangnan made it significantly harder to stir up class hatred against the actual exploiters than was the case in north China. In the south the real hatred of the common people was directed against the resident agents and rent collectors for absentee landlords.[19] Indeed, in at least some districts, the majority of those targeted and struggled against were not landlords at all. For example in Shanghai county, of the 779 individuals subjected to mass struggle sessions in 1951, only a quarter (200) were landlords. Local bullies accounted for 140, counter-revolutionaries for 239, and a catch-all category of "other" for 213.[20] Nevertheless, despite the

18. On the difficulties of classifying individuals, see William Hinton, *Fanshen: A Documentary of Revolution in a Chinese Village* (Vintage Books, 1968), esp. pp. 285–87, 303–305. Even in north China these categories can be questioned, as there was relatively little economic stratification compared to the south; in northern rural China almost everyone was poor in absolute terms.

19. Shanghai Municipal Archives (SMA) A71/1/71, "Shanghai shi jiaoqu tudi gaige zongjie" ("Comprehensive summary of land reform in suburban Shanghai"), 25 November 1952, pp. 2–5 of internal report.

20. Minhang District Archives (MHA) 13-1-37. "Shanghai xian jiesu tugai gongzuo douzheng tongjibiao" ("Shanghai county statistical table: struggle work on the completion of land reform"), dated 18 November 1951.

objective special circumstances and social complexity of the region and cadres' own awareness of the importance of avoiding mistaken oversimplification through "pure struggle against landlords" (*danchun douzheng dizhu* 单纯斗争地主) when those who rented land were often themselves middling smallholders, in the final analysis the same categories of Marxian class analysis and targets of struggle were applied to the greater Shanghai area with only minor modifications.

Regime self-confidence, articulated through a particular version of morality and socio-economic justice, was also manifested in the way in which a range of different social groups was brought in to support and implement land reform. The young People's Republic made extraordinary efforts to mobilize the patriotic and moral commitments of basic-level cadres of poor peasant background (many of whom were not Party members at all), middle school and university students, representatives from democratic parties, and even scholars from the higher reaches of academia in Beijing. Land reform went hand in hand with a substantial expansion of the ranks of basic-level cadres in the countryside. In the Shanghai suburbs alone, 4,616 activists were identified and trained, of whom over one-fifth (1,042) were promoted to the ranks of regular cadres, and overall some 6,481 cadres were promoted, with the vast majority (6,005) from poor and middle peasant backgrounds.[21] But it wasn't only poor and middle peasants who were drawn in to the state's basic structures and agenda.

Special teams of local-level and nationally known academics and social science researchers were also inculcated into regime norms of Marxian categories through ideological training, and sent to the countryside first to record the "objective" social and economic conditions of "feudal" impoverishment and stratification, and then deployed on behalf of the state to implement the regime's programme of land reform. Academics from Beijing's elite universities were sent to the Jiangnan as special land reform teams to investigate conditions and participate in land reform, eventually writing up widely disseminated reports on their experiences for the rest of the country.[22] In the spring of 1951 another special team – this time representatives of China's democratic parties – was chosen by the Political Affairs Department of the Central People's Government to follow suit.[23] A much larger number of 460 lecturers from local universities and senior

21. SMA B14/1/80, "Shanghai shi jiaoqu xunlian ganbu shu peiyang jijifenzi qingkuang" ("Situation on Shanghai municipal outlying district cadre training division's activist training"), and "Sheng tudi gaige qianhou xiangcun jiceng ganbu bianhua qingkuang tongjibiao" ("Statistical form on changes in basic level rural cadres before and after land reform") both p. 13 of internally numbered file dated 31 December 1951.

22. "Beijing ge daxue jiaoshou huadongqu tudi gaige canguan tuan zongjie" ("General summary of Beijing universities' professorial group visiting tour of the Eastern China region land reform"), *Wo suodaode sunan tugai yundong* (Shanghai: Shanghai jiaoqu he sunanqu tudi gaige weiyuanhui, 1951).

23. Jiangsu Provincial Archives (JPA) 3006-2-224 "Guanyu canjia sunan tugai ge zhong minzhupai qingkuang" ("Situation on democratic groups' participation in land reform in South Jiangsu"), 16 May 1951.

middle schools in the greater Shanghai area were similarly trained and organized into special teams to carry out land reform directly in the countryside surrounding Shanghai, and students and recent graduates were especially sought out for land reform teams as well – at least in part because their literacy could be counted on.[24] While it is impossible to evaluate whether these individuals actually believed in the new categories of social understanding such as "feudalism" and "exploiting classes" or whether their reports and memoirs were edited to reflect regime objectives, what does stand out is the degree to which many non-Marxist academics and intellectuals so quickly adapted to behaving and writing *as if* they really did accept these new categories of Marxian diagnosis of social problems. Testimonials from the time and an enormous memoir literature may be epistemologically suspect, but behaviour suggests that many did actively participate in the land reform campaign, pushing through the regime policy "cure" of land reform through identification of class enemies, mass struggle sessions, redistribution of land and overcoming poverty through the beginning of voluntary co-operativization.[25] As it set about inculcating a set of new, revolutionary norms in tandem with the nuts and bolts of state reintegration, the regime's didactic self-confidence in the historical correctness of the categories by which it understood social and economic relations was surely an important component of its willingness to mobilize the emotional affect and moral outrage of its citizens at polar ends of society – from poor peasant to privileged intellectual.[26]

The concurrent and partially overlapping Campaign to Suppress Counter-revolutionaries was run through the regular institutions of the party-state rather than specially detached work teams and newly recruited local cadres, but it exemplified state strengthening in two other respects: stiffening the resolve and overcoming the natural scruples of provincial and sub-provincial cadres, while expanding the directly coercive institutions of the state.[27] In the key announcement that launched the campaign on 10 October 1950, the Party sharply reversed its earlier policy of "excessive lenience" (*kuanda wubian* 宽大

---

24. The reports and experiences of individuals in the special Beijing team were published in a variety of places, including *People's Daily*, and then put together into a special published collection *Wo suo kandao de sunan tudi gaige yundong* (*The Land Reform in Southern Jiangsu I Witnessed*), edited by Sunan renmin gongshu tudigaige weiyuanhui, and brought out by the Shanghai outlying district committee on land reform in late 1951. On the special training and organization of lecturers and senior high school teachers in work teams to carry out land reform, see SMA B14-1-6 and passim "Jiaoshi canjia tudi gaige di'yi xiaozu mingdan ji duiyuan dengjibiao" ("Registration form for the first small group of instructors participating in land reform: name lists and group members") (1951).

25. Lisa Wedeen, "Acting 'as if' symbolic politics and social control in Syria," *Comparative Studies in Society and History*, Vol. 40, No. 3 (1998), pp. 403–423.

26. Shi Wenqi, "Wo suo jiandaode su'nan tudi gaige yundong" ("The land reform movement in Sunan that I saw"), in *The Land Reform in Southern Jiangsu I Witnessed*, pp. 88–89.

27. Some of the information below on the Campaign to Suppress Counter-revolutionaries is also covered in much greater detail in Strauss, "Paternalist terror."

无边) in favour of "combining suppression and lenience" (*zhenya kuanda jiehe* 镇压宽大结合) and exhorted local cadres to enact a harsh policy of "executing some, imprisoning some and putting some under house arrest."[28] The problem for local cadres was that the slogan of "combining suppression with lenience" was vague enough to mean almost anything. Many couldn't understand why it was necessary to crack down so hard on counter-revolutionaries, especially as most of the political counter-revolutionaries who had held high positions in security or party organizations for the KMT had already been promised lenience if they came forward and registered with authorities. At least in the Jiangnan, a natural reluctance to be the instruments of state violence led to significant foot-dragging in campaign implementation. Until Luo Ruiqing went on tour and publicly reprimanded most of the big cities of the south in late March 1951, many local cadres felt that counter-revolutionaries could be won over by intensive re-education, wondered why the Party was so abruptly cancelling its own promises of lenience to those who came forward and registered, doubted the necessity of shooting people, and denied that their own offices could possibly harbour counter-revolutionaries.[29]

The Campaign to Suppress Counter-revolutionaries also led to a direct and significant expansion of the security and coercive instruments of the state, which grew hand-in-hand with a new culture of informing and obsession with secrecy. In the general atmosphere of panic and hysteria about counter-revolutionaries and sabotage, local cadres were exhorted to strengthen security work, extend surveillance, and build up the police by recruiting the young and politically reliable to phase out the then more numerous KMT leftovers. Local security committees set up ad hoc sites to register free-floating counter-revolutionaries, and began what would turn out to be a lengthy process of directly imposing vertically integrated lines of security reporting in large factories, government offices and schools. In the late spring of 1951, the Eastern China military region security headquarters sent over 400 cadres to important factories in Shanghai

28. The "Double Ten" Directive that launched the campaign is reproduced in *Jianguo yilai zhongyao wenxian xuanbian*, Vol. 1 (Beijing: Zhongyang wenxian chubanshe, 1992), p. 421, and Luo Ruiqing's formula of "executing some, imprisoning some and confining some to house arrest" in "Zhonggong zhongyang pizhun zhongyang gong'an bu 'guanyu quanguo gong'an huiyi de baogao'" ("The Chinese communist central approved and circulated central Ministry of Public Security 'Report on the national public security conference'"), 28 December 1950, *ibid.* p. 443.

29. See in particular SMA A22/2/50, "Shifu jiguan ganbu buchong tianbiaozhong de xuanchuan jiaoyu gongzuo zongjie" ("General report on propaganda and education work for municipal organization cadres' supplementary form completion"), 31 July 1951, and SMA S64-4-134, "Shanghai shi zaoqi gongye tongye gonghui, 'Benhui huiyuan xuexi zhenya fangeming shi zhengci de xuexi jihua he zongjie baogao'" ("Shanghai municipal preliminary same industry society 'General report and study plan for society's members study of the principles for the suppression of counterrevolutionaries'"), 5 June 1951.

to set up these committees and provide advice and support on the implementation of the campaign.[30] But of course once these footholds were established the CCP presence did not fade; it only became stronger, and much expanded with subsequent campaigns. In both urban areas and the countryside the campaigns of 1951 led directly to the expansion of the state in terms of its numbers of agents, and to the beginnings of its direct intrusion on the everyday workings of the work place.

Bringing in the Masses: Campaign as Show

By either Leninist or Chinese traditions of statecraft, the young PRC was unusual in the degree to which it openly solicited the participation and support of its urban and rural populations, and the degree to which this took place in open, public space. Both land reform and the Campaign to Suppress Counter-revolutionaries had, as their dénouement, a form of populist participatory theatre in the form of *kongsu hui* (控诉会), public mass accusation sessions against defined class enemies. The public accusation meeting was, quite literally, a show put on by the new state, replete with staging, props, stock characters, rough working scripts, dramatic peaks and a good round of final applause. Mass accusation meetings against both counter-revolutionaries and landlords (in the Jiangnan the two categories frequently overlapped) were not the formalized, bureaucratic affairs of woodenly delivered show trials of the Soviet Union, they were deliberately used as a heuristic devise to engage the emotions of the public, whip up hatred against designated class enemies and mobilize the masses into positive support for the regime. Every urban area held mass accusation meetings against counter-revolutionaries, as did most villages against landlords; and when sufficient landlords could not be produced, "local bullies" and other power holders under the old regime, particularly those who had actively collaborated with the Japanese, filled in.

This account of an accusation meeting in Mulan (木兰) county in rural Heilongjiang gives a sense of the public face of these events:

On August 14 [1951], the public judgement of Wang Hanwu and the others was held in the county seat's people's primary school.

At around 7.00 to 8.00 am, group by group the masses began to filter in. There were weathered old people, children closely following their parents ... over 150 women with babies in their arms walked for 20 or 30 kilometres to come to the occasion. People came from all corners, filling the schoolyard, packed into the surrounding neighbourhood, and looked out from every nearby window.

At 9.00 am, Chair Xie Wanzhun opened the meeting. 14,000 pairs of eyes avidly focused on the rostrum. The chair explained the significance of the meeting, and the chief prosecutor, Zhu Hong, read out the charges:

30. SMA C1/1/28, "Shanghai gongren canjia zhenya fangeming yundong zongjie baogao" ("Summary report on Shanghai worker's participation in the campaign to suppress counter-revolutionaries"), July or August 1951.

"Wang Hanwu, Sun Shengye and other traitorous thieves, under the Japanese occupation you cruelly oppressed the people, impressed forced labour, drafted soldiers, commandeered grain, suppressed our anti-Japanese soldiers and people, and killed who knows how many. As leader of the intelligence association, Wang Hanwu accused 100+ people and arrested over 20."

Prosecutor Song continued: "*tewu* group leader Sun Fujiang arrested over 70 anti-Japanese resisters. Head of police Wang Jiadong set up a bandit area, terrorized villagers into fleeing, and killed many." He concluded "Puppet county chief Ji Liang not only did the bidding of the Japanese, he even continued his counter-revolutionary activities after the Japanese were vanquished, scheming to establish a bandit military ... fighting against the liberation of Mulan. These guys have blood debts piled high, whose evil crimes reach the sky – without the death penalty the people's hatred will never be settled."

[Then] the people's accusations began. Fourteen-year-old Yu Jiangji mounted the stage, and with tears flowing pointed to Sun Shengye: "You grabbed my father, killed my grandmother, and forced my mother out of her home." Zhao Wanjin then got on stage, grinding his teeth, "My family had five people in it. You beat my father to death, put me in jail for three years, oppressed my mother to death, starved my two younger sisters to death ..." He was unable to go on for the tears choking his throat. [With this], weeping copiously, all present accused [the counter-revolutionaries] without rest, with sounds that filled the yard.

The people indignantly requested the people's government to put the people first, and execute Wang Hanwu, Sun Yesheng and the others by firing squad. As the death sentence was being carried out, the yard filled with the endless cries of: "Thanks to the Chinese Communist Party!" "Thanks to Chairman Mao!" "Thanks to the People's Government!"[31]

In Mulan county, as elsewhere throughout the country, the CCP staged real theatre in which spectacle, state-sanctioned morality and audience participation coalesced into one remarkable show. What evidence we have suggests that in most cases, the accused were roundly condemned, the unjustly victimized given a chance to speak, the emotions of the crowd were engaged, and the event concluded with mass public support for the regime and its actions, with the incidental effect of all present implicitly bloodying their hands in their collusion with the state's violence.

In 1951, the members of the public brought to public accusation meetings were probably not aware that they were part of a show put on by the state, with an appointed supporting role as chorus and object of ideological instruction. Despite the real enough emotions that *kongsu hu* unleashed, these were heavily stage managed affairs, not the spontaneous events they seemed to be at the time. Only a small proportion of counter-revolutionaries were actually put before the public in this way, and local cadres saved those with the most heinous crimes most likely to be hated by the people for this purpose. Cases against the accused were processed and decided on far in advance of the mass accusation meeting. The individuals who got up to confront

31. Wu Yunfe, "Yi yici gong shenhui" ("Remembering a public trial"), *Riwei tongzhi de Mulan* (*Mulan under Japanese Puppet Rule*), *Mulan wenshi ziliao*, No. 4 (1989), pp. 49–50.

the accused and "speak bitterness" were specially chosen for the degree to which they would be likely to engage the emotions of the crowd and tended to represent the very old, the very young and women, and they were all coached beforehand as to what to say and when.[32]

The new state-defined morality, sanctions against regime-determined transgressors and participatory "show" all coalesced in the dénouement of the mass campaign. The combination of harshness in dealing with class enemies, and the very public manner in which *kongsu hu* were played out made for maximal education into regime norms at minimal cost. After the mobilizational phase of the Campaign to Suppress Counter-revolutionaries was over in the late summer of 1951, the CCP almost immediately extended the basic principle by preparing for the next round of mass campaigns to isolate, destroy and reincorporate those other potential social and economic competitors whose services were still to some degree needed by the state: leftover bureaucrats, private entrepreneurs and intellectuals. All were subjected to a similar mix of warning propaganda, sudden arrest, enforced self criticism and on occasion mass accusation meetings between the autumn of 1951 and 1953 – this time with no killing, but also with virtually no resistance being offered.

Limits of Campaigns: Sufan (肃反) in 1955 and Beyond

Once these preliminaries of regime consolidation were met, the revolutionary People's Republic moved from asserting control over different sectors of society by campaign to envelopment of society with the establishment of the key interlocking institutions of socialism: a *hukou* that fixed the population, and a centrally managed grain supply system that discriminated heavily in favour of the city over the countryside as the institutional underpinnings of the First Five-Year Plan. The subsequent rapid nationalization of remaining industry and enterprises in urban areas (1955) and collectivization in the countryside (1955–56) were then implemented through bureaucratic campaigns of intense policy push rather than through broadly based campaign mobilization of society.

Yet the CCP was unable simply to give up on its attachment to the notion of mass mobilization and participation, now under the quite different dynamics of work and politics within a work unit. A *sufan* ("Cleaning Out of Counter-revolutionaries") campaign was launched in 1955, with later surges in 1957–58 (when it overlapped with the Anti-Rightist Campaign) and 1960 (when it overlapped with the "Little Leap"). The initial campaign was geared at checking

32. SMA C21/1/98, "Shanghai gongren canjia zhenya fangeming yundong zongjie baogao" ("Summary report on Shanghai worker's participation in the campaign to suppress counterrevolutionaries"), July or August 1951.

the unverified credentials of large numbers of people who overnight found themselves working for the state. In theory, the campaign was to have been carried out in the time-honoured manner of stirring up the masses (*fadong qunzhong* 发动群众): the preparation of materials and struggle sessions, this time carried out within the confines of the small group, with the suggested number of counter-revolutionaries to be rooted out at around 5 per cent per work unit. In practice, things worked quite differently. The guidelines for determining who was a counter-revolutionary (as opposed to the much more common categories of someone with "historical questions" or a "backward political attitude") were so ambiguous that in many work units a minority of activists (*jiji fenzi* 积极分子), eager to prove themselves and win possible promotion to the Communist Youth League, simply ran away with the process and succeeded in designating upwards of 20 per cent of the work unit as counter-revolutionary.[33] Worse, despite the best efforts of unit leadership to engage and mobilize the commitments of the masses by the leadership in small group study and accusation sessions, the rank and file resolutely refused to be "stirred up." In 1951, when campaigns and accusation were played out with real drama in public space, most in the participating audience did not understand that their role was that of a chorus in a show put on by the state – albeit one with real consequences for those unfortunate enough to be singled out as enemies. In the summer of 1955, however, with the process of accusation and struggle in the narrower confines of the work place with its more visible hierarchies of power and status, most grasped that campaigns were displays of power put on by the state. They understood that the class-based categories of the redeemable and the enemy were flexible and porous depending on the moment, that individuals could be crushed at any time, and that despite the CCP's adherence to its formula of "stirring up the masses" and criticism and struggle sessions against enemies, it was in not in their interest (except for activists) to draw attention to themselves. It was small wonder that the majority chimed in with only formulaic and timid criticism of designated "targets." As early as 1955, participation in campaigns became rote for the majority, and tied to the prospect of specific reward in an emerging status hierarchy for a designated minority.

Worse, as designated enemies moved from the clearly definable "other" in society to a much less definable "inner" of the work unit, so too did the standards of demarcation become broader and vaguer. In the earliest months of *sufan* in 1955, beyond the issuing of a vague target of "around 5 per cent" per work unit, there was no way to

---

33. SMA B123/2/1036, "Di'yi shangye ju zhuanmen xiaozu guanyu liangge duoyue laide suqing ancang fangeming douzheng de chubu zongjie" ("Preliminary report of the first commerce bureau's special small group on the struggle against hidden counter-revolutionaries over the last two plus months"), 30 September 1955. After repeated rounds of "adjustments," the final numbers of counter-revolutionaries "cleaned out" was infinitesimally small, at only one or two per work unit.

distinguish between those with "historical questions" from those with more serious "political questions," or either from counter-revolutionaries, and all criteria were subject to drastic revision in either a more stringent or more accommodating direction depending on signals from above that could and did change at any time. In retrospect, the trajectory over the course of the 1950s was towards greater vagueness and increasing breadth of targeting. In 1951, one really had to have either done something or very recently been a visible part of an organization that was openly and plausibly designated counter-revolutionary. In 1955, one only had to have not come fully clean about prior involvement in an organization deemed counter-revolutionary or suspect; simply refraining from action was enough. By 1957, one only needed to have ever said something that could be construed as counter-revolutionary to be so targeted, and by the end of the 1950s a simple accusation of having thought the wrong kinds of thoughts sufficed.

Conclusion: The Paradoxical Lessons of Success and the Outcome of Failure

This article considers the period that was by any account the most successful in the history of the revolutionary People's Republic of China: the years of regime consolidation and the establishment of socialism (1949–56). It suggests that the revolutionary state's primary agenda (the integration of the unitary state) and the key vehicle by which it achieved that integration (the campaign) had precedents in the Republican period and contemporary referents in Stalin's Soviet Union, but the particular ways in which campaigns were launched and worked through were very much the product of the Chinese Communist Party's particular ethos of morality paired with popular participation. It argues that campaigns – in their four different forms – were at the heart of the mechanics of regime consolidation and the establishment of socialism, and insofar as these great challenges were met successfully between 1949 and 1956, campaigns were an important part of that aggregate success, however crude, brutal and coercive they might have been towards individuals.

This leaves an important question. If the years between 1949 and 1956 are thought to be in aggregate "successful" (at least in comparison with later periods in the history of the revolutionary PRC), was this a success that was later squandered, and if so, why? Was the ultimately tragic trajectory of the revolutionary PRC something built into the very institutions and ideology of its consolidation in the early to mid-1950s; or, as the official Party historiography would have it, was there a sharp wrong turn made some time after the Eighth Party Congress of autumn 1956? This question is perhaps unanswerable, but the focus on campaigns and their limits suggests some provisional responses. Campaigns in combination with CCP direction from above were such an effective mechanism of regime consolidation and the establishment of socialism that this strategy became a victim of its own success when social, political and economic conditions changed. Campaigns did concentrate the implementing power of the bureaucracy, push through a wide range of policies, and even, particularly in the early years of regime consolidation, mobilize significant sectors of the population in support of regime-determined political goals to isolate and destroy those deemed to be "other." Those unfortunate enough to be the targets of campaigns (counter-revolutionaries, landlords, "corrupt" businessmen, "corrupt" cadres, intellectuals of suspect background) suffered severely, but the regime's goals of educating the public in new revolutionary norms, engaging mass support, and destroying both real and potential sources of political, social or economic competition were by and large met. The post-1949 years of consolidation and the establishment of socialism were years in which the CCP's own understanding of what won the civil war continued to serve them well. The mechanics of (re)establishing a vertically integrated state with a revolutionary leadership played out in a policy environment in which, like the civil war itself, enemies were visible and the CCP's own skill at mobilizing the majority against what it defined as the minority resulted in an almost unbelievably rapid set of clearly definable, measurable successes. And even in contemporary China, campaign methods still have significant traction in policy areas where enemies have been clearly definable as a minority "other" (such as the *falun gong* 法轮功) or as an external enemy to be wiped out (SARS, bird flu).

But when appropriate targets are not both clearly identifiable and compelling, campaigns run into trouble, and these are exactly the kinds of conditions with which the CCP had to deal after the mid-1950s. With the social and economic power of alternative social groups destroyed through mass campaigns, coercive domination of society secure and exit options closed off, the CCP's key programmes of consolidation and the establishment of the basic political and economic institutions of socialism had been pushed through much more quickly than anyone had imagined possible. The very improbability of such rapid and thorough successes ultimately made more extravagant forms of voluntarism plausible (if we could win the civil war, tame the economy, push through land reform, wipe out all forms of social and political competition, *and* both collectivize agriculture and nationalize all private enterprise with so little resistance in such a short period of time, why *not* be able to leap directly into communism?) and the continued use of the tactics of success (the campaign) unquestioned. The use of campaign methods in a very different policy environment against much less obvious targets combined with other, often contingent, elements: external shocks from de-Stalinization elsewhere in the Leninist world, real objective problems with continuing in a Stalinist trajectory of one-man management and the continued imbalances in the planned economy, Mao's own bias against the obvious signs of the domestication of the revolutionary impulse and the collective inability of the CCP leadership to contain his more extravagant impulses, and the CCP's abandonment of its earlier materialist tradition of careful investigation and diagnosis of economic and social relations. All these components reinforced political norms that gave strong incentives to increasingly leftist impulses on the part of local cadres. Tellingly, campaigns continued and in fact intensified, with very different and highly negative aggregate results. The later "mistakes" of the Anti-Rightist Campaign, the Great Leap Forward and even the Cultural Revolution were neither a dramatic wrong turn nor bred in the bone. They resulted from a set of norms and practices that were fused to the successes of the civil war and 1949–56. Inseparable from the leadership's own myths and understanding of its own successes, campaigns and the uses to which they were put were unable to adapt to the changed environment of the all-enveloping work unit, the collective and the planned economy. Ultimately and ironically, the presumptive lessons of success resulted in later failure, while on the other side of the Taiwan Straits, the presumptive lessons of failure laid a foundation for future success.

Dilemmas of Inside Agitators: Chinese State Feminists in 1957*

Wang Zheng

ABSTRACT   In 1957 the All-China Women's Federation shifted its emphasis on gender equality and embraced a conservative theme "diligently, thriftily build the country, and diligently, thriftily manage the family" for its work report at the Third National Women's Assembly. Based on archival research and interviews, this article examines gender contestations in the CCP's central power structure and argues that formation of the conservative line was a result of strategic manoeuvres by the top women's federation leaders and Deng Xiaoping with the goal of sustaining a gender-based organization in a time of political turbulence. The article emphasizes the importance of informal relations in the formal decision-making process. Informal relations do not fall in the usual analytical categories neatly and defy historical analysis with little historical evidence for empirical studies. Yet they can be crucial in determining historical events, as is demonstrated in the article.

In the past two decades scholarship on Chinese women's history in the 20th century has complicated our understanding of gender politics in the Chinese Communist Party (CCP).[1] Slogans such as women's liberation and equality between men and women (*nannü pingdeng* 男女平等) have been embraced by the CCP since its inception, while structural inequality and dismissal or even suppression of gender issues were perennial phenomena in the Party's history. In much of the Revolution era the subordination of women's interests was justified by either a Marxist theory that gave priority to class struggle, or the necessity of circumstances, such as the unity required for the war against Japanese invaders. While feminists in the CCP never stopped their cautious negotiations and manoeuvres, their efforts in promoting women's interests secured legitimacy only in the beginning of the People's Republic of China (PRC).

The founding of the All-China Women's Federation (ACWF) in April 1949 marked the beginning of a golden, though brief, period for

* The author wishes to thank Elisabeth Croll, Gail Hershatter and Kimberley Ens Mannings for their comments on early drafts of this article.

1. For feminist critique of the Chinese Communist Party's gender policies, see Kay Ann Johnson, *Women, the Family, and Peasant Revolution in China* (Chicago: University of Chicago Press, 1983); Phyllis Andors, *The Unfinished Liberation of Chinese Women, 1949–1980* (Bloomington: Indiana University Press, 1983); Judith Stacey, *Patriarchy and Socialist Revolution in China* (Berkeley & Los Angeles: University of California Press, 1983); Sonia Kruks, Rayana Rapp and Marilyn B. Young (eds.), *Promissary Notes: Women in the Transition to Socialism* (New York: Monthly Review Press, 1989); and Christina K. Gilmartin, *Engendering the Chinese Revolution: Radical Women, Communist Politics, and Mass Movements in the 1920s* (Berkeley & Los Angeles: University of California Press, 1995).

feminists in the CCP. In order to consolidate the support of women in the liberated areas and to reach women in the Nationalist controlled regions, the top Party leaders unequivocally endorsed the establishment of the federation. Receiving the mandate from the Party, women leaders such as Deng Yingchao (邓颖超) and Cai Chang (蔡畅) wasted no time in setting up a national women's organization as an institutional base for the women's liberation movement in new China. Many young women communists were transferred from various posts unrelated to women-work (*funü gongzuo* 妇女工作) to different levels of the women's federation throughout the country. By September 1950, women's federations were set up in 83 cities. By 1953 there were already over 40,000 officials of the ACWF system nationwide working at and above the district level.[2] And by 1954 women in many cities had been organized into women's congresses, the grassroots organization of the ACWF. In a matter of a few years, women communists had successfully developed this gender-based organization into the only mass organization that reached down to rural villages and urban neighbourhoods.[3]

Even in this initial euphoric stage ACWF officials' dedicated work to promote equality between men and women was not without obstacles and challenges. As each level of the ACWF was subordinate to the Party committee of the same administrative level, women officials were often confronted with Party bosses who showed little interest in equality between men and women or women-work. Chairman Mao was apparently well aware of this situation. On 12 November 1952 in a meeting with the leaders of the ACWF, he taught them how to deal with different levels of Party committees in these colourful words: *yi song* (一送) (first, submit proposals to the Party committee); *er cui* (二催) (second, push for the Party committee to reply); *san maniang* (三骂娘) (if the first two methods did not work, third, just curse and swear).[4] Apparently, neglecting women's interests, though never a formal policy, was a common practice within the Party that continued into the socialist period. Still, in this early stage the ACWF was able to forge ahead. Their undaunted

2. The figure appears in Deng Yingchao's report to the second ACWF national congress in 1953. See "Sinianlai zhongguo funü yundong de jiben zongjie he jinhou renwu" ("A summary of the Chinese women's movement in the past four years and future task"), in Chinese Women Cadres School (ed.), *Zhongguo funü yundong wenxian ziliao huibian* (*An Anthology of Source Material on the Chinese Women's Movement*) (Beijing: Chinese Women's Press, 1988), Vol. 2, p. 171. The two-volume anthology is classified as an internal document, which is not for public circulation.

3. For a discussion of the early institutional development of the ACWF, see Wang Zheng "State feminism? Gender and socialist state formation in Maoist China," *Feminist Studies*, Vol. 31, No. 3 (2005), pp. 519–551. For a study of the ACWF in the post-Mao era, see Ellen Judd, *The Chinese Women's Movement between State and Market* (Stanford: Stanford University Press, 2002).

4. Luo Qiong and Duan Yongqiang, *Luo Qiong fangtan lu* (*Interviews with Luo Qiong*) (Beijing: Chinese Women Press, 2000), p. 126. Mao's original phrase *san maniang* was changed by women officials into *san piping* (third, criticize) in their public talks, perhaps because of the apparent gender offensiveness of the original.

stance could be illustrated by a high point in this period when Deng Yingchao and Cai Chang each gave a speech at the Eighth Party Congress in September 1956, reiterating the goal of women's liberation as well as providing critical assessment of the state of equality between men and women.[5]

The Women's Federation system's impressive efforts in addressing gender inequality – from drafting and implementing the Marriage Law and breaking gender boundaries in employment to mobilizing women's participation in public affairs and local governance – constituted a large part of what was new about the new China in the initial stage of the CCP's tenure. However, in 1957 the ACWF suddenly made a conservative turn at the Third National Women's Assembly, departing from its previous policy of mobilizing women to participate in production as a means of achieving women's liberation, and adopting *qinjian jianguo, qinjian chijia* (勤俭建国，勤俭持家, diligently, thriftily build the country, and diligently, thriftily manage the family) as its central task. In her careful study of women-work of the ACWF, Delia Davin pointed out that "a striking feature of the documents of the 1957 Congress was the unprecedented emphasis on the importance of women's family and household duties brought in under the slogan." She related this conservatism in the women's movement to conservative economic policy, while acknowledging the difficulty of finding traces that might indicate debates behind the formulation of new policies and aims for women-work.[6] Feminist scholars have noticed the significant change in the objectives of women-work in 1957, but so far it has remained unclear why the ACWF embraced such an apparently regressive line.[7]

Based on documents from the Shanghai Archives and ACWF's archives as well as published works including memoirs by ACWF officials, this article attempts to trace the process of the ACWF's alleged "change of heart" so as to illuminate internal workings of gender politics of the CCP in the late 1950s. As the article demonstrates, political tensions within the Party were played out in unexpected ways in the volatile time of 1957, a period in which scholars have examined confrontations between intellectuals and the Party, and workers and the Party.[8] Gender, I argue, no less than class, was a focal point for many in the power game. Constructing a

5. See Deng Yingchao, "Zai dangde lingdao xia, tuanjie he fahui guangda funü quanzhong de liliang" "(Under the Party's leadership, unite and utilize the power of women masses"), and Cai chang, "Jiji peiyang he tiba gengduo genghao de nüganbu" ("Actively train and promote more and better women cadres"), in *An Anthology*, Vol. 2, pp. 262–68.

6. Delia Davin, *Woman-Work: Women and the Party in Revolutionary China* (London: Oxford University Press, 1976), pp. 65–68.

7. See Zhang Naihua, "The All China Women's Federation, Chinese women and the women's movement: 1984–1993," PhD dissertation, Michigan State University.

8. See Elizabeth Perry, "Shanghai's strike wave of 1957," *The China Quarterly*, No. 137 (1994), pp. 1–27; Jackie Sheehan, *Chinese Workers: A New History* (London & New York: Routledge, 1998); and Merle Goldman, *Literary Dissent in Communist China* (Cambridge, MA: Harvard University Press, 1967).

narrative of Chinese state feminists' contentions, negotiations and compromises in a particular historical context, this article also raises questions about methods for studying the gender history of the PRC.

Deng Xiaoping's Instructions?

Several years ago when I was working in the Shanghai Archives on a different project, I happened to see a curious document dated 22 October 1957, entitled "Notes of Luo Qiong (罗琼) conveying the important directives on women-work by the leading comrades of the Secretariat and the Political Bureau of the Central Committee."[9] It had a disclaimer at the beginning, stating that the text was put together from one or two comrades' note-taking; it had been checked by some leaders but without Luo Qiong's personal proofreading; the text was just meant to be reference material for internal discussion; and it should be returned after reading. Apparently, this was an informal transmission of internal talks. To date, this document remains the only one I have found that directly quoted the top Party leaders' talks on women-work in that critical historical period. It struck me as a curious piece because it recorded those talks verbatim, but without an introduction to the context. The only broad context is that the talks were given during the Anti-Rightist Campaign. The specific context of the talks and their meanings remained vague.

The document has two parts: one contains directives from the Secretariat of the Central Committee and the other has directives from the Political Bureau of the Central Committee. The directives from the Secretariat address three issues, *qinjian jianguo, qinjian chijia*, women's liberation and equality between men and women, and methods of women-work. From these directives, it is clear that Deng Xiaoping was the one who instructed that *qinjian jianguo, qinjian chijia* should be the theme of the Women's Assembly. He gave a long talk elaborating the significance of *qinjian jianguo, qinjian chijia* in the construction of socialism and women's important role in *qinjian chijia*. With this evidence one could reach the conclusion that Deng Xiaoping had imposed the patriarchal policy on women-work and the ACWF succumbed to the power of the patriarchal state. Case closed.

However, in her memoir published in 2000, Luo Qiong, one of the co-authors who drafted the report for the Third National Women's Assembly, recalled the experience of following Deng Xiaoping's instruction 42 years before and unequivocally expressed her deep gratitude to Deng. This is how she describes her feelings when the Political Bureau approved the final version of the report: "Holding

9. "Luo Qiong tongzhi chuanda zhongyang shujichu, zhongyang zhengzhiju fuze tongzhi duiyu funü gongzuo jiao zhongyao zhishi de jilu zhengli" ("Notes of Luo Qiong's conveying the important directives on women-work by the leading comrades of the Secretariat and the Political Bureau of the Central Committee"). C31-1-169, Shanghai Municipal Archives.

the report draft in my hands, all kinds of emotions came through my heart. I was deeply grateful to the guidance of the Central Committee and comrade Deng Xiaoping in the important historical moment. I was also deeply sorry that we had been unable to grasp the key to the problems at first. I will forever remember comrade Deng Xiaoping's instruction."[10] Such overflowing gratitude to Deng Xiaoping could be more a reflection of the author's mind in 2000 than in 1957. Nevertheless, given that Deng Xiaoping had just replaced gender equality with a two-diligences policy, why would Luo Qiong be so grateful to him? What was the inner logic behind this demonstrated gratitude, past and/or present? What was so inspiring about Deng's instruction? Certainly Luo Qiong was not just talking about the two-diligences policy that had subsequently been abandoned shortly after the Great Leap Forward began. So what valuable instruction did Deng give to the ACWF officials?

The Work Report for the Third National Women's Assembly

The Third National Women's Assembly was scheduled to take place in September 1957. Luo Qiong and Dong Bian (董边), both members of the standing committee of the ACWF, were assigned to draft the work report for the Assembly, and the vice-chair of the ACWF Zhang Yun (章蕴) was in charge of the report writing. The work report, setting the agenda for the whole women's federation system in the following four years, is the centrepiece at the National Women's Assembly when representatives of women from all walks of life throughout the country convene in Beijing. As such, it is a crucial part of the preparation for the assembly. But on this occasion, the team began writing in the spring of 1957 but was unable to finalize the report in six months. According to Luo Qiong, by early August they had already revised the report ten times yet could not reach agreement after much debate. Luo Qiong's memoir does not specify what they were debating about. But it does summarize in a tone of self-criticism the reasons for being unable to produce a report over such a long period. In Luo's view, they did not handle well the relationship between fulfilling the Party's central task and raising women's status; they did not regard the Party's main work as the central task of women-work; they mistakenly thought that when the economic system changed to public ownership the conditions to achieve complete equality between men and women had arrived; in the draft they drew a parallel between building a socialist country and achieving equality between men and women in the title, and they accentuated the latter in the content of the report; and they confused work policy with work methods.[11]

10. Luo Qiong and Duan Yongqiang, *Interviews with Luo Qiong*, p. 148.
11. *Ibid.* p. 144.

Documents found in the ACWF's archives confirm Luo Qiong's memory. The title of the fourth draft was "Strive further to achieve equality between men and women." Vice-chair Zhang Yun edited the draft carefully but did not change the title and its main theme. Late in July 1957 Zhang Yun conveyed the instructions of Cai Chang and Deng Yingchao to ACWF officials working on the preparation for the Assembly:

On the fundamental issue of women-work in the construction period after the victory of socialist revolution, [they] agreed to say mobilizing women in the whole country to participate in socialist construction, striving for complete equality between men and women. We will not propose striving for women's thorough liberation. Three ways of phrasing may be considered: one, mobilizing women to participate in socialist construction and striving for complete equality between men and women, paralleling the two parts; two, participating in socialist construction so as to achieve equality between men and women; and three, highlighting the mobilization of women to participate in socialist construction as the general principle, followed by concrete tasks. The two elder sisters are inclined to the third way and would like the ACWF's Party group to discuss the issue.[12]

Clearly, the focus of the debate was whether to insist on gender equality as a theme of the report or not. The first two suggestions by "the elder sisters" for the title already expressed compromise when compared with the title of the fourth draft, which singularly emphasized gender equality. Cai Chang and Deng Yingchao opted for the third suggestion, which actually removed the phrase from the title. And they made a firm suggestion not to propose striving for women's thorough liberation. Why had pursuing gender equality and women's thorough liberation become problematic at this time? Why did Cai Chang and Deng Yingchao, two veteran communists and top CCP leaders' wives who had openly advocated gender equality at the Party's Congress a year before, not even dare to highlight gender equality in the title of the work report? What was at stake behind these anxious discussions?

In May that year Mao Zedong turned the Party's rectification movement into the Anti-Rightist Campaign. The sudden change of political direction not only startled people outside the Party but also disoriented many Party officials such as the ACWF top leaders. In the eight years since the founding of the PRC, women communists in the ACWF and the whole women's federation system had worked very hard to advance gender equality. From implementing the Marriage Law, encouraging women to break gender boundaries in employment, and improving women's health and literacy, to setting up women's organizations at the grassroots level nationwide, the women's federation officials, many of whom were young women in their 20s or early 30s, actively, even vehemently, promoted women's interests and social advancement. Many of them firmly, though naively,

12. "Zhang Yun tongzhi chuanda Cai dajie he Deng dajie de zhishi" ("Comrade Zhang Yun conveys instructions from Sister Cai and Sister Deng"), ACWF archives.

believed that with the victory of socialist revolution it was time for women to cash in the Party's promissory note of women's liberation. Even veteran communists such as Zhang Yun had high expectations of women's liberation in the socialist country and held achieving gender equality as a sacred mission.[13] Luo Qiong's self-criticism was to the point in that they "mistakenly thought that when economic system had changed to public ownership the conditions for achieving complete equality between men and women had arrived."

The Anti-Rightist Campaign, unlike previous campaigns that simply required women's participation, not only diverted the ACWF's energy and resources from women-work, but also posed serious challenges to it. Since the founding of the ACWF, the rationale for the necessity of such a gender-based organization could be summarized in two points: first, socialist revolution and socialist construction require women's participation, and the ACWF was to organize and mobilize women to work for the Party's general tasks; and secondly, there were still feudal remnants in socialist China that oppressed women, so women needed such an organization to help them break free from feudal bondage to achieve gender equality. In ACWF official talks, publications and workshops for training women activists, feudal bondage, women's oppression, equality between men and women, and women's liberation were almost always mentioned, and as a result the terms quickly entered the PRC's public discourse. In the early 1950s when their efforts to set up grassroots women's organizations were questioned or resisted by local male officials, ACWF officials would always appeal to such rhetoric, emphasizing the reality of gender inequality or even abuses of women so as to stress the necessity of a women's organization for the ultimate goal of women's liberation.[14]

But after the internal circulation of Mao Zedong's article dated 15 May 1957, entitled "Things are beginning to change" and signalling his offence over "bourgeois rightists," things changed rapidly. Now merely talking about problems in socialist China could qualify one as a rightist. ACWF officials were quick to realize that they could no longer say women in socialist China were still oppressed or not yet liberated. But if women were not oppressed and were already liberated, what should be the tasks of the ACWF? Or an even more troubling but logical question could be, was there any need for the existence of a gender-based organization if there was no more gender oppression? The suggestion by Cai Chang and Deng Yingchao to drop gender equality in the title reveals their astute awareness of the new taboo. But even if the report drafters followed this compromising suggestion, they would still have been faced with the dilemma of how to articulate the goals of the ACWF in a manner that both conformed

13. See All-China Women's Federation, *Huainian Zhang Yun dajie* (*Remembering Sister Zhang Yun*) (Beijing: Chinese Women's Press, 1996).
14. See Wang Zheng, "State feminism?"

to the current political atmosphere and justified the existence of the women's federation. In any case, the drafters apparently were not ready to give up the theme of gender equality, as Luo Qiong revealed in her memoir.

The deadline for submitting the report to the Secretariat of the Central Committee for approval was 7 August. The top officials of the ACWF were unable to reach a consensus when it was due. A draft with the title "Report on women-work" was submitted to the Secretariat for their instruction on revision. The document had no other title, which could be read either as indicating that the drafters were too disoriented to present a clear theme or as an uncompromising compromise, that is, the drafters tried to gloss over what they did not want to give up with a vague title. By informing the Secretariat that they needed the top Party leaders' instruction on revision, the ACWF officials removed their liability for making political mistakes at this critical moment.

According to Luo Qiong, a few days after the draft was submitted, Deng Yingchao called her from Beidaihe where the top Party leaders were spending their summer, telling her that comrade Deng Xiaoping told them not to argue any more, just come to Beidaihe to discuss how to revise the report. "Sister Deng also told me to take with me materials on diligently, thriftily building the country, and diligently, thriftily managing the family."[15] Receiving the call, Luo Qiong "was elated" and immediately reported to Zhang Yun. The writing group went to Beidaihe straight away. Luo Qiong must have known that the heavy burden of producing a politically correct report was not on the shoulders of the writing group any more.

On 14 August, General Secretary Deng Xiaoping hosted a meeting of the Secretariat to discuss the draft submitted by the ACWF. Luo Qiong recalls, "Comrades Cai Chang and Deng Yingchao expressed their views first. Comrade Zhang Yun gave some explanations on the draft. All the participating comrades of the Secretariat talked, giving comments or suggestions. Not a single comrade gave positive views on our draft."[16] Even in her memoir published in 2000, Luo Qiong would not reveal what the members of the Secretariat said. What did she hide and why? Here that curious document I found in the Shanghai Archives fills in the blank. The first part of the document was actually a set of notes on the comments of the members of the Secretariat on the draft in that meeting. It could have been from Luo Qiong's notes in the meeting since she was the one conveying the "directives of leaders of the Secretariat." A full quotation of Party leaders' comments on women's liberation and equality between men and women recorded in this document will help reveal what adversity the ACWF officials were confronting in the summer of 1957.

---

15. Luo Qiong and Duan Yongqiang, *Interviews with Luo Qiong*, p. 145.
16. *Ibid.*

The leading comrades of the Secretariat unanimously think that now women are already liberated, and men and women are already equal. They think whether women are liberated and having equality should be mainly judged by the social system. Judging from the socialist ownership, men and women have already achieved economic equality. Women are already participating in state politics, and the numbers are not small. Since women already have equality, why still demand equality? What else do you want? One leading comrade says: equality between men and women is a slogan of anti-feudalism. Capitalist society has faked equality. The socialist system has genuine equality. Raising [the slogan of] equality between men and women again at present will cause ideological confusion.

Leading comrades also point out: are there any phenomena of inequality? There are. These should be gradually resolved in the process of socialist construction. Therefore, in the Assembly [you] should emphasize what short-comings women still have; what efforts they themselves should make to overcome them; and how to achieve equal rights they already have. Moreover, the extant phenomena of inequality will not be entirely eliminated in a short period of time, and they are just remnants in the whole society. If [you] singularly raise the issue, it would cause ideological confusion. It is incorrect to parallel [equality between men and women] with socialist construction.[17]

Luo Qiong's notes did not name who said what in this section, a significant contrast to the way she mentioned Deng Xiaoping in a different section. Did she sense that such hostility to gender equality would make male leaders lose face one day if publicized? Whatever motivation she or other ACWF officials had, the anonymous way they presented these top male leaders' directives reveals their disapproval if not disdain. The male Party leaders' "unanimous" criticism of ACWF leaders' insistence on gender equality revealed their tremendous ignorance or disavowal of deeply entrenched structural inequality still existing not only in rural but also urban China, a reality that the ACWF officials had been making great efforts to publicize and to change. The stern warning of causing ideological confusion by raising the issue of equality between men and women was certainly made against the specific context of the Anti-Rightist Campaign, thereby giving it extra coercive and manipulative effects.

Following the quotation of comments by Party leaders, Zhang Yun's words are quoted in parentheses:

Comrade Zhang Yuan added: inequality between men and women is the problem of class society. Some phenomena in the socialist society should be resolved gradually, and they exist because of individuals' mishandling, or problems, mistakes, shortcomings in work, not as a fundamental issue relating to equality between men and women. The saying that [there is still] inequality is inappropriate.[18]

17. "Notes of Luo Qiong's conveying the important directives on women-work by leading comrades of the Secretariat and the Political Bureau of the Central Committee."
  18. *Ibid.*

It is not known in what tone Zhang Yun said these words. Probably, as the one responsible for the draft that insisted on gender equality, she felt pressure to make a self-criticism in front of the Party leaders. A veteran women-work official who had bravely confronted masculinist challenges in her exploration of the format of grassroots organization of women a few years before, and who possibly was the key person insisting on keeping the demand for equality between men and women in the draft, Zhang Yun in the summer of 1957 had to give in. Previously she had criticized male chauvinism as politically incorrect. Now, as masculinist views were shielded in the dominant hymn to socialism by male leaders, Zhang Yun had neither the language nor the power to fight back. Significantly, the notes did not record how Cai Chang and Deng Yingchao, the two more senior women leaders present, responded to male leaders' attack on gender equality. It could be that they kept silent. In any case, Zhang Yun was then the executive chair of the ACWF and therefore the legitimate person to bear the brunt of the attack and to give a conciliatory response on behalf of the ACWF.

The male leaders did not stop at an assault on gender equality. They also criticized ACWF officials for complaining about working on central tasks of the Party and for "treating it as doing odds and ends." They stressed that only in the process of completing central tasks could the ACWF do a good job on women-work. In the first eight years' history of the women's federation, the conflict between the Party's central work and the ACWF's women-work had been a dominant theme. The ACWF had been called on to mobilize women to work on each campaign and each task set by the CCP, in addition to directly transferring ACWF officials to work on those tasks. In most cases, those central tasks had no relation to addressing gender hierarchy or women's needs and interests. Women's federation officials at different levels found they worked more for the central tasks than for women, and many were troubled by such a situation. For example, the Shanghai Women's Federation's officials expressed their discontent in the mid-1950s with these sharp questions: "It is correct to mobilize women to participate in the central political campaigns called by the Party. But what have women gained through these campaigns? What have they given to women? What can we say about our special work for women?"[19] Contrasting these critical questions with male Party leaders' criticism, the different gender positions of the ACWF and the male-dominated Secretariat are clear.

In essence, the controversy over the central tasks and women-work was a contest to make the ACWF a tool of the Party on the part of the male leaders and to make it a genuine women's organization for women's interests on the part of its own officials. Seen in this light, the

19. "Shanghai minzhu fulian 1953 nian xiabannian gongzuo zongjie" ("Shanghai Democratic Women's Federation's review of work in the second half of 1953"), 1954, C31-1-75.

title of the fourth draft of the report, "Strive further to achieve equality between men and women," almost amounted to a declaration by the ACWF that it would focus on gender issues. The top ACWF officials must have hoped that with the completion of the nationalization of industry and commerce, the Third National Women's Assembly in 1957 would mark a turning point at which the ACWF would begin to shift its central attention to gender equality. However, the turning point was diverted by the Anti-Rightist Campaign. The changed political setting provided a golden opportunity for masculinist power in the Party effectively to block any feminist move, and to exert tighter control over this gender-based organization.

Cai Chang and Deng Yingchao, wives of top leaders, must have had a better sense of masculinist sentiment in the Party's leading body than Zhang Yun, who had been widowed in her 20s. Their inclination towards the third title, which did not mention equality between men and women but highlighted the central task of socialist construction, proved to be a shrewd assessment of the current situation. Apparently, the report-writing group, including Zhang Yun, still tried to cling to their original goal in a drastically changed political environment. Their unyielding insistence on equality between men and women must have looked outrageous to the male leaders, arousing strong negative reaction from everyone in the Secretariat except for Deng Xiaoping. This was one of those moments that laid bare the deep gender gap within the Party.

It must have been devastating for Zhang Yun, Luo Qiong and Dong Bian to hear male leaders denouncing their report draft in such blatant male chauvinist language. But there is no record of how they felt at that moment, besides the above-quoted self-criticism by Zhang Yun. What we do know is that this terrible situation did not last too long. This is how Luo Qiong described in her memoir what happened after the male leaders' criticism:

Comrade Xiaoping was sitting on the side, smoking and listening quietly. In the end comrade Xiaoping gave a summarizing talk. He had a well-thought-out plan and came straight to the point. His first sentence was: "Revisions could be small, medium or large. It seems your draft requires a large revision." His second sentence was: "Your labour will not be wasted as some parts can be used in the revised version." He clearly pointed out: "It seems that you did not grasp the general task of constructing a socialist country set by the Eighth National Congress of the Party. Your assembly should be one that mobilizes women in the whole country to diligently, thriftily build the country, and diligently, thriftily manage the family in order to strive for the construction of socialism. Your report should use this as its title." He confirmed: "The principle of women-work in the period of socialist construction should be diligently, thriftily building the country, and diligently, thriftily managing the family in order to strive for the construction of socialism." He said once, and then said again with emphasis: "This principle is not wrong and it should be the fundamental principle for a long time."[20]

20. Luo Qiong and Duan Yongqiang, *Interviews with Luo Qiong*, p. 145.

According to Luo Qiong, Deng Xiaoping gave a long talk on the two-diligences policy and quoted Chairman Mao twice. Deng also gave detailed instructions on the structure of the report, telling them to organize it into seven parts and specifying the theme for each part. He told them how many words they were supposed to write for each part and asked them to limit the length to 20,000 characters. "From the principle and task to the structure and length, comrade Xiaoping told us everything clearly," Luo Qiong said in her memoir. Obviously, Deng Xiaoping had done his homework before hosting this meeting of the Secretariat.

Following Deng's instructions, the writing group finished revisions in one week and sent it back to the Secretariat. Besides centring on the two diligences, the revised version also included the Secretariat members' view on gender equality. It stated: "Since the socialist revolution was completed, women in our country have already achieved equal rights with men in political, economic, cultural and social aspects and family life. They have forever ended thousands of years of sad history of being oppressed and subjugated, and achieved women's liberation."[21] A second meeting of the Secretariat on reviewing the report was scheduled. Luo Qiong was very uneasy on that day. But this time Deng Xiaoping was the first to talk and he said, "this version is basically fine now." Then other leaders followed to give their consent. They only offered some minor editorial suggestions before they approved it. Then the draft was ready to be submitted to the Political Bureau of the Central Committee.

Before following the draft to another setting, we should look closely at Deng Xiaoping's role in this critical moment. It is clear that he was the only male leader in the Secretariat who did not attack the ACWF that day. Instead, he had spent time beforehand working out a "politically correct" theme to break the impasse. Judging from Luo Qiong's description, Deng Xiaoping did not mention "equality between men and women" at all, either positively or negatively. We have no way of discerning his personal position on the issue. His agenda was unmistakably to propose a new principle for women-work, that is, the two diligences. This principle was a retreat from the goal of striving further for gender equality since it did not address gender hierarchy but rather consolidated the gender division of labour and reinforced gender roles. It also strengthened the masculinist Party position of using the ACWF as a tool for the central tasks of the Party. As such, it received the unanimous approval of the Secretariat.

But was this proposal totally siding with the masculinist power in the Party? Why were Luo Qiong and other ACWF officials so grateful to Deng? What was the key to the problems that Luo Qiong regretted

21. "Qinjian jianguo, qinjian chijia, wei jianshe shehuizhuyi er fendou" ("Diligently and thriftily build the country, diligently and thriftily manage the family, striving for socialist construction"), in Chinese Women Cadres School, *An Anthology of Source Material on the Chinese Women's Movement*, Vol. 2, p. 316.

they had not grasped at first, while apparently Deng Xiaoping did? The clues to these puzzles can be found in the second part of the curious document, that is, the part recording the discussions of the revised draft by the Political Bureau. The document set out the Political Bureau leaders' discussion under three topics. The first, problems in the Anti-Rightist Campaign, recorded Party leaders' discussions about how rightists attacked socialism and their suggestions on how the report should include denouncement of rightist theses by using examples from work on women and children (the final report of the ACWF included some direct quotations from leaders' discussions on this issue). The second topic, about the two diligences, expressed leaders' agreement and approval of this "very important issue." The third topic was about the question of whether the ACWF should exist or not and its function. In this crucial part, the document did not note opposing views at all, but simply quoted Liu Shaoqi's favourable view of the ACWF. The length of the quotation showed that the Political Bureau spent quite a while on this issue.

Liu Shaoqi's views as recorded in the document, apart from registering his approval of the revised report, focused on refuting the view that the ACWF should be eliminated. This is a direct quotation:

To the question of whether we want Fulian or not, I think we should not say such words any more. Some people have thought that women's liberation is a task of one period, a task of a historical stage. As if since women are liberated, Fulian is not needed. In my view, not only at present, but also in the future, Fulian still should exist. With the existence of Fulian, [we] can carry out work among the women masses.

Liu repeated at the meeting:

As to the question of how much longer Fulian should exist, Fulian should exist for a long time. Don't bring up the question of whether it should be eliminated or not any more.[22]

The political environment for the ACWF in 1957 is clear now. The contention was not simply over gender equality, but more seriously, over the very existence of the organization. This explains why ACWF officials wanted to insist on striving for equality between men and women even though they knew that the slogan might sound problematic in that particular political context. How could this gender-based organization legitimize its existence without a gender-specific goal and function? Seen in this light, Deng Xiaoping's ingenuity also came into relief. His proposal of the two diligences provided a gender-specific function to legitimize the existence of the ACWF. And better yet, he used politically correct rhetoric to present a traditional role for women to play, rhetoric that would shield him from any possible attack.

22. "Notes of Luo Qiong's conveying the important directives on women-work by leading comrades of the Secretariat and the Political Bureau of the Central Committee."

The formulation of the two diligences first appeared in Chairman Mao's writings. Mao in 1955 was editing a volume of reports on the development of rural co-operatives nationwide. He wrote 104 small commentaries on more than 170 reports. One report, entitled "Diligently and thriftily running the co-ops," stimulated Mao's comment of "diligently and thriftily running everything."[23] During the following years he would mention the point of diligence occasionally. In the context of promoting rural collectivization, he gave a talk on rural co-ops at the Sixth Congress of the Central Committee in 1955. One of the fifteen points he made was on diligence: "We should advocate diligently and thriftily managing the family, diligently and thriftily running the co-ops, and diligently and thriftily building the country. Our country needs diligence first, and thrift second; we don't want laziness, and we don't want sumptuousness. Laziness would lead to decline, which is not good."[24] According to Luo Qiong, this was one of the two sayings by Chairman Mao quoted by Deng Xiaoping at the Secretariat meeting. In July 1957 Mao wrote an article that was circulated among provincial Party secretaries who were convening in Qingdao. In it he again mentioned diligently running the co-ops. But this time, he specifically mentioned women's role in diligence: "In order to resolve the issue of diligently and thriftily managing the family, [we should] chiefly rely on women's groups to do such work."[25] This was the second quotation cited by Deng Xiaoping in his speech on the two diligences, followed with his own emphasis that this was the historical responsibility of Fulian.[26]

In the beginning of 1957 the Party centre launched a campaign of zengchan jieyue (增产节约, increase production and practise economy) as a response to the overheated economy of 1956.[27] In publicity on this campaign, Mao's quotation of "diligently and thriftily running everything" was widely circulated. In the women's federation system officials at different levels began to emphasize women's role in the campaign of increasing production and practising economy, and together with Chairman Mao's quotation, an emphasis on women's role in "diligently and thriftily running the family" also emerged.[28] In other words, by the time of Deng Xiaoping's selection of the couplet,

23. "Zhongguo nongcun de shehuizhuyi gaochao de xuyan" ("Preface to 'The high tide of socialism in rural China'") September and December 1955, in *Mao Zedong xuanji* (*Selected Works of Mao Zedong*), Vol. 5 (Beijing: People Press, 1955), p. 249.

24. "Nongye hezuohua de yichang bianlun he dangqian de jieji douzheng" ("A debate on agricultural collectivization and current class struggles"), 11 October 1955, in *Selected Works of Mao Zedong*, p. 213.

25. "Yijiuwuqi nian xiaji de xingshi" ("The situation in summer 1957"), July 1957, in *ibid.* p. 459.

26. Luo Qiong and Duan Yongqiang, *Interviews with Luo Qiong*, p. 146.

27. Mao Zedong, "Duizhongyang guanyu yijiuwuqi nian kaizhan zengchan jieyue yundong de zhishi gao de piyu ("Comment on the directive draft on the Party Central launching the campaign of increasing production and practicing economy in 1957"), in *Jianguo yilai Mao Zedong wengao* (*Mao Zedong's Papers Since the Founding of the PRC*) (Beijing: Zhongyang wenxian chubanshe, 1990), Vol. 6, pp. 302–303.

28. *Renmin ribao* (*People's Daily*), 26 March 1957, p. 6.

"diligently, thriftily build the country, and diligently, thriftily manage the family" had been circulated in the public discourse though not yet often appeared as a pair. And it was one of the ACWF's multiple tasks following the current central task.

Deng Xiaoping did not initially decide on the theme of two diligences for the ACWF. The July instructions from Deng Yingchao and Cai Chang on the report also included Deng Xiaoping's directives. At that time, he told the ACWF that "following Chairman Mao's instruction at the meeting of provincial Party secretaries, the theme of the report should be the issue of women passing the test of socialism."[29] The term "passing the test of socialism" first appeared in one of Mao's talks in January 1957 when he said: "Some party members have passed all kinds of tests in the past, but it is difficult for them to pass the test of socialism."[30] Mao's attention at this point was on Party members and high officials who disagreed with his collectivization and nationalization policies. Although passing the test of socialism was originally not intended for people outside the Party, in July when the Anti-Rightist Campaign peaked, it did not sound far-fetched to include women. Everyone in China seemed to face the issue of passing the test of socialism. The ACWF followed Deng's instruction to prepare their report and other designated presentations. Consequently, Song Qingling's talk at the Assembly was entitled "Women should resolutely pass the test of socialism."[31] The theme, however, only worked in one way, that is, it followed the political tempo. It did not help address the specific dilemma of the ACWF. Therefore, in the leading body of the ACWF the debate over the central theme of the work report continued.

Deng's instruction in July showed that he was informed of the process of the preparation for the Third National Women's Assembly and was involved in decision-making. The liaison between Deng and the ACWF was either through Deng Yingchao or Cai Chang, or both. It was Deng Yingchao who informed Luo Qiong of Deng Xiaoping's invitation to the writing group to go to Beidaihe. And on the phone, Deng Yingchao asked Luo Qiong to take some materials on two diligences with her. Deng Yingchao had obviously informed Deng Xiaoping of the dilemma of the ACWF and it was this information that made Deng Xiaoping look for a different theme for the report. We don't know how Deng Xiaoping discussed the new theme with Deng Yingchao, but when he decided to get the writing group to Beidaihe he had already thought of the new theme and had told Deng

29. "Comrade Zhang Yun conveys instructions from Sister Cai and Sister Deng."
30. "Zai shengshi zhizhiqu dangwei shuji huiyi shang de jianghua" ("Talk on the conference of provincial Party Committee secretaries"), January 1957, in *Selected Works of Mao Zedong*, Vol. 5, p. 335.
31. See Song Qingling, "Funü yao jianjue guohao shehuizhuyi zhe yiguan" ("Women should resolutely pass the test of socialism"), in Chinese Women Cadres School, *An Anthology of Source Material on the Chinese Women's Movement*, Vol. 2, p. 308.

Yingchao what it was about. By switching the theme from passing the test of socialism to two diligences, Deng Xiaoping showed his astute understanding of what was at stake in drafting the report. And with this switch he simultaneously succeeded in saving the women's federation, appeasing masculinist power in the Party and showing his faithful following of the highest authority, Chairman Mao. At any rate, Deng Xiaoping should be credited with finding those two short quotations from Mao's many long talks and writings and applying them to practices with such creativity at this critical moment.

Interestingly, at the meeting of the Political Bureau, when Liu Shaoqi defended the ACWF he tried to use the same strategies. He also invoked Mao to legitimize the existence of the women's federation. According to him, Mao at the Supreme State Conference had said: "In the old society there were matchmakers for marriage. The new society has abolished the feudal system but young men and women have difficulty in getting married, that is, they cannot find a partner. Shouldn't we have a department for introducing [partners] and [providing] guidance?" After quoting Mao, Liu Shaoqi then emphasized that issues of marriage, women and children were most pervasive social issues that deserved research so as to create healthy social ethics and common practices: "Creating lively social practices and healthy ethics is beneficial to socialism. If Fulian could shoulder this task, it would play a good role." Searching for a "politically correct" role for the women's federation to play, Liu Shaoqi, just like Deng Xiaoping, expressed narrowly defined functions for the women's organization while appealing to Chairman Mao's authority. It is ironic, though not surprising, that these women-friendly Party leaders protected the women's federation by placing it within the parameters approved by masculinist power. Were they conscious of the conservative nature of their proposals? Probably not. The act of appealing to Mao's authority in those circumstances seems not so much to seek protection from possible criticism of their conservative stance on gender issues as to add weight to their ingenious proposals. The practice of quoting Mao for legitimacy, which would be pervasive in the whole country a decade later, seemed already to be a common practice among top Party officials in the late 1950s.

Highlighting the two male Party leaders' role in this historical moment, I would like to point out a pattern of the working strategy of the ACWF. The two male leaders did not jump to the rescue of the ACWF on their own initiative. Although I have not yet found evidence to establish a connection between the ACWF and Liu Shaoqi at this point, I have already shown that Deng Yingchao, who had known Deng Xiaoping since the early 1930s, played a crucial role in obtaining Deng Xiaoping's support. Informal relations are always important in the formal decision-making process. To Chinese state feminists – the ACWF officials who were used to long-term marginalization of women in the Party's power structure – informal relations were crucial channels of access to the male-dominated power centre. It would not be an exaggeration to claim that in the first decade of the PRC every important state policy promoting women's interest was a result of successful manoeuvres by these inside feminist agitators with the help of crucial informal relations fostered by the wives of top Party leaders. The two-diligences policy, seemingly a setback, should be regarded as representing one of those successful manoeuvres behind the scenes.

The Third National Women's Assembly and Beyond

Embracing the two diligences as its central principle, the ACWF thus survived 1957. It must have been a huge relief for the women's federation top officials that with this new principle the Third National Women's Assembly smoothly sailed through the rough sea of the Anti-Rightist Campaign. There is no record to show if they ever discussed among themselves the full implications of accepting this protective but confining new principle for women-work. The published materials demonstrate that the ACWF seriously devoted itself to the implementation of the two diligences nationwide after the Third National Women's Assembly. They even enthusiastically presented a proposal to the Central Committee to begin nationwide propaganda activities on diligently and thriftily managing the family, and the Central Committee approved their proposal, issuing directives to Party branches all over the country to include such propaganda activities in their agenda. Thus, instead of being eliminated, the ACWF emerged in the spotlight, gaining support from various Party and government branches, and creating a hype on diligently and thriftily managing the family before the Spring Festival of 1958.[32]

But this hype was soon swept aside by another even greater hype, the Great Leap Forward in 1958. Suddenly people in the whole country were mobilized to speed up socialist construction, and women were portrayed as an important labour force in social production rather than frugal managers of families. Moreover, it seemed that individual families might be abolished very soon, as collective dining halls were set up in rural communes. Socializing housework and liberating women's productivity were in vogue. The ACWF had quickly to host a national conference on women-work attended by provincial women's federation leaders to adjust its agenda and principles. Documents on this one-month-long conference reveal that local women's federation officials raised a lot of challenging questions to the work report of the Third National Women's Assembly. Was it problematic to adopt the two diligences as the principle for women-work? How come the report said women had already been liberated and had already achieved equality between men and women? Why was women's thorough liberation not mentioned? Why was socialization

---

32. Luo Qiong and Duan Yongqiang, *Interviews with Luo Qiong*, pp. 149–150.

of housework not mentioned? Didn't such lack of mention reflect a lack of vision? And so on. In a talk by Dong Bian, the co-author of the report, we can see that the ACWF officials were put in an awkward situation trying to justify the theme of the report written less than a year before. The talk also demonstrates how the ACWF officials swiftly responded to the changed setting. Dong Bian basically broke all the taboos set by the Secretariat a year before and returned to the pre-1957 rhetoric of the existence of inequality between men and women and feudal remnants: "Women's thorough liberation and genuine equality between men and women will have to follow the development of socialism and be achieved completely in a communist society." She admitted the expediency to local officials who might not understand the pressure the ACWF had experienced a year before at the time of the Third National Women's Assembly: "The whole country was just in the most intense period of struggling against bourgeois rightists. The circumstances required us to concentrate all our efforts to call on women in the whole country to go firmly on the socialist road."[33]

As to the two diligences, Dong Bian explained that the productivity of the time had required that women diligently and thriftily manage the family for the construction of socialism. Now that social productivity had developed, she claimed, it thus became appropriate to turn individual housework into collective enterprises so as to liberate women from housework to devote themselves to socialist production, although the spirit of diligently and thriftily running everything should be maintained. In the dominant craze of "running to communism," Dong Bian neither explained nor any official asked how social productivity could have developed so fast in less than a year. Thus, the Great Leap Forward enabled the ACWF to leap out of the role of a diligent housekeeper for women in the whole country and leap back to the role of a socialist producer. Ironically, when women's productivity was "liberated" (meaning, when massive mobilization of women into the labour force was accomplished), the necessity of a gender-based organization was once again questioned. In some locations women's federations at the county level were disbanded in the second half of 1958. The ACWF officials hastily manoeuvred to confront another crisis, a story to be told in a different article.[34]

Facing serious crises in 1957, ACWF officials managed to sustain the gender-based organization, an accomplishment achieved with compromises. Several points can be drawn from the short history of

33. Dong Bian, "Zai quanguo funü gongzuo huiyi shangde fayan" ("Talk on the national conference on women-work"), in Chinese Women Cadres School, *An Anthology of Source Material on the Chinese Women's Movement*, Vol. 2, p. 364.
34. In her recent article Kimberley Ens Manning gives an account of the disbanding of local women's federations in 1958. See "The gendered politics of woman-work: rethinking radicalism in the Great Leap Forward," *Modern China*, Vol. 32, No. 3 (2006), pp. 1–36.

the ACWF in 1957. First, the gender contentions over gender equality and women's liberation analysed here deconstruct the myth of a benevolent patriarchal socialist state. The Party has been a machine of masculinist power that values women only for their utility to the goal of the party-state. But within the Party there were women communists who held a position that differed from the Party's masculinist position. Pursuing gender equality was their goal, a goal they, at first, genuinely believed could be achieved in socialism, and which they thought justified the existence of the women's organization. The progressive policies and laws on gender issues passed in the first decade of the PRC were manifestations of the effective efforts of these communist women, inside feminist agitators.

Secondly, 1957 was the moment when the ACWF officials realized the huge cognitive gap between themselves and the male Party leaders, and dispelled the fantasy of focusing the organization on gender equality in the socialist state. It was not only that they had different understandings of gender equality; fundamentally, gender equality was no longer on the agenda of the Party, and the ACWF was only needed to fulfil the Party's tasks. In other words, in order for the ACWF to exist, the Party's central tasks had to be the top priority of the organization. If previously the relationship between the Party's central tasks and women-work had been ambiguous or subject to debate within the ACWF, the Secretariat in 1957 defined it point-blank. Closely following the Party's central tasks remained the theme of all the official reports and talks of the ACWF until 1983, when protecting the legal rights of women and children became the principle of women-work. The year 1957 in this sense did mark a setback of state feminists and a substantial victory of masculinist power in the Party.

Thirdly, if we compare the ACWF with the All-China Federation of Trade Unions (ACFTU) in 1957, the ACWF leaders' compromising stance is shown in relief. Pressed by workers' agitation to form independent organizations, as Jackie Sheehan observes, the ACFTU leaders "began to formulate a role for the unions in which they would concern themselves mainly or exclusively with the interests and demands of the workers."[35] While both the ACWF and ACFTU often found themselves sandwiched between "the masses" they were supposed to represent and the Party, historically the ACWF leaders never took chances to be openly confrontational with the Party. The ACWF was different from the ACFTU, which represented the working class, in that it only represented women, who had historically been secondary to "working class" and never even been in the rhetorical position of a "leading class" in the proletarian revolution. It was not just the awareness of their subordinate position in the larger scheme of revolution that made the ACWF leaders conciliatory. More importantly, it was also the Party's long history of suppressing

35. Sheehan, *Chinese Workers: A New History*, p. 79.

so-called "bourgeois feminism" that made the ACWF leaders fully aware of the implications of the male Party leaders' criticism in 1957. They were once again warned that pursuing women's interests could never stand alone or apart from serving a "larger" purpose if they were not to be accused of committing bourgeois feminist mistakes. By closely following the Party leaders' instructions, the subordinate and compromising ACWF was able to prove its loyalty to the Party in that eventful year, in contrast to the ACFTU which transgressed in each crucial historical moment. Such meaningful historical records certainly play a role in the fact that the ACWF receives much less state surveillance in its promoting of women's interests than the ACFTU does for workers in the post-Mao era.[36]

Fourthly, the crucial role of informal relations in this story poses theoretical and methodological questions to historians. How do we theorize such informal relations that cut across the gender line (and presumably class, race or any other divide in other cases)? In real life, men's support or backing might be found in most cases of women's social and political advancement for the simple reason that power holders were, and still are, predominantly men. Gaining male power holders' support by utilizing informal relations is certainly not a patent of women, but given that women as a social group lack formal channels to the power centre, informal relations were of paramount importance to them.[37] Conversely, the pro-women state policies issued in the PRC must have a lot to do with how informal relations have been utilized. Unfortunately, activities around such informal relations were rarely documented, and hence are forever lost to historians when the involved parties die. In other words, the material basis to theorize the role of informal relations in historical processes may not exist. What the historian can do is to call attention to the importance of such informal relations and associated manoeuvres by inside feminist agitators in China.

36. The similar contrasting pattern between the ACWF and the ACFTU re-emerged in the 1989 democracy movement. The ACFTU openly supported students' demonstration but the ACWF remained silent until after the crack-down when it was among the earliest to issue a statement condemning the democracy movement.

37. On informal relations among the Chinese elite and their influence on historical processes, see Jin Qiu, *The Culture of Power: The Lin Biao Incident in the Cultural Revolution* (Stanford: Stanford University Press, 1999).

Aspects of an Institutionalizing Political System: China, 1958–1965*

David Bachman

ABSTRACT This article uses newly available Chinese sources to take a different look at aspects of the Chinese political system and the Chinese state during 1958 to 1965. While not challenging the literature on elite power issues, it demonstrates that much more was going on within the Chinese state than has been widely appreciated. In particular, the article focuses on the formal legal process, where it appears that the use of courts was extensive throughout the pre-Cultural Revolution period and where the verdict of not guilty, not punished occurred more frequently in China than it did in American federal criminal cases; on the growing breakdown of the Party elite; and on China's preparation for war, basically an ongoing process of the Chinese state from 1962 on, with extensive militarization even earlier.

The prevailing narrative framework for understanding the political history of the People's Republic of China (PRC) from 1958 to 1965 is overwhelmingly focused on elite politics and developments giving rise to the Cultural Revolution. More specifically, studies of this period examine the radicalism that emerged out of the Anti-Rightist Campaign and culminated in the Great Leap Forward, with a special focus on Mao Zedong. The Leap depression and famine forced a return to more moderate, semi-institutionalized patterns of recovery, economic rehabilitation and new development. Liu Shaoqi (刘少奇), Deng Xiaoping (邓小平), Zhou Enlai (周恩来) and Chen Yun (陈云) are seen as playing critical roles during the early 1960s, with Mao stepping back to reflect on what had happened. He became increasingly dissatisfied with Liu and Deng's policies and their long-term implications, and he began to inject greater concerns with "class struggle" on to the political agenda. But these initiatives did not achieve Mao's goals, and his frustration and dissatisfaction with Liu, Deng and the central party-state grew. Ultimately, he found all of them unreformable and concluded they must be purged. Thus, by late 1965, Mao was "alone with the masses, waiting," about to launch the Cultural Revolution.[1]

The English-language scholarship on this period is not at the forefront of current academic research on contemporary China. MacFarquhar's trilogy (specifically volumes two and three),

* I wish to thank Ketty Loeb for research assistance, and Susan Whiting and the participants in the *China Quarterly* workshop on the history of the PRC 1949–1976, especially Julia Strauss, for comments on an earlier draft.

1. André Malraux, *Antimemoirs* (trans. Terence Kilmartin) (New York: Holt, Rinehart and Winston, 1968), p. 375.

supplemented by Teiwes and Sun, generally represent the state of the art for English-language work on this period or parts of it.[2] A number of scholars made contributions prior to the completion of MacFarquhar's work, but with the exception of Teiwes and Sun, none has published an overview political history of even part of this period since MacFarquhar's third volume appeared in 1997.[3] Additional light has been shed on the politics and effects of the Great Leap famine, on central–provincial relations during the Leap, on family law and society, and on politics at the village level during the Leap and after, but academic research has generally moved in other directions.[4]

This general lack of attention to the 1958 to 1965 period by scholars working in English is particularly unfortunate because a vast number of new Chinese books and articles have appeared which shed significant new light on it. Authorized biographies of top leaders, chronologies of their lives, memoirs by some leading figures and the sporadic release of new primary materials all promise major pay-offs for those who explore these sources. The burgeoning Chinese academic community and specialized journals on Party or PRC history regularly provide new insights into the 1958 to 1965 period. Provincial and lower-level gazetteers, published in great profusion, provide a greater sense of regional variation, if nothing else (and they usually do provide much more than this).[5]

2. Roderick MacFarquhar, *The Origins of the Cultural Revolution, Vol. 1: Contradictions among the People, 1956–1957; Vol 2: The Great Leap Forward, 1958–1960;* and *Vol. 3: The Coming of the Cataclysm, 1961–1965* (New York: Columbia University Press, 1974, 1983 and 1997, respectively); Frederick C. Teiwes, *Politics and Purges in China* (Armonk: M. E. Sharpe, 1979; 2nd ed., 1993); and Frederick C. Teiwes with Warren Sun, *China's Road to Disaster* (Armonk: M.E. Sharpe, 1999).

3. Earlier, important works covering the 1958 to 1965 period included: Peter R. Moody, Jr., *The Politics of the Eighth Central Committee of the Communist Party of China* (Hamden: Shoestring Press, 1973); Parris H. Chang, *Power and Policy in China* (University Park: Pennsylvania State University Press, 1974); Byung-joon Ahn, *Chinese Politics and the Cultural Revolution* (Seattle: University of Washington Press, 1976); and Kenneth Lieberthal, "The Great Leap Forward and the split in the Yenan leadership," in Roderick MacFarquhar and John K. Fairbank (eds.), *The Cambridge History of China, Vol. 14: The People's Republic, Part I: The Emergence of Revolutionary China, 1949–1965* (Cambridge: Cambridge University Press, 1987), pp. 293–359.

4. On the famine, see Dali L. Yang, *Calamity and Reform in China* (Stanford: Stanford University Press, 1996) and Jasper Becker, *Hungry Ghosts* (London: J. Murray, 1996). On other aspects of the history of this period, see Alfred L. Chan, *Mao's Crusade* (Oxford: Oxford University Press, 2001); Neil Diamant, *Revolutionizing the Family* (Berkeley: University of California Press, 2000); Edward Friedman, Paul G. Pickowicz and Mark Selden with Kay Ann Johnson, *Chinese Village, Socialist State* (New Haven: Yale University Press, 1991); and Friedman, Pickowicz and Selden, *Revolution, Resistance, and Reform in Village China* (New Haven: Yale University Press, 2005).

5. Some particularly important examples of these new materials include: Pang Xianzhi and Jin Chongji (chief eds.), *Mao Zedong zhuan (1949–1976)* (*Biography of Mao Zedong*), 2 vols. (Beijing: Zhongyang wenxian chubanshe, 2003); *Zhou Enlai nianpu, 1949–1976* (*Chronology of Zhou Enlai, 1949–1976*), 3 vols. (Beijing: Zhongyang wenxian chubanshe, 1997); Bo Yibo, *Ruogan zhongda juece yu shijiande huigu*

This article draws on a limited subset of these new Chinese materials. Instead of focusing on elite interactions, it looks at aspects of political institutionalization of the revolutionary Chinese state. This is done by examining three areas: the use of law and the courts during this period (with comparisons to the 1950–57 period); the ongoing and accelerating transformation of the Chinese political elite from late 1957 to late 1965; and more interpretatively, it begins to outline the story (and an emerging political agenda) of China's preparation for war in a very insecure international environment. These areas hardly exhaust the varieties and dimensions of institutionalization in China, nor do they show uniform trends. What each section suggests is that there were many aspects of human activity organized by the Chinese state during the 1958–65 period that were not connected all that directly to elite power considerations. Some could be recovered after 1976, others rejected, but all served to shape the nature of the state.

The Cultural Revolution (CR) profoundly colours how scholars think about the 1958 to 1965 period. Given its titanic and traumatic nature, the question of why a cultural revolution is so compelling that the search for antecedents, causes and key choices in the period leading up to it has appropriately dominated scholarly inquiry. While that agenda should continue, particularly in light of new materials and research opportunities, new avenues of research can and should be opened up if scholars try to imagine that there was no CR. What trends, patterns and agendas were developing in Chinese politics and society that did not connect directly to it? If Mao had died on 31 December 1965, how might China's history been different? Just because Mao called for putting politics in command, did it mean that society and the rest of the political system took him at his word? How did people try to live ordinary lives, build futures for their families and work the political system from 1958 to 1965 without any expectation that there would be a cultural revolution? What cultural practices and repertoires emerged in China prior to the CR, and which were not the product of the state, or wholly internalized as the state intended? How did developments in the 1958–65 period contradict or reinforce patterns emerging in the early years of Chinese Communist Party (CCP) rule? Of course we cannot answer these questions unequivocally or definitively, but studies of this period would be greatly enhanced if we tried to, and this article makes a small attempt to

---

footnote continued

(*Recollections of Some Major Policies and Events*), 2 vols. (Beijing: Zhonggong zhongyang dangxiao chubanshe, 1991, 1993); *Jianguo yilai Mao Zedong wengao* (*Manuscripts of Mao Zedong since the Founding of the Country*), 13 vols. (Beijing: Zhongyang wenxian chubanshe, 1987–98); Chen Donglin, *San xian jianshe* (*Third Front Construction*) (Beijing: Zhonggong zhongyang dangxiao chubanshe, 2003). The most useful Party and PRC history journals include *Dangdai Zhongguo shi yanjiu* (*Research on the History of Contemporary China*), *Dangde wenxian* (*Party Documents*) and *Zhonggong dangshi ziliao* (*Materials on CCP History*).

suggest some of the doors that might be opened if we tried to ask new questions, tried to pursue new points of departure, or at least move away from the foregrounding effect of the Cultural Revolution.

Use of Legal Institutions

Until recently, there was very limited discussion of the use of legal institutions and practices in the entire Mao period. With no real access to Chinese society, the small number of legal scholars working on China analysed formally promulgated laws and regulations, evaluated legal processes discussed in the Chinese press (almost always for didactic purposes) and gleaned insights from refugees. The result was a series of studies that emphasized how little formal judicial processes mattered in China. Law was done "without lawyers," mediation was preferred to formal court proceedings and administrative punishments were more important than formal criminal procedures.[6] With the reform period, China became more open, promulgated many more laws and appeared to desire to build the rule of law. Thus, scholars of the Chinese legal system concentrated almost all their attention on the post-Mao legal system. Only Diamant's work has begun to challenge this research focus.[7]

In 2000, the court system published statistics on court proceedings covering the period from 1950 to 1998. These statistics did not define terms, provided no clarification of categories and used different categories in different years. No geographic breakdown of the data was provided. In many ways, the two volumes on court statistics were example of how not to compile statistical material.[8] Nevertheless, they are the only known sources of court statistics stretching back to the founding of the PRC currently available. As shown below, they open up new questions about the role of law and politics and law and society for the pre-CR period.

First, it is clear that no matter how flawed the administration of justice was in Chinese courts, judicial proceedings were frequent in the pre-1966 period, as Table 1 shows.[9] About 24.5 million court cases were opened between 1950 and the end of 1965, with civil cases (the "civil law" volume appears to include all non-criminal cases, such as those involving administrative law, not usually thought of as civil law)

6. For example, Victor H. Li, *Law Without Lawyers* (Boulder: Westview Press, 1978); Stanley B. Lubman, "Mao and mediation," *California Law Review*, Vol. 55, No. 5 (1967), pp. 1284–1359; and Jerome Alan Cohen, *The Criminal Process in the People's Republic of China, 1949–1963* (Cambridge, MA: Harvard University Press, 1968).

7. Diamant, *Revolutionizing the Family*.

8. *Quanguo renmin fayuan sifa tongji lishi ziliao huibian, 1949–1998: minshi bu fen; xing shi bufen* (*Compendia of Historical Material on the Administration of Justice by the People's Courts of the Whole Nation: Civil and Criminal Volumes*) (Beijing: Renmin fayuan chubanshe, 2000). Hereafter these sources will be cited as Criminal Stats and Civil Stats for the appropriate volume.

9. Civil Stats, p. 1, Criminal Stats, p. 1.

Table 1: **Cases Opened in Chinese Courts, 1950–1965**

Year	Total	Criminal	Civil
1950	1,154,081	475,849	678,232
1951	1,866,279	959,398	906,881
1952	2,202,403	723,725	1,478,678
1953	2,202,815	344,909	1,857,906
1954	2,186,826	896,666	1,290,160
1955	2,098,655	1,077,716	1,020,939
1956	1,523,344	722,557	800,787
1957	1,796,391	868,886	927,505
1958	2,372,808	1,899,691	473,117
1959	960,838	560,157	400,681
1960	864,686	543,868	320,818
1961	1,074,249	437,750	636,499
1962	1,187,850	317,769	870,081
1963	1,238,816	415,648	823,168
1964	929,030	262,199	666,831
1965	818,520	237,660	580,860
Cumulative total, 1950–65	24,477,591	10,744,448	13,733,143

constituting more than 55 per cent of all cases opened. Some 61 per cent of all cases during the entire period were opened between 1950 and 1957 (56 per cent of all criminal cases and 65 per cent of all civil cases). Despite the decline in the absolute number of cases opened in 1958–65 compared to 1950–57, almost 9.5 million cases were started, with the cases evenly divided between civil (51 per cent) and criminal (49 per cent), compared to 40 per cent criminal and 60 per cent civil in the first seven years of court statistics.

There was great variability in the frequency of cases, as detailed in Table 2.[10] With the exceptions of 1951, 1955 and 1958–60, civil cases were always more common than criminal cases. 1958 was an extraordinary year for criminal courts, with 17.5 per cent of all criminal cases for the entire 1950–65 period opened then. Indeed, more criminal cases were opened in 1958 than in any other year prior to 1999. Yet after the high tide during the Great Leap, the number of criminal cases diminished fairly consistently between 1961 and the end of 1965. Whether labour re-education or other administrative punishments were more frequently employed during this period remains unknown. In contrast, there is significant fluctuation in civil cases, but in all years in the 1960s, more than half a million civil cases were opened.

Of civil cases, marriage disputes and divorce cases were by far the most prominent (see Table 3).[11] The civil law volume does not provide

10. Calculated on Civil Stats, p. 1 and Criminal Stats, p. 1.
11. Based on Civil Stats, pp. 4–33.

Table 2: **Percentage of Civil and Criminal Cases**

Year	Civil cases as % of all cases	Criminal cases as % of all cases
1950	58.77	41.23
1951	48.59	51.41
1952	67.14	32.86
1953	84.34	15.66
1954	59.00	41.00
1955	48.65	51.35
1956	52.57	47.43
1957	51.63	48.37
1958	19.94	80.06
1959	41.70	58.30
1960	37.10	62.90
1961	59.25	40.75
1962	73.25	26.75
1963	66.45	33.55
1964	71.78	28.22
1965	70.96	29.04

Year	% of all cases 1950–65, by year	% all criminal cases by year	% all civil cases, by year
1950	4.71	4.43	4.94
1951	7.62	8.93	6.60
1952	9.00	6.74	10.77
1953	9.00	3.21	13.53
1954	8.93	8.35	9.39
1955	8.57	10.03	7.43
1956	6.22	6.72	5.83
1957	7.34	8.09	6.75
1958	9.69	17.68	3.45
1959	3.93	5.21	2.92
1960	3.53	5.06	2.34
1961	4.39	4.07	4.63
1962	4.85	2.96	6.34
1963	5.06	3.87	5.99
1964	3.80	2.44	4.86
1965	3.34	2.21	4.23

information on court findings, such as how many divorces were granted. But it does reveal that, again with the exception of the Great Leap years, nearly a million Chinese per year were in court trying to solve marriage disputes one way or another. After 1958, marriage disputes were never less than 70 per cent of all civil court cases, and almost all were cases of divorce (or attempts to divorce by at least one party). Marriages can only end in divorce in a legal finding issued by a

Table 3: **Civil Cases**

Year	Civil	of which marriage disputes	% of all civil cases	of which divorce	% of all civil cases
1950	678,232	281,049	41.44	197,060	29.05
1951	906,881	487,574	53.76	409,500	45.15
1952	1,478,678	941,618	63.68	837,900	56.67
1953	1,857,906	1,109,191	59.70	940,369	50.61
1954	1,290,160	678,691	52.61	597,933	46.35
1955	1,020,939	579,366	56.75	–	–
1956	800,787	514,669	64.27	–	–
1957	927,505	522,671	56.35	–	–
1958	473,117	298,009	62.99	–	–
1959	400,681	309,675	77.29	–	–
1960	320,818	268,860	83.80	263,707	82.20
1961	636,499	549,251	86.29	535,710	84.17
1962	870,081	654,751	75.25	624,426	71.77
1963	823,168	581,262	70.61	543,323	66.00
1964	666,831	474,647	71.18	448,106	67.20
1965	580,860	417,907	71.95	395,665	68.12

court of law. And we do not know what percentage of unhappy marriages is shown by the 400,000 divorce cases in 1965. Yet, these data support Diamant's conclusions about the significance of divorce prior to the Cultural Revolution.[12] They further suggest that the surge in divorce in the reform period was not a new phenomenon. Rather, there were enough pre-CR marriage dispute and court cases to hypothesize that divorce and going to court were fairly well-established social practices. The CR may have fundamentally attacked courts and divorce, but once the CR era ended and courts were restored, divorce proceedings quickly returned as (remembered) social practice.

The material on criminal law also casts domestic developments in new light. For example, we can provide some information on the number of counter-revolutionary trials held, types of crimes, class background of the accused for a number of years and sentencing practices (see Table 4).[13] Cases involving counter-revolutionary activities were particularly prominent in the years 1951, 1953, 1955 and especially 1958. Indeed, nearly one-third of all cases involving counter-revolutionary crimes were opened in 1958. This is a particularly surprising finding because it is generally assumed that most "rightists" capped in the Anti-Rightist Campaign were punished according to administrative acts (labour re-education) rather than the formal criminal process. However, the Ministry of Public Security

12. Diamant, *Revolutionizing the Family*.
13. Based on Criminal Stats, pp. 1, 6, 10, 19, 26, 33, 39, 44, 52, 60, 65, 68–69, 73, 80, 84, 92 and 100.

Table 4: **Criminal Cases and Counter-Revolutionary Activities**

Year	Criminal cases	of which counter-revolutionary activities	% of criminal cases
1950	475,849	58,470	12.29
1951	959,398	435,812	45.43
1952	723,725	16,705	2.31
1953	344,909	114,034	33.06
1954	896,666	69,720	7.78
1955	1,077,716	273,074	25.34
1956	722,557	138,347	19.15
1957	868,886	180,555	20.78
1958	1,899,691	822,853	43.32
1959	560,157	105,831	18.89
1960	543,868	104,632	19.24
1961	437,750	96,314	22.00
1962	317,769	18,448	5.81
1963	415,648	52,027	12.52
1964	262,199	34,420	13.13
1965	237,660	27,229	11.46
Total	10,777,748	2,548,471	23.65

appears to have taken campaigns aimed at political deviance as a reason to intensify general "law and order" work across the board, arresting those on the borderline between acceptable and unacceptable behaviour who in other years might have been left alone. Given the premium on suppressing political deviance during campaigns, there were incentives within the political-legal system to blur distinctions between "ordinary" crime and political deviance, and to over-report (arrest and try) cases of counter-revolutionary crime.[14]

Also of interest, throughout the early 1960s counter-revolutionary activities were not a particularly high proportion of all criminal cases, suggesting that political crimes as reflected in court statistics were not very salient, in turn suggesting more limited political polarization than is usually portrayed: seemingly, public security personnel did not give uncovering counter-revolutionary activity an especially high priority.[15] Political struggle was immanent with Mao's call never to forget class struggle, but discerning what constituted revisionism in practice, and crimes stemming from it, was not clear, and apparently not acted upon by the police and the courts all that much.

There was substantial variability in the types and numbers of counter-revolutionary crimes throughout the pre-CR period. These

14. My thanks to Michael Schoenhals and especially Julia Strauss for heightening my appreciation of this point.
15. For some support for this position, see Michael Dutton, *Policing Chinese Politics* (Durham: Duke University Press, 2005), pp. 205–217.

Table 5: **Types of Criminal Cases**

Year	Criminal	Of which property related crimes	Of which crimes against people	Of which murder	% murder violent crime	Rape	% rape violent crime
1950	475,849	51,553	109,228	11,260	10.31	4,358	3.99
1951	959,398	70,539	92,427	16,887	18.27	19,060	20.62
1952	723,725	64,872	159,384	13,193	8.28	41,118	25.80
1953	344,909	70,900	211,101	17,606	8.34	44,349	21.01
1954	896,666	5,350	25,718	–	–	16,559	64.39
1955	1,077,716	34,763	24,034	–	–	17,815	74.12
1956	722,557	75,834	126,948	8,066	6.35	21,094	16.62
1957	868,886	133,467	166,760	8,315	4.99	24,938	14.95
1958	1,899,691	360,547	114,833	17,621	15.34	48,641	42.36
1959	560,157	108,891	46,288	7,931	17.13	16,499	35.64
1960	543,868	161,687	29,170	10,727	36.77	11,050	37.88
1961	437,750	153,045	30,878	9,096	29.46	6,472	20.96
1962	317,769	26,412	40,518	5,457	13.47	6,974	17.21
1963	415,648	105,584	192,702	5,393	2.80	13,822	7.17
1964	262,199	39,531	65,067	4,960	7.62	11,988	18.42
1965	237,660	33,929	61,473	4,599	7.48	12,639	20.56

fluctuations are themselves indications of the political nature of "counter-revolutionary" crimes. Without changing political contexts, or cadres "encouraged" to arrest people for counter-revolutionary activities some years and not others, how else can these fluctuations be explained?

As with many aspects of the court statistics, it is not clear whether the cases involving counter-revolutionary crimes are counted in other statistics. The criminal volume does provide information on numbers of cases of crimes against property (economic crimes), and crimes against people (violent crime). As is obvious from Table 5, economic crimes and crimes against people do not equal the total number of criminal cases opened in a particular year.[16] Particularly large numbers of murder and rape cases took place during the Leap high tide. After the bottoming out of the famine, the murder rate dropped, with the fewest murder cases tried over the 1962–65 period on a yearly basis. There does not appear to be any clear pattern in the relationship between property related crimes, like theft, and violent crime. Property crimes are significantly more common during the Leap famine period, but why violent crime cases dropped so sharply in the same period is unclear.

16. Calculated from Criminal Stats, pp. 6–107.

Table 6: **Class Background of Accused**

Year	Good	Bad	Other	Total	% good	% bad	% other
1950	119,406	10,629	39,812	169,847	70.30	6.23	23.41
1951	–	–	–	–	–	–	–
1952	–	–	–	–	–	–	–
1953	–	–	–	–	–	–	–
1954	–	–	–	–	–	–	–
1955	–	–	–	–	–	–	–
1956	197,184	78,913	173,281	449,378	43.88	17.56	38.56
1957	303,235	134,794	89,332	527,361	57.50	25.56	16.94
1958	894,570	388,793	439,557	1,722,920	51.92	22.57	25.51
1959	182,775	261,113	58,511	502,399	36.38	51.97	11.65
1960	188,163	212,364	77,947	478,474	39.33	44.38	16.29
1961	87,155	221,255	11,212	319,622	27.27	69.22	3.51
1962	72,605	91,491	117,942	282,038	25.74	32.44	41.82
1963	182,339	81,729	27,884	291,952	62.46	27.99	9.55
1964	76,192	24,438	14,740	115,370	66.04	21.18	12.78
1965	68,608	101,937	13,362	183,907	37.31	55.43	7.27

The courts statistics provide information on the class and social background of defendants for some years (Table 6).[17] Here there is a connection between periods of political mobilization and people from bad "status" (*chengfen* 成分) as defendants. In 1959–61 and 1965, people with bad class status were the largest category of defendants, even though they formed a smaller percentage of the population than those with good class status. Nevertheless, there is considerable fluctuation in class background which makes discerning trends for the 1956–65 period (when the data are most complete) difficult, if not impossible.[18]

17. Calculated from Criminal Stats, pp. 6–107. Categories changed over time. I have aggregated various categories as follows. For 1950, I treated poor and middle peasants, military personnel, workers and urban poor as "good"; landlord, bureaucratic capitalist, puppet troops as "bad"; and rich peasant, petit bourgeoisies, minorities and others as "other." For 1956–58, worker, staff, collective peasants and poor were "good"; landlords, rich peasants, capitalists and floating individuals (vagabonds, *liumin*) "bad"; and individual peasants, collective handicraft workers, individual handicraft workers and others as "other." For 1959–65, office workers and state bureaucrats, students, peasants, workers, workers who became degenerate elements, and cadres as "good"; landlords and rich peasants, counter-revolutionary elements, bad elements, rightists, capitalists, escapees from labour reform who commit additional crimes, opponents of the revolution, hooligans, capitalists and former puppet soldiers as "bad"; and vagabonds, small business owners, idle individuals, and others as "other."

18. Richard Curt Kraus, *Class Conflict in Chinese Socialism* (New York: Columbia University Press, 1981) provides a thorough discussion of class categories and statuses. But he does not provide percentages of the population in each category. The 1964 Chinese census did ask about class status. Kenneth Lieberthal, *Governing China, 2nd Edition* (New York: W.W. Norton, 2004), p. 304, states that there might have been about 50 million people who suffered from forms of class category discrimination. But no definitive figures exist publicly, and as a result of the Cultural Revolution decade, large numbers of people who had previously not been in negative class/status categories were labelled as enemies of the regime (to varying degrees).

Table 7: **Verdicts**

Year	Number of defendants	Five years to death sentence	% of all verdicts	Less than five years	% of all verdicts	Other punishment	% of all verdicts
1950	169,847	15,465	9.11	122,749	72.27	31,633	18.62
1951	134,011	21,365	15.94	57,187	42.67	51,466	38.40
1952	661,789	129,554	19.58	280,664	42.41	93,360	14.11
1953	675,476	96,285	14.25	263,329	38.98	102,884	15.23
1954	805,279	91,106	11.31	385,141	47.83	114,225	14.18
1955	965,828	319,941	33.13	375,320	38.86	101,932	10.55
1956	473,042	132,799	28.07	175,812	37.17	44,949	9.50
1957	552,782	77,350	13.99	213,950	38.70	215,889	39.05
1958	1,682,446	482,241	28.66	571,884	33.99	602,954	35.84
1959	532,772	151,688	28.47	128,057	24.04	230,561	43.28
1960	500,727	183,805	36.71	105,335	21.04	202,204	40.38
1961	460,052	136,669	29.71	110,428	24.00	152,662	33.18
1962	291,190	66,321	22.78	88,484	30.39	83,079	28.53
1963	335,477	77,897	23.22	96,032	28.63	110,759	33.02
1964	131,217	28,431	21.67	27,331	20.83	59,435	45.30
1965	118,279	34,028	28.77	24,572	20.77	32,488	27.47

Year	Not guilty or not punished	% of all verdicts
1950	–	–
1951	3,993	2.98
1952	158,211	23.91
1953	212,978	31.53
1954	214,807	26.67
1955	168,635	17.46
1956	119,482	25.26
1957	45,593	8.25
1958	25,367	1.51
1959	22,466	4.22
1960	9,383	1.87
1961	60,293	13.11
1962	53,306	18.31
1963	50,789	15.14
1964	16,020	12.21
1965	27,191	22.99

Finally, the criminal court statistics provide material on verdicts (Table 7).[19] Several points are of interest here. First, in every year, it appears that "other" is the most common form of punishment. This includes probation, fines and unspecified "other" verdicts. Secondly, over time, the most severe sentencing category became more common,

19. Calculated from Criminal Stats, pp. 2–3.

and after 1957 was never less than 20 per cent of the verdicts in all cases, averaging over 25 per cent for the 1958–65 period. Concomitantly, lesser prison sentences declined. Finally, and most intriguingly, a surprisingly large number of defendants were either found not guilty or were not punished. There was considerable variability over time on this dimension, with the 1957–60 period having particularly low rates of not guilty/not punished verdicts, but overall, it seems that at least 14 per cent of all defendants received no sanctions. In criminal cases tried between 1950 and 1965 in US federal courts (a small proportion of all criminal cases tried in the US), 12 per cent of all defendants were not convicted.[20] This high rate of not guilty/not punished verdicts in China during the 1950–65 period does not conform to many images of the criminal justice system in China.

These statistics on court actions allow us to begin to construct new ideas and patterns about law, politics and society in the pre-CR era. They must be taken with more than a grain of salt, stripped of context and detail. Even with these caveats in mind, however, it appears that law and legal procedures in the 1958 to 1965 period were more important than previously thought: they engaged lots of people, there were lots of trials (however brief), and the legal system might have been less affected by political campaigns than hitherto suspected. Moreover, continued resort to legal procedures to handle marriage disputes and criminal behaviour is particularly remarkable in light of the attack on law and lawyers that took place in the Anti-Rightist Campaign. The number of cases certainly declined in the 1958–65 period compared to the 1950–57 period, and large numbers of political or criminal infractions were handled administratively by the Ministry of Public Security. Nevertheless, law, or at least formal legal institutions and practices, seem to have been an integral part of CCP rulership prior to the CR. In this sense, these findings would seem to support much recent historical scholarship that suggests that 1949 should not be seen as a sharp divide. These data, and the limited interpretations of them put forward here, suggest that the pre-Cultural Revolution period can be seen as a continuation of some of the trends highlighted in the scholarship on law and society in pre-PRC China. It is the Cultural Revolution that marks the sharp break, and a briefer interruption of pre-1949 trends, at least in this field, than is commonly portrayed.

20. Michael J. Hindelang, Michael R. Gottfredson, and Timothy Flanigan (eds.), *Sourcebook of Criminal Justice Staistics 1980* (Washington: US Department of Justice, Bureau of Justice Statistics, 1981), p. 429. On p. 389, this source notes that "although the Uniform Crime Reports and the National Prisoner Statistics program provide nationwide data on specific law enforcement and correctional activities, no comparable uniform nationwide data exist for the collection and dissemination of state and local judicial processing statistics." In 1975, there were 1.8 million criminal cases disposed of in the US. Less than 50,000 of them were federal criminal trials. The vast majority of criminal cases thus are state and local matters, but there is no standard reference for accessing data for state and local trials.

Elite Transformation

This section looks at emerging patterns of leadership change in China, largely comparing the Seventh Central Committee (CC) with the Eighth, at least until the end of 1965. In contrast to the argument suggested above – that in the realm of law and society the use of the law appears to reflect earlier trends emergent in Chinese society – in terms of elite transformation, there appears to be a sharper break in patterns of change within the established elite (as defined by membership in the CCP Central Committee and top Party, state and military positions). While many have looked at the social background characteristics of various CCP central committees, and on occasion compared one committee with the preceding one, less has been done comparing the Seventh with the Eighth Central Committee than with other cases. This partly reflects the (until recently) lack of authoritative information about individuals, and the relatively small number of scholars doing contemporary China studies during the period of the Eighth Central Committee's existence (1956–69). My argument here is that there was remarkable stability within the Seventh Central Committee (1945–56). But both demographic and political developments occurred during the Eighth CC prior to the CR. The effect of these developments is that even without a CR there would have been a significant changing of the political elite whenever the CCP got around to holding the Ninth Party Congress and selecting the Ninth Central Committee (which should have taken place in 1961). This analysis relies heavily on *Zhongguo gongchan dang lijie zhongyang weiyuan dacidian, 1921–2003*,[21] as well as individual biographies and earlier biographical reference sources.

The Seventh CC had 44 full and 33 alternate members. Of these 77 top CCP leaders, five would die before 1956 (one died even before the Seventh CC was selected, unknown to Party headquarters). Five others would be removed from the Central Committee (purged). Several also suffered persistent ill health and were inactive for a significant fraction of the term of the Seventh CC. Thus, the Seventh CC had a mortality rate of 6.5 per cent, the same percentage as the removal/purge rate. In short, biological and political mortality affected 13 per cent of the Seventh CC over its 11-year span – or 1 per cent change per year. Those with instances of poor health (Xu Xiangqian 徐向前, Lin Biao 林彪 and Zheng Weisan 郑位三) were all selected to the Eighth CC (Zheng was in persistent ill health from 1948 on, and never held a leadership position from 1949 to 1969). Moreover, only one member of the Seventh CC died after 1949 (three died together in a plane crash in 1946). Of the five removed from the CC and/or purged, one committed suicide and one remained imprisoned until his death, but the other three all were ultimately

21. *Biographical Dictionary of All Members of the CCP Central Committee, 1921–2003* (Beijing: Zhonggong dangshi chubanshe, 2004). Hereafter CC Bio Dictionary.

either fully or partially rehabilitated prior to the CR. Li Yu (黎玉) and Liu Zijiu (刘子久) were removed as CC alternates in 1950, but their careers resumed an upward trajectory after a brief hiatus. Zeng Jingbin (曾镜冰), associated with Gao Gang (高岗) and Rao Shushi (饶漱石), was out of prison by 1956, and held a largely honorific and powerless position prior to the CR.[22] None of the three was returned to the CC. Thus, there was little turnover in the Seventh CC during the course of its tenure. With the exception of Gao and Rao, removals/purges were not terribly punitive, and norms about re-education and rehabilitation may not have been fundamentally undermined by the Gao–Rao case. There was no need for the CCP leadership to think all that seriously about rejuvenating the Party leadership or preparing the next generation of CCP leaders in 1956, when it came time to select the Eighth CC.

The Eighth CC of 97 full and 73 alternate members chosen in 1956 was supplemented by an additional 25 alternates in 1958. A total of 195 individuals served on the CC at some point from 1956 to 1965. The mortality rate of CC members did not increase significantly from the Seventh CC. Fifteen of the 195 members died prior to 1966, or 7.7 per cent. However, demotions and purges (but not removal from the CC) may have affected as many as 29 members.[23] An additional 13 were ill or inactive at the end of 1965. Thus up to 57 members of the CC had died, were in poor health and elderly, or had seen their status in the leadership downgraded; that is, nearly 30 per cent of the Central Committee were affected by political or physical problems by 1966. However, none of those removed or purged from office by 1966 was stripped of CC membership (unlike those purged/removed in the Seventh CC), and all were given some sort of work after their removal. In some cases the job was fairly trivial; in other cases, more significant work was assigned, though the purgees' level of activity and influence appears generally to be limited. But even Peng Dehuai (彭德怀) and Huang Kecheng (黄克诚) had responsible positions by

22. Information on CC members in this paragraph from *ibid*.
23. Those purged or demoted are: Deng Hua, Deng Zihui, Feng Baiju, Gu Dacun, Hong Xuezhi, Huang Kecheng, Jia Tuofu, Li Fuchun, Li Lisan, Luo Ruiqing, Pan Fusheng, Peng Dehuai, Shu Tong, Su Yu, Tan Qilong, Wan Yi, Wang Heshou, Wang Jiaxiang, Wang Shusheng, Wu Zhipu, Xi Zhongxun, Xiao Ke, Yang Shangkun, Yang Xianzhen, Zeng Xisheng, Zhang Wentian, Zhang Zhongliang, Zhao Jianmin and Zhou Xiaozhou. Of these, six cases are potentially ambiguous. Li Lisan was generally inactive after 1957, though still holding relatively important positions; Li Fuchun had much of his power and authority as head of the State Planning Commission stripped from him with the establishment of the "Small Planning Committee" under Yu Qiuli in 1965; Wang Heshou was moved from being Minister of Metallurgy to being Party secretary of Anshan, Liaoning, and the Party secretary for the Anshan Iron and Steel Works; Wang Jiaxiang was criticized for advocating moderation in Chinese foreign policy, became ill and was inactive, but was never formally removed from his positions prior to 1966; Wang Shusheng was transferred from heading the People's Liberation Army's Armaments Department to becoming a vice-chairman of the Academy of Military Science in 1959, and Yang Xianzhen was severely criticized in 1964 for philosophical "mistakes" but was never formally removed from his positions prior to the CR.

1965. Zhang Wentian (张闻天) and Zhou Xiaozhou (周小舟) were given jobs within a year of their purges in 1959. While Peng's purge may have violated Party norms, other norms, such as curing the illness to save the patient, seem to have held tenuously. Nevertheless, the persistence of any of these ill, inactive, demoted or purged members of the CC on the subsequent CC is problematic. Even if there were no Cultural Revolution, there would have been considerable turnover within the CCP elite.

The upper levels of the People's Liberation Army (PLA) were particularly affected by power and health issues. Of the ten PLA marshals, one died, one was clearly purged, two saw their influence reduced and two were ill for extended periods.[24] Of the ten full, or four-star, generals in 1955, one died, four were removed or purged, and one saw his status downgraded.[25] Yet of the 57 three-star generals in 1955, five died before 1966, and four had their status downgraded or were purged. All military figures who were purged, removed or downgraded were part of the central military apparatus, and all military leaders on the Party Secretariat were purged over the 1958 to 1966 period. Again, with so much attrition in the top tiers of the PLA, there was likely to be extensive jockeying for a position of power and influence among the 48 remaining three-star generals and the two-star ones. Personnel politics in the PLA was going to be intense.

The State Council premiers and vice-premiers saw the second highest rate of political and physical effects. Of the 20 officials who served as premier and vice-premier in the First and Second National People's Congresses periods (1954–59, 1959–65), one died (Ke Qingshi 柯庆施), three were purged (Peng Dehuai, Xi Zhongxun 习仲勋, Luo Ruiqing 罗瑞卿) two were demoted or removed (Deng Zihui 邓子恢 and Li Fuchun 李福春), and two were often in ill health (Chen Yun and Lin Biao). Also, the top economic officials had all been severely criticized at the outset of the Great Leap (Zhou Enlai, Chen Yun, Li Fuchun, Li Xiannian 李先念, and Bo Yibo 薄一波), though only Bo would be purged in the CR.

In contrast to the role of the law in the PRC, where it appeared that pre-1949 trends of a significant role for formal legal institutions were continued during the years leading up to the CR, major discontinuities were emerging in terms of the CCP leadership system. Mortality rates among the elite were slightly increasing, and by the early 1960s, as the oldest CCP leadership cadres were approaching their 70s, the issue of generational succession was tacitly if not explicitly on the agenda. In many areas this could have been an orderly process had the CR not intervened. Younger, able administrators had risen to prominence and could have been co-opted to the

24. Respectively, Luo Ronghuan, Peng Dehuai, Liu Bocheng, Zhu De, Xu Xiangqian and Lin Biao.
25. Again, respectively, Chen Geng, Su Yu, Huang Kechang, Tan Zheng, Luo Ruiqing and Wang Shusheng.

CC (such as Zhao Ziyang 赵紫阳). But politics was already shaking the structure of the high command, with Liu Bocheng (刘伯承), Su Yu (粟裕), Wang Shusheng (王树声) and Xiao Ke (肖克) attacked in 1958, and Peng Dehuai, Huang Kecheng, Hong Xuezhi (洪学智), Deng Hua (邓华), Wan Yi (万毅) and also Wang Shusheng attacked at Lushan and after. If only because of the frequency and number of military leaders attacked and replaced within the central military command, military politics and the competition for promotion was likely to be fierce, and as accounts of rivalries among the remaining top military leaders suggest (as between Lin Biao and Luo Ruiqing, or Nie Rongzhen (聂荣臻) and He Long (贺龙), as well as Nie and Luo), this was indeed what happened. The CR of course greatly exacerbated already existing rivalries, jealousies and hostilities. But even without it, growing turnover within the elite for reasons related to health and "ordinary" communist politics was beginning to create a large number of vacancies in top positions. Elite transition and transformation was a process that was already getting under way when the CR broke out.

War and War Preparations

As noted in the introduction, the search for the origins of the Cultural Revolution dominates scholarly discussions of the 1958 to 1965 period. And while, indeed, in 1966, politics in command was truly trumps, the Chinese state and its leaders devoted a huge amount of their time, attention and state resources to preparing the Chinese state for war, and fighting in several. Without a Cultural Revolution, the effects of the militarization of society and the economy might have been the key story of China from the Great Leap to 1966. Even with the CR, the decisions made about preparing for war in the late 1950s and early 1960s have legacies felt to this day. Part of this story has begun to come to light with the pathbreaking contributions of John Wilson Lewis and his collaborators and students, and by Barry Naughton, but much more can be added to those works.[26]

26. John Wilson Lewis and Xue Litai, *China Builds the Bomb* (Stanford: Stanford University Press, 1988), *China's Strategic Seapower* (Stanford: Stanford University Press, 1994), and "China's search for a modern air force," *International Security*, Vol. 24, No. 1 (1999), pp. 64–94; John Wilson Lewis and Hua Di, "China's ballistic missiles program," *International Security*, Vol. 17, No. 2 (1992); Evan A. Feigenbaum, "Soldiers, weapons and Chinese development Strategy," *The China Quarterly*, No. 158 (1999), pp. 285–313, and *China's Techno-Warriors* (Stanford: Stanford University Press, 2003); Barry Naughton, "The Third Front," *The China Quarterly*, No. 115 (1988), pp. 351–386, and "Industrial policy during the Cultural Revolution," in William A. Joseph *et al.* (eds.), *New Perspectives on the Cultural Revolution* (Cambridge, MA: Harvard University Press, 1991), pp. 153–181. One fine, and totally unexpected, example of the long-term impact of war, war preparation, and defence industrialization on the Chinese body politic is found in Susan Greenhalgh, "Population science, missile Science," *The China Quarterly*, No. 182 (2005), pp. 253–276.

William Kirby in his profound discussion of Republican China's relationship with the world noted that "nothing mattered more."[27] One can almost say the same thing about 1958 to 1965, in a perhaps perverse way. China was little integrated into the institutions and practices of the international system, but almost every development in China had deep connections to the world outside its borders. The PLA was on a war footing for much of the 1958–65 period. It fought or participated in at least five major campaigns and engaged in numerous smaller engagements and skirmishes. China tested its first nuclear weapons (after perhaps being given the plans to them by the Soviets), and by 1964 its national economy had been put in the service of defence industrialization. Whole new lines of industry were created to provide new weapon systems, and higher education was put at the full disposal of the military industrial system. During the Great Leap, major efforts were devoted to providing basic levels of military training for a militia in the "Everyone a soldier" campaign. PLA enlistments appear to have increased in the early 1960s. PRC grand strategy was substantially changed, and fundamentally new foreign policy orientations were developed; at times, foreign policy lines were debated. Even as the effects of the Great Leap famine greatly reduced China's foreign trade, its trade orientation increasingly shifted towards Europe and Japan, with precursors to the foreign economic policies of the 1970s and early 1980s considered. Despite increased commitment to self-reliance after the break with the Soviet Union, Mao wanted to import more foreign technology. Some of these themes are elaborated on below.

Prior to the Great Leap, defence industrialization figured prominently in Chinese industrial planning, and many of the "156" Soviet supplied projects in the First Five-Year Plan were weapons production plants.[28] Mao and Zhou argued for a reduction in conventional defence industry and defence expenditures in 1956 to fund nuclear weapons development, and this appears to have been followed through during at least the early stages of the Great Leap. New projects, with or without Soviet help, were started during the Leap, especially in the aviation and nuclear fields. New ship designs and support were also transferred from the Soviets in 1959. While the Soviets did not provide the PRC with promised sample atomic bombs, they did apparently tell the Chinese how to design and build them.

From 18 June to 2 August 1958, Soviet nuclear weapons developers from Arzamas-16, the classified Soviet nuclear research town, traveled to Beijing. Prior to the trip, they had been instructed by N.I. Pavlov [a Soviet nuclear weapons industry official]....He explained that the Chinese wished to make an atomic

---

27. William C. Kirby, "The internationalization of China," *The China Quarterly*, No. 150 (1997), pp. 433–458. The quotation is the first sentence of the article.
28. Bo Yibo, *Recollections of Some Major Policies and* Events, Vol. 1, pp. 296–301 and Chen Ping *et al.* (eds.), *Xin Zhongguode jiben jianshe – guogfang gongye juan* (*New China's Capital Construction – Defence Industry Volume*) (Beijing (?): Guofang gongye chubanshe, 1987), *passim*.

bomb, and they (the specialists from Arzamas-16) were to go to China and explain to the Chinese how the bomb was designed. The specialists did as they were told. During their visit, the Chinese also expressed interest in other practical issues, including Arzamas's Structural Design Bureau, how it organized cooperation with Soviet industry, the atomic bomb's design, and how the bombs were tested at the experimental stage.[29]

After Soviet assistance began to decline in mid-1959, and even after the withdrawal of all Soviet advisors in the summer of 1960, there continued to be Soviet support for certain weapons systems to China. It was in 1961–62 that the Soviets provided China with plans for MiG 21 fighters (Jian 歼 7). Chinese nuclear scientists were still allowed to go and work at the Joint Nuclear Research Centre in Dubna, and in at least one case stay for three years, to return to work in China's nuclear weapons programme.[30]

While the break with the Soviets on defence technology might have been less sharp than is commonly believed, there is no doubt that the Great Leap was a disaster for China's defence industries (as well as the rest of China). The commander of the Chinese air force, Liu Yalou (刘亚楼), urged the Shenyang Aircraft Factory to rush into serial production of the MiG 19 (Jian 6) supersonic fighter. He was paraphrased as saying in December 1960, "the air force dares to fly Chinese-built aircraft. Even if they are dangerous, we are not afraid." It was not a dare to take up. Safety and product quality was so fundamentally flawed that the Jian 6 was grounded from 1961 to 1964.[31] During that entire time, China's only jet fighter was the subsonic Jian 5, of early 1950s vintage. This had significant implications for air defence. In addition, in 1960, the newly appointed PLA chief of staff Luo Ruiqing made an inspection trip to Chengdu to assess whether the quality of the construction of the Chengdu Aircraft Factory and the Chengdu Jet Engine Factory were able to be fixed, or whether the plants simply had to be scrapped.[32] He Long and

29. E. Negin and Iu. Smirnov, "Did the USSR share its atomic secrets with China?" in *Science and Society. History of the Soviet Atomic Project (40s–50s), Vol. 1* (in Russian), pp. 310–11, as quoted in Viktor M. Gobarev, "Soviet policy towards China: developing nuclear weapons 1949–1969," *Journal of Slavic Military Studies*, Vol. 12, No. 4 (1999), pp. 1–53, on p. 25. While there may be some exaggeration or hazy recollections after many years, colleagues in Soviet studies have assured me that Negin and Smirnov are authoritative figures.

30. Duan Zijun (chief ed.), *Dangdai Zhongguo de hangkong gongye* (*The Aviation Industry of Contemporary China*) (Beijing: Zhongguo shehui kexue chubanshe, 1988), p. 139 and the entry for Qian Shaojun in CC Bio Dictionary, p. 579.

31. Lin Hu (chief ed.), *Dangdai Zhongguo kongjun* (*The Air Force of Contemporary China*) (Beijing: Zhongguo shehui kexue chubanshe, 1989), p. 302, Duan Zijun, *The Aviation Industry*, pp. 46–47, and Yu Yongbo (chief ed.), *Dangdai Zhongguo de guofang keji shiye, xia* (*The Defence Science and Technology Endeavours of Contemporary China, Vol. 2*) (Beijing: Dangdai Zhongguo chubanshe, 1992), pp. 181–83.

32. Zhang Yu and Cai Guangang, "Luo Ruiqing yu guofang gongye" ("Luo Ruiqing and national defence industry"), *Research on the History of Contemporary China*, No. 5, pp. 54–64; see pp. 54–55.

Zhou Enlai highlighted grave defects in PLA equipment caused by the Leap in the 1960–62 period.[33]

The Great Leap collapse caused Mao to be quite conservative in his military thinking and planning. One history of military affairs notes that in the early 1960s, Mao ordered that US spy plane overflights should in general not be attacked. No US aircraft was successfully intercepted by Chinese aircraft between 1955 and 1965.[34] While the PLA air defence forces continued to shoot down Kuomintang (KMT) reconnaissance aircraft, none of the three aircraft brought down between late 1959 and late 1963 was lost due to air interception. China had little or no ability to defend itself from the air, and was subject to frequent aerial observation.[35]

Mao's caution in not responding to US overflights, the transfer of MiG 21 technology to China and apparent restoration of Chinese nuclear scientists participating in the Dubna nuclear research centre suggest that interpretations of Wang Jiaxiang's (王稼祥) famous recommendations about moderating Chinese foreign policy need to be reconsidered. Mao may de facto have been reducing tensions with the US, the Soviet Union and to a lesser extent India, and reducing foreign aid in the 1960–62 period.[36]

Despite caution with regard to the great powers and India, China did deploy troops across its borders in late 1960 and 1961.[37] Upon concluding a border demarcation agreement in 1960, Burma agreed to allow China to attack KMT forces in Burma. Between November 1960 and February 1961, more than 10,000 PLA troops were involved in two separate operations to attack KMT forces, with considerable success. These operations in Burma, along with continuing efforts to pacify the rebellion in Tibetan regions of China from 1958 to early 1961 and an ongoing rebellion in the Liangshan Yi (凉山彝) region of

33. For example, *He Long junshi wenxuan* (*Selected Writings of He Long on Military Affairs*) (Beijing: Jiefang jun chubanshe, 1989), pp. 577–81, and *Zhou Enlai junshi wenxuan, di si juan* (*Selected Writings of Zhou Enlai on Military Affairs, Vol. 4*) (Beijing: Renmin chubanshe, 1997), pp. 421–37.

34. Liao Guoliang *et al.* (eds.), *Mao Zedong junshi sixiang fazhan shi* (*A History of the Development of Mao Zedong's Military Thought*) (Beijing: Jiefang jun chubanshe, 1991), p. 460 and Han Huaizhi and Tan Jingqiao (chief eds.), *Dangdai Zhongguo jundui de junshi gongzuo, shang* (*The Military Affairs of Contemporary China's Armed Forces, Vol. 1*) (Beijing: Zhongguo shehui kexue chubanshe, 1989), pp. 594–609.

35. *Ibid.* pp. 360–69.

36. *Wang Jiaxiang xuanji* (*Selected Works of Wang Jiaxiang*) (Beijing: Renmin chubanshe, 1989), pp. 446–460; Xu Zehao, *Wang Jiaxiang zhuan* (*Biography of Wang Jiaxiang*) (Beijing: Dangdai Zhongguo chubanshe, 1996), pp. 553–569. Mao, prior to the CR, only criticized the three reductions to foreign visitors, and only starting more than a year after they were presented to him. See Cong Jin, *Quzhe fazhan de suiyue* (*Times of Torturous Advance*) (Zhengzhou: Henan renmin chubanshe, 1989), pp. 575–581.

37. Han and Tan, *The Military Affairs of Contemporary China's Armed Forces*, pp. 376–379; and Yu Hui, *Wushinian guoshi jiyao: junshi juan* (*Outline of 50 Years of National Affairs: Military Affairs Volume*) (Changsha: Hunan renmin chubanshe, 1999), pp. 387–406.

Sichuan (active between 1955 and 1961), suggest that China saw its security situation as deteriorating.[38]

The lack of air defence led to severe strains within the Military Affairs Commission, with He Long and Luo Ruiqing (and Zhou Enlai lending some support) arguing for greater priority for conventional weapons, especially fighter aircraft, and Nie Rongzhen (backed by Mao) arguing for continued priority for the nuclear weapons and missile programmes. Nie and Mao won the debate, but over the course of the early 1960s, Luo and He gained greater bureaucratic control over all defence industries.[39] Thus, throughout the early 1960s, China had little or no air defence, it was making few new investments in the defence industry, and the quality of weapons was a big problem. Moreover, the international situation from China's perspective was growing increasingly tense.

It is not clear when the Chinese leadership knew that Chiang Kai-shek (Jiang Jieshi 蒋介石) hoped to attack China. On 10 June 1962, the Central Committee issued an order for the PLA to prepare for a KMT invasion, and mobilize for the defence of the mainland.[40] Already by late February 1962, Zhou Enlai had called on the army to rectify itself and prepare for war.[41] (And even prior to Zhou's call, Sichuan began to have some of its civilian plants meet military needs.[42]) Zhou concluded that the defence industries could not meet the military's needs, and argued that defence mobilization production lines be established in and among civilian factories. Such endeavours had existed during the Korean War, but 1962 marked their revival. Over the course of the next 25 or so years, substantial new investments, machinery and personnel were added to civilian factories. More than 3,000 civilian factories nationwide were organized into defence industrial production mobilization lines, most to meet the needs of ground force units. Zhou took personal charge of this work, implemented by the State Economic Commission. By the end of 1962, 57 mobilization production lines had been established nationwide.[43] There were high tides in the creation of mobilization lines after 1964 and the onset of the Third Front policy, and in 1969.

38. *Ibid.* pp. 330–386 and *Sichuan sheng zhi: junshi zhi* (*Sichuan Provincial Gazetteer: Military Affairs Volume*) (Chengdu: Sichuan renmin chubanshe, 1999), pp. 294–300, 317–19.

39. On this, see Zhang and Cai, "Luo Ruiqing and national defence industry," *Selected Writings of He Long on Military Affairs*, *Selected Writings of Zhou Enlai on Military Affairs*, and *Nie Rongzhen huiyi lu, xia* (*Memoirs of Nie Rongzhen, Vol. 2*) (Beijing: Renmin chubanshe, 1986), pp. 810–11.

40. Zhang Yutao (chief ed.), *Xin Zhongguo junshi dashi jiyao* (*Outline of Major Military Affairs of New China*) (Beijing: Junshi kexue chubanshe, 1998), p. 180.

41. *Selected Writings of Zhou Enlai on Military Affairs*, pp. 425–27, 433–37.

42. *Sichuan sheng zhi: jixie gongye zhi* (*Sichuan Provincial Gazetteer: Machinery Industry Volume*) (Chengdu: Sichuan cishu chubanshe, 1993), pp. 325, 327.

43. *Dangdai Beijing guofang gongye* (*The National Defence Industry of Contemporary Beijing*) (Beijing: Beijing ribao chubanshe, 1990), pp. 14–15, 179–181, 184–86 and 191–94, and Wang Lei *et al.* (chief eds.), *Dangdai Zhongguo de bingqi gongye* (*The Ordnance Industry of Contemporary China*) (Beijing: Dangdai Zhongguo chubanshe, 1993), pp. 373–76.

Information on these lines is sporadic. At their height, Beijing had ten lines, Hebei 33, Guangdong 13 and Gansu at least ten. Some 62 enterprises were involved in mobilization production in Sichuan, 500–600 in Hebei, 143 in Guangdong and at least 100 in Gansu.[44] Usually located in cities, these lines could provide the ordnance necessary for either guerrilla war or conventional defence.

Again, even prior to the formal development of the Third Front policy, parts of China's defence industrial system were put on an emergency mobilization basis. The Second Ministry of Machine Building, charged with nuclear weapons production, started its own Third Front strategy in late 1963. As Sino-Soviet relations deteriorated, and the US became more involved in the war in Vietnam, key nuclear weapons facilities in Baotou (包头), Inner Mongolia, Hengyang (衡阳), Hunan, Lanzhou and Jiuquan (酒泉) prefecture in Gansu were increasingly vulnerable to attack. The Ministry, closely supervised by Zhou Enlai and Nie Rongzhen, began plans to build additional key nuclear installations in Sichuan and one in Guizhou.[45] China had no effective air defence from 1961 to 1964, but Chinese radar could track U-2 reconnaissance flights. Whether Chinese leaders knew about US discussions to destroy China's nuclear programme is not known. But they did know where spyplanes were flying.[46]

Some time in early 1964, deputy PLA Chief of Staff Yang Chengwu (杨成武) asked the Operations Department of the General Staff to evaluate the effects of a bombing campaign on China's ability to wage war. The report Yang received on 25 April 1964 stated that the 14 cities in China with a population of one million or more accounted for about 60 per cent of all major civilian industry, 73 per cent of the aviation industry, 78 per cent of the shipbuilding industry, 59 per cent of military electronics (which was most electronics in the 1960s), and

44. *Ibid.* for overall figures, and *The National Defence Industry of Contemporary Beijing* for the Beijing figures. For the Sichuan figures, see *Sichuan Provincial Gazetteer*. On Hebei, Guangdong and Gansu, see *Hebei sheng zhi: di 34 juan: guofang keji gongye zhi* (*Hebei Provincial Gazetteer, Vol. 34: National Defence Science, Technology, and Industry Volume*) (Beijing: Zhongguo shuji chubanshe, 1995), pp. 155–164; Xi Zhiwei (chief ed.), *Guangdong jungong shiliao, 1949–1987* (*Historical Materials on Military Industry in Guangdong*) (n.p., 1990 (?)) pp. 8–10 and 125–130; and *Gansu sheng zhi: di sishisan juan. junshi gongye zhi* (*Gansu Provincial Gazetteer, Vol. 43: Military Industry*) (Lanzhou: Gansu renmin chubanshe, 1992), pp. 81–93.

45. Li Jue *et al.* (chief ed.), *Dangdai Zhongguo de he gongye* (*The Nuclear Industry of Contemporary China*) (Beijing: Zhongguo shehui kexue chubanshe, 1987), pp. 413–14 and *Zhongguo da san xian* (*China's Big Third Front*) (Beijing: Zhongguo huabao chubanshe, 1998), p. 17.

46. For an idea about the information gathered by aerial and space surveillance and the uses to which it could be put, see William Burr and Jeffrey T. Richelson, "Whether to 'strangle the baby in the cradle',"*International Security*, Vol. 25, No. 3 (2000–2001), pp. 54–99 (additional material supporting this essay is found on the National Security Archive's website: www. nsarchive.org. See also *Tracking the Dragon: National Intelligence Estimates on China during the Era of Mao* (n.p.: Government Printing Office, n.d.), pp. 365–374 and NIE 13-2-62 and SNIE 13-2-63 on the CD-Rom that is part of this publication. This material can also be found at www.cia.gov/nic.

44 per cent of the ordnance industry.[47] Thus, most of China's ability to provide the material foundation to wage war was almost completely vulnerable to aerial bombardment in a relatively small number of places. This report makes much clearer why Mao intervened to alter the Third Five-Year Plan fundamentally and develop the Third Front policy of defence industrialization in China's interior.[48] Mao's ability to override the preliminary proposals for the Third Five-Year Plan conclusively demonstrated that his power had not been significantly eroded by the Great Leap. He intervened as he saw fit in policy making. And when Li Fuchun, the chairman of the State Planning Commission, seemed less than anxious to develop the Third Front, Mao established a small planning commission under Yu Qiuli (余秋里) who was more responsive to his direction.[49]

More important than the fact of the reassertion of Mao's political dominance by the Third Front was the effect of that decision. Simply put, the Third Front turned an already highly militarized economy into a pure war economy. Of the 157 ordnance enterprises under the central government in 1990, 96 were the product of the Third Front period. The same was true for more than 100 of the 143 aviation enterprises in China in 1985 and more than half of all missile factories in 1985. Prior to the Third Front, Guizhou had no defence industries, and of its 175 medium and large enterprises in 1985, only 46 were started prior to 1965. The rest were Third Front projects, of which 81 were defence enterprises. And while no other province was as deeply affected by the Third Front as Guizhou, every provincial level unit except Tibet was heavily involved in the policy.[50]

47. "Fu: zongcan zuozhan bu de baogao" ("Supplement: report of the operations department of the General Staff Department") , *Dangde wenxian* (*Party Documents*), No. 3 (1995), pp. 34–35.

48. For primary documentary material on the Third Front, see *ibid.* pp. 33–42. The leading PRC author on the Third Front is Chen Donglin; see his *Sanxian jianshe: beizhan shiqi de xibu kaifa* (*Third Front Construction: Opening up the West during the Era of Preparing for War*) (Beijing: Zhonggong zhongyang dangxiao chubanshe, 2003).

49. Fang Weizhong and Jin Chongji (chief eds.), *Li Fuchun zhuan* (*Biography of Li Fuchun*) (Beijing: Zhongyang wenxian chubanshe, 2001), pp. 618–647.

50. A list of 157 centrally managed ordnance factors is found in *Zhongguo bingqi nianjian (1986–1990)* (*China Ordnance Industry Yearbook, 1986–1990*) (Beijing: Bingqi gongye chubanshe, 1991), pp. 911–920. From numerous scattered sources I have been able to find approximate or actual starting dates for all of them. Numbers of factories in the space and aviation industries are found in *Zhonghua renmin gongheguo 1985 nian gongye pucha ziliao, di san ce* (*Material on the 1985 Industrial Census of the PRC, Vol. 3*) (hereafter 1985 Ind Census, followed by the volume number) (Beijing: Zhongguo tongji chubanshe, 1988), pp. 122–25. On Guizhou, see 1985 Ind Census, Vol. 2, (this volume provides data on individual large and medium enterprises), *passim.* On defence industrialization in Guizhou, see Chen Yongxiao (chief ed.), *Guizhou sheng jingji dili* (*The Economic Geography of Guizhou Province*) (Beijing: Xinhua chubanshe, 1992), pp. 264–68. Overall statistics for the number of large and medium enterprises in the 1985 industrial census in 1985 Ind Census, Vol. 1, pp. 8–12.

The Third Front had multiple national security dimensions, and while it supported a grand strategy of people's war (which emerged in the mid-1960s from an early, active defence of the border strategy)[51] it was not guerrilla war. Cloning nuclear facilities was not to fight a guerrilla war, nor was developing missile production bases in Shaanxi, Guizhou, Hubei and Sichuan. Developing a submarine production base in Fuling (涪陵), Sichuan is hardly an example of guerrilla war. The big Third Front – the centrally directed drive – to build large-scale defence industrial production facilities in the interior was to fight a relatively high tech, conventional and perhaps nuclear war. The small Third Front, the provincial programmes to develop self-reliant weapons production systems for local forces, was more suited for guerrilla war. And the defence industrial production lines fell somewhere in between.

It is far from clear that the Third Front projects did anything to make China fundamentally more secure, despite the immense effort they entailed. Moreover, the provincial level units that received very high levels of Third Front investment during the period had among the lowest per capita incomes in China at the turn of the millennium: for example Guizhou, Sichuan, Chongqing and Shaanxi all ranked in the bottom ten in terms of per capita income.

While the national economy was mobilized to prepare for war, so too was much of the rest of China. The early to mid-1960s was a period of bureaucratic consolidation and slow growth, except with regard to defence industry management. Bureaucratic mobility had been quite high in the 1950s, as the state system was fleshed out and the national administrative apparatus put in place. With the Great Leap famine and depression, and the high prior staffing of the bureaucracy, recruitment greatly slowed.[52] However, the defence industrial bureaucratic management and research sector was the great exception to this. Between 1961 and 1965 separate ministries of machine building were established to plan and administer defence industrial sectors. The Second Ministry of Machine Building existed in the 1950s, and managed the nuclear industry. Other defence industrial ministries of machine building were established to build aircraft, electronics, ordnance, ships and missiles in the early 1960s.[53] This bureaucratic elaboration was accompanied by the proliferation

51. Hu Zhefeng, "Jianguo yilai ruogan junshi zhanlue fangzhen tanxi," ("An analysis of some of the guiding principles of military strategy since the founding of the PRC"), *Dangdai Zhongguo shi yanjiu* (*Research on the History of Contemporary China*), Vol. 7, No.4 (July 2000), pp. 21–32.

52. The implications of this development are brought out in the major works on the social origins of the CR. See Jonathan Unger, *Education under Mao* (New York: Columbia University Press, 1982); Susan L. Shirk, *Competitive Comrades* (Berkeley: University of California Press, 1982); and Lynn T. White, III, *Policies of Chaos* (Princeton: Princeton University Press, 1989).

53. Dates based on the time of the appointment of the first minister in charge. See *Zhongguo gongchan dang zhizheng sishinian (zeng ding ben)* (*The Chinese Communist Party's 40 Years of Exercising Power, revised edition*) (Beijing: Zhonggong dangshi chubanshe, 1991), pp. 599–600.

of research institutes and academies to try to compensate for the departure of Soviet advisors and experts.

In addition, after 1963 it appears that the PLA began to increase in numbers. Full details are not available, but by 1965, the PLA exceeded 5 million soldiers and by the early 1970s it exceeded 6 million. In 1965, border troops were 83 per cent larger than they were in 1958, and reserves increased by 41 per cent over the same period.[54] Publicly announced defence spending (in later statistical yearbooks) shows that in 1961 defence spending was 13.6 per cent of all government spending. But the next year it rose to more than 18 per cent, and did not drop below 18 per cent until after Richard Nixon's visit to China in 1972.[55] Coupled with Third Front investment after 1964, China's military industrial complex was probably consuming more than half of all government spending.

Border or external conflict was almost constant from 1962 to the CR. In addition to the war with India, American and Taiwanese overflights of China picked up. By mid-1964, Mao removed his ban on intercepting US aircraft. KMT commando raids on the coast were also ongoing. China built roads in Laos to aid the Pathet Lao, and sent troops to North Vietnam to man air defences and keep supplies flowing. CIA-supported Tibetan exiles continued military actions in Tibet, and the Soviet Union began to militarize its border with China. China attempted to promote revolution in much of South-East Asia. It also considered coming to Pakistan's military assistance during its 1965 war with India.[56]

By the end of 1965, China was a highly militarized society preparing for war. The best and the brightest graduates of the educational system were dispatched to work in defence-related research or production. Defence production and weapons development, especially nuclear weapons and missiles, had the highest priority in the country. Mao made these allocational choices his highest economic priorities, and met little resistance from other top leaders. While there are many reasons why this was so, one is that planned economies seem to have a particular strength in defence industrialization. The Soviet Union became a war economy in the 1940s, and while trying to move away from it at various points in the 1950s, it was never really able to do so. China, especially from 1964 to the early to mid-1970s, was moving far along the same road of building a gigantic defence industrial complex.

54. Yu Hui *Outline of 50 Years of National Affairs*, pp. 411–12, and Zhang Aiping (chief ed.), *Zhongguo renmin jiefang jun, xia* (*The Chinese People's Liberation Army, Vol. 2*) (Beijing: Dangdai Zhongguo chubanshe, 1994), p. 132.

55. *Statistical Yearbook of China, 1986* (Oxford: Oxford University Press, 1986), pp. 520 and 518.

56. On these activities, see Han and Tan, *The Military Affairs of Contemporary China's Armed Forces*, Vol. 1; *Mao Zedong junshi huodong jishi* (*Record on Mao Zedong's Military Activities*) (Beijing: Jiefang jun chubanshe, 1994), p. 938; John Kenneth Knaus, *Orphans of the Cold War* (New York: Public Affairs, 1999); Jay Taylor, *China and Southeast Asia* (New York: Praeger, 1974), and John W. Garver, *Protracted Conflict* (Seattle: University of Washington Press, 2001), pp. 194–204.

With reform, China was able to move along a different path. But the legacy of the war economy permeates the Chinese economy to this day. It is not simply that large state-owned enterprises (SOEs) are inefficient. It is that many of those that remain are or were defence industrial producers. The interior is backward not just because most of its industry is SOEs but because it is home to a large number of defence factories and facilities. Banks are effectively bankrupt not just because the state orders them to subsidize SOEs, but also because many of the bailouts go to defence producers. China avoided being as deeply militarized an economy as the Soviet Union for several reasons which need not be discussed here, but it is not because it did not try.

Conclusion

This article, however superficially, reveals aspects of the institutionalization of the Chinese revolution during 1958 to 1965 that have not been a central focus for scholarship. It tries to demonstrate new possibilities for recapturing elements of the history of the period without being overwhelmed by the catastrophe that followed. It shows some of the variety of trends present in China bearing on the political. Some may have been inexorably linked to the CR, but others much less so. Law as an institution or process was more integrated into the Chinese political system than most thought. Leadership turnover and perhaps generational transition was looming, even without the CR. China's political economy and its polity were being mobilized for war, but not directly for the kind of war that broke out in 1966. If the data and arguments presented here convince readers that there is much more to the 1958–65 period than the origins of the CR, it will have achieved one of its main purposes.

This article has focused on (in retrospect), three core process related to the Chinese state in 1958–65, taking advantage of a variety of the newly available Chinese sources that reveal little-known or previously underappreciated aspects of Chinese political history. These processes – related to leadership, administration and policy – illustrate there was more to the Chinese state and its relationship with its people than power politics and class struggle. They suggest different trends extant within the Chinese political system that interacted sometimes independently, sometimes coincidentally, and sometimes as a direct result of elite power politics.

Each of these processes highlights different aspects of CCP rule in the 1958 to 1965 period. The activities of the courts speak to aspects of state–society relations that are not likely to be recaptured through retrospective interviewing of people who lived through this period. Nor is the information about the criminal process readily discernable from other sources. To the extent that court activity mirrors actual social behaviour, divorce was reasonably common in China, crime was down and crimes involving people with bad class backgrounds were generally a low number of all criminal cases, suggesting relatively low levels of political polarization until the end of 1965. Most surprisingly, the data suggest that a higher percentage of Chinese criminal defendants were found not guilty and not punished than was the case in US federal criminal trials for the same period.

The changing composition of the political elite suggests a somewhat countervailing tendency. In all political systems, the question of who governs is a central question of political analysis. We see within the political elite probably more polarization than within state–society relations. But even here, Party norms and practices (at least on the surface) persist. No member of the Eighth Central Committee lost his or her membership in the CC prior to 1966. All who were removed from power for political reasons were given new positions after a period of time, during which they were subject to various forms of rectification, or "curing the illness to save the patient" (those purged in late 1965 are exceptions). Limited institutionalization even in the highest realm of political power continued. Mortality, declining health, advancing age and political struggles were opening up new opportunities and creating new potentials for struggles for personal advancement (whether ruthless or not).

In an era, at least from 1962 to the CR, when politics was in command, and when the central military elite was subject to more political turmoil than any other segment of the elite, it is remarkable how limited were the effects of elite political concerns on defence industrialization and war preparation. China devoted a considerable amount of state treasure, the lives of its citizens and the attention of its leaders to the prospect of international conflict involving China. It is true that rivalries, jealousies, ambitions and other human dimensions of politics were at stake as China mobilized for war, but politics was constrained by national security considerations (however idiosyncratic some of the responses to national security crises were).

These three processes – the activities of Chinese courts, elite change and imminent transformation, and preparing for war – speak to a Chinese state that was proceeding on its business prior to 1966, of trying to institutionalize its mechanisms of rule, maintain (some) norms about managing elite conflict and meeting pressing challenges. One probably could have identified other core processes of Chinese state-building, studied them and found many new and surprising things to say about them. The three discussed here are of high salience, involved millions of people (at least in two of the cases) and testify to the wide range of activities where various degrees of institutionalization were taking place. The Cultural Revolution put an end (for a time) to many of those attempts to deepen this institutionalization, but in all three areas, it only delayed that institutionalization, with the Chinese state developing newer, more professional ways to handle the same questions after 1976 (or 1989).

Squeezing the Peasants: Grain Extraction, Food Consumption and Rural Living Standards in Mao's China*

Robert Ash

ABSTRACT   At the end of Mao's life farmers still accounted for some 80 per cent of China's population. Its declining share in GDP notwithstanding, agriculture continued to carry a heavy developmental burden throughout the Mao era. The production and distribution of grain – the wage good par excellence – held the key to fulfilling this role. But despite a pragmatic response to the exigencies of famine conditions in 1959–61, state investment priorities never adequately accommodated the economic, let alone the welfare needs of the farm sector. Thanks to the mechanism of grain re-sales to the countryside, the Chinese government's extractive policies were less brutal in their impact than those pursued by Stalin in the Soviet Union. Even so, a detailed national, regional and provincial analysis of grain output and procurement trends highlights the process of rural impoverishment which characterized China's social and economic development under Maoist planning.

The role of institutional change in agriculture – in particular, its ability to promote rapid and sustained farm development – has long been debated. The experience of China under the leadership of the Chinese Communist Party (CCP) is something of a *cause célèbre* in this respect. In less than three decades, the Chinese countryside underwent two institutional upheavals – collectivization in the 1950s, decollectivization in the 1980s – whose policy thrusts ran in exactly opposite directions.

Economists have long recognized the importance, even necessity, of institutional change as a source of farm output and productivity growth. But the conventional wisdom, strongly supported by empirical evidence, is that institutional change is only one of several elements that must be mobilized in support of such growth. In particular, economic measures and technical initiatives are thought to be at least as important as "getting institutions right." Changing the organizational framework of agriculture may have a positive impact on efficiency and growth. But the effect is likely to be one-off and short-term, and the effect of subsequent institutional adjustments may be merely incremental. By contrast, the potential benefits of *economic*

* I am grateful to the participants of the *China Quarterly* Conference (October 2005), at which a very different version of this article was initially presented, for comments and advice on how I might go about making a very diffuse paper more focused. I also take special pleasure in thanking Professor Colin White (La Trobe University, Melbourne, Australia) – a dear friend of almost half a century – for his insightful and encouraging comments from afar on an interim version of this article.

policy initiatives and technical progress are less constrained, and offer a basis on which to make continuous improvements.

Insufficient recognition of the beneficial, mutually-reinforcing complementarity between institutional, economic and technological measures characterized Chinese government thinking on farm policy between the 1950s and 1970s. For a time, collectivization was thought to be impossible until China's agriculture had been mechanized. By the time Mao made his speech that launched the first "high tide of co-operativization,"[1] the relationship between the two had been reversed, with collectivization now a prior condition of farm mechanization. Implicit in the new emphasis was the belief that technical progress in agriculture should not be solely identified with the use of modern capital-intensive technology. Labour-intensive improvements – close planting, more multiple cropping, better use of organic fertilizers – were also important. So was the Nurksean prescription of rural capital formation based on mass labour mobilization. Such measures were most effectively pursued in an institutional framework which afforded tight control over the farm workforce. In China the outcome of this one-sided emphasis on institutions was a legacy of technological backwardness in agriculture. The economic implications of this for a sector which in the 1970s still accounted for well over three-quarters of total employment, and which provided 70 per cent of light industry's material inputs and about half of the state's budgetary revenue, were serious.

In 1949 its ideological and historical roots committed the CCP to a strategy of institutional change as the main engine of growth in the rural sector. The first major post-1949 campaign was an increasingly radicalized land reform, which destroyed the political and economic power base of the landlord-gentry class. Through the distribution of land and other assets to poor and landless peasants, it also consolidated mass support for the Party in the countryside. Land reform was, however, a temporizing measure: the first step of a series of agrarian changes that would lead to full collectivization. As the experience of the Soviet Union had already demonstrated, implement-ing collectivization in a framework of dirigiste, central planning without simultaneously damaging farm incentives and undermining efficiency posed a formidable challenge. But for the Chinese government, such considerations were less important than the promise of unprecedented control over the labour force and agricultural output, offered by further expropriation, socialization and the creation of new and larger organizational forms. By such means, the government's all-important extractive role vis-à-vis the peasants would be fulfilled. Thereby too, the priority goal of rapid industrialization – which depended on securing from farmers a real

---

1. Mao Zedong, "Guanyu nongye hezuohua wenti" ("On the question of agricultural co-operativization"), 31 July 1955 (printed in *Xinhua yuebao* (*New China Monthly*), Vol. 73, No. 11 (1955), pp. 1–8).

surplus (food, raw materials and exportable goods) and a financial surplus – would also be achieved. Except when, in the early 1960s, famine forced a temporary adjustment of investment priorities, the imperative of heavy industrialization was the ultimate determinant of farm policy throughout the Mao period.

The main concern of this article is with the impact of the government's extractive policies on Chinese peasants, with some consideration also given to the nature and rationale of agricultural policy. I offer a brief review of farm production, but it is with peasants *as consumers* that I am more concerned in an attempt to assess changes in their living standards during the Mao era. Given the pervasive nature of rural poverty that was part of the legacy of this period, much of my analysis necessarily focuses on grain.

Other authors have of course investigated these issues. Perhaps the most notable contributions are those of Nicholas Lardy and Kenneth Walker,[2] which remain hugely insightful more than 20 years after their publication, offering valuable comment on the impact of Maoist farm policies on rural consumption and living standards. Neither writer had access, however, to consistent time-series estimates of grain output, procurement and urban and rural-resales for the entire Mao era, which became available only after the publication of their books.[3] As far as I am aware, this is the first article to make use of these data to investigate the rural implications of grain extraction throughout the planning period up to Mao's death.

Agricultural Development in the Mao Period

Tables 1 and 2 seek to capture critical dimensions of the physical profile, resource endowment and performance of China's agriculture between 1952 (the eve of the First Five-Year Plan [FFYP]) and 1976. The two tables are highly revealing. Concealed in them is the essence of the labour mobilization approach, without which – given the disproportionate allocation of government budgetary spending[4] and investment to sectors other than agriculture – the impressive

2. E.g., Nicholas R. Lardy, *Agriculture in China's Modern Economic Development* (Cambridge: Cambridge University Press, 1983), esp. ch. 4. Kenneth R. Walker, *Food Grain Procurement and Consumption in China* (Cambridge: Cambridge University Press, 1984). Also useful is Thomas Lyons, *Economic Integration and Planning in Maoist China* (New York: Columbia University Press, 1987).

3. Walker did subsequently gain access to these materials, of which he made extensive use in a study, published posthumously, of the Great Leap Forward ("Food and mortality in China during the Great Leap Forward," in Robert F. Ash (ed.), *Agricultural Development in China, 1949–1989: The Collected Papers of Kenneth R. Walker* (Oxford: Oxford University Press, 1998), pp. 106–147).

4. Table 1 shows that throughout the period of the FFYP tax revenue from agriculture exceeded government budgetary spending in support of farming. Not that the proceeds of agricultural taxes shown in the table capture the full extent of agriculture's fiscal burden: from 1953 onwards, the compulsory sale to the state of farm produce (above all, grain – par excellence, the wage good) at prices fixed by the state below the market level was a much more important source of development support.

Table 1: **China's Agriculture – Supply of Land, Labour and Capital, 1952–76**

	1952	1957	1965	1976
Population (m)				
Total population (TP)	574.8	646.5	725.4	937.2
Rural population (RP)	503.2	547.0	594.9	773.8
RP as % TP	87.5	84.6	82.0	82.6
Employment (m)				
Total employment	207.3	237.7	286.7	388.3
Rural employment	182.4	205.7	235.3	301.4
Agricultural employment	–	192.0	225.0	286.5
Agric. share of total employment (%)	–	80.8	78.5	73.8
Agric. share of rural employment (%)	–	93.3	95.6	95.1
Area (m ha)				
Arable area	107.9	111.8	103.6	99.4
Irrigated area	20.0	27.3	33.1	45.0
Irrigated area as % arable area	18.5	24.4	31.9	45.3
Total sown area	141.3	157.2	143.3	149.7
Multiple cropping index (%)	131.0	140.6	138.3	150.6
Farm mechanization				
Agricultural machine power (m kw)	–	1.2	10.9	117.5
Number of large and medium tractors (units)	1,307	14,674	72,599	397,000
Number of small (incl. hand) tractors (units)	–	–	3,956	825,000
Chemical fertilizers				
Total application (m tons, nutrient)	0.04	0.15	1.73	5.24
Av. application per sown ha (kg)	0.28	0.95	12.07	35.00
Fiscal resource flows to and from agriculture (m *yuan*)				
Government expenditure on agriculture	904.0	2,350.0	5,498.0	11,049.0
As % of total government expenditure	4.03	7.94	11.95	13.71
Tax revenue from agriculture	2,751.0	2,967.0	2,578.0	2,914.0
As % of total tax revenue	22.99	19.16	12.62	7.14
Investment in agriculture (m *yuan*)				
Agricultural capital construction investment	774.0	1,187.0	2,497.0	4,104.0
As % total capital construction investment	8.6	8.3	13.9	10.9

Sources:
Ministry of Agriculture, *Zhongguo nongcun jingji tongji dachuan, 1949–86* (*Compendium of Rural Economic Statistics for China, 1949–86*), hereafter *Dachuan*, (Beijing: Nongye chubanshe, 1989); National Bureau of Statistics (NBS), *Xin Zhongguo wushi nian nongye tongji ziliao* (*New China – 50 Years of Agricultural Statistical Materials*), hereafter *50NNYZL* (Beijing: Tongji chubanshe, 2000); NBS, *Xin Zhongguo wushi nian tongji ziliao huibian* (*Comprehensive Collection of Statistical Materials for 50 Years of New China*), hereafter *50NTJZL* (Beijing: Tongji chubanshe, 1999); NBS, *Zhongguo nongcun tongji nianjian* (*China Rural Statistical Yearbook*) (Beijing: Tongji chubanshe, various issues); NBS and Ministry of Labour and Social Security, *Zhongguo laodong tongji nianjian, 2004* (*China Labour Statistical Yearbook, 2004*) (Beijing: Tongji chubanshe, 2004); NBS, *Zhongguo guding zichan touzi tongji ziliao, 1950–1985* (*Statistical Materials on Fixed Capital Investment in China, 1950–85*), hereafter *ZGGD* (Beijing: Tongji chubanshe, 1987).

Table 2: **China's Agricultural Performance, 1952–76**

	1952	1957	1965	1976
Gross value output (GVAO) (m yuan)*				
All agriculture	41,700	53,670	58,960	79,930
Crop cultivation	36,490	45,550	48,480	64,140
Forestry	290	930	1,200	1,510
Animal husbandry	4,790	6,900	8,270	11,370
Fisheries	130	290	1,010	1,510
With all agriculture as 100.0				
Crop cultivation	87.5	84.9	82.2	80.2
Forestry	0.7	1.7	2.0	1.9
Animal husbandry	11.5	12.9	14.0	14.2
Fisheries	0.3	0.5	1.7	1.9
Average GVAO per head of agricultural employed labour (yuan)				
All agriculture	240.7†	279.5	262.0	279.0
Crop cultivation	221.7‡	249.7‡	226.8‡	235.7‡
Total output (m tons)				
All food grains	163.9	195.1	194.5	286.3
Oilseeds	4.2	4.2	3.6	4.0
Cotton	2.3	2.6	1.9	2.1
Meat (incl. poultry)	3.4	4.0	5.5	7.8
Aquatic products	1.7	3.1	3.0	4.5
Sugar	7.6	11.9	15.4	19.6
Average yield (kg/ha)				
All food grains	1,322	1,460	1,626	2,371
Oilseeds	734	605	702	693
Cotton	234	284	419	417
Sugar	34,839	27,918	29,454	21,785
Average output per head of total population (kg)				
All food grains	285.1	301.8	268.1	305.5
Oilseeds	7.3	6.5	5.0	4.3
Meat (incl. poultry)	5.9	6.2	7.6	8.3
Aquatic products	3.0	4.8	4.1	4.8
Sugar	13.2	18.4	21.2	20.9

Notes:
   * These figures are based on constant 1957 prices.
   † Assuming that agricultural employment was 95% of rural employment.
   ‡ Assuming that crop cultivation absorbed 95% of all agricultural employed.
Sources:
   Table 1; Ministry of Agriculture, *Compendium of Rural Economic Statistics, 1949–86; New China – 50 Years of Agricultural Statistical Materials*

expansion in irrigated area and multiple cropping shown in Table 1 could not have taken place. The institutional bias of farm policy in the 1950s is highlighted in the relative neglect of the use of modern farm inputs. This applied to both working capital, represented by chemical fertilizers,[5] and fixed capital (such as tractors) in promoting agricultural growth. Given existing resource constraints, this entailed a significant cost. For example, despite their mobilizational capacities, the collectives failed to generate sufficient labour and draught animals to meet the demands for increased output placed upon them.[6] The fact that there were on average fewer than two tractors per hundred collectives merely highlights the potential impact of delayed farm mechanization.

The fiscal burden carried by the farm sector during the 1950s is captured in the finding that state spending on agriculture was less than tax revenue from this source (from the mid-1960s this was reversed). The farm sector's low investment share was dispropor-tionate to the developmental burden it carried, especially since the meagre resources it received for capital construction under the FFYP were mainly directed to water control construction on the Yellow River, the gains from which were questionable.[7] However, there are two qualifications to this gloomy picture. First, it takes no account of the farm sector's own potential for investment, which the central government believed was considerable (during the FFYP period farm households were reported to have undertaken net capital investment of more than 10 billion *yuan*, almost half the value of basic capital construction investment in agriculture in the same period).[8] Secondly,

5. In 1965, China's average consumption of chemical fertilizer per hectare of arable area was about two-thirds of the world average and at about the same level as in the USSR. At the time of collectivization, the gap between China and many parts of the world, though not India, was even greater.

6. K.R. Walker, "Organization of agricultural production," in A. Eckstein, W. Galenson and Ta-ching Liu (eds.), *Economic Trends in Communist China* (Chicago: Aldine Publishing Co., 1968), pp. 397–358. The shortage of labour and draught animals was exacerbated by the negative impact of collectives on labour incentives, and by the slaughter and ill-care of large numbers of oxen and water buffaloes.

7. E.g. see Judith Shapiro, *Mao's War Against Nature: Politics and the Environment in Revolutionary China* (Cambridge: Cambridge University Press, 2001), pp. 49–51. A revealing comment on irrigation problems during the FFYP is available in *Jihua jingji* (*Planned Economy*), No. 10 (1957), pp. 15–17. See also Choh-Ming Li's comment, "22 large irrigation projects have been initiated during the 5 years (1953–57), each requiring 2 to 4 years for completion; by the end of 1957 only a few had been completed – with poor results," *Economic Development of Modern China: An Appraisal of the First Five Years of Industrialization* (Berkeley & Los Angeles: University of California Press, 1959), p. 67. After 45 years, Li's analysis still repays careful reading and offers valuable insights into the rationale and impact of the FFYP.

8. The estimate of farm household investment is from *Jihua jingji*, No. 10 (1957), pp. 1–2. This figure is, however, likely to refer to *fixed* investment, since another Chinese source indicates that "farmers' self-investment, incl. additions to working capital, totalled 17 b. *yuan*" during 1953–57 (Nicholas R. Lardy, *Agriculture in Modern China's Development* (Cambridge: Cambridge University Press, 1983), p. 138). Annual estimates of capital construction investment in agriculture are given in National Bureau of Statistics (NBS), *Zhongguo guding zichan touzi tongji ziliao, 1950–85* (*Statistical Materials on Fixed Capital Investment in China, 1950–85*), hereafter *ZGGD* (Beijing: Tongji chubanshe, 1987), p. 97.

the central budget was not the only source of budgetary support for farming. Official NBS estimates show, for example, that during 1953–57, 735 million *yuan* were invested in the chemical fertilizer and farm machinery industries.[9]

A striking feature of Table 1 is the interruption of progress that occurred between 1957 and 1965. This was of course a reflection of the Great Leap Forward, the social and economic impact of which prompted a marked change in the thrust of China's farm policy through the reversal of sectoral investment priorities. This has sometimes been interpreted as a shift towards an "agriculture first" strategy. But if the new approach showed the CCP's concern with "the welfare of the masses,"[10] the underlying motivation was less one of altruism than of realpolitik. The fundamental imperative that the Party sought to fulfil was that of maintaining its authority in the wake of the great famine of 1959–61. What is undeniable is that from the early 1960s, not only was there a significant rise in agricultural investment itself,[11] but the allocation of *industrial* investment also favoured the farm sector by prioritizing agricultural machinery and chemical fertilizer production. Significant too was the launch of small-scale rural industrialization, which gave farmers access to low-grade, but cheap and serviceable additions to fixed and working capital.

These were important departures from previous farm policies, and although they were prompted by the exigencies of the time, it would be wrong to regard them as mere tactical expedients. As Table 1 suggests, increased availability of mechanized power, greater use of chemical fertilizers and irrigated area expansion all continued through and beyond the 1960s. However, the increased supply of fixed and working farm capital is not necessarily an accurate guide to their economic impact. Introduction of farm machinery favoured a small number of regions to the near exclusion of many others.[12] Nor was

9. I.e. 465 m *yuan* in chemical fertilizers, 270 m *yuan* in production and repair facilities for farm machinery (*ibid.* p. 103).

10. Robert F. Dernberger, "Agriculture in communist development strategy," in Randolph Barker and Radha Sinha (eds.) with Beth Rose, *The Chinese Agricultural Economy* (Boulder, CO: Westview Press, 1982), p. 74.

11. In contrast to the FFYP years, when agriculture received a mere 7.1% of aggregate capital construction investment, in 1958–62 the corresponding figure was 11.3%, and for the recovery years (1963–65) 17.6%. For the rest of the Mao period, it averaged between 10% and 11%.

12. E.g. in 1978 Hebei, Henan, Shandong and Jiangsu accounted for 34% of total agriculture machine power (NBS, *Xin Zhongguo wushi nian tongji ziliao huibian* (*Comprehensive Collection of Statistical Materials for 50 Years of New China*), hereafter *50NTJZL* (Beijing: Tongji chubanshe, 1999), p. 120), while over 37% of all large and medium-sized tractors were in Hebei, Shandong, Heilongjiang and Liaoning (NBS, *Xin Zhongguo wushi nian nongye tongji ziliao* (*New China – 50 Years of Agricultural Statistical Materials*), hereafter *50NNYZL* (Beijing: Tongji chubanshe, 2000), p. 120). Average grain yields in 1978 in these 6 provinces ranged from 22%, 20% and 18% below the corresponding national figure in Heilongjiang, Hebei and Henan, to 1%, 14% and 44% above it (Shandong, Liaoning and Jiangsu) (*50NNYZL*, p. 242). These ratios hardly point to farm mechanization's uniformly positive impact on land productivity, although estimating the relationship between farm mechanization and

farm machinery always used for agricultural production: tractors were often valued more as a means of transport than for cultivation purposes.[13] That chemical fertilizers had a significant positive impact on yields in the 1960s and 1970s is not in doubt. But at first fairly crude nitrogenous fertilizers produced in local, small-scale factories were often used as a means of securing rapid rises in yields. By contrast, insufficient attention was given to crucial long-term considerations of soil types, nutrient requirements and application techniques, and the demands of complementarity between seed varieties, water availability and agricultural chemicals. In the 1970s, the situation changed, as policy makers began to address such deficiencies, and at the end of the decade much of the sown areas of maize, wheat and – especially – rice was planted under high-yielding fertilizer-responsive seed varieties.[14] Most impressive of all and central to the gains from agricultural technical progress was the impressive expansion in irrigated area. During 1965–76, the "effectively-irrigated area" rose from 33.1 million to 45 million hectares.[15] From a longer-term perspective, this was probably the most important infrastructural legacy of developments that took place during the Mao period.[16]

It would be misleading to describe these developments as merely cosmetic. Whether they signified the implementation of a lasting "agriculture first" strategy depends on how one interprets the available evidence. From a sectoral perspective, state investment continued to be directed overwhelmingly to industry, not agriculture.

---

footnote continued

productivity is enormously complicated. On Kit Tam's study (*China's Agricultural Modernization: The Socialist Mechanization Scheme* (London: Croom Helm, 1985)) remains an essential source for anyone wishing to explore the rationale and impact of farm mechanization – especially tractorization – in China.

13. This applied even to the small "walking tractors," produced in large numbers in order to accommodate the smallness of scale of Chinese farming. The use of tractors for purposes other than ploughing may have reflected the more critical transportation bottleneck: "moving bulky manures, seeds, seedlings, harvested crops, etc. consumes more labour power than ploughing," Thomas Wiens, "Technological change," in Barker and Sinha, *The Chinese Agricultural Economy*, p. 112.

14. Over 80% of rice was sown under such varieties in 1978. Bruce Stone, "Basic agricultural technology under reform," in Y.Y. Kueh and R.F. Ash (eds.), *Economic Trends in Chinese Agriculture: The Impact of Post-Mao Reforms* (Oxford: Clarendon Press, 1993), p. 335.

15. Ministry of Agriculture, *Zhongguo nongcun jingji tongji dachuan, 1949–86* (*Compendium of Rural Economic Statistics for China, 1949–86*), hereafter *Dachuan* (Beijing: Nongye chubanshe, 1989), p. 318. In 1952 the corresponding figure was 20 m ha. "Effectively-irrigated" (*youxiao guangai*) means "level land which has water sources and complete sets of irrigation facilities to lift and move adequate water for irrigation purposes under normal conditions" (Stone, "Basic agricultural technology under reform," p. 312, Table 9.1). Reference to "normal" conditions is significant, since floods and drought frequently precipitated *abnormal* conditions. E.g. in ten out of the 15 years for which data are available between 1960 and 1976, over 30 m ha were affected by natural disasters (and 20–30 m ha in three more) (*50NNYZL*, p. 29).

16. The case is argued vigorously by Chris Bramall in his *Sources of Chinese Economic Growth, 1978–1996* (Oxford: Oxford University Press, 2000), esp. pp. 132–147.

At the same time, although the farm sector's share of such investment fell off from the level of 1958–65, and especially the record high in the immediate aftermath of the Leap (1962–65), between the mid-1960s and the end of the 1970s, it remained significantly higher than during the FFYP (1953–57).[17] In addition, the share of heavy industrial development in agriculture-support industries, such as chemical fertilizers and farm machinery, ran at record levels between 1965 and the end of the Mao period.[18]

The view that institutional constraints – inefficiencies associated with the persistence of the three-tier system of commune, production brigade and production team – were more serious than irrational sectoral allocations of state investment in undermining accelerated farm output growth is one which I share. A return to price planning, the re-opening of rural markets and, most radically, the sanctioning of contracts between individual farm households and production teams[19] were central to the rural sector's recovery, in the early 1960s, from previous famine conditions. But the retreat from core Maoist and socialist values was only temporary, and in the second half of the 1960s there was a return to the collectivist ethos and to production planning which lasted until Mao's death. That this should have occurred just as the Cultural Revolution was unfolding is not coincidental.[20] Nor is the emergence of a renewed emphasis on local and regional rural self-sufficiency, in terms of both consumption and investment, encapsulated in the Cultural Revolution's "*dazhai* model" of agricultural development.

The data in Table 2 highlight some of the strengths and weaknesses of agricultural policies during the Mao era. At the most aggregative level, they show that there was a distinct slowing in the rate of agricultural growth after 1957 that was not only the product of the disastrous Great Leap Forward – recovery had, after all, taken place by 1965 – but that continued throughout the Cultural Revolution decade (1966–76).[21] Bearing in mind that population growth continued after 1965,[22] the adverse implications of this are clear. Given the steady contraction in

17. Relevant data can be found in Ash, "The peasant and the state," *The China Quarterly*, No. 127 (1991), esp. pp. 496–502.

18. *Ibid.*

19. For evidence of these precursors of the responsibility systems of the early 1980s, see C.S. Chen and C.P. Ridley, *Rural People's Communes in Lien-Chiang: Documents Concerning Communes in Lien-chiang County, Fukien Province*, 1962–63, esp. Documents V and VI; also K.R. Walker, "Chinese agriculture during the period of readjustment, 1978–83," *The China Quarterly*, No. 100 (1984), p. 786.

20. Cf. Nicholas R. Lardy: "increased direct planning ... coincided with a sharp political shift to the left that drastically reduced rural periodic markets in most of China," *Agriculture in China's Modern Economic Development* (Cambridge: Cambridge University Press, 1983), p. 46.

21. The estimates in Table 2 indicate an average rate of GVAO increase of 5.2% p.a. (1952–57), and 2.1% p.a. (1957–76). The corresponding figure for 1965–76 is 2.8% p.a.

22. The average rate of natural increase of total population was 2.4% p.a. during 1965–76

arable area that took place after 1957,[23] a comparison of the output growth of individual products points to a mixed assessment of China's agricultural performance. On the one hand, increases in grain production were sustained by quite impressive improvements in yields, especially after 1965. On the other hand, the yield performance of cotton and oilseeds was much more disappointing; and increased output of sugar was only made possible by a major expansion in its sown area.

Another striking finding is the absence of any significant degree of economic diversification in the farm sector. In the early 1950s agriculture was dominated by grain; at the end of the 1970s, although the extent of such dominance had declined, conditions remained basically unchanged. The contrast here with post-1978 rural economic diversification is very noticeable. It reflects the role of grain as the basic wage good – a role that was underlined in the Cultural Revolution by the imperative, on geo-strategic security grounds, of local as well as national grain self-sufficiency.

But in the end, the clearest evidence of Chinese agriculture's inability to fulfil all its developmental demands is captured in trends in per capita grain production. Having peaked at 307 kilograms in 1956, average per capita grain output did not re-attain this level until 1975. Between the last three years of the FFYP (1955–57) and the last three years of Mao's life (1974–76), it increased from 302.6 to 305.5 kg, a cumulative increase of less than one percentage point. Given the heavy burden of extraction on the agricultural sector – and bearing in mind that rural food self-sufficiency in China required 275–300 kg of raw grain to be made available per head[24] – the welfare implications of the failure to achieve more rapid and sustained output growth start to become clear.

Grain Extraction and Its Impact on Farmers in China

Its extraordinarily erratic nature is one of the more arresting features of economic development in the People's Republic under the leadership of Mao Zedong. However, a constant throughout the period was the commitment to industrialization,[25] and agriculture's contribution was fundamental. The goal would be jeopardized unless

23. From 111.83 m ha (1957) to 99.39 m ha (1976) – a decline of over 11% – according to *50NNYZL*, p. 21 (though these figures take no account of the retrospective need for upward revision of arable area data, highlighted in China's First (1997) National Agricultural Census.

24. A benchmark figure at the higher end of this range is applicable to rural China throughout the Mao years. Authoritative Chinese sources (incl. Chen Yun) confirm this. See K.R. Walker, *Food Grain Procurement and Consumption in China* (Cambridge: Cambridge University Press, 1984), p. 3.

25. "The stark contrast in productivity between industry and agriculture reflects the consistent concentration of investment resources in the former over many years in search of maximum industrial growth" (Y.Y. Kueh, "China's new industrialization strategy," *The China Quarterly*, No. 119 (1989), p. 422.

an agricultural surplus[26] could be generated and made available to the government. Despite being poor, China's agriculture even before 1949 was probably capable of generating a potentially significant surplus, captured in the shares of farm output marketed and remitted as rent. Increasing that surplus was of course a major policy goal of the government after 1949. But an even greater concern was the need to secure control over the available supply of farm products (above all, grain). The importance of extraction was no doubt impressed upon Chinese leaders by the experience of the Soviet Union. Stalin's decision to launch collectivization at the end of the 1920s had, after all, been prompted by concerns about how to control grain supplies, and the movement had begun with a grain procurement campaign. It is no coincidence that the Chinese government's monopoly procurement and distribution – Central Purchase and Central Supply (*tonggou tongxiao* 统购统销) – system was introduced in November 1953 against the background of an increasingly serious grain deficit resulting from a rapid rise in demand.[27] Nor is it coincidental that Mao's advocacy, in July 1955, of accelerated co-operativization took place against the background of a loss of control over grain supplies.[28]

National Trends

The following analysis attempts to measure the procurement burden that was placed on Chinese farmers during the Mao era, and to consider its implications for their welfare, measured in terms of grain consumption.[29] Table 3 sets out estimates of grain procurement for every year between 1953 and 1976, with allowance made for re-sales to farmers. The figures are given in terms of raw grain. Table 4 shows the extraction burden (for convenience, I have averaged the figures for each sub-period, although data for each of the famine years are also shown individually).

A comparison between grain procurement in China and in the Soviet Union during their FFYPs provides a telling indication of the

26. The particular emphasis on *heavy* industrialization meant that the role of agriculture as a source of labour was less important.

27. Unwilling either to sanction a slower rate of industrial growth or to let grain prices rise, the government opted for the introduction of compulsory quotas. The *locus classicus* for consideration of the rationale of the CPCS system remains Dwight H. Perkins, *Market Control and Planning in Communist China* (Cambridge, MA: Harvard University Press, 1965).

28. The supposed benefits of co-operatives extended beyond tighter control over farm output to the ability to dictate the allocation of sown area between different crops and planting methods. The essential basis of the Marxist belief in the need to nurture a socialist agriculture through collectivization lay in the perceived benefits of the *large scale* in farm production.

29. At the low levels of per capita income that prevailed throughout the Mao period, food consumption offers the best proxy for living standards of the subsisting population. The focus on grain reflects the fact that the rural diet was dominated by the direct ingestion of grain (cereals, coarse grains [incl. potatoes] and beans).

Table 3: **Grain Production and Procurement, and Rural Grain Supplies**

	Total grain output (m tons)	Gross procurement (m tons)	Grain re-sales to farmers (m tons)	Net procurement (m tons)	Rural grain supplies (m tons)
First Five-Year Plan					
1953	166.83	47.46	11.58	35.88	130.95
1954	169.52	51.81	20.23	31.58	137.94
1955	183.94	50.75	14.57	36.18	147.76
1956	192.75	45.44	16.74	28.70	164.05
1957	195.05	48.04	14.17	33.87	161.18
Great Leap Forward					
1958	197.65	58.76	17.04	41.72	155.93
1959	169.68	67.41	19.84	47.57	122.11
1960	143.85	51.05	20.16	30.89	112.96
1961	136.50	40.47	14.67	25.80	110.70
1962	154.41	38.15	12.43	25.72	128.69
Recovery					
1963	170.00	43.97	13.34	30.63	139.37
1964	187.50	47.43	15.58	31.85	155.65
1965	194.53	48.68	15.09	33.59	160.94
Third Five-Year Plan					
1966	214.00	51.58	13.34	38.24	175.76
1967	217.82	49.36	11.62	37.74	180.08
1968	209.06	48.70	10.83	37.87	171.19
1969	210.97	46.68	12.85	33.83	177.14
1970	239.96	54.44	12.42	42.02	197.94
Fourth Five-Year Plan					
1971	250.14	53.02	13.20	39.82	210.32
1972	240.48	48.30	14.38	33.92	206.56
1973	264.94	56.12	15.12	41.00	223.94
1974	275.27	58.07	14.10	43.97	231.30
1975	284.52	60.86	16.92	43.94	240.58
1976	286.31	58.25	17.53	40.72	245.59

Source:
50NYTJZL, p. 37 (output); Ministry of Agriculture, Planning Office, *Nongye jingji ziliao, 1949–83* (*Materials on the Agricultural Economy, 1949–83*), hereafter *NYJJZL*, pp. 342–43 (procurement and re-sales). No date of publication is given in the copy of the document available to me, but it is likely to have been 1984.

heavy burden carried by Chinese farmers. Under the Soviet First Plan (1928–32), which coincided with the first great collectivization drive,[30] state procurement of grain absorbed 24.7 per cent of total production.

30. Between 1928 and 1932 the proportion of peasant households in collectives (*kolkhozy*) rose from 1.7% to 61.5%. Lynne Viola, *Peasant Rebels under Stalin: Collectivization and the Culture of Peasant Resistance* (New York & Oxford: Oxford University Press, 1996), p. 211.

Table 4: **The Burden of Grain Extraction on Chinese Farmers**

	Total grain output	Gross procurement	Grain re-sales to farmers	Net procurement	Rural grain supplies
	All output and procurement figures in m tons of raw grain. Figures in brackets show procurement and re-sales as % of total output.				
First Five-Year Plan	181.62	48.70	15.46	33.24	148.38
(1953–57 av)	(100.00)	(26.81)	(8.51)	(18.30)	(81.70)
Great Leap Forward	160.42	51.17	16.83	34.34	126.08
(1958–62 av)	(100.00)	(31.90)	(10.49)	(21.41)	(78.59)
1959	169.68	67.41	19.84	47.57	122.11
	(100.00)	(39.73)	(11.69)	(28.04)	(71.96)
1960	143.85	51.05	20.16	30.89	112.96
	(100.00)	(35.49)	(14.01)	(21.47)	(78.53)
1961	136.50	40.47	14.67	25.80	110.70
	(100.00)	(29.65)	(9.11)	(18.84)	(81.10)
Recovery years	184.01	46.69	14.67	32.02	151.99
(1963–65 av)	(100.00)	(25.38)	(7.97)	(17.40)	(82.60)
Third Five-Year Plan	218.36	50.15	12.21	37.94	180.42
(1966–79 av)	(100.00)	(22.97)	(5.59)	(17.37)	(82.63)
Fourth Five-Year Plan	263.07	55.27	14.74	40.53	222.54
(1971–75 av)	(100.00)	(21.01)	(5.60)	(15.41)	(84.59)
1976	286.31	58.25	17.53	40.72	245.59
	(100.00)	(20.35)	(6.12)	(14.22)	(85.78)

Source:
  Table 3.

The corresponding Chinese figure (26.8 per cent) was higher, despite the fact that average per capita grain output in China was more than 40 per cent lower than in the Soviet Union.[31]

With average per capita grain output not significantly above subsistence level, farm conditions in China could not sustain such a high procurement ratio. So much is clear from Table 4, which shows that, on average, more than 18 million tons a year were returned to

---

31. I estimate average per capita grain production (excl. potatoes) in 1930 in the USSR to have been about 530 kg (output from *ibid*. p. 232, Table 23; total population from Jerzy F. Karcz, *The Economics of Communist Agriculture: Selected Papers* (Bloomington: International Development Institute, 1979), p. 479). In China in 1955 – also the mid-point of its FFYP and a bumper harvest year – the corresponding figure was about 300 kg.

the rural sector in order to maintain adequate nutritional standards there. As a result, China's net procurement ratio was significantly lower than the gross ratio.[32]

The most striking feature of the two tables is the remarkable increase in the burden of extraction that occurred during the Great Leap Forward. As it happens, the procurement ratio in the USSR also rose sharply in its Second FYP period (1933–37).[33] But whereas the famine that took place in the wake of the increasing procurement burden in the USSR (especially the Ukraine) reflected a knowing wilfulness on the part of Stalin, famine conditions in China – in terms of their impact on human life, far more serious than in the Soviet Union – had their origin in misguided extraction policies based on serious misinformation about the true level of the grain harvest in 1958.[34] As shown below, raising the procurement ratio to new heights while total grain output was falling sharply was to have disastrous consequences for farmers' nutritional standards. Meanwhile, the misguided nature of such policies is also highlighted in trends in China's grain trade during these years. In 1959 and 1960, when total output had fallen by 53.8 million tons, China remained a net exporter of grain to the tune of 6.81 million tons; only in 1961 – by which time the output decline had risen to 61.2 million tons – did China revert to being a net grain importer.[35]

Reference was made above to the adoption of an "agriculture first" strategy in the early 1960s. The pragmatism inherent in this new stance of associated policies was reflected in procurement quota adjustments. Despite the food security concerns, the Cultural Revolution decade saw a small but steady decline in both gross and net grain procurement ratios. Throughout the period under consideration here, China's rural population continued to rise quite rapidly. With this in mind, Table 5 seeks to investigate the welfare implications – here defined in terms of food supplies – of the data presented in Tables 3 and 4.

On the basis of a self-sufficiency norm of 275–300 kg of raw grain per head,[36] grain production was sufficient to meet the basic requirements of the Chinese population – though barely adequately – during the periods of the First and Fourth FYPs. Between 1959 and 1970, even this most basic criterion could not be fulfilled. Except for 1960–63, however, domestic output would readily have accommodated the needs of the *rural* population throughout the period. In fact, as the figures in the final column show, only during the last few years

32. Concealed in the figures shown in Tables 3 and 4 was a complex pattern of inter-provincial grain transfers from surplus to deficit regions. This is analysed in great detail, at least for 1953–57, in Walker, *Food Grain Procurement and Consumption*, ch.
33. To 37.7% (excl. potatoes) (Viola, *Peasant Rebels Under Stalin*, p. 250, Table 27).
34. Whether or not the worst consequences of the famine would have been avoided had the confrontation between Mao and Peng Dehuai at the Lushan Conference (July 1959) not occurred is a tantalizing question.
35. In 1961 China imported 4.45 m tons (net) (see *Dachuan*, pp. 520 and 534).
36. See above, p. 9. The 300 kg figure would have been sufficient at prevailing low levels of income to provide for basic human food consumption needs, as well as leaving a small surplus for seed and livestock feed.

Table 5: **Per Capita Availability of Grain in the Rural Sector**

	Average per capita output of grain (kg)		Average potential forfeiture of grain to rural population as result of procurement (net procurement divided by rural population) (kg)	Average availability of grain after re-sales (total output less gross procurement plus re-sales) per head of rural population (kg)
	Total population	Rural population		
First-Five Year Plan				
1953	283.74	333.21	71.66	261.55
1954	281.29	332.15	61.88	270.25
1955	299.26	352.85	69.40	283.45
1956	306.79	364.88	54.33	310.55
1957	301.69	361.00	62.68	298.32
1953–57 av	294.83	349.14	63.90	285.24
Great Leap Forward				
1958	299.50	367.49	77.57	289.92
1959	252.47	316.33	88.68	227.65
1960	217.27	274.13	58.87	215.26
1961	207.26	255.41	48.27	207.13
1962	229.45	275.61	45.91	229.71
1958–62 av	241.19	297.77	63.74	234.03
Recovery				
1963	245.76	295.20	53.19	242.01
1964	265.96	318.76	54.15	264.61
1965	268.18	321.98	55.60	266.39
1963–65 av	260.14	312.19	54.30	257.86
Third-Five Year Plan				
1966	287.09	344.04	61.48	282.56
1967	285.22	341.78	59.22	282.56
1968	266.20	316.85	57.40	259.46
1969	261.52	309.03	49.55	259.48
1970	289.14	341.18	59.75	281.44
1966–70 av	277.74	330.34	57.40	272.94
Fourth Five-Year Plan				
1971	293.49	348.00	55.40	292.60
1972	275.85	326.98	46.12	280.86
1973	296.98	352.22	54.51	297.72
1974	302.96	358.52	57.27	301.25
1975	307.86	364.11	56.23	307.88
1971–75 av	295.65	350.23	53.96	296.27
1976	305.50	361.50	51.41	310.09

Sources:
    Table 4; *50NTJZL*, p.1 (total and rural population).

of Mao's life did per capita grain supplies to the rural population fulfil the 300 kg norm. From this perspective, one way of interpreting the net procurement estimates shown in the penultimate column of Table 3 would be to regard them as a crude proxy for the import gap that would have had to be filled in order to provide for the subsistence needs of the Chinese population in the absence of the CPCS system.[37]

On the basis of Piazza's study of food consumption and nutrition at the level of total population,[38] Table 6 attempts to estimate average daily energy intake for China's rural population. These are no more than proxy indicators, but they offer a sufficiently robust basis on

37. I stress the crude nature of this argument, which takes no account, for example, of food supplies available to rural households from private plots or concealed land sown under grain, or from diverting feed and seed supplies to human consumption. The implications of the decline in grain production in the aftermath of the Great Leap Forward emerge clearly from the data. It is possible, for example, to compare actual rural grain availability with the volume of grain that would have been required to provide for China's rural population:

	Projected rural grain needs (m tons)	Actual rural grain supplies (m tons)	Grain surplus (+) deficit (−) (m tons)
1958	161.35	155.93	+9.26
1959	160.92	122.11	−38.81
1960	157.43	112.96	−44.47
1961	160.33	110.70	−49.63

An even bigger gap between availability and needs would emerge if we were to project a revised population series based on average rural population growth during 1953–57 (i.e. 1.9% p.a.). Alternatively, one might compare the number of peasants that could, *ceteris paribus*, have been supported ("potential subsisting population") by the output levels of 1959–61 with the number that production in fact sought to provide for ("actual subsisting population"):

	Potential subsisting population (m)	Actual subsisting population (m)	Difference (m)
1958	658.83	537.84	120.99
1959	565.60	536.40	29.20
1960	479.50	524.76	−45.26
1961	455.00	534.44	−79.44

These estimates are purely hypothetical. But they intimate the enormity of the food security threat inherent in mismanagement of the Great Leap Forward. In the event, the apocalypse suggested in the figures did not happen, although the finding that up to 30 million excess deaths occurred during 1959–61 leaves no doubt as to the unprecedented scale of the drama that unfolded. Note too that in addition to 30 m excess deaths, declining sexual activity and the effects of "amenorrhea of hunger" (the failure to menstruate by women of childbearing age) caused a "birth deficit" of a further 30 m babies who otherwise would have been born.

38. Alan Piazza, *Food Consumption and Nutritional Status in the PRC* (Boulder, CO: Westview Press, 1986).

Table 6: **Estimated Energy Intake Among the Rural Population**

	Average rural per capita grain production (kg)	Average rural daily per capita energy intake (Kcal)	Average rural daily per capita energy requirements (Kcal)	Intake as % of requirements
First Five-Year Plan (1953–57 av)	285.24	2,119	2,092	101.3
Great Leap Forward (1958–62 av)	234.03	1,779	2,116	84.1
1959	227.65	1,668	2,111	79.0
1960	215.26	1,587	2,116	75.0
1961	207.13	1,644	2,121	77.5
Recovery (1963–65 av)	257.86	1,939	2,135	90.8
Third Five-Year Plan (1966–70 av)	272.94	2,020	2,149	94.0
Fourth Five-Year Plan (1971–75 av)	296.27	2,157	2,172	99.3
1976	310.09	2,257	2,203	102.5

Notes and Sources:
  I have estimated rural energy intake on the basis of output:energy conversion ratios derived from annual estimates in Alan Piazza, *Food Consumption and Nutritional Status in the PRC* (Boulder, CO: Westview Press, 1986), p. 77, Table 4.3. Energy requirements are those shown by *ibid*. p. 92, Table 4.8. Rural per capita grain production from Table 5.

which to draw two conclusions. The first is to reinforce the severity of the rural food crisis in the wake of the Great Leap Forward. The second is to highlight the closeness to the margin of subsistence in which Chinese peasants lived throughout the Mao era. Viewed from the national level, not only was there no appreciable improvement in food consumption during the period, but only in its final years did standards re-attain the level of the FFYP years.[39]

Regional Trends

  A shortcoming of the foregoing analysis is that it takes no account of regional variations in rural conditions. The need to consider the 27 provinces "proper"[40] makes a detailed analysis of provincial trends in grain output, extraction and rural consumption impossible within this short section. Nevertheless, the estimates presented here are derived

39. In physical terms, only in the very year of Mao's death (1976) did per capita grain supplies to the rural population finally re-attain the previous peak level of 1956. But per capita energy supplies in 1976 were probably still lower than in 1956.
  40. I.e. excluding the three municipalities with provincial-level status (Beijing, Tianjin and Shanghai). Data for Tibet are also excluded. In referring to "provinces" I also mean to include the autonomous regions.

from an exhaustive statistical analysis of the total and per capita output, procurement (gross and net) and residual agricultural supply of grain in every province for every year between 1953 and 1976.[41]

The egalitarian thrust of the Maoist development strategy did not prevent the persistence of wide inter and intra-regional differences in rural economic and welfare conditions. Widely differing inter-regional levels of population and farm productivity dictated the need for a complex nexus of grain transfers between surplus and deficit provinces, which was reflected in major differences in provincial net procurement ratios. Such differences were, however, far from stable, causing the regional profile of grain transfers to change quite significantly during the Mao era.

Table A1 in Appendix A sets out comprehensive time-series data relating to total output, net procurement and residual supplies of grain available to the farm population in every province of China between 1953 and 1975. From these figures I have derived summary estimates for each of seven regions, shown in Table 7. A common, although not universally consistent, pattern emerges from these figures (see Figure 1). Throughout the Mao era, the highest rate of extraction was in the north-east, a reflection of large surpluses produced by Heilongjiang and, at least until the mid-1960s, Jilin. More surprising is the finding that in the 1950s, the second-highest rate of extraction was in the north-west, an inherently poor agricultural region, albeit one with a small population. This did not, however, persist, and by the second half of the 1970s, the net procurement rate had fallen below that of every other region. What also emerges is that by the end of Mao's life, in virtually every region the rate was lower than it had been in the 1950s and early 1960s. This reflects China's change of status from a net grain exporter to a net importer in and after 1960 in the wake of the food crisis precipitated by the Great Leap Forward. Allowing urban food needs – above all, those of Beijing, Tianjin and Shanghai (which accounted for 12.6 per cent of China's urban population in 1957) – to be met from overseas suppliers significantly eased the procurement burden on farmers and left them with larger amounts for subsistence, feed and seed. I return to the impact of the Leap on rural living standards below.

Changes in the *rate* of extraction assume meaning only when they are related to changes in output that have meanwhile occurred. That is, depending on whether total grain output has risen or fallen, a decline in the net procurement rate may generate a greater or smaller transfer of grain, in absolute terms. This is highly relevant to China's

---

41. For valuable insights into inter-provincial grain flows, see also Walker, *Food Procurement and Consumption in China*; and Thomas P. Lyons, *Economic Integration and Planning in Maoist China* (New York: Columbia University Press, 1987). A remarkable provincial analysis of the implications for food consumption of the Great Leap Forward is given by Walker in "Food and mortality in China during the Great Leap Forward."

Table 7: **Total Output, Net Procurement Rate and Residual Supplies of Grain Available to Peasants: A Regional Perspective**

	Total output of grain (raw weight in m tonnes)					Net procurement rate (%)					Residual supplies available to peasants (raw weight in m tonnes)				
	53–57	58–62	63–65	66–70	71–75	53–57	58–62	63–65	66–70	71–75	53–57	58–62	63–65	66–70	71–75
North	35.21	29.96	34.48	43.70	55.40	12.10	15.79	–	10.76	12.17	30.95	25.23	–	39.00	48.66
North-east	18.76	16.24	18.68	24.02	28.72	28.89	35.28	27.84	33.26	28.24	3.34	10.51	13.48	16.03	20.61
North-west	14.39	13.62	15.93	17.59	21.03	24.53	25.18	19.33	13.93	11.89	10.86	10.19	12.85	15.14	18.53
Centre	25.44	24.64	28.63	33.28	41.20	17.14	20.33	17.67	16.11	14.39	21.08	19.63	23.57	27.92	35.27
East	27.77	24.22	29.88	36.48	45.65	17.39	19.69	17.57	16.61	14.06	22.94	19.45	24.63	30.42	39.23
South	14.54	13.14	16.18	18.27	21.92	18.57	20.55	24.91	20.25	16.65	11.84	9.92	12.15	14.57	18.27
South-west	35.65	29.87	34.52	40.08	47.94	19.72	21.73	15.59	15.09	12.56	28.62	23.38	29.14	34.03	41.92

Sources:

See Appendix A, Table A1. Regional classification – north: Henan, Hebei, Shanxi, Shandong (Beijing and Tianjin excluded); north-east: Heilongjiang, Jilin, Liaoning; north-west: Inner Mongolia, Gansu, Ningxia, Shaanxi, Xinjiang, Qinghai; centre: Hunan, Hubei, Jiangxi; east: Anhui, Zhejiang, Jiangsu (Shanghai excluded); south: Fujian, Guangdong; south-west: Guizhou, Sichuan, Yunnan, Guangxi.

Figure 1: **Net Procurement Rates**

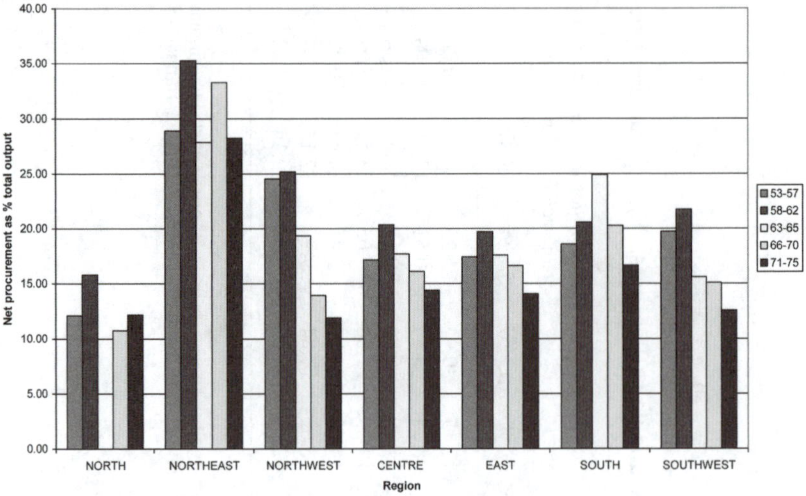

experience under planning, estimates of absolute levels of procurement showing that with two exceptions – in the south and south-west – by the first half of the 1970s, despite a fall in the net extraction rate, the amount of grain released through procurement by each region was greater than it had been in the 1950s and early 1960s.

It is a truism that the Great Leap Forward marked a watershed in China's economic performance and policy formulation, especially in regard to the agricultural sector. The trauma of the Leap is suggested in the sharp rise in both the rate and level of grain extraction that occurred after 1958 against the background of what was initially thought to have been a doubling of output in 1958. In fact, total production of grain rose only marginally in this year: the precise increase is still a matter for debate.[42] Worse, in the three years that followed (1961–63), while grain output fell by 61.15 m tonnes – a decline of over 30 per cent – the rate of net procurement increased to an unprecedented level in almost every province (see Table 8).

Throughout the Mao era, levels of grain consumption among farmers were determined by three main factors: output growth, net procurement and population growth. It is beyond the scope of this article to consider the separate effect on consumption of each of these factors. But as a preliminary to that exercise, I have converted the aggregate data shown in Table A1 (Appendix) to estimates of average output and availability, after procurement, per head of farm

42. The most recent time-series data available to me show national grain output to have risen by a mere 1.3% in 1958 (from 195.045 m tones to 197.65 m tonnes). See NBS, Department of Comprehensive Statistics, *Xin Zhongguo wushiwu nian tongji ziliao huibian* (*China Compendium of Statistics, 1949–2004*) (Beijing: Tongji chubanshe, 2005), p. 45.

Table 8: **The Impact of the Leap on Net Procurement Rates**

	Net procurement rate (%), 1953–57	Net procurement rate (%), 1959–61
Henan	13.28	13.10
Hebei	3.60	20.55
Shanxi	19.58	21.63
Shandong	15.09	16.07
Inner Mongolia	35.70	35.53
Gansu	20.47	20.96
Ningxia	21.34	26.42
Shaanxi	19.20	22.87
Xinjiang	24.23	25.92
Qinghai	20.42	24.40
Heilongjiang	39.62	28.45
Jilin	34.76	44.08
Liaoning	11.35	20.90
Hunan	13.79	18.66
Hubei	16.09	19.47
Jiangxi	24.23	30.25
Anhui	18.41	19.47
Zhejiang	17.99	22.16
Jiangsu	16.32	20.94
Fujian	20.55	28.66
Guangdong	17.76	26.75
Guizhou	17.08	20.92
Sichuan	23.00	27.70
Yunnan	17.33	19.57
Guangxi	12.75	18.20

Source:
  NYJJZL, pp. 354–407.

population in each province (provincial details are in Table A2). The regional findings in Table 9 are derived from these provincial figures. In interpreting these figures, it should be borne in mind that in the economic circumstances of the early Mao years, 275 kilograms of raw grain provided a reasonable level of self-sufficiency among Chinese farmers.[43] The left-hand side of the table reveals that except in the north, per capita output throughout the period was sufficient to meet this benchmark, and even to generate a surplus above subsistence needs (see also Figure 2). By contrast, as shown in Figure 3, the data to the right indicate that until the second half of the 1960s (and in the north and south-west even later) rural per capita availability was often

---

43. Walker's own chosen definition of grain self-sufficiency fell within a range of 275–309 kg (see *Food Grain Procurement and Consumption*, p. 3.) Note that he cites a 1955 speech by Chen Yun to the effect that 280 kg offered "sufficient" supplies to meet personal consumption, feed and seed needs (*ibid.*).

Table 9: **Output and Availability of Grain per Head of Farm Population by Region**

	Output of grain per head of agricultural population (raw weight in kg)					Availability of grain per head of agricultural population (raw weight in kg)				
	53–57	58–62	63–65	66–70	71–75	53–57	58–62	63–65	66–70	71–75
North	258.84	213.76	227.82	262.98	303.40	227.52	180.01	161.48	234.70	266.48
North-east	584.61	469.91	455.94	519.91	534.72	415.71	304.11	329.02	346.97	383.73
North-west	367.65	317.19	330.02	322.34	334.77	277.47	237.31	266.21	277.44	294.97
Centre	353.82	330.25	351.46	362.09	396.00	293.18	263.10	289.34	303.78	339.00
East	332.57	287.72	324.96	351.51	387.88	274.73	231.05	267.86	293.12	333.33
South	382.43	324.68	357.57	357.81	375.41	311.42	245.12	268.51	285.35	312.90
South-west	326.44	277.58	297.87	304.47	313.44	262.06	217.27	251.45	258.51	274.08

Sources:
As Table 7.

Figure 2: **Average Grain Output per Head of Farm Population: A Regional Perspective**

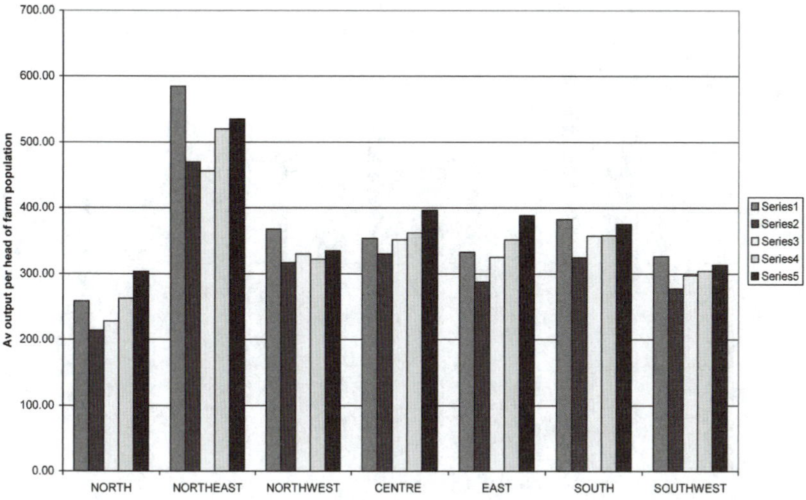

unable to meet even basic subsistence requirements. As far as I know, there is no evidence that the Chinese leadership deliberately targeted farmers in the way in which the government under Stalin did during the Soviet collectivization campaigns.[44] In the USSR, re-sales to the farm sector were unknown,[45] and what saved many peasants from starvation in the mid-1930s was the produce available from their private plots. In China, grain re-sales to farmers were their salvation – something that can easily be demonstrated by subtracting rural re-sales from the provincial and regional estimates of total supplies shown in Table A1. In the absence of transfers back to the villages, hunger and starvation would have been more common occurrences in many parts of China before and after the great famine of 1959–61.[46]

Nevertheless, the findings presented here do suggest that quite widespread rural impoverishment was one of the effects of the central

44. E.g. I do not think that the simple statement that "peasant terror derived from and was conditioned by state terror," which captures the reality of conditions in the Soviet countryside in the late 1920s and early 1930s, can be applied to conditions in China. The quotation is Lynne Viola's: see *Peasant Rebels under Stalin*, p. 130.

45. In 1941 (the first full year of war against Germany), slightly less than 5% of compulsory deliveries and payments in kind to Machine Tractor Stations were held as food reserves and welfare supplies for orphans, invalids, etc. (*ibid.* p. 286). I am grateful to Colin White for his insights into the impact of collectivization on rural consumption in the Soviet Union.

46. Unfortunately, the tyranny of the word limit makes it impossible to consider, in detail, the implications for rural consumption of the Great Leap Forward. The estimates shown in Tables A1 and A2 are eloquent testimony to the enormity of the food crisis that faced the rural sector during 1959–61. E.g. it is no coincidence that the rural population of the south-west should have shown an absolute decline between 1953–57 and 1958–62 – a reflection of the catastrophic famine in Sichuan, where some 5 m "excess deaths" are thought to have occurred.

Figure 3: **Average Grain Availability Per Head of Farm Population: A Regional Perspective**

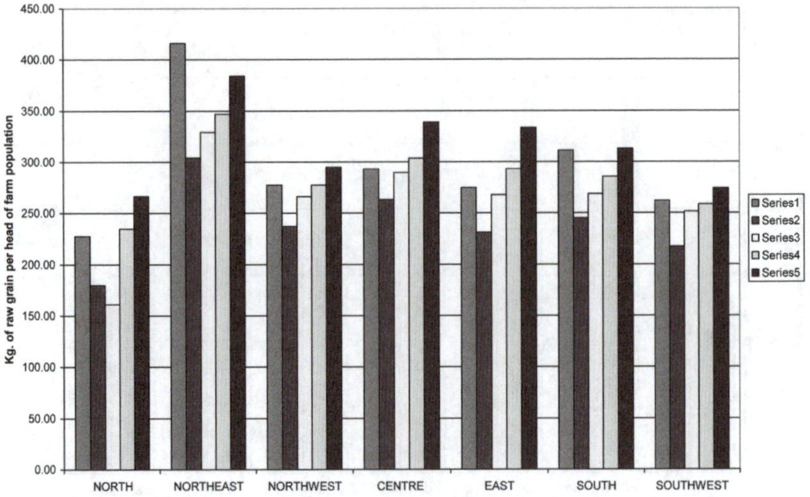

government's extractive policies – and by implication of the economic strategy of which these policies were a part.[47] It is difficult to know to what extent below-subsistence average per capita grain availability actually resulted in malnourishment. The more likely immediate consequence was to reduce feed to draught animals in order to provide more for human consumption. In addition, as in the USSR, private plots were an important source of supplementary energy.[48]

There is a policy inference too to be drawn. Throughout the Mao era, Beijing sought to implement a forced industrialization strategy, one that placed the highest premium on maximizing heavy industrial growth. In this, agriculture had a vital facilitating role to play: most directly through the provision of cheap food (grain) for the growing urban proletariat. In fulfilling this role without recourse to overseas purchases of grain, at least until 1961 when China reverted to being a net grain importer, the farm sector minimized its claims on scarce foreign exchange. In the absence of significant farm modernization, it also minimized its claims on central budgetary funds, thereby maximizing industry's investment capacity. The achievement was in many ways a remarkable one, not least when compared with the much

47. Until the mid-1960s, the only region that enjoyed average per capita grain supplies that were comfortably in excess of subsistence was the north-east (though one or two provinces in other regions occasionally also exceeded this basic level). Interestingly, the population growth in the north-east greatly outstripped that of all other regions between 1963–65 and 1958–62: could this have reflected the desirability of the region as a refuge for hungry migrants from northern provinces?

48. In interpreting the figures in Tables 9 and A2, note that "200 kg of unhusked grain, after provision for seed and some livestock feed, could provide 1,200–1,400 calories, depending on the type of grain …" (Walker, *Food Grain Procurement and Consumption*, p. 3).

greater violence and rural dislocation that had accompanied the implementation of a similar strategy in the Soviet Union. But it was not without its cost, captured most eloquently in the stagnation of farm consumption and welfare. Even allowing for increased rural grain availability, at the end of Mao's life food consumption for most farmers remained within the subsistence range. The scale of rural impoverishment that characterized China during the Mao era was ultimately unsustainable, and the failure to generate more significant improvements in farmers' living standards was an important driver of the first rural reforms of the Deng era.

Table A1 shows that the regional estimates conceal wide inter-provincial variations in rural grain output and consumption. No less important are intra-provincial differences; after all, many Chinese provinces have populations to rival those of large European countries. From this perspective, the publication since the 1990s of grain "gazetteers" is an important development that has made available detailed statistical data and other information relating to grain production, procurement and distribution at county level throughout China. A few examples from these sources highlight some of the micro-level regional variations in rural living conditions associated with different net procurement burdens.

Table 10 provides indicators of per capita grain availability[49] in seven counties in five Chinese provinces during the Mao era. They include counties in northern, eastern, southern and south-western regions, but given that there were more than 2,000 counties in China at the end of the 1970s, it would be silly to claim that they constitute a representative sample. What is perhaps most striking is the commonality of experience which they display (incidentally confirming the picture shown in the national figures presented earlier).

The estimates in Table 10 highlight the dramatic impact of the events of the Great Leap Forward and its immediate aftermath (1958–62) on China's peasants. Despite the government's imposition of tight control over grain, re-sales to the countryside through the CPCS system guaranteed adequate supplies to the rural population. Indeed, for many peasants 1956 marked an historic high point in grain consumption. But the collapse of the statistical system in 1958 presaged three years in which a savage deterioration in China's rural food security precipitated terrible famine in the countryside. Table 10 underlines the strong regional dimension of famine conditions in 1959–61, as well as differences in the chronology of the famine. Among the seven counties, average grain availability in 1961 ranged from 134 kg in Pucheng (Fujian) to 254 kg in Fangcheng (Henan), a gap wide enough to embrace severe famine in one case and adequate

---

49. Great care must be taken in interpreting these figures. E.g. they take no account of grain produced on farm households' private plots (although this is unlikely to have been significant in the 1950s when official policy sought to prevent farmers from growing grain on their plots). Nor can I be sure that every estimate shown is given in terms of raw, as opposed to trade, grain.

Table 10: Per Capita Grain Availability in Seven Counties in China

Average per capita grain supplies in each of the following counties (kg)

	Guanyun 灌云 (Jiangsu)	Haining 海宁 (Zhejiang)	Leqing 乐清 (Zhejiang)	Pucheng 浦城 (Fujian)	Fangcheng 方城 (Henan)	Nanyang 南阳 (Henan)	Yuanjiang 元江 (Yunnan)
1949	–	192.5	–	–	–	–	234
1950	–	190.0	–	–	–	–	218.5
1951	–	238.5	–	–	–	–	209.5
1952	–	230.5	–	–	–	–	198
1949–52 av	–	212.9	–	–	–	–	215.0
1953	240.4	220.5	–	283.0	316.0	256.0	205
1954	241.6	237.0	–	353.0	409.0	302.0	225.5
1955	236.9	278.0	263.0	318.0	455.0	303.0	233
1956	255.2	293.5	–	314.0	397.0	311.0	281.5
1957	244.2	244.5	260.0	260.0	337.0	253.0	250.5
1953–57 av	243.66	254.7	261.5 *	305.6	382.8	285.0	239.1
1958	261	284.0	221.0	277.0	328.0	222.0	228
1959	212.9	264.0	188.0	179.0	217.0	199.0	188.5
1960	199.7	191.0	195.0	134.0	254.0	176.0	193.5
1961	189.6	238.5	186.0	214.0	215.0	178.0	176
1962	176.1	280.0	191.0	252.0	308.0	218.0	236
1958–62 av	207	251.5	196.2	211.2	264.4	198.6	204.4
1963	169	266.0	236.0	289.0	297.0	224.0	223.5
1964	214.2	264.5	241.0	303.0	310.0	229.0	255
1965	261.1	260.5	234.0	312.0	344.0	254.0	297.5
1963–65 av	214.5	263.7	237.0	301.3	317.0	235.7	258.7

Table 10: (Continued)

Average per capita grain supplies in each of the following counties (kg)

	Guanyun 灌云 (Jiangsu)	Haining 海宁 (Zhejiang)	Leqing 乐清 (Zhejiang)	Pucheng 浦城 (Fujian)	Fangcheng 方城 (Henan)	Nanyang 南阳 (Henan)	Yuanjiang 元江 (Yunnan)
1966	279.2	297.5	247.0	240.0	392.0	209.0	301
1967	266.4	275.5	223.0	289.0	269.0	231.0	305
1968	269.2	270.0	212.0	197.0	301.0	231.0	264.5
1969	265.3	275.0	211.0	231.0	280.0	192.0	269
1970	258.6	272.0	261.0	318.0	298.0	228.0	301
1966–70 av	270.4	278.0	230.8	255.0	308.0	218.2	288.1
1971	288	271.0	250.0	268.0	333.0	262.0	290
1972	276.2	292.0	312.0	294.0	331.0	255.0	314
1973	300.2	284.5	216.0	291.0	348.0	264.0	301
1974	298.2	271.0	208.0	322.0	315.0	237.0	302.5
1975	296.7	252.5	194.0	328.0	337.0	288.0	292
1971–75 av	291.2	274.2	236.0	300.6	332.8	261.2	299.9
1976	314.5	285.5	195.0	283.0	384.0	293.0	289.5

Note:

* Average for 1955 and 1957 only.

Sources:

The figures are calculated, or cited directly, from – Guanyun: *Guanyun xian liangshi zhi (Grain Gazetteer for Guanyun County)* (Nanjing: Jiangsu kexue jishu chubanshe, 1993), pp. 107–09; Haining: *Haining liang you zhi (Grain and Edible Oil Gazetteer for Haining County)* (Hangzhou: Zhejiang renmin chubanshe, 1991), pp. 62–63; Leqing: *Leqing xian liangshi zhi (Grain Gazetteer for Leqing County)* (Beijing: Zhongguo guoji guangbo chubanshe, 1991), pp. 49–50; Pucheng: *Pucheng xian liangshi zhi (Grain Gazetteer for Pucheng County)* (Zhengzhou: Zhongzhou guji chubanshe), 1992, p. 111; Nanyang: *Nanyang xian liangshi zhi (Grain Gazetteer for Nanyang County)* (Zhengzhou: Zhongzhou guji chubanshe, 1991), pp. 77–78; Yuanjiang: *Yuanjiang Hanizu Yizu Daizu zizhixian liangshi zhi (Grain Gazetteer for the Autonomously-Administered County of Yuanjiang Minority Peoples)* (Kunming: Yunnan renmin chubanshe, 1994), pp. 45–47.

food supplies in the other. It also emerges that for some, the worst point of famine occurred in 1960, whereas for others it was in 1961.[50] It is also interesting that for the two counties – Haining (Zhejiang) and Yuanjiang (Yunnan) – in which such data are available, per capita grain supplies during the Great Leap Forward fell significantly below the level of 1949.

The county estimates throw into sharp relief the tragedy that unfolded in the Chinese countryside at the end of the 1950s and beginning of the 1960s. In Fushun in Sichuan – the worst affected of all Chinese provinces[51] – sweet potatoes made up 30–50 per cent of grain supplies, while the monthly supply of fine grains (rice and/or wheat) to babies less than 12 months old was reduced to a mere 1.5 kg.[52] As conditions deteriorated, not only did net outflows of grain from previous surplus regions cease but national reserves were also depleted. In the first half of 1960, procurement targets from major commercial grain bases in Heilongjiang, Jilin and Sichuan were only half fulfilled; in the second half of the year supplies dried up altogether. As a result, large amounts of grain had to be sent from the state granaries to deficit regions. Within a 12-month period from the end of June 1959, central reserves fell from 17.15 million tons to 6.35 million tons.[53] After 1958 grain supplies for draught animals inevitably also declined. In Guanyun (灌云) in North Jiangsu, as feed grain was reallocated to human consumption, supplies fell from 4,130 tons in 1958 to 2,080 tons in 1959 – and to a mere 440 tons in 1960.[54] The impact of the decline on animals' health and survival capacity was profound.

Thanks to a revision of policy priorities, after 1961 recovery was quite rapid, although in five of the seven counties average per capita grain supplies in 1963–65 remained below the corresponding FFYP level. Thereafter, for farmers at least, the impact of the Cultural Revolution on consumption was nowhere near as serious as that of the Leap. That said, the evidence of county-level data confirms the finding of Table 5 that the Cultural Revolution's most radical and economically disruptive phase (1967–69) coincided with a renewed, albeit relatively small and short-lived, decline in rural grain availability. But although the trend growth of average per capita

50. In Guanyun the worst point was apparently reached in 1962. It would be interesting to know to what extent this experience was repeated elsewhere (i.e. beyond North Jiangsu).

51. Walker estimated that 5.952 m excess deaths occurred in Sichuan during 1959–61 ("Food and mortality," p. 109, Table 3.1).

52. Fushun County Grain Bureau, *Fushun xian liangshi ju zhi* (*Grain Bureau Gazetteer for Fushun County*) (n.p., 1988), p. 91.

53. Chu Han, *Zhongguo 1959–1961: Sannian ziran zaihai* (*China 1959–1961: Three Years of Natural Disasters*) (Chengdu: Sichuan renmin chubanshe, 1996), p. 72. The same source notes that the dislocation of normal distribution practices bringing some large cities close to exhaustion of grain supplies for their urban populations.

54. *Guanyun xian liangshi zhi* (*Grain Gazetteer for Guanyun County*) (Nanjing: Jiangsu kexue jishu chubanshe, 1993), p. 107. Each of the counties illustrated in Table 7 experienced a sharp contraction in feed supplies between 1959 and 1961.

grain supplies was positive during the Fourth FYP period (1971–75), by the last year of Mao's life (1976) the previous peak level of grain availability had been re-attained in only three counties.

Rural Diet, Income and Consumption Spending

The most detailed source of information on rural income during the Mao period and under the impact of the early reforms is contained in the statistical survey compiled and published by the Planning Office of the Ministry of Agriculture, mentioned above,[55] which provides a valuable overview of the allocation of collective income among various uses during 1956–65 and from 1970 onwards. Table 11 reproduces the relevant data. The figures show that the share of net income (minus taxes) directed to collective farm investment via the public accumulation fund rose from 4.5 per cent in 1956 – the year in which fully-socialist collectivization took place – to an astonishing 15.5 per cent in 1959. In the aftermath of the Leap, both tax and internally generated investment were curtailed, as a result of which in 1965 the public accumulation fund's income, net of tax payments, had fallen to 9 per cent. Subsequently, its burden once again increased, and in 1976 it was just over 11 per cent of net income (less taxes). By contrast, the share of the public *welfare* fund was much more stable and never exceeded 3 per cent of net income. More meaningfully, however, average per capita funding availability out of the public welfare fund was minimal, rising from 0.4 *yuan* (1956) to a peak of 2.2 *yuan* in 1975. Most striking of all are the figures in the final column, which highlight the very slow growth of per capita cash income: by 1.7 per cent per annum between 1956 and 1976.[56]

I have already drawn attention to the downturn in agricultural growth that took place after 1958 and, more interesting, the persistence of this trend *after 1965*. The likelihood that this reflected the Cultural Revolution imperative of grain self-sufficiency seems to be borne out in the finding (see Table 2) that in contrast to an agricultural growth rate of 2.8 per cent per annum between 1965 and 1976 – and a mere 2.6 per cent for the cropping sector as a whole – total *grain* production grew by almost 3.6 per cent a year. Underlying this quite buoyant growth were steady improvements in average grain yields: from 1,626 kg per hectare (1965) to 2,012 kg (1970) and an average 2,332 kg (1974–76). During the same period, the sown area under grain expanded much less. In short, the increase in output was carried more by higher yields – a much more secure basis for output growth in a land-scarce country like China – than by area extension. At the same time, however, the expansion of inappropriate triple-cropping of grain entailed significant economic and welfare costs in some regions.[57]

55. *Nongye jingji ziliao 1949–1983.*
56. But by 2.3% p.a., comparing 1956–58 with 1974–76.
57. Cf. Lardy, *Agriculture in China's Modern Economic Development*, p. 83.

Table 11: **Income, Expenditure and Accumulation in Collectives**

	Gross income (m yuan)	Expenditure Total (m yuan)	(of which, production spending) (m yuan)	Net income (m yuan)	State tax (m yuan)	Collective retained income Public accumulation fund (m yuan)	Public welfare fund (m yuan)	Income for distribution Income for distribution to collective members Total (m yuan)	Per capita (yuan)	(of which, cash income distributed to collective members) Total (m yuan)	Per capita (yuan)
1956	34,390	7,870	(7,700)	26,520	3,380	1,030	210	21,900	43.01	(5,407)	(10.62)
1957	36,752	9,728	(9,235)	27,024	3,617	1,802	457	21,148	40.54	(5,216)	(10.00)
1958	41,020	10,930	(10,460)	30,090	3,900	4,060	620	21,450	41.39	(5,296)	(10.22)
1959	38,400	10,280	(9,560)	28,120	3,840	3,960	690	19,470	37.60	(4,867)	(9.40)
1960	36,770	10,650	(9,930)	26,120	3,640	1,100	370	20,860	41.25	(5,146)	(10.18)
1961	41,230	11,010	(10,100)	30,220	2,640	1,730	820	24,780	48.12	(6,170)	(11.98)
1962	42,330	11,960	(10,960)	30,370	2,750	1,870	610	24,860	46.06	(6,091)	(11.29)
1963	44,050	12,470	(11,570)	(31,580)	2,880	2,270	670	25,610	46.16	(6,323)	(11.40)
1964	48,960	14,140	(13,330)	(34,820)	3,320	3,500	830	26,930	47.52	(6,622)	(11.69)
1965	53,166	14,977	(13,320)	(38,189)	2,980	3,492	758	30,460	52.28	(7,724)	(13.26)
1966	—	—	—	—	—	—	—	—	—	—	—
1967	—	—	—	—	—	—	—	—	—	—	—
1968	—	—	—	—	—	—	—	—	—	—	—
1969	—	—	—	—	—	—	—	—	—	—	—
1970	72,726	22,415	(20,319)	50,311)	3,292	4,757	1,228	39,903	59.47	(10,027)	(14.94)
1971	77,874	23,469	(21,243)	54,405	3,456	4,554	1,321	43,557	62.94	(10,088)	(14.58)

Table 11: **(Continued)**

	Gross income (m yuan)	Expenditure		Net income (m yuan)	State tax (m yuan)	Collective retained income		Income for distribution			
		Total (m yuan)	(of which, production spending) (m yuan)			Public accumulation fund (m yuan)	Public welfare fund (m yuan)	Income for distribution to collective members		(of which, cash income distributed to collective members)	
								Total (m yuan)	Per capita (yuan)	Total (m yuan)	Per capita (yuan)
1972	79,655	25,546	(23,959)	54,109	3,521	4,610	1,262	43,767	61.77	(11,128)	(15.71)
1973	86,381	27,035	(25,470)	59,346	3,701	5,642	1,423	47,340	65.36	(12,064)	(16.66)
1974	90,933	29,299	(27,414)	61,636	3,748	6,421	1,531	48,744	65.76	(12,326)	(16.63)
1975	92,451	31,073	(28,871)	61,378	3,712	6,918	1,630	47,591	63.22	(11,509)	(15.29)
1976	97,593	33,413	(30,767)	61,005	3,673	6,444	1,587	47,891	62.80	(11,652)	(14.88)

Source:
NYJJZL 1949–83, pp. 510–11.

In the end, however, the most serious cost of the Cultural Revolution in the countryside was the failure to follow the dictates of the principle of comparative advantage in order to reverse the previous stagnation of farm incomes and rural living standards.[58] Tables 12 and 13 seek to capture changes in material living standards by comparing average annual consumption by rural (*xiangcun* 乡村) residents of major farm products in 1955–57, 1963–65 and 1974–76. The corresponding figures for the urban population are also included for comparative purposes, as are those for 1981–83 in order to show the effect of early post-1978 rural reforms.

During the last three years of Mao's life, farmers' access to most basic items not only was less than during the second half of the FFYP – almost 20 years earlier – but had also fallen further behind that of their urban counterparts. In short, inter-sectoral differentials had widened. In addition, the estimates of grain consumption conceal a *qualitative* deterioration in the rural diet. By the end of the Mao period, peasants were consuming fewer fine grains (rice and wheat) and more coarse grains (including potatoes) than they had 20 years previously.[59]

The estimates in Table 12 demonstrate the dramatic effect of early post-1978 rural reforms. By the beginning of the 1980s, rural grain consumption per head had risen to a record level, had overtaken that of the urban sector and was characterized by a much higher intake of fine grains.[60] Consumption of edible oil, meat and poultry, eggs, sugar and alcohol also increased sharply.[61] The same picture – one of stagnation or decline between the 1950s and late 1970s but of major improvements in the wake of the first rural reforms – is shown in analysis of the structure of farm consumption spending (Table 13).

Although relevant data are not available for 1976, it is clear that in the final year of Mao's life, the pattern of consumption expenditure among the rural population was almost exactly the same as it had been in the mid-1950s and mid-1960s. Consumption spending was overwhelmingly directed towards food (which accounted for over two-thirds of total spending) and other essentials, such as clothing and fuel. When expenditure on housing was deducted, the balance left to purchase other items was minimal. By the early 1980s, the situation had already changed significantly, with food accounting for less than 60 per cent of spending and a major boom in housing under way.

58. E.g., see Liu Suinian and Wu Qungan (eds.), *"Wenhua da geming" shiqi de guomin jingji* (*The National Economy during the period of the "Cultural Revolution"*) (Harbin: Heilongjiang renmin chubanshe, 1986), who refer to grain cultivation being forced on cotton and vegetable farmers (p. 38). Incomes from cotton and vegetables were significantly higher than from grain cultivation (traditionally, the lowest-return farm activity).

59. *NYJJZL*, pp. 548–49. The shift towards potatoes reflected their high energy yields per unit area.

60. Between 1978 and 1983, average per capita consumption of rice and wheat rose from 245.01 kg to 392.51 kg while consumption of coarse grains fell from 250.65 kg to 127.3 kg (*NYJJZL*, p. 549).

61. *Ibid.*

Table 12: **Changes in Consumption in Urban and Rural China**

| | Average per capita consumption per annum | | | | |
	Food grains (kg)	Vegetable oil (kg)	Sugar (kg)	Pork (kg)	Cotton cloth ("feet"*)
China					
1953–57	404	4.8	2.9	9.8	22.3
1963–65	353	2.8	2.9	10.8	15.4
1974–76	379	3.4	4.5	14.6	23.3
1981–83	451	7.0	8.5	23.5	30.6
Urban					
1953–57	407	10.3	7.3	18.0	38.7
1964–65	400	7.7	7.0	19.6	29.5
1974–76	417	9.1	11.5	29.1	46.2
1981–83	436	16.6	64.7	35.1	46.9
Rural					
1953–57	403	3.8	2.1	8.3	19.5
1963–65	343	1.8	2.1	9.0	12.5
1974–76	372	2.2	3.2	11.8	18.9
1981–83	455	4.7	6.3	20.8	26.9

Note:
* That is, *chi*.
Source:
    NYJJZL, *1949–83*, pp. 538–542.

Table 13: **The Changing Structure of Rural Consumption Spending in China**

| | Share of rural consumption spending allocated to each category (%) | | | | | |
| | Material consumption | | | | | "Cultural" and other services |
	Food	Clothing	Fuel	Housing	Daily articles	
1954	68.59	13.08	6.58	2.06	6.97	2.72
1957	65.75	13.44	10.04	2.10	6.94	1.73
1965	68.46	10.51	8.31	2.83	7.18	2.71
1978	67.71	12.70	7.14	3.16	6.57	2.72
1983	59.30	11.13	5.43	11.10	10.83	2.21

Source:
    NYJJZL, *1949–83*, pp. 544–46.

Conclusion

Two comparative perspectives highlight the deficiencies of Chinese agricultural policy during the Mao era. One is provided by China's agricultural record under the impact of the post-1978 reforms, especially in the early 1980s. Another is offered by the experience of agricultural development in Taiwan between the 1950s and 1970s.

Between 1928 and 1937, the economic policy options available to the Kuomintang (KMT) government on the mainland were largely determined by the nature of the base from which it derived its political support. The same can be said of the Chinese Communist Party, which relied heavily on poor tenants and landless farm workers to maintain its position in parts of rural China. This alliance was congruent with the Communist Party's ideological roots in a sense in which the KMT's reliance on landowners in the countryside was not.[62] In any case, the KMT's commitment to redistributing land ownership rights and promoting farm modernization was largely formulaic. This proved to be a critical weakness, one that was exacerbated by the remoteness of senior KMT officials from the reality of socio-economic conditions in rural China. With the benefit of hindsight, the social and political consequences of the KMT government's failure to address land problems were incalculable.

The contrast between the KMT's agricultural record in China during the Nanking decade and in Taiwan between the 1950s and 1970s is an extraordinary one. In Taiwan, the implementation of a policy package that, allowing for interim agronomic and technological advances, was essentially the same as had been advocated – but never implemented – some 20 years previously, had a markedly positive and lasting impact on agricultural output and productivity growth, as well as on farmers' living standards.

But no less remarkable is the contrast on the mainland between the economic impact of the mainly one-dimensional emphasis on institutional change – that is, farm collectivization – that characterized Mao's approach to agricultural policy, and that of a more pragmatic attitude towards agricultural development that was evident after 1978. Inherent in post-1978 policies was an explicit awareness of the urgent need to raise consumption and living standards in the Chinese countryside, as well as to promote more rapid and sustained economic growth in the farm sector. This concern with the welfare aspects of agricultural growth was one that had been almost entirely lacking, except when rural conditions posed a threat to the political basis of Party rule, throughout the Mao period.[63]

Mao's refusal to countenance a retreat from the collectivist thrust of farm policy, except as a temporizing measure following the collapse of the Great Leap Forward, was enormously costly. Even after the events of the early 1960s, China's investment strategy remained basically unchanged. For Mao, as for Stalin, the imperative of heavy

---

62. The ideological thrust of some aspects of Sun Yat-sen's rural economic policy was, after all, quite radical.

63. Concern shown in recent years by the Chinese government towards *san nong* – the problems associated with unfavourable developments in the countryside (*nongcun*), agriculture (*nongye*) and among farmers (*nongmin*) – also highlights worries about their social and political, more than the economic, effects.

industrialization was a veritable shibboleth. Unlike Liu Shaoqi, Deng Xiaoping, Chen Yun and other far-sighted Chinese leaders, Mao viewed the introduction of accommodating policies towards the farm sector in the early 1960s as a tactical expedient, not a strategic adjustment. In the event, neither in its pure nor in its modified form did the Soviet development model prove itself capable of meeting the difficult challenges confronting China's farm sector. From the 1950s to the death of Mao in 1976, Chinese agriculture failed to generate a level and pattern of growth that was capable simultaneously of raising farm productivity and efficiency, generating higher living standards for farmers, and fulfilling agriculture's developmental burden to the benefit of the entire economy and society. Such was the closeness to the margin of subsistence that throughout the Mao period, China's economy remained tied to the apron strings of the agricultural sector. Not until Mao was dead and a new ethos had emerged, grounded in an awareness of the virtues of balance,[64] did agriculture cease to be a drag on economic growth and improved living standards. From this perspective, although the agricultural sector has continued to be the source of serious problems until the present day, the breaking in the early 1980s of the symbiotic link between the performance of agriculture and that of the rest of the economy must be judged one of the defining moments of China's reform era.

64. "Balance" in the sense not only of more balanced growth between economic sectors, but also of the simultaneous pursuit of economic *and welfare* objectives.

Appendix: Provincial Grain Output and Grain Procurement

Table A1: **Total Output, Net Procurement Rate and Residual Supplies of Grain Available to Peasants in 25 Chinese Provinces and Autonomous Regions, 1953–75**

	Total output of grain (raw weight in m tonnes)					Net procurement rate (%)					Residual supplies available to peasants (raw weight in m tonnes)				
	53–57	58–62	63–65	66–70	71–75	53–57	58–62	63–65	66–70	71–75	53–57	58–62	63–65	66–70	71–75
North	35.21	29.96	34.48	43.70	55.40	12.10	15.79		10.76	12.17	30.95	25.23		39.00	48.66
Henan	11.75	9.43	11.12	13.63	17.90	13.28	14.14	2.71	10.98	9.72	10.19	8.10	10.82	12.13	16.16
Hebei	7.27	6.91	7.55	11.03	13.87	3.60	16.40		9.58	10.42	7.01	5.78		9.97	11.65
Shanxi	4.05	3.91	4.56	4.77	5.88	19.58	20.36	16.96	14.11	15.99	3.44	3.11	3.79	4.10	4.94
Shandong	12.14	9.71	11.25	14.27	17.75	15.08	15.09	12.59	10.35	10.40	10.31	8.24	9.83	12.79	15.90
North-east	18.76	16.24	18.68	24.02	28.72	28.89	35.28	27.84	33.26	28.24	3.34	10.51	13.48	16.03	20.61
Heilongjiang	7.39	6.64	7.62	10.67	12.10	39.62	42.62	34.37	41.69	31.77	4.46	3.81	5.00	6.22	8.26
Jilin	5.14	4.57	5.06	6.21	7.64	34.76	41.47	30.02	33.82	31.45	3.35	2.67	3.54	4.11	5.24
Liaoning	6.23	5.03	6.00	7.14	8.98	11.35	19.99	17.77	20.15	20.76	5.52	4.02	4.93	5.70	7.12
North-west	14.39	13.62	15.93	17.59	21.03	24.53	25.18	19.33	13.93	11.89	10.86	10.19	12.85	15.14	18.53
IMAR	3.72	3.88	3.83	4.15	4.59	35.70	32.04	28.46	11.16	4.98	2.39	2.64	2.74	3.69	4.36
Gansu	3.21	2.47	3.22	3.64	4.65	20.47	19.91	10.69	11.13	11.30	2.55	1.98	2.88	3.23	4.12
Ningxia	0.60	0.55	0.76	0.79	0.96	21.34	23.57	17.61	26.22	12.01	0.47	0.42	0.63	0.58	0.84
Shaanxi	4.85	4.35	4.99	5.62	7.05	19.20	20.61	15.12	13.65	15.13	3.92	3.45	4.24	4.85	5.98
Xinjiang	1.48	1.90	2.49	2.79	2.97	24.23	25.45	25.59	19.29	15.33	1.10	1.41	1.85	2.25	2.51
Qinghai	0.53	0.47	0.64	0.60	0.81	20.42	38.59	18.59	11.84	12.95	0.42	0.29	0.52	0.53	0.71
Centre	25.44	24.64	28.63	33.28	41.20	17.14	20.33	17.67	16.11	14.39	21.08	19.63	23.57	27.92	35.27
Hunan	10.52	9.93	10.33	13.29	16.64	13.79	18.06	12.15	11.69	12.37	9.07	8.14	9.07	11.74	14.58

Table A1: (Continued)

	Total output of grain (raw weight in m tonnes)					Net procurement rate (%)					Residual supplies available to peasants (raw weight in m tonnes)				
	53–57	58–62	63–65	66–70	71–75	53–57	58–62	63–65	66–70	71–75	53–57	58–62	63–65	66–70	71–75
Hubei	8.70	8.49	11.16	11.48	14.61	16.09	18.12	17.42	15.63	14.11	7.30	6.95	9.22	9.69	12.55
Jiangxi	6.22	6.22	7.14	8.51	9.95	24.23	27.00	26.01	23.63	18.22	4.71	4.54	5.28	6.50	8.14
East	27.77	24.22	29.88	36.48	45.65	17.39	19.69	17.57	16.61	14.06	22.94	19.45	24.63	30.42	39.23
Anhui	9.55	7.12	8.25	10.56	14.74	17.99	22.07	18.26	14.37	12.28	7.93	5.55	6.74	9.04	12.93
Zhejiang	7.36	7.20	8.70	10.19	11.97	13.62	18.61	15.66	16.23	14.62	6.36	5.86	7.34	8.54	10.22
Jiangsu	10.86	9.90	12.93	15.73	18.94	20.33	20.17	18.76	18.39	15.09	8.65	8.04	10.55	12.84	16.08
South	14.54	13.14	16.18	18.27	21.92	18.57	20.55	24.91	20.25	16.65	11.84	9.92	12.15	14.57	18.27
Fujian	4.08	3.71	4.28	4.67	6.17	20.55	25.59	19.46	15.28	14.77	3.24	2.76	3.45	3.96	5.26
Guangdong	10.46	9.43	11.90	13.60	15.75	17.76	24.04	26.85	21.97	17.42	8.60	7.16	8.70	10.61	13.01
South-west	35.65	29.87	34.52	40.08	47.94	19.72	21.73	15.59	15.09	12.56	28.62	23.38	29.14	34.03	41.92
Guizhou	4.47	3.91	4.39	4.91	5.34	17.08	20.59	15.65	15.17	11.43	3.71	3.10	3.70	4.17	4.73
Sichuan	19.88	15.51	18.52	21.43	25.21	23.00	25.25	17.32	15.64	13.06	15.31	11.59	15.31	18.08	21.92
Yunnan	5.43	5.15	5.77	6.40	7.37	17.33	18.26	14.48	16.28	12.80	4.49	4.21	4.93	5.36	6.43

Table A1: **(Continued)**

	Total output of grain (raw weight in m tonnes)					Net procurement rate (%)					Residual supplies available to peasants (raw weight in m tonnes)				
	53–57	58–62	63–65	66–70	71–75	53–57	58–62	63–65	66–70	71–75	53–57	58–62	63–65	66–70	71–75
Guangxi	5.87	5.30	5.84	7.34	10.02	12.75	15.58	11.13	12.42	11.74	5.12	4.47	5.19	6.43	8.84

Notes and Sources:

Output and procurement (both urban and rural re-sales) data for every Chinese province in every year can be found in a uniquely comprehensive source, published as an internal document by the Planning Office of the Ministry of Agriculture (*NYJJZL*, pp. 354–407). Because the output and procurement estimates are measured differently (the former are given in terms of raw grain, the latter in trade grain), I have converted all the figures to a common measure through the use of conversion ratios for 11 provinces, cited by Walker in his "Interpreting Chinese grain consumption statistics" (originally published in *The China Quarterly*, No.92 (1982), republished in Ash (ed.), *Agricultural Development*, p. 214). For provinces for which I have no direct evidence of conversion ratios, I have applied the ratios of contiguous regions. I am aware that since the ratios cited by Walker are taken from local newspaper sources published between 1956 and 1959, the figures shown in my Table 7 fail to take account of structural changes in grain production in the 1960s and 1970s. However, even if allowance could be made for such changes, it would be unlikely to materially affect the picture given here. For ease of exposition, figures for individual years have been averaged into groups of years coinciding with significant sub-periods of economic policy and development.

In order to convert aggregate figures to per capita estimates, I have used the comprehensive provincial agricultural population data (*nongye renkou*, except for Inner Mongolia, where I have adjusted "village" (*xiangcun*) population estimates for 1953–70 *nongye renkou* figures) given in NBS, *Quanguo gesheng, zizhiqu, zhixiashi lishi tongji ziliao huibian, 1949–1989* (*Compendium of Historical Statistical Materials for Every Province, Autonomous Region and Directly Administered Municipality, 1949–1989*) (Beijing: Tongji chubanshe, 1990), passim.

Table A2: **Output and Availability of Grain per Head of Farm Population in 25 Chinese Provinces and Autonomous Regions, 1953–75**

	Output of grain per head of agricultural population (raw weight in kg)					Availability of grain per head of agricultural population (raw weight in kg)				
	53–57	58–62	63–65	66–70	71–75	53–57	58–62	63–65	66–70	71–75
North	258.84	213.76	227.82	262.98	303.40	227.52	180.01	161.48	234.70	266.48
Henan	272.81	212.29	235.79	259.27	299.48	236.55	182.21	229.40	230.81	270.35
Hebei	227.05	205.23	206.45	277.00	320.18	218.87	171.59	211.66	50.38	286.84
Shanxi	311.06	280.49	290.08	278.13	308.18	249.99	223.35	241.15	238.94	258.77
Shandong	253.39	201.75	216.76	251.99	284.64	215.19	171.33	189.49	225.83	254.95
North-east	584.61	469.91	455.94	519.91	534.72	415.71	304.11	329.02	346.97	383.73
Heilongjiang	858.30	636.63	599.53	760.51	682.46	518.33	365.34	393.47	443.55	465.59
Jilin	597.67	512.33	466.79	507.77	548.85	390.27	299.92	326.76	336.06	375.98
Liaoning	418.68	330.70	344.43	358.07	407.07	371.11	264.47	283.31	285.88	322.64
North-west	367.65	317.19	330.02	322.34	334.77	277.47	237.31	266.21	277.44	294.97
IMAR	551.93	501.29	407.45	390.40	369.27	354.77	340.66	291.73	346.66	350.72
Gansu	308.65	230.63	285.97	281.73	293.19	245.46	184.72	255.13	250.39	273.94
Ningxia	400.00	323.53	415.30	369.16	375.00	312.59	249.02	343.66	270.77	330.73
Shaanxi	329.93	266.87	273.27	283.12	317.42	266.59	211.69	231.72	244.25	269.25
Xinjiang	349.88	394.19	432.29	400.29	364.42	265.30	293.11	321.47	323.21	308.32
Qinghai	337.58	281.44	363.64	291.26	333.33	267.52	170.99	294.51	255.12	290.58
Centre	353.82	330.25	351.46	362.09	396.00	293.18	263.10	289.34	303.78	339.00
Hunan	335.89	317.35	304.81	348.09	385.99	289.42	260.13	267.69	307.47	338.32
Hubei	341.98	315.85	379.08	348.20	395.72	287.07	258.66	313.05	293.80	339.84
Jiangxi	410.83	378.35	393.82	409.92	414.41	311.34	276.16	291.23	313.10	338.91

Table A2: (Continued)

	Output of grain per head of agricultural population (raw weight in kg)					Availability of grain per head of agricultural population (raw weight in kg)				
	53–57	58–62	63–65	66–70	71–75	53–57	58–62	63–65	66–70	71–75
East	332.57	287.72	324.96	351.51	387.88	274.73	231.05	267.86	293.12	333.33
Anhui	327.62	262.34	290.19	325.52	383.75	267.24	209.57	244.32	278.63	333.96
Zhejiang	365.08	335.82	351.80	366.94	387.88	299.46	261.69	287.39	314.23	340.32
Jiangsu	31764	278.09	333.33	361.03	391.16	265.91	226.35	281.18	302.36	333.90
South	382.43	324.68	357.57	357.81	375.41	311.42	245.12	268.51	285.35	312.90
Fujian	341.99	295.15	299.30	288.09	325.25	271.91	219.80	240.97	244.09	277.14
Guangdong	389.42	337.99	384.49	390.24	399.54	320.39	256.59	281.21	304.53	330.01
South-west	326.44	277.58	297.87	304.47	313.44	262.06	217.27	251.45	258.51	274.08
Guizhou	305.95	269.28	282.13	274.61	253.80	253.58	213.79	238.06	214.16	224.62
Sichuan	331.50	271.49	306.62	311.94	315.52	255.28	202.99	253.52	263.10	274.30
Yunnan	333.54	306.55	307.41	303.03	299.96	275.75	250.58	262.83	253.59	261.54
Guangxi										

Sources:
As Table A1.

Local Cadres Confront the Supernatural: The Politics of Holy Water (*Shenshui*) in the PRC, 1949–1966*

Steve A. Smith

ABSTRACT This article examines incidents in which the miracle-working properties of a source of water or other substance are discovered, thereby sparking unauthorized visits by hundreds or thousands of people to gain access to it. The article examines: the meanings of holy water and the motivations of those who set off in search for it; the sociological dimension of these quests; the extent to which such episodes were a deliberate attempt by enemies of the regime, principally redemptive religious sects (*huidaomen*), to sow disorder; the reaction of the authorities to outbreaks of holy water fever and the measures they took to deal with it; and what such outbreaks reveal about the nature of the local state and about popular attitudes to it in the first decade-and-a-half of the People's Republic of China.

On the Double Nine festival (*chongyangjie* 重阳节) of 1956 in the first district of Shunde (顺德) county in Guangdong province, relatives of Chen Yuan (陈远), accompanied by nuns and monks, went to sweep Chen's grave in Nangang (南岗) village. Chen had been a fruit seller who had dispensed herbal medicine to sick people free of charge. After his death, those whom Chen had helped collected money to build him a fine tomb, which was erected in a valley through which a mountain stream flowed. In order to protect the tomb, two subterranean channels were laid to take water around the grave and to deposit it in two small pools. While the grave-sweeping was taking place, peasant bystanders drank water from the pools and commented on how delicious it tasted. Soon rumours began to circulate that the pools had magical properties. The galvanizing moment came when a young boy, tending cows in the vicinity of the tomb, had a dream in which an unknown person told him to take water from the pools to give to his sick mother. He did so and his mother was miraculously cured of a chronic illness. Thereafter, "superstitious women" from Nangang village began to visit the grave and to spread the tale that "three immortals have come down to earth to save the people" and that "their holy water will cure any disease." Soon 300 to 400 people were visiting the pools each day, and by July 1957 the number had risen to 8,000 to 9,000 per day.[1]

* This article is from my project "Struggling with 'superstition': communism versus popular culture in Russia (1917–41) and China (1949–76)," which is generously funded by the UK Arts and Humanities Research Council.

1. This account is based on Shunde District Archive, 19-4-4. The files concerning this incident in the Guangdong provincial archive are closed.

This incident was typical of hundreds that occurred in the People's Republic of China (PRC) in the years prior to the Cultural Revolution, incidents in which local people discovered the miracle-working properties of a local source of water, spread tales of the wonders it could perform, and thereby sparked quests by hundreds and sometimes thousands of people to go off in search of the holy water (*shenshui* 神水).[2] Quests for holy or sacred water (*xianshui* 仙水), or for holy or sacred medicine (*shenyao* or *xianyao* 神藥, 仙藥), were one of the most pervasive forms of what the communist authorities called "feudal superstitious activity" in this period.[3] They occurred throughout China, among both Han Chinese and ethnic minorities, and with considerable frequency.[4] Their incidence seems to have been particularly intense in the years 1953–54, 1957 and, possibly, 1963–64.[5] The quests most commonly centred on sources of water, but quite often they involved more specific sources of sacred power such as holy trees (*shenshu* 神树), sacred herbs (*xiancao* 仙草) or sacred pills (*xianwan* 仙丸). Water is the source of life, essential to plants, animals and humans, and the ascription of sacred properties to it is a phenomenon found in most cultures. The symbolic meanings of water vary from positive (water as a cleansing, purifying, dissolving agent) to negative (water as a destructive agent), but its identification with life-bearing forces and with fecundity is widespread.[6] In China water carried all of these associations but, more specifically, holy water and holy mineral or vegetable substances were believed to have preternatural efficacy by virtue of the fact that a god or gods had chosen them as instruments through which to make their spiritual power (*ling* 靈) efficacious in the world. The quest for such substances

2. To the best of my knowledge, this phenomenon has not been studied before. In her pioneering article on rural violence in socialist China, Elizabeth Perry briefly mentions "holy water" incidents. Elizabeth J. Perry, *Challenging the Mandate of Heaven: Social Protest and State Power in China*, (Armonk, NY: M. E. Sharpe, 2002), p. 281.

3. Because of its etymological connotations with health and wholeness, I have chosen to translate *shen* as "holy." I have translated *xian* as "sacred," since this is more in line with the meaning of the Chinese than the English "immortal." However, where *xian* refers to individuals or spiritual beings I have retained the conventional translation of "immortal." Some writers make sharper distinctions between these terms as appertaining, respectively, to gods (*shen*), immortals (*xian*) and living saints (*sheng*). See Wu Bing'an, *Zhongguo minjian xinyang* (*Chinese Popular Belief*) (Shanghai: Shanghai renmin chubanshe, 1995), p. 222. It should be noted that in official sources these terms are always in inverted commas.

4. All the incidents I have discovered occurred in rural areas, but they also occurred in urban areas. For a holy water incident in Taiyuan city sometime in the 1970s see Guo Chunmei, Zhang Qingjie, *Shisu mixin yu Zhongguo shehui* (*Superstitious Customs and Chinese Society*) (Beijing: Zongjiao wenhua chubanshe, 2001), p. 347.

5. This is an impression based on the clustering of reports I have been able to find. It is not clear whether the higher frequency of reported incidents reflects heightened concern on the part of the authorities or a real increase in frequency, brought about by health epidemics, economic uncertainties or other threats. I am indebted to an anonymous referee for pointing to this issue, but am unable to resolve it on the basis of the evidence at my disposal.

6. "Water," in Mircea Eliade (ed.), *Encyclopedia of Religion*, Vol. 15 (London: Macmillan, 1987), pp. 350–58.

was thus motivated by a desire to benefit from the divine (*shen* 神) power they contained.

This article seeks, first, to explore the meanings of holy water and medicine in order to deepen understanding of what motivated those who set off in search of these sacred substances. Secondly, it examines the social dimension of these quests, looking at their size, composition and spatial dimensions. Thirdly, it asks how far such episodes were a deliberate attempt by enemies of the regime, principally redemptive religious sects (*huidaomen* 会道门), to sow disorder and to foment popular disaffection. Fourthly, it examines the reaction of the authorities and looks at the measures they took to deal with outbreaks of holy water fever. Finally, the article asks what such outbreaks reveal about the nature and strength of the local state and about popular attitudes to it in the first decade-and-a-half of the PRC.

The Meanings of Holy Water

The discovery of holy water always produced a ferment of stories designed to demonstrate and authenticate its efficacy, usually stories of miracles of one sort or another. The communist authorities typically characterized these tales as "rumours" (*yaoyan* 谣言).[7] In a review of large-scale holy water episodes in 1953 and 1954, the Public Security Bureau of Rehe province observed:

As a general rule, before people start to seek holy medicine many rumours circulate, and female spirit mediums (*wupo* 巫婆) and immortals-come-to-earth become active, enticing the minority of the masses who are sick to seek holy medicine. If a person whose illness is not serious fully recovers, then rumours run wild and the masses, seeing what has happened, start to believe. At this point the numbers seeking medicine rise sharply.[8]

Typical of such stories was one that circulated in Zhejiang province in 1953. On the second day of the first lunar month, Shi Chunzhang (施春樟), an old man of poor peasant status who lived alone, told his neighbours in Changshan (常山) township in Jinhua (金华) prefecture that the previous night he had had a dream in which an apparition on the Shiren (石人) mountain had urged him to collect 50 *jin* of rice in order to repair the road up the mountain side. The apparition explained: "The old buddha in the Shiren temple was damaged by the PLA and the militia and has now moved into a rock at the summit of the Shiren mountain. If you go and worship there he will bless and protect this area." The buddha seems to have been the Stone Man after whom the local mountain was named and to which the temple was dedicated. Villagers quickly collected 50 *jin* of rice and within a few days repaired the road. Soon people began to climb to the summit

7. S. A. Smith, "Talking toads and chinless ghosts: the politics of 'superstitious' rumors in the People's Republic of China, 1961–65," *American Historical Review*, Vol. 111, No. 2 (2006), pp. 405–427.
8. Hebei Provincial Archive, 684-2-432.

to burn incense at the rock in the belief that the "Stone Man is manifesting its power" (*Shiren xian ling* 石人显灵). Stories quickly abounded:

Today the bodhisattvas have descended on to Shiren mountain to hold a meeting (*kaihui* 开会). For five *li* (2.5 kilometres) around the mountain sacred grasses and herbs are growing that can cure a hundred illnesses. Children who eat them will become strong. Hunchbacks will become straight, the dumb will speak, those who are not ill will enjoy robust health if they eat the medicine.

During March about 300 to 400 people a day visited the mountain from adjacent counties. Du Jinhai (杜金海), an old peasant from Lanqi (兰溪) county who suffered from acute tuberculosis, hobbled to the top of the mountain to eat the sacred herbs and ran the five *li* back without stopping. His story impelled scores of people in his township to undertake the pilgrimage. At first, those who came to worship the buddha and to pick the sacred herbs were people suffering from diseases or chronic ill ill-health, but pilgrims soon came to seek blessings of other kinds. Those who ate the herbs returned full of stories of the potency of the Stone Man. "Chairman Mao has only five medals (*jiangzhang* 奖章), but the Lord (Buddha) has seven and wears them very prettily." By 11 April, the number of worshippers at the Shiren mountain had grown to between 1,500 and 2,000 a day, reaching 3,000 on some days. Pilgrims came from nine counties, and a few from as far away as Hangzhou and Shanghai. Wearing straw sandals, they sacrificed incense, candles and paper money on the mountain top and returned bearing herbs, tree branches, mud balls and grass seed, so that the mountain was soon stripped of all vegetation.[9]

As the incident suggests, the principal, but not exclusive motivation spurring people to seek holy medicine was the desire to be cured of disease or to be guaranteed good health. When questioned by the authorities, pilgrims made this clear. In the Shiren mountain episode, they told propagandists sent to the site: "You officials from the people's government have five or six *jin* of rice every day, but we common people have nothing to eat. We can only trust in the bodhisattvas. If you haven't bank notes to pay the doctor what can you do?"[10] In March 1953 at Huacao (华漕) farm in Xinjing (新泾) district near Shanghai, a water hole was discovered whose sacred properties quickly became the object of a large cult. Doctors at the site who tried to discourage pilgrims from drinking the water were told: "Everyone here is led by Chairman Mao … But you must let us drink the sacred water, for there is no one to look after us when we are ill." "The workers have hospitals but we don't. If you won't let us drink the water, then give us 500,000 *yuan* for a hospital." "We rely on the government, but we also rely on the sacred water." A work team at

9. *Neibu cankao* (*Internal Reference Materials*) (hereafter *NBCK*), 8 May 1953, pp. 75, 81–82.
10. *NBCK*, 8 May 1953, p. 81.

the site carried out a detailed survey of the motivations of pilgrims. It estimated that 40 per cent could not be dissuaded under any circumstances from drinking the water. These included the poor who had no means to pay for medical treatment for themselves or their families; families who were not necessarily poor but who had members who were chronically sick; those who were suffering from illness, regardless of ability to pay; and those who were redeeming a pledge to the gods. The work team concluded that in general it was harder to dissuade the poor than the prosperous, the old than the young, women than men, and the sick than the healthy from drinking the water.[11] The motivations of pilgrims, however, were not always related to health concerns. In Langdai (朗岱) county in Guizhou in 1957, several hundred peasants visited a sacred tree in Yunpan (云盘) township every day. When asked by local officials why they came, only a minority said they hoped to be cured of illness; the largest group said that they were seeking happiness (*tao le* 讨乐), while others said they were petitioning the gods for something to eat, petitioning to have children or petitioning to find a spouse.[12]

These essentially practical motivations would suggest that holy water pilgrimages can be typed as "instrumental," according to the six-fold typology of pilgrimage developed by Alan Morinis.[13] However, holy water pilgrimages were imbricated by a rich and diverse religious culture that invested these events with a complex set of meanings. First, the sites where holy water or medicine were discovered were assumed ipso facto to be sacred, set apart from contiguous space by virtue of the fact that a god had chosen the place to manifest its *ling*. This broadly fits Mircea Eliade's paradigm of a sacred place as an *axis mundi*, a vertical along which the upper, earthly and nether worlds intersect. Not all such sites accorded with the cultural stereotype that identified them with awe-inspiring locales such as mountains or lakes. Nothing could have been less prepossessing than the village duck pond in Huangjianzhen (黄尖镇) in Sheyang (射阳) county in Jiangsu, where holy water was discovered in 1985. However, locals dubbed it the "precious jade pool and sacred ground" (*yaochi shengdi* 瑶池圣地), since for them it had become a site transfigured by numinous power, a site where mortals could commune with the gods.[14] Although holy water was occasionally

---

11. Shanghai Municipal Archive, A22-2-137.
12. *NBCK*, 8 May 1957, p. 11. The vast majority of women who climbed Mount Tai wanted to have a child. Brian R. Dott, *Identity Reflections: Pilgrimages to Mount Tai in Late Imperial China* (Cambridge MA: Harvard University Press, 2004), p. 81.
13. Alan Morinis, "Introduction: the territory of the anthropology of pilgrimage," in A. Morinis (ed.), *Sacred Journeys: the Anthropology of Pilgrimage* (Westport CN: Greenwood Press, 1992), p. 11.
14. Li Changren, *Jiekai mixin guishen jiemu* (*An Exposé of Superstitious Gods and Ghosts*) (Changchun: Jilin renmin chubanshe, 1987), p. 6. This name may suggest the influence of the redemptive sects, one of which was called the Precious Jade Pool Sect (Yaozhimen).

found at a temple, it was mainly discovered at sites that hitherto had had no religious significance.[15]

Secondly, travelling to a sacred site to take water or medicine was modelled on the cultural template of the pilgrimage, in the loose sense that it was a journey to a sacred place. As Susan Naquin and Chün-gang Yü point out, pilgrimage did not occupy a central place in Chinese culture as it did in Islam, Christianity, Judaism, Hinduism or monastic Buddhism; yet certain pilgrimages, such as climbing the five sacred mountains, were of great cultural import.[16] In comparison with these culturally valorized pilgrimages, however, trips to holy water sites were modest affairs, lacking the elaborate meanings associated with sacred mountains or major temples.

Thirdly, as acts normally undertaken by individuals, these pilgrimages were qualitatively different from rituals such as temple procession festivals which involved all the households in a particular neighbourhood and which symbolically marked the bounds of the community.[17] Fourthly, the act of taking holy water was structured according to the basic ritual of Chinese popular religion: making an offering to a god in the hope of a gaining a favour. Visitors to a sacred site first burned incense and offered a sacrifice to the god who presided over it before availing themselves of the substance into which the god had infused its *ling*. Generally, worshippers described their actions as "burning incense" (*shao xiang* 烧香), the term used for everyday worship, rather than as "presenting incense to the mountain" (*chao shan jin xiang* 朝山进香), the term used for sacrifice on specialized pilgrimages.[18]

Finally, the act of seeking holy water was sometimes structured as a vow, involving not merely the exchange of offerings in the hope of a favour, but an explicit promise of repayment to the god if a wish were granted.[19] A hole containing clear blue water, about 1.8 metres deep, was discovered at the foot of a large mountain in Qinglong (青龙) county in Rehe province in spring 1954. A female spirit medium said that Yuanshenye (元神爷) had taken up residence in the pool. When Wang Yucheng, a baojia head under the Japanese, looked into the pool and saw two sparks of fire, he took this to be a bad omen. He

15. In 1954 in Kangping county in western Liaoning, 40 to 50 people from three villages set off for the lama temple in Lindong in Inner Mongolia to collect holy water. In the same year in Quwo county in Shanxi province, two Yiguandao leaders claimed that the "god who appears in dreams is manifesting its power" at the temple in Zheng village, causing locals to throng there to seek medicine from the god. *Gongan shouce* (*Public Security Handbook*), No. 21, 1954, p. 1. I thank Michael Schoenhals for this reference.

16. Susan Naquin and Chün-gang Yü, *Pilgrims and Sacred Sites in China* (Berkeley: University of California Press, 1992), p. 2.

17. Stephan Feuchtwang, *Popular Religion in China: the Imperial Metaphor* (Richmond: Curzon, 2001), pp. 63–65, 83–84. The case of Bazhong county in Sichuan discussed below may be an exception to this generalization, for holy water in this instance was a feature of a regular temple fair.

18. Naquin and Yü, *Pilgrims and Sacred Sites*, pp. 11–12.

19. Dott, *Identity Reflections*, p. 12.

thus made a vow to Yuanshenye that if he were spared whatever ills lay in store for him, he would make a sacrifice to him. Evidently, the ills were averted, for Chen later "redeemed his vow" (*huanyuan* 还愿) by sacrificing a pig's head and eggs at the pool.[20] In a Christian context the vow is often interpreted as a way in which the laity can bypass the monopoly of spiritual authority of the clergy.[21] In Chinese popular religion, of course, there was no professional clergy, but vows such as Wang's may be seen as permitting the individual access to the divine without the mediation of ritual specialists or of the community.[22]

The other cultural context that imbricated the taking of holy water and medicine was that of popular health practice. Ordinary folk, especially in the countryside, had limited access to Chinese medicine based on the classical texts, ancient theories and pharmacopoeia of the indigenous tradition. Instead they relied on a variety of healers, including female and male spirit mediums (the latter usually called *shenhan* 神汉), Daoist priests, herbalists, midwives and itinerant hucksters, and on a variety of therapies, including drugs, acupuncture, moxibustion, charms, spells, amulets, divination, incantations and, above all, exorcism.[23] In popular health practice medicine and exorcism were barely separable, especially in types of illness perceived to be demonic in aetiology.[24] At the heart of much popular thinking was the notion that disease was caused by vengeful spirits, an idea that can be traced back to a millennium before the common era; and though this notion would later compete with a powerful conception of disease as rooted in the desires of the self, it continued to represent a "thematic pole to which reflection on sickness would repeatedly return."[25] Since the demons that cause illness cannot be propitiated through sacrifice, they have either to be prevented from entering the body by means of signs that demonstrate an alliance with superior supernatural forces, or be removed from the body with the help of spells or magical substances.[26] In this context the ingestion of holy substances has a decidedly exorcistic function. In 1980 in Wushan (吴山) commune in Changxing (长兴) county in Zhejiang province, a woman who was having a difficult pregnancy visited a female spirit

20. Hebei Provincial Archive, 684-2-432.

21. William Christian, *Local Religion in 16th-Century Spain* (Princeton NJ: Princeton University Press, 1981), pp. 31–43.

22. Robert Hymes, *Way and Byway: Taoism, Local Religion, and Models of Divinity in Song and Modern China* (Berkeley: University of California Press, 2002), p. 67.

23. On the absence of a unified theoretical approach to health care and the pluralism of therapies, see Paul U. Unschuld, *Medicine in China: A History of Ideas* (Berkeley: University of California Press, 1985).

24. J. J. M. de Groot, *The Religious System of China*, Vol. 6 (Leiden: Brill, 1910), p. 1071.

25. Kuriyama Shigehisa, "Concepts of disease in East Asia," in Kenneth F. Kiple (ed.), *The Cambridge World History of Human Disease* (Cambridge: Cambridge University Press, 1993), p. 52.

26. Paul U. Unschuld, "History of Chinese medicine," in *ibid.* p. 20.

medium who diagnosed that there was a demon living in her stomach and gave her a tin of sacred water to expel it. Sadly, this brought on a miscarriage.[27]

Holy water and drugs also took their place among the mystical therapies, often referred to as "prescriptions from the spirits" (*xianfang* or *shenfang* 仙方, 神方) or "efficacious pills and sacred drugs" (*ling dan xian yao* 灵丹仙药) that derived from vernacular Daoist tradition. This posited that celestial beings sent herbal and animal substances down to earth as sacred medicine, and that the ingestion of such substances, along with various dietary, respiratory and sexual techniques, could help reverse the steady loss of vital energy that was the normal course of life. Such sacred substances, by virtue of the *ling* they embodied, could invigorate the vital spiritual forces (*jingshen* 精神) of those who consumed them and thus help prolong life, possibly forever. In 1953 in Shanghai, a "living immortal" (*huoshen xian* 活神仙) claimed to possess an elixir (*xian dan* 仙丹) and sacred charms (*shen fu* 神符) that could cure any illness.[28] In 1957 in Zhenhai (镇海) county in Zhejiang, Xia Agen (夏阿根), a blind man from Shijiao (石礁), went to Daxie (大谢) for five days to seek out an immortal who had acquired fame curing illness. He took away with him stones touched by the immortal, claiming they contained an elixir, and sold them to the 700 to 800 people who each day queued up to see him.[29] In Bazhong (巴中) county in Sichuan, temple fairs were held on the Yinling (阴灵) mountains on the 19th day of the second, sixth and ninth lunar months. The locals believed that on these days the water on the mountain was pure water from Guanyin, Goddess of Mercy, and that grasses and leaves on the trees could cure any disease. At the temple fairs of 1965, a female spirit medium from Pingliang (平梁) commune sold holy drugs at four *yuan* a pack; another from Zaolin (枣林) commune sold holy water at five *jiao* a bowl; while a Daoist priest sold "holy peaches" that would enable a woman to give birth to a son.[30] The peach symbolized fertility because the flowering of the peach tree in spring is seen to represent the triumph of the bright *yang* principle over the dark *yin* principle.[31] Decoctions of peaches, moreover, were supposed to be effective in expelling demons from the body and were thus used to cure diseases such as convulsions, spasm or lethargy believed to have a

27. Guo Chunmei, *Superstitious Customs*, p. 341. Ruth Harris notes how those who were cured at Lourdes in late 19th-century France spoke of their illness as a kind of alien force expelled from the body as a result of bathing in the sacred water. She notes the parallel with exorcism. Ruth Harris, *Lourdes: Body and Spirit in the Secular Age* (London: Penguin, 1999), p. 319.

28. "'Huo shenxian' xian yuanxing" ("The true shape of the 'living immortal' revealed"), *Xinmin wanbao*, 12 February 1963. It turned out that this "immortal" had worked for the security organs of the Kuomintang and was sentenced to seven years in jail

29. *NBCK*, 8 May 1957, p. 11.

30. Sichuan Provincial Archive, 50–377.

31. J. J. M. de Groot, *The Religion of the Chinese* (Westport CN: Hyperion Press, 1980 (orig. 1912)), p. 37.

diabolical pathology.[32] In sum, holy substances of all types, suffused as they were with the *shen* qualities of gods, were believed to be efficacious both in strengthening the patient's spiritual vitality and in exorcising demons, since *shen* stands diametrically opposed to *gui* (鬼) in the universal order.[33]

In spite of connecting to ancient beliefs that the ingestion of *shen* substances can promote immortality or expel demons, I have not found evidence that quests for holy water constituted a clearly defined form of religious practice with a long pedigree. De Groot cites a tale from Ge Hong (葛洪) (283–343CE), the philosopher who attempted to fuse an immortality-centred Daoism with Confucianism, about the discovery of sacred water at a grave, in which the scholar-officials of the time responded very much like communist cadres in the 1950s, by filling in the water hole.[34] But the standard works on Chinese religion have little to say on quests for holy water and medicine per se, which may imply that the surge in these was of relatively recent origin, linked perhaps to the rapid growth of redemptive sects amid the social and economic turmoil of the 1930s and 1940s.[35] Certainly, the communist authorities associated the phenomenon with those sects they promiscuously lumped together as *huidaomen*. By 1949, these consisted of more than 300 different groups, whose doctrines and rituals varied considerably, but which shared the characteristics of being congregations that defined membership in terms of belief, rather than of residence or descent, and of being oriented to individual salvation.[36] The largest of them, the Yiguandao (一贯道), was estimated to have 178,000 followers in Beijing, at least 140,000 in Tianjin, and 187,000 in Shaanxi province at the time of Liberation.[37] Practices of magical healing were important in the ritual life of some but not all these redemptive sects. The Yiguandao, for example, believed that the Maitreya, or Buddha of the Future Era, was already on earth and poised to inaugurate the third and final *kalpa*, so its principal concern was with prophylaxis against calamities of an eschatological kind rather than with mundane health care. Nevertheless in Cangzhou (沧州) district in Hebei province, it seems that the most common reason for people to join the Yiguandao was a

32. de Groot, *Religious System*, Vol. 6, p. 958.

33. *Ibid*. p. 961.

34. *Ibid*. p. 1092.

35. That said, in her valuable account of Kuomintang campaigns against "superstition" in popular health practice in the 1930s, Rebecca Nedostup makes no mention of holy water. R. A. Nedostup, "Religion, superstition and governing society in Nationalist China," PhD, Columbia University, 2001, pp. 516–542.

36. Joseph Bosco, "Yiguan Dao: 'heterodoxy' and popular religion in Taiwan," Murray A. Rubinstein (ed.), *The Other Taiwan, 1945 to the Present* (Armonk, NY: M. E. Sharpe, 1994), pp. 423–444.

37. Shao Yong, *Zhongguo huidaomen* (*The Heterodox Sects of China*) (Shanghai: Shanghai renmin chubanshe 1997), p. 472; Thomas David DuBois, *The Sacred Village: Social Change and Religious Life in Rural North China* (Honolulu: University of Hawai'i Press, 2005), p. 134.

desire for healing.[38] And in Tianjin, as late as 1966, various masters in the Yiguandao, the Jiugongdao (九宫道, Nine Temples Way) and the Zhongmen Zhengjiao (中门正教, True Teaching of the Central Gate) were said to be able to call on the gods to cure illness through *qigong*, incantations and holy water.[39] That said, the standard work on the redemptive sects in the 1930s and 1940s does not suggest that the provision of holy water and medicine was a central element in their repertoire; and in general, communal forms of healing do not appear to have been as important to these sects as they are to healing cults in China today.[40]

The Social Dimensions of Quests for Holy Water

The majority of incidents in which people went in search of holy medicine were small in scale and relatively localized. Thomas DuBois, writing of Hebei province, suggests that "stories concerning the role of the spirits in the physical health of the individual generally remain within a very small area, the limit usually being about thirty *li*." This he equates with the "sphere of local culture."[41] In March 1953 in Hebei there were over 80 episodes of people seeking holy water and medicine in 17 counties. Of these, 36 incidents involved less than 50 people, 28 involved between 50 and 500, ten involved 500 to 1,000, and only six involved more than 1,000.[42] Nevertheless the discovery of holy water in one place often led to its speedy discovery elsewhere in the vicinity. The number of incidents in Hebei continued to rise after March 1953, and by summer 26 counties were affected, no fewer than 57 holy water sites appearing in Cang (沧) and Yanshan (盐山) counties alone.[43] In Rehe province in the same year, holy water was discovered in more than 30 different spots in 13 counties and banners, and at its peak about half the province was affected by the movement. On any one day, it was estimated that 20,000 people were seeking holy water.[44] In Guangdong in August 1954, holy water was discovered in Huiyang (惠阳) county and by the spring festival of 1955 holy water mania had spread to more than 80 counties and municipalities.[45] So if the numbers visiting any single site were often relatively small, cumulatively the impact of the discovery of holy water on a region could be enormous. Similarly, if in most cases pilgrims travelled quite

38. A more systematic survey in Dai county in Shanxi province in 1947, however, suggested that the largest proportion (46%) of "poor peasants" who joined the sect did so in order to "escape disaster" (*duozai tainan*), followed by 14% who wished to get rich. DuBois, *Sacred Village*, pp. 146–47.

39. Jilin Provincial Archive, 16-18-10.

40. Shao Yong, *The Heterodox Sects, passim*. Nancy N. Chen, "Healing sects and anti-cult campaigns," *The China Quarterly*, No. 174 (2003), pp. 505–520.

41. *Ibid.*

42. DuBois, *Sacred Village*, p. 66.

43. *NBCK*, 8 May 1953, p. 87.

44. Hebei Provincial Archive, 684-2-365; *NBCK*, 103, 8 May 1953, p. 80.

45. *Renmin ribao*, 7 July 1955. *Survey of the China Mainland Press* (*SCMP*), 1092, 20 July 1955.

short distances to visit a sacred site, this did not preclude some coming from far afield. In 1953 in Chaoyang (朝阳) in Rehe some old women accompanied a sick friend to the Jiaoding mountain, walking there and back, a distance of more than 40 kilometres. Li Wen, who lived in the ninth district of Lingyuan (凌源) county, travelled to the same mountain by train in order to get water for his sick daughter, but by the time he returned home his child was dead.[46] The following year people in Rehe rode by donkey, horse, ox cart or bicycle to sacred sites, taking with them offerings of fruit, pigs' heads and incense.[47] The work team sent to the holy water hole at Huacao farm near Shanghai discovered that on 23 April 1953 alone, some 20,000 visitors arrived at the site on foot, on 2,498 three-wheeled carts and on 2,224 bicycles.[48] It is likely that with the implementation of household registration, travel became more difficult, but it did not end the unauthorized movement of people. In 1964 during one temple fair in Suining (遂宁) county in Sichuan, more than 25,000 people visited the Lingquan (灵泉) and Guangde (广德) monasteries for holy water, exorcism and fortune-telling.[49]

The authorities were eager to know about the class status of seekers after holy water and holy medicine. In 1953, the 200,000 visitors to the water hole at Huacao farm near Shanghai were said to comprise "mainly peasants, shack dwellers and the poor (*pinmin* 贫民) from the neighbourhood, but also some townsfolk, workers, school pupils, and a small number of landlord elements, employees from government organs, senior staff, members of capitalist families, Catholics, Protestants, Yiguandao and White Russians."[50] In the same year, seekers after holy water in Rehe included ordinary masses, militiamen, village leaders, Communist Party members, communist youth league members and dependants of cadres.[51] In Guizhou in 1957, 70 per cent of peasants in Yanjiao (岩脚) district in Langdai county were reported to have visited a sacred tree in neighbouring Afang (阿方) township, the majority of them young people of both sexes, but including officials from the agricultural producer co-operatives and Party members.[52] Officials claimed that visitors to the Linquan and Guangde monasteries in Sichuan in 1964 were mainly peasants, the urban poor and handicraftsmen, but included workers, students, retired cadres, Party and communist youth members from rural areas, as well as local officials.[53] It is hard to make firm generalizations based on such impressionistic data. A broad cross-section of the population seems to have been drawn into the search for holy water

46. *NBCK*, 8 May 1953, p. 80.
47. Hebei Provincial Archive, 684-2-432. Rehe province was largely absorbed into Hebei province in 1956.
48. Shanghai Municipal Archive, A22-2-137.
49. Sichuan Provincial Archive, 50–174.
50. Shanghai Municipal Archive, A22-2-137.
51. Hebei Provincial Archive, 684-2-365.
52. *NBCK*, 8 May 1957, p. 11.
53. Sichuan Provincial Archive, 50–174.

and medicine, but peasants obviously constituted the majority and townsfolk were possibly under-represented.

Women were more likely to be pilgrims than men, and women could be instrumental in constituting the holy water event. In 1954 in Jiangsu province the old wife of Li Zunqing (李尊青) announced following the spring festival that she had a vat of holy water that could cure a hundred illnesses. Soon up to 300 people a day, drawn from eleven townships in Gaochun (高淳) and Longgang (陇港) counties, were flocking to drink the water.[54] In 1985 a fisherman heard strange sounds emanating from the sluice gate at the Huangjianzhen duck pond in Jiangsu, whereupon his aunt, Mrs Huang née Chen (黃陈氏), a woman of 76, and her female friend set out to find out the cause of the noise by using chopsticks as a form of divination. Soon they announced to the village that seven immortals had taken up residence in the pool, including Chen Zhijia (陈治家), a doctor from Yangzhou who had enjoyed great esteem among the people of Subei in the late Qing era.[55] Mrs Huang's friend then inaugurated a cycle of miracles which served to publicize the spiritual efficacy of the duck pond by curing a Mr Cai (蔡) of tuberculosis with 49 cups of water from the pond (seven being a magic number). Meanwhile Old Lady Ding (*Ding laotaitai* 丁老太太) from Huachuan (花川) village set about exploiting the commercial potential of the site by erecting a stall where she sold incense, carried out chopstick fortune-telling, and charged people a "registration fee" (*guahao fei* 挂号费).[56] This incident, at least, suggests that women, far from being duped by nefarious elements, as the authorities liked to insist, were central actors in constituting the sacred scenario.[57]

The involvement of cadres in "feudal superstition" is evident from reports already cited, and was a cause of great concern to higher-level authorities. It is something of a truism that basic-level cadres were the agents of the state within the village, obliged to carry out central policy, yet under constant pressure from their communities to interpret and implement central policy in ways that would do least damage to local interests. Since the struggle against "feudal super-stition" was a relatively low priority of the party-state – compared, for example, with grain requisitioning or collectivization – it was an issue on which local cadres were likely to compromise with their constituents. We know, for example, that some cadres tried to shield practitioners of superstition from the prying eyes of

54. *Gongan shouce*, No. 21 (1954), p. 2.
55. Li Changren, *Exposé of Superstitious Gods*, p. 6. Between 1964 and 1965, a rumour spread from Yunnan to Sichuan that seven female immortals had descended to earth and were offering sacred medicine, moving from place to place, spending seven days in each. Sichuan Provincial Archive, 50–377.
56. Li Changren, *Exposé of Superstitious Gods*, pp. 7–8.
57. That said, the sardonic account of this incident refers cryptically to over 200 women who were subjected to acts of indecency and insult by lads who "caught a fox to behead a demon" on their behalf. *Ibid.* p. 8.

outsiders.[58] But it is also clear that significant numbers of cadres themselves engaged in practices they knew to be proscribed by the Party and state organs to which they were accountable. Many reports mention this in general terms, but are sparing in detail. Along the Fujian coast, where superstition was said to be rampant in the wake of the famine (1959–61), it was reported of Lianjiang (连江) county: "some cadre members and their families have led the way in participating in superstition, crying 'Freedom of Belief' and 'Superstition is the Demand of the Masses'."[59] In 1963 in Sichuan, out of 291 female cadres who attended a three-level cadre conference, 149 were deemed to have "ordinary problems," of which 95 related to superstitious activities, chief of these being use of holy water; and of nine said to have "serious problems," three related to involvement in superstitious activity, although no details were given.[60] Furthermore, if officials tried to resist pressure from their constituents to condone superstitious activity, they risked provoking popular opposition. In the Stone Man mountain episode of 1953, the township head in Shiren was beaten up when he refused to lend "the masses" lamps so that they could climb the mountain at night.[61] In Changle (长乐) county in Fujian province in spring 1954, a district Party secretary was roughed up by a mob when he refused to declare that worship of the gods was legal. In Youqi (尤溪) county in the same province, a crowd of more than 30 people tried to make the work team sent to Huashang village sign a "treaty of surrender" (touxiang shu 偷降书) to allow superstitious activity; when it refused, the crowd showered it with faeces.[62]

Before going on to examine further the political implications of these holy water incidents, it is worth noting that the authorities took exception to them on a number of grounds. First, the exodus of sizeable numbers of people from collectives and communes adversely affected production. In Ding (定) county in Hebei in 1953, spring sowing and anti-drought measures were allegedly undermined by searches for holy water.[63] In 1957 spring ploughing in ten counties of eastern Guizhou was said to have been seriously disrupted because "thousands of households have been running hundreds of li to find holy water and medicine."[64] In Shahe (沙河) county in Hebei in the same year advanced co-operatives lost 2,100 days production, costing

58. Li Shengxian, *Anfang wuyi: wuyi pianshu jiemi* (*Secret Visits to Witch Doctors: Exposing the Secret Ruses of the Witch Doctors*) (Beijing: Zhongguo shehui chubanshe, 2000), p. 223.
59. C. S. Chen (ed. and intro.), *Rural People's Communes in Lien-Chiang: Documents Concerning Communes in Lien-chiang County, Fukien Province, 1962–63* (trans. Charles Price Ridley) (Stanford CA: Hoover Institution Press, 1969), p. 110.
60. Sichuan Provincial Archive, 29–170.
61. *NBCK*, 8 May 1953, p. 84.
62. *NBCK*, 12 June 1954, p. 173.
63. *NBCK*, 8 May 1953, p. 88.
64. *NBCK*, 8 May 1957, p. 11.

over 1600 *yuan*, as a result of members going off in search of holy water.[65] In addition, the arrival of hundreds and sometimes thousands of visitors at a sacred site had a deleterious impact on surrounding land. In 1953 visitors to the water hole at Huacao farm near Shanghai were said to have dug up six *mu* of farmland in their search for holy water and "sacred *qi*" (marsh gas) and to have trampled young crops over an area of four *mu*.[66] In 1956 in De (德) county in Shandong a mound where holy medicine was found "has been stripped of all its bushes and grasses and tracks have been made across all the surrounding farm land."[67]

Secondly, the authorities objected to holy water pilgrimages because they were wasteful, in that pilgrims spent money on travel to the sites and on buying religious paraphernalia. According to the report on the Stone Man incident, "many peasants are dissipating their incomes buying incense and candles and other offerings and going on pilgrimage to get medicine, and the number of people who have fallen ill has actually risen as a result of drinking unboiled water and eating mud." Some were said to have borrowed money for their fare and to have hired casual labourers to work their land so that they could go on pilgrimage.[68]

Thirdly, not least of the concerns of the authorities was that in a few cases people actually died from drinking infected water or eating poisonous herbs. In Chaoyang and neighbouring counties of Rehe in 1953, nine people were said to have died: five because they had not been taken to a doctor after taking holy drugs; three because they had been poisoned by "worms" said to be holy medicine; and one who had fallen from a cliff while gathering sacred herbs.[69] One of the fatalities was a girl from Caozhangzi (草杖子) village who died after taking holy drugs made from insects, frozen hawthorn, flour and ice.[70] In the holy water event that hit Guangdong province in 1954–55, it was claimed that in just three out of the 80 counties affected, 33 persons died as a result of taking holy water.[71]

The Political Implications of Holy Water Incidents

Such essentially practical concerns aside, the principal, indeed obsessive concern of the authorities was that holy water incidents were manufactured by enemies of the regime, in particular by the redemptive religious sects, in order to sow confusion and undermine public order. The *huidaomen* operated in secret and this, combined with their occult and sometimes millenarian beliefs, made them

65. *Ibid.* p. 8.
66. Shanghai Municipal Archive, A22-2-137.
67. *NBCK*, 28 March 1957, p. 542.
68. *NBCK*, 8 May 1953, p. 75, p. 83.
69. Hebei Provincial Archive, 684-2-365.
70. *NBCK*, 8 May 1953, p. 74.
71. *Renmin ribao*, 7 July 1955. *SCMP*, 1092, 20 July 1955.

suspect in the eyes of the authorities. The Yiguandao, for example, was organized hierarchically around clandestine "altars," each headed by an altar master (*tanzhu* 坛主), often located in people's homes. Disciples were initiated by means of the "three secret treasures" (a mantra, a hand position and a symbolic opening of a door in the body so that the soul might depart through a proper exit).[72] Their suspicious character was greatly compounded by the fact that the Communists believed the *huidaomen* had collaborated extensively with the Japanese and backed the Kuomintang to the hilt. This made them outright counter-revolutionary organizations in the eyes of the Party, even if it recognized that the mass of ordinary members had no political animus against the regime. Upon coming to power, it set about prosecuting a vigorous "withdraw from the sects" (*tuidao yundong*) campaign between 1951 and 1953. In Tianjin alone, where the first Yiguandao altar was set up in 1935, 209,000 were said to have withdrawn from the sects by June 1952.[73] The campaign broke the back of the *huidaomen* organizationally but by no means eliminated their influence, and they showed remarkable capacity to revive sporadically in the ensuing years.

Although there was a degree of paranoia on the part of the authorities about the *huidaomen*, there is evidence that some sects did exploit holy water incidents for subversive ends. In Hebei 34 out of the 42 instigators of the holy water epidemic in March 1953 were said to be leaders of the Yiguandao, the Xiantiandao (先天道, Way of Former Heaven), the Hunyuanmen (混元门, Primordial Chaos sect), and the Shengxiandao (圣贤道, Sacred Sage teaching), the rest being monks, nuns and female spirit mediums.[74] That there was deliberate sabotage by hostile political forces during this holy water epidemic is indubitable: between 7 and 20 April, 56 irrigation carts (*shuiche* 水车), belonging to village officials, Party and youth league members, were destroyed in seven villages of Ding county.[75] In Shandong province in spring 1957, in the course of the holy water events that affected eleven counties, over 100 disturbances took place in Liaocheng (聊城) prefecture in which peasants demanded to leave the advanced co-operatives. The report on these disturbances admitted that *huidaomen* were not behind all the protests, but noted the involvement of some 20 redemptive sects.[76] In Moli township in Guan county, Yang Minggui, leader of the White Lotus cult (Bailian jiao, 白莲教), and 16 of his disciples incited 36 households to leave the co-operative and beat up two township cadres.[77] In Madian (马店) township in Linqing (临清) county:

72. Bosco, "Yiguan Dao," pp. 423–444.
73. Kenneth P. Lieberthal, *Revolution and Tradition in Tientsin, 1949–1952* (Stanford CA: Stanford University Press, 1980), p. 112; DuBois, *Sacred Village*, p. 129.
74. *NBCK*, 8 May 1953, p. 87.
75. *Ibid.* p. 88.
76. *NBCK*, 28 March 1957, pp. 540–41.
77. *Ibid.* p. 541.

Fan Jingnan (范景南) and Fan Mingnan (范明南), bandits with blood debts, who escaped the net during the anti-counter-revolutionary movement, seeing that the administration of the advanced co-operatives was not initially sound, and seeing that as a result of last year's disaster (*zai* 灾) co-operative members were dissatisfied, seized on this to encourage middle peasants to "speak bitterness" and to demand to leave the co-operative.[78]

Most of the 43 ringleaders arrested by the Provincial Public Security Bureau in Shandong in 1957 were members of the Shengxiandao "who operate by exploiting superstitious thinking, inciting the backward masses by preying on the sick and thereby disrupting the work of the advanced co-operatives."[79] In what appears to have been the most dramatic but probably an isolated action, sectarians in Guangdong took advantage of holy water disturbances to plan an actual uprising against the Communists. In spring 1957 during an influenza epidemic in Xinyi (信宜) and Dianbai (电白) counties, a female spirit medium announced that holy water had been discovered at the Yangong temple in Dianbai township, prompting 80,000 people to flock to the temple from six counties. Taking advantage of the unsettled conditions, a band of sectarians, landlords and former Kuomintang officers allegedly formed a 14th Corps of the Chinese National Revolutionary Army, which prophesied that Guanyin would descend to earth on her birthday when the holy water at the Yangong temple would be particularly efficacious. It also predicted that three urns of silver would be unearthed close to the temple. In Xinyi city, either on or around that day, Corps members seized guns from public security officers, beat them up and tried to stage an armed attack on the CCP headquarters.[80]

Generally more important than the *huidaomen* were local spirit mediums, usually known as *wupo* or *shenhan*, who played a central role in constituting the holy water scenario. Faced by a new outbreak of "seeking the gods and begging for medicine" (*qiushen taoyao* 求神 讨药) in spring 1954, the Rehe provincial CCP sent out a directive on 19 April to all Party branches. This delivered the standard warning that counter-revolutionaries were using the situation to spread rumours, disrupt spring ploughing and sowing, and undermine public order, but conceded that many holy water incidents arose from widespread dissatisfaction with inadequate medical provision, limited understanding of hygiene and medicine, and "general superstition," which caused people to turn to spirit healers known as *xiangtou* (香头) and to female spirit mediums in order to ask them to "arouse the gods" (*tiao dashen* 跳大神) or "impart a prescription" (*chuan pianfang*

78. *Ibid*. p. 540.
79. *Ibid*. p. 541.
80. This is pieced together from Maoming shi difang zhi bangong shi, *Maoming shi da shiji* (Maoming City Local Gazetteer Office, *Chronicle of Events in Maoming City*) (Guangzhou: Zhongshan daxue chubanshe, 1997), p. 64; *SCMP*, 1588, 2 August 1957, pp. 31–32. The ten documents on the incident in the Guangdong provincial archive are closed. Guangdong provincial archive, 214–127.

传偏方).[81] *Xiangtou* are men and women who use animal spirits, usually the fox spirit, to heal disease, and are particularly associated with the north-eastern region. In Cang county in Hebei peasants distinguish between ordinary sicknesses of the body (*shi* 實) and those of supernatural origin (*xu* 虛), and believe that *xiangtou* are effective in curing *xu* sickness, which is often attributed to retribution for past evil deeds, spirits of the dead, animal spirits or celestial beings calling their heavenly children home.[82] In 1953 the holy water movement in Lingyuan county in Rehe was triggered by a *xiangtou* who proclaimed that: "The gate of heaven is wide open and all the gods have come down to earth to offer holy medicine." In the same county a woman announced that: "On the third day of the third lunar month, the Old Fox Spirit (*lao hu xian* 老狐仙) moved to the Wanglou mountain where he is dispensing holy medicine."[83] In the north-east corner of Rehe in 1954, a man styling himself an "official" *xiangtou* (*guan xiangtou* 官香頭) claimed that he had been authorized by the district authorities to practise for two months in order to rid the area of measles, using a fox spirit (*huli xian* 狐狸仙), a great spirit (*da xian* 大仙), a yellow spirit (*huang xian* 黃仙), a toad spirit (*hama xian* 蛤蟆仙), a wolf spirit (*lang xian* 狼仙), a white spirit (*bai xian* 白仙) and a snake spirit (*she xian* 蛇仙).[84]

As the example of the "official" *xiangtou* implies, spirit mediums were eminently capable of deploying the regime's rhetoric to suit their own ends. A female spirit medium in Wudan (乌丹) county in Rehe, where 102 people had died of measles, justified doling out holy water "brought to earth by the gods," by saying that the medical co-operatives required patients to pay a fee which many poor people could not afford, whereas the gods gave their services for free. The gods, she reasoned, were serving the people, and added that when dispensing holy water herself, she always gave priority to members of PLA and revolutionary martyr families.[85] Xin Liu argues that use of the language of state by ordinary folk should not necessarily be construed as evidence of the state's ideological power; rather such language "can be employed by anyone on an occasion for which the employment of it may generate certain effects."[86] Such usage testifies to a form of "creative accommodation" with the regime on the part of people eager not to abandon a source of spiritual power that they believe is helpful to them.[87] At the same time, spirit healers were not afraid to stand up to the local authorities. In Wudan county a female

81. Hebei provincial archive, 684-2-432. *Tiao dashen* is a shamanic ritual to summon ghosts in north-east China. Liu Delong (ed.), *Minjian suxin yu kexue wenhua* (*Popular Beliefs and Scientific Culture*) (Jinan: Shandong jiaoyu chubanshe, 2002), p. 325.

82. DuBois, *Sacred Village*, ch. 3.

83. Hebei Provincial Archive, 684-2-365.

84. *Ibid.*

85. *Ibid.*

86. Xin Liu, *The Otherness of Self: a Genealogy of the Self in Contemporary China* (Ann Arbor, University of Michigan Press, 2002), p. 104.

87. I am indebted to Vivienne Shue for this insight.

spirit medium claimed she had the permission of the county women's federation to practise and that the district authorities had no right to stop her. Two female medical officers from the county town arrived in the village while she was conducting an exorcism, but turned tail when she shrieked at them: "Oh, I knew you would come. I was thinking of going to fetch you myself!"[88] Despite such political manipulation, the Rehe provincial Party committee warned against treating spirit healers as if they were counter-revolutionaries. Those who failed to "wash their hands" should be set to regular work and made to account for their actions and to apologize before the masses. Model *xiangtou* who reformed themselves should be used to explain to the masses the error of believing in supernatural cures. In cases where a *xiangtou* refused to abandon her avocation, she should be sentenced by due process to a term of reform through labour, but this should not be done indiscriminately.[89]

The Reaction of the Authorities

Virtually all circulars from national, provincial and sometimes county authorities were critical of the way in which local officials dealt with holy water outbreaks. During the Stone Man mountain episode in 1953, it was said:

Township leaders and village cadres were at a loss to know what to do and took a negative attitude, allowing the phenomena to expand in scope. For example, in Jinhua county, Xianqiao (仙桥) district, the leaders and cadres in Huangni (黄泥) village, after discovering that the villagers were worshipping and taking sacred medicine, took no measures whatsoever and didn't even organize any propaganda teams to stand by the pool side.[90]

It fell to "progressive peasants," the report claimed, to compel officials to take action: "People drinking the sacred water are falling ill, but what are our officials doing to stop it?" In Longshan (龙山) township on 24 April, over 300 locals, disgusted at the fact that pilgrims coming to take holy water from a local pond were defecating by the side of the pond, surrounded the township government office and refused to leave until officials took action. They insisted, moreover, that township leaders make a public self-criticism, which they had no choice but to do.[91] In the first holy water episode in Rehe in 1953, the provincial Public Security Bureau criticized county-level cadres in the 13 counties and banners affected for regarding the episodes as "pure superstition" and failing to take swift action. It also upbraided basic-level cadres for their reluctance to act against class enemies, although it conceded that this sprang in part from the fact that they had earlier been criticized for "coercion and commandism."[92]

88. *Ibid.*
89. Hebei provincial archive, 684-2-432.
90. *NBCK*, 8 May 1953, p. 83.
91. *Ibid.* p. 84.
92. Hebei Provincial Archive, 684-2-365

The best-coordinated official intervention in a holy water episode occurred at the Huacao farm in Xinjing in 1953. Because it took place so close to Shanghai, where Communists were numerous and well organized, and because the episode was huge in scale, the authorities resolved to mount a text-book operation to suppress it. Initially, the Xinjing district Party committee took the view that the eruption of holy water fever would soon exhaust itself and failed to inform the Shanghai municipal committee of the CCP. When the latter learned of the disturbances two weeks later, its propaganda bureau was initially divided on how to respond, some wanting to fill in the water hole and prevent visitors from getting to the site, others preferring to exploit the situation for propaganda purposes. In the end, the bureau called for a twin-track approach to what it defined as a struggle against both the "backward thinking" of the masses and the disruptive activities of "bad elements."[93] On 22 April, Huang Min (黄敏) from the Shanghai municipal committee delivered a report to the Xinjing committee, calling for unified thinking on the part of officials, the formation of a leadership organ, to be headed by Huang himself, and the sending of a work team to the holy water site. The leadership organ, divided into a secretariat, a bureau for propaganda and a bureau for public order, comprised no fewer than 95 operatives, including 20 from the propaganda bureau of the municipal committee, eight from the Xinjing district committee and 66 from the Public Security Bureau. The task of the latter was discreetly to keep an eye on "suspicious elements" (ke yi fenzi 可疑分子). Huang Min explained that the number of police would be reduced once they had control of the situation. Trade unions were also mobilized to talk to the drivers who brought many of the 200,000 pilgrims to the site. Despite fears of counter-revolutionary subversion, the work team later acknowledged that there was no political group behind the events. Only one potentially dangerous incident occurred when early on the morning of 29 April, the day the work team began filling in the water hole, some 700 to 800 people broke through the cordon at two of the five propaganda stations. "For half an hour, things looked bad, but the people were persuaded to withdraw from the water hole." The work team carried out extensive propaganda, principally about the harmful effects of drinking unboiled water. The non-Party Shanghai Association for the Dissemination of Science provided useful facts, such as that there were 4,260,000 colon bacilli in one cubic centimetre of the holy water. For the literate, blackboards and charts were set up explaining the harmful effects of bacteria, although the work team concluded that these proved rather ineffective. More valuable was the provision of magnifying glasses, bought from a peddler at 3,000 yuan each, which allowed the curious to look at the microbes living in the water. For some, the sight of these "celestial insects" merely confirmed their faith in the water's miraculous properties, while

93. Shanghai Municipal Archive, A22-2-137.

others sagely concluded that they would need to boil the water before they could drink it. At the same time, propagandists both on site and in neighbouring schools and factories stressed the damage done to production by pilgrims absenting themselves from farming, the waste of resources involved, and the fact that they were being overcharged by greedy drivers. According to the work team, propagandists addressed young and old in respectful tones, but its report is frank to the point of self-parody about the brusqueness with which they harangued individuals through megaphones: "You, young woman with permed hair, wearing a red *qipao*, why are you going to drink the thick muddy water?" "You, young man about to ladle water, you should be ashamed of yourself!"[94]

By no means all authorities responded to holy water incidents in so co-ordinated a fashion. The ever-present fear that such incidents would be exploited by counter-revolutionaries meant that many local authorities inclined to repression rather than education: "Several hundred PLA men with machine guns are preventing people from going to worship the Buddha."[95] Moreover, whenever leftism was in the ascendant in national policy, local authorities were more likely to treat holy water events as politically motivated. In December 1958, the government finally conceded that counter-revolutionary elements were "not many"; yet the Great Leap Forward that was then proceeding apace saw a lurch towards leftism in public security policy, with the number of those arrested for counter-revolutionary activity rising substantially.[96] Following the débâcle of the Great Leap Forward, the Ministry of Public Security campaigned against "leftist excesses" in public security work and urged its organs to handle contradictions among the people correctly. In line with this, a circular of 22 August 1961 stressed the need to distinguish between superstitious activity fomented by counter-revolutionaries and super-stitious activity in which peasants were seeking "spiritual solace" (*jingshen anwei* 精神安慰) as a result of "the calamities and difficulties."[97] At the 7,000 Cadres Conference from 11 January to 7 February 1962, Liu Shaoqi condemned the use of dictatorial methods to deal with contradictions among the people, saying this was tantamount to the "Kuomintang style" and to "standing on the people, pressuring the people."[98] This easing of control led to an upsurge in superstitious activity between 1962 and 1965.

94. This account is based on the report of the work team and on two reports by the propaganda bureau of the Shanghai municipal committee of the CCP. Shanghai municipal archive, A22-2-137.
95. *NBCK*, 8 May 1953, p. 82.
96. *Zhongguo renmin gongan shigao* (*Draft History of Chinese People's Public Security*) (Beijing: Jingguan jiaoyu chubanshe, 1997), pp. 439, 299.
97. *Ibid.* p. 311.
98. *Ibid.* p. 315.

Popular Attitudes to the State

Holy water incidents were almost certainly the most widespread form of unauthorized mass activity in the first decade of the PRC. And although such incidents were certainly not new, they appear to have increased in frequency during this period. At the same time, we should not rule out the possibility that the new communist authorities were simply more vigilant than their predecessors, and that their practices of surveillance, monitoring, interrogation, accusation and confession gave greater definition to what had hitherto been scattered and inchoate phenomena. Holy water incidents suggest that while the power of the party-state was far stronger in China at the grassroots than it had been, for example, in the Soviet Union between 1918 and 1933, it was less secure than it appeared. For one thing, activity by those dubbed "counter-revolutionaries" was certainly more long lasting than many scholars have appreciated. The redemptive sects may have been destroyed in organizational terms by 1953, but their capacity to engage the needs and desires of the rural population in ways they could understand proved strong at least until the Great Leap Forward.[99] For another, it is clear now that the higher authorities had little confidence in the capacity of local agents to deal with such incidents. The inability or unwillingness of basic-level cadres to stop hundreds of thousands of people abandoning production and setting off – sometimes on long journeys – testifies to the real limits of state power in this period. Party, government and security organs could inveigh against the reduction in farming output, the waste of money on travel and purchase of ritual items, the unauthorized movement of people and, above all, the exploitation of "superstitious" thinking by politically harmful elements, but they could do little to prevent them. This was not least because many basic-level cadres themselves subscribed to superstitious thinking or were fearful of those, such as *xiangtou*, who claimed power on the basis of their ability to engage the supernatural. Over time, the capacity of the party-state to impose its will doubtless increased, especially with the establishment of the communes and the imposition of the *hukou* (户口) policy. But any short-term lifting of controls, such as took place following the devastating famine in the early 1960s, led to the immediate revival of superstitious activity.

The authority of the party-state was also less secure in this period than was once assumed because its rural policies, certainly those that followed land reform, were far from popular, and created considerable anxiety in sections of the peasantry. While the period up to the Great Leap Forward may still be considered one of general optimism compared with the situation prior to 1949, we now know that in the

---

99. Stephen Jones goes further and argues that the sects continued to organize in China throughout the 1950s and even into the Cultural Revolution period. Stephen Jones, *Plucking the Winds: Lives of Village Musicians in Old and New China* (Leiden: Chime Foundation, 2004), p. 107.

countryside, especially, many of the policies of the regime created widespread anxiety.[100] Vivienne Shue noted the fear that the creation of year-round mutual aid teams created in all sections of the rural populace.[101] In 1954 and 1955, the implementation of the unified procurement and supply programme encountered nationwide resistance when the state failed to limit procurements and to sell enough grain back to the peasants. And in 1956 and 1957 rural contention reached a peak when the peasants were forced to join collective farms.[102] Relations between rural communities and the authorities look to have been anything but smooth in these years. Indeed it seems possible that the entire period between 1951 and 1962 was one in which many peasants felt troubled that requisitioning and collectivization were undermining their traditional way of life. Certainly, the circumstances surrounding the discovery of holy water often reflect anxiety about official policies. The mood of the people in the Stone Man mountain area in Zhejiang in 1953 was described as "uneasy" (ren xin bu an 人心不安), and in Hebei in the same year as "fearful."[103] Yet we must assume that obtaining holy water inspired pilgrims with some hope. The stories that accompanied the discovery of holy water served to remind people that the power of the gods was still at work in the world, still a resource that could be accessed in order to deal with their tribulations. Amid general uncertainty, then, the quest for holy water attested to the belief of millions that the only forces on which they could rely were supernatural in nature; and they showed impressive determination to uphold rituals they believed could energize relations between the spirit and human worlds and thus ease their plight. Communities were not afraid to act in defence of their right to worship and seek favour from the gods; nor were they afraid to voice their dissatisfaction, not least with dismal medical provision; nor most significantly, were they afraid to disobey local officials and set out in search of holy water. Whether this makes the quest for holy water a form of resistance, however, is moot. Seeking holy water was essentially an individual rather than a community response to trials and anxieties, even if in some circumstances a majority of villagers were involved. Individuals demonstrated their unwillingness to acquiesce in their fate; but ultimately, with the

100. I discuss the extent of fear in the rural population in this period in "Fear and rumour in the People's Republic of China, 1949–58," *Cultural and Social History*, 2008 (forthcoming).

101. Vivienne Shue, *Peasant China in Transition* (Berkeley: University of California Press, 1980), pp. 176–77.

102. Huaiyin Li, "The first encounter: peasant resistance to state control of grain in east China in the mid-1950s," *The China Quarterly*, No. 185 (2006), pp. 145–163; Thomas P. Bernstein, "Cadre and peasant behavior under conditions of insecurity and deprivation: the grain supply crisis of the spring of 1955," in A. Doak Barnett (ed.), *Chinese Communist Politics in Action* (Seattle: University of Washington Press, 1969), p. 371.

103. *NBCK*, 8 May 1953, pp. 81, 88.

exception of committed members of the sects, they were not out to make trouble for the authorities.

The sheer scope of the holy water phenomenon is a reminder of a truism: the CCP carried out a revolution in a society where a majority still clung, at least in part, to a magico-religious world-view. The frustration expressed by the authorities at the pervasiveness of holy water incidents highlights the gulf that existed between the scientific rationality and materialist epistemology of the party-state and the beliefs of millions of its subjects. Yet not too much should be made of this gulf. For one thing, the "masses" were perfectly capable of combining magico-religious elements with secular elements from the Party's own discourse, as the examples of the politically inventive *xiangtou* suggest, so if their world-view was rooted in an essentially religious cosmology, it was nevertheless powerfully shaped by revolutionary policies and by official propaganda. For another, thousands of the agents of the party-state at the grassroots themselves subscribed to magico-religious beliefs and were undoubtedly a conduit through which many of the supposedly proscribed idioms and symbols of popular religion entered official political culture. Many have noted the powerfully religious character of Maoism, with its god-like leader, its struggle to realize a heavenly vision, its sacred texts, its demonized enemies, and its "ceremonies of innocence and rituals of struggle."[104] Given the popularity of holy water, it comes as no surprise to learn that Mao himself could provide holy water as efficacious as that of any god. Red Guards, for example, would scoop up "happiness water" from the Gold Water Bridge in front of Tiananmen before setting out from Beijing to "share revolutionary experience" during the Cultural Revolution.[105] And when Mao presented the workers of the capital with mangoes he had been given by the foreign minister of Pakistan on 5 August 1968, his doctor, who was then living at a Beijing textile factory, recalls how the workers there held a huge ceremony, "rich in the recitation of Mao's words, to welcome the arrival of the mango" donated to the factory. The workers sealed the mango in wax, hoping to preserve it for posterity. Unfortunately, no one thought to sterilize it, and after a few days it began to rot. The revolutionary committee at the factory then decided to boil the flesh of the mango in a huge pot of water. "Another ceremony was held, equally solemn. Mao was again greatly venerated and the gift of the mango was lauded as evidence of the Chairman's deep concern for the workers. Then everyone in the factory filed by and each worker drank a spoonful of the water in which the sacred mango had been boiled." When the doctor told the Chairman about this veneration, Mao merely laughed. "He had no problem with the

104. Richard Madsen, *Morality and Power in a Chinese Village* (Berkeley: University of California Press, 1994).

105. Ban Wang, *The Sublime Figure of History: Aesthetics and Politics in 20th-Century China* (Stanford: Stanford University Press, 1997), p. 206.

mango worship and seemed delighted by the story."[106] This incident, in some ways trivial, nicely illustrates the shift in the political culture of the Maoist regime as it came to incorporate more and more elements of the popular culture it purported to despise. If in the early 1950s, the party-state had endeavoured to eliminate popular reliance on magical power, by the time of the Cultural Revolution, it sought to exploit such reliance by generating its own sources of magical power. Its success in utilizing idioms from popular culture, such as that of holy water, provides a clue as to how, despite the traumatic changes it unleashed, it managed to retain the loyalty of millions of ordinary people.

106. Zhisui Li, *The Private Life of Chairman Mao* (London: Arrow Books, 1996), p. 503

Factional Conflict at Beijing University, 1966–1968*

Andrew G. Walder

ABSTRACT For two years after the summer of 1966, Beijing University was racked by factional conflict and escalating violence. Despite the intensity of the struggle the factions did not express differences in political doctrine or orientation towards the status quo. Nie Yuanzi, the veteran Party cadre who advanced rapidly in the municipal hierarchy after denouncing both the old Beida Party Committee and the work team, fiercely defended her growing power against opponents led by several former allies. Compromise proved impossible as mutual accusations intensified, and interventions by national politicians served only to entrench the divisions. The conflicts were bitter and personal not because they expressed differences between status groups, but because the rivals knew one another so well, had so much in common, and because the consequences of losing in this struggle were so dire.

From 1966 to 1968 China was torn apart by factional struggles that escalated into armed conflict and persisted until the imposition of martial law. The ubiquity and intensity of these conflicts suggested that they were deeply rooted in China's political and social structures. Factions were typically distinguished by their reputed orientation towards the status quo. "Conservatives" presumably viewed existing political and social arrangements more favourably, and considered the Party's traditions and institutions to be basically sound. "Rebels" or "radicals," on the other hand, presumably viewed these institutions more critically.[1] Some, noting that these struggles often seemed to be about power rather than doctrine or policy, have balked at the distinction.[2]

* I am grateful to Michael Schoenhals for his generous help with sources and critical comments on an earlier draft.

1. See Hong Yung Lee, *The Politics of the Chinese Cultural Revolution: A Case Study* (Berkeley: University of California Press, 1978), and Tang Shaojie, "Qinghua daxue liangpai kan 'wenhua da geming' zhong qunzhong zuzhi de duili he fenqi" ("Antagonisms and splits among mass organizations during the 'Cultural Revolution': the case of the two factions at Qinghua University"), in Zhang Hua and Su Caiqing (eds.), *Huishou "wenge": Zhongguo shinian "wenge" fenxi yu fansi (The "Cultural Revolution" in Retrospect: Analysis and Reflections on China's Ten-year "Cultural Revolution"*), 2 vols. (Beijing: Zhonggong dangshi chubanshe, 1999), pp. 774–788.

2. Xu Youyu finds the distinction meaningless after the rebel factions split in early 1967. See his *Xingxing sese de zaofan: Hongweibing jingshen suzhi de xingcheng ji yanbian (Rebellion of All Hues: The Formation and Evolution of Red Guard Mentalities)* (Hong Kong: Zhongwen daxue chubanshe, 1999).

Many observers suspected a social basis for factions: conservative factions should have appealed to those in favourable positions, while rebel factions should have attracted those in less favourable positions.[3] The idea was elaborated in studies of particular groups, and had obvious validity in certain well-known cases.[4] The Shanghai Scarlet Guards, for example, mobilized workers through the official trade union structures to defend the Shanghai Municipal Party Committee against rebel attacks in the autumn of 1966.[5] The early high school Red Guards were dominated by students from revolutionary cadre households, and resisted escalating attacks on senior officials.[6]

Beijing University (Beida 北大) was at the epicentre of the Cultural Revolution, and it also experienced severe internal factionalism. Yet the course of this two-year struggle remains unexamined to this day. Only recently has it been possible to reconstruct the origins of the factions, the identities of their leaders, the nature of the dispute between the two sides, and the course of their escalating conflict.[7] To a surprising extent, the two sides were similar in their leadership and political orientation. They disagreed vociferously about political tactics and personalities, but there were no doctrinal or programmatic differences that would mark either faction as conservative or radical. Once the Beida factions allied with other groups across the city and became embroiled in the manoeuvrings of national-level politicians, the stakes for the two sides escalated, divisions hardened and violence ensued. This micro-history suggests that violent factionalism could be a competitive struggle between similar claimants to power rather than an expression of structural cleavages in Chinese society.

3. See Ezra Vogel, *Canton Under Communism* (Cambridge, MA: Harvard University Press, 1969), pp. 339–340, and Lee, *Politics of the Cultural Revolution*, pp. 1–6.

4. See Gordon White, "The politics of *Hsia-hsiang* youth," *The China Quarterly*, No. 59 (1974), pp. 491–517, and "The politics of demobilized soldiers from liberation to Cultural Revolution," *The China Quarterly*, No. 82 (1980), pp. 187–213; Andrew G. Walder, "The Chinese Cultural Revolution in the factories: party-state structures and patterns of conflict," in Elizabeth Perry (ed.), *Putting Class in its Place: Worker Identities in East Asia* (Berkeley: Institute of East Asian Studies, University of California, 1996), pp. 167–198.

5. Elizabeth J. Perry and Li Xun, *Proletarian Power: Shanghai in the Cultural Revolution* (Boulder, CO: Westview, 1997), Andrew G. Walder, *Chang Ch'un-ch'iao and Shanghai's January Revolution* (Ann Arbor: University of Michigan Center for Chinese Studies, 1978).

6. Anita Chan, Stanley Rosen and Jonathan Unger, "Students and class warfare: the social roots of the Red Guard conflict in Guangzhou (Canton)," *The China Quarterly*, No. 83 (1980), pp. 397–446, and Gordon White, *The Politics of Class and Class Origin: The Case of the Cultural Revolution* (Canberra: Contemporary China Centre, Australian National University, 1976).

7. For a survey of the new sources that make this research possible, see Joseph W. Esherick, Paul G. Pickowicz and Andrew G. Walder, "The Chinese Cultural Revolution as history: an introduction," in Joseph W. Esherick, Paul G. Pickowicz and Andrew G. Walder (eds.), *The Chinese Cultural Revolution as History* (Stanford: Stanford University Press, 2006), pp. 1–28.

The Wall Poster of 25 May 1966

On 25 May 1966, in an act that is often viewed as the opening salvo of the Cultural Revolution, Nie Yuanzi (聂元梓) and six philosophy department colleagues denounced Beida Party secretary Lu Ping (陆平) and two municipal Party committee officials – Song Shuo (宋硕) and Peng Peiyun (彭珮云) – for obstructing the Cultural Revolution at Beida. Although this wall poster is considered the precursor of the Red Guard movement, none of the authors was a student. All of them were cadres or instructors of Marxism-Leninism, and all but one were veteran Party members.[8]

Nie Yuanzi, the most senior of the group, was in fact a middle-aged cadre with extensive elite connections. Sitting on the university's Party committee, she was among the school's top 30 officials. At the time, she was 45 and married to an official in the Central Discipline Inspection Commission 23 years her senior.[9] She and her husband regularly socialized with officials of ministerial rank.[10] Her brother Nie Zhen (聂真) was vice-Party secretary of People's University and married to an ex-wife of Liu Shaoqi. Nie's elder sister worked in the CCP north China bureau's propaganda department, where her husband was vice-head.[11] Nie joined the Party as a middle school student in 1938 and spent the war years in Yan'an (延安). Although she never completed high school, she attended a series of cadre schools in later years. In the 1950s she served in several Party posts in Harbin, and was married to Wu Hongyi (吴宏毅), a vice-mayor on the standing committee of the Harbin municipal Party committee. After their divorce in late 1959, Nie transferred to Beida, serving as vice-chair of economics until 1963, when she was promoted to the post of general branch secretary in the philosophy department.[12]

The famous wall poster revived an intra-Party split that appeared during the Socialist Education Movement (SEM). In July 1964 Kang Sheng (康生) ordered Zhang Panshi (张磐石), vice-head of the CCP propaganda department, to investigate the school.[13] After interviewing a number of disgruntled cadres and instructors who had been

---

8. Mu Xin, "'Quan guo diyizhang dazibao' chulong jingguo" ("How the 'nation's first wall poster' was cooked up"), *Zhonggong dangshi ziliao* (*Materials on Chinese Communist Party History*), No. 75 (2000), pp. 166–67, and Wang Xuezhen, Wang Xiaoting, Huang Wenyi and Guo Jianrong (eds.), *Beijing daxue jishi (yibajiuba-yijiujiuqi) (Beijing University Chronology (1898–1997))* (2 vols.) (Beijing: Beijing daxue chubanshe, 1998), p. 640.

9. Wu Gaizhi, who joined the Party in 1924, attended the Whampoa Military Academy, took part in the Northern Expedition, Nanchang uprising and Long March: Nie Yuanzi, *Nie Yuanzi huiyilu (Nie Yuanzi's Memoirs)* (Hong Kong: Shidai guoji chuban youxian gongsi, 2004), p. 94.

10. For example, with the head of the CCP Organization Department, An Ziwen; *Nie Yuanzi's Memoirs*, pp. 95–99.

11. *Ibid.* pp. 18–19, and *Xin Beida bao*, 30 August 1967, p. 3.

12. *Nie Yuanzi's Memoirs*, pp. 69–71, 74–79.

13. Beijing University Party History Office, "Beida shejiao yundong de shishi jingguo" ("The course of the socialist education movement at Beida"), *Zhonggong dangshi ziliao*, No. 81 (2002), pp. 90–91.

involved in a series of conflicts with the Beida Party leadership since
the late 1950s, they concluded that there were many "politically
impure elements" and "foreign spies" active in the university.[14] By
January 1965 Zhang was holding public struggle sessions against
alleged class enemies, including numerous Party secretaries and
standing committee members who had bourgeois backgrounds or
family members with overseas or Nationalist connections.[15] The
campaign seemed excessive to many on the work team and in the
Beijing and central Party apparatus, and a heated debate ensued, with
Beijing Party secretary Peng Zhen (彭真) strongly criticizing the work
team. Deng Xiaoping (邓小平) agreed. He criticized Kang Sheng,
certified Beida and Lu Ping as politically sound, and ordered a
rectification campaign.[16]

The tables were turned on militant work team members and their
Beida supporters, now criticized for "leftist errors." Beida's SEM
activists were forced to make self-criticisms: Nie Yuanzi, philosophy
department instructors Kong Fan (孔繁), Yang Keming (杨克明),
Zhang Enci (张恩慈), Sun Pengyi (孙蓬一) and others.[17] Their most
forceful critics were Chang Xiping (常溪萍), work team vice-head and
Party secretary of East China Normal University,[18] Song Shuo, vice-
head of the education and cultural department of the Beijing
municipal Party committee, and Peng Peiyun, who worked in
Song's department.[19] Beida's "leftists," now disgraced, began
transferring elsewhere.[20]

Nie's challenge to Lu Ping in May 1966 was orchestrated by Kang
Sheng. Zhang Enci, who had recently transferred from Beida to
Kang's central theoretical research group, submitted a report on 5
May 1966 calling for a reversal of the SEM verdicts. Kang sent the report
to Mao, who was away from Beijing during Politburo meetings at which
Peng Zhen and other ranking leaders were purged. On 11 May, Mao had
it reprinted and circulated to the Party leadership.[21] Three days later
Kang Sheng sent a task force to Beida to instigate denunciations of Lu
Ping. His wife, Cao Yi'ou (曹轶欧), chaired the group, which included
anti-Lu Ping members of the SEM work team and their supporters.[22]

14. See *Beijing University Chronology*, p. 614. These earlier conflicts are described
in *Xin Beida*, 22 and 27 September 1966, *Nie Yuanzi's Memoirs*, pp. 79–89, and Yang
Xun, *Xinlu: Liangzhi de mingyun* (*Tolerance: The Destiny of Knowledge*) (Beijing:
Xinhua chubanshe, 2004), pp. 115–147.
15. "The course of the socialist education movement at Beida," pp. 90–92.
16. *Ibid.* pp. 94–95, and *Beijing University Chronology*, pp. 621–27.
17. *Youguan Chang Xiping tongzhi zai Beijing daxue shejiao zhong de yixie cailiao*
(*Some Materials on Comrade Chang Xiping during the Beida SEM*), "Xin xiang dong"
Huadong shifan daxue zhandou dui, 5 October 1966, pp. 19–39; *Nie Yuanzi's
Memoirs*, pp. 88–89.
18. See *Some Materials on Comrade Chang Xiping*, pp. 10–19.
19. Peng's efforts are detailed in *Dazibao xuan (liu)* (*Selected Wall Posters, 6*),
Beijing daxue gongzuozu bangongshi, 1 July 1966.
20. Nie was herself preparing to transfer; *Nie Yuanzi's Memoirs*, pp. 89 and 100.
21. *Ibid.* p. 89; *Jianguo yilai Mao Zedong wengao, Di shier ce* (*Mao Zedong's Post-
1949 Manuscripts, Vol. 12*) (Beijing: Zhongyang wenxian chubanshe, 1987), p. 57.
22. *Beijing University Chronology*, p. 642, and *Materials on Chang Xiping*, pp. 19–25.

The group initially approached Chen Shouyi (陈守一), member of the Beida Party standing committee, who declined.[23] Cao's group then turned to Nie and the instructors in her department.[24] Nie was a likely candidate: in late 1965 she had submitted a report to Mao, protesting at the way the SEM activists had been used by the work team and then betrayed.[25] Coincidentally, only weeks before she had established a direct relationship with Kang Sheng after meeting him to report her suspicions that An Ziwen was leaking state secrets to his mistress, whom Nie suspected of being a spy. Kang instructed her to keep an eye on the couple and submit regular reports.[26] Mindful of her SEM experience, Nie agreed to denounce Lu Ping only after seeing the 16 May circular and receiving assurances from Cao.[27]

Lu Ping's supporters initially denounced Nie's group as anti-Party conspirators.[28] The school's top leaders split. Two powerful figures – first vice-Party secretary Ge Hua (戈华) and standing committee member Cui Xiongkun (崔雄崑) – sided with Nie. They wrote to the Central Committee accusing Lu Ping of an attempt to "suppress revolution," and demanded that another work team be sent to Beida.[29] The issue was settled on 1 June when Mao abruptly ordered nationwide publication of the wall poster.[30] Zhang Chengxian (張承先), member of the Hebei provincial Party committee secretariat, was hastily appointed to head a new work team. He arrived that evening to announce that Lu Ping was out and a work team was on its way.[31]

23. *Beijing University Chronology*, p. 642; and Beida dangshi xiaoshi yanjiushi dangshi zu, "Kang Sheng, Cao Yi'ou yu 'di yizhang dazibao'" ("Kang Sheng, Cao Yi'ou and the 'first wall poster'"), *Bainian chao*, No. 9 (2001), pp. 32–38. See also Chen Shouyi, "Lishi shi gongzheng de: Beida jiaoshou yi 'wenge'" ("History is impartial: a Beida professor's memoir of the 'Cultural Revolution'"), *Zhongguo yanjiu* (*China Studies*), No. 1 (1995), pp. 161–184.

24. See *Beijing University Chronology*, p. 642, and Mu Xin, "How the 'nation's first wall poster' was cooked up," pp. 167–68.

25. She submitted the report to Mao's secretary, Tian Jiaying, through her older sister, who knew him; *Nie Yuanzi's Memoirs*, pp. 88–89.

26. *Ibid.* pp. 101–104. Nie and her husband played mah-jong regularly with An and his mistress.

27. *Ibid*, pp. 111–18, *Beijing University Chronology*, p. 642. Recent accounts disagree about Nie's role in writing the wall poster and whether Cao initiated it. A critical overview of the extant accounts is Liu Yigao, "Cong quanguo 'di yi zhang dazibao' he xiaogang 'hongshou yin' tanqi" ("About the nation's 'first wall poster' and the Xiaogang village 'red handprint'"), *Zhonggong dangshi ziliao*, No. 87 (2003), pp. 144–160.

28. "Beijing daxue wenhua da geming dashiji,1966.5.25–1966.8.8" ("Chronicle of major events of Beijing University's Cultural Revolution, 25 May–8 August 1966), in *Wuchan jieji wenhua da geming dazibao xuan (yi)* (*Selected Wall Posters of the Great Proletarian Cultural Revolution, 1*), Wenhua geming weiyuanhui dazibaozu bian, 20 September 1966, pp. 43–44, *Nie Yuanzi's Memoirs*, pp. 122–128, and *Renmin ribao*, 5 June 1966.

29. *Beijing University Chronology*, p. 643.

30. Mao wrote to Kang Sheng and Chen Boda, "... it is absolutely essential to circulate this in newspapers nationwide. Now we can start to smash the stronghold of reaction at Beijing University." *Mao Zedong's Post-1949 Manuscripts*, Vol. 12, pp. 62–63.

31. Zhang Chengxian, "'Wenhua da geming' chuqi de Beida gongzuozu" ("Beijing University's work team in the early stages of the 'Cultural Revolution'"), *Zhonggong dangshi ziliao*, No. 70 (1999), pp. 17–18.

The Beida Work Team

This was a complete victory for the Nie group. Cao Yi'ou became the work team's vice-head, and was its liaison with the Central Cultural Revolution Group (CCRG), where she also headed the staff office.[32] Liu Yangqiao (刘仰峤), an anti-Lu Ping member of the SEM work team, was in its leading group along with Ge Hua and Cui Xiongkun, the Beida Party standing committee members who sided with Nie over the wall poster. Nie became director of the work team's staff office, and Zhang Enci vice-director. Yang Keming, who helped draft the wall poster, became vice-director of the staff office in charge of propaganda. Kong Fan, philosophy department instructor and a Nie ally in the SEM, joined the work team's policy research group.[33]

The work team implemented the agenda of the SEM dissidents. It targeted prominent administrators and faculty for impure class origins or foreign connections, and anyone who sided with Lu Ping in earlier battles.[34] By early July the Beida leadership was devastated. Only one out of 20 general branch secretaries (Nie Yuanzi) was judged reliable, and 16 were judged to be class enemies. Fewer than 8 per cent of all the cadres were judged to be without error, and two-thirds were said to have committed errors serious enough to remove them from their posts.[35] Only one-third of the cadres emerged from this ordeal unscathed.

Despite its militance, the work team was abruptly withdrawn at the end of July and its leader, Zhang Chengxian, was denounced for its efforts to curtail student violence. Having declared open season on the Beida Party and faculty, the work team found it difficult to control the students. During proliferating struggle sessions, the accused wore tall hats, placards were hung from their necks, they were shoved about violently on the stage, their hair pulled, arms fixed behind them while kneeling in the "jet plane" position, big character posters pasted on their bodies, and sometimes were beaten severely. By 17 June the work team counted 178 cadres, teachers and students who were treated in this manner; after one session a vice-chair of the history department committed suicide.[36]

32. *Beijing University Chronology*, pp. 645 and 647, and Guo Yingqiu and Wang Houyi, "Guo Yingqiu linzhong koushu: 'wenge' qinliji" ("Guo Yingqiu's deathbed testimony: a personal account of the 'Cultural Revolution'"), *Yanhuang chunqiu*, No. 128 (2002), p. 49.

33. See *Beijing University Chronology*, pp. 647–49, *Wuchan jieji wenhua da geming dazibao xuan (si)* (*Selected Wall Posters of the Great Proletarian Cultural Revolution, 4*), Wenhua geming weiyuanhui dazibaozu bian, 1 March 1967, pp. 31–34, *Dazibao xuan, zengkan (ershi) zhiyi* (*Selected Wall Posters, Supplement 12, Part 1*), Beijing daxue wenhua geming weiyuanhui dazibaozu bian, 28 November 1966, pp. 7–11, and Zhang Chengxian, "Beijing University's work team," p. 22. Nie contradicts the last two sources cited above, and denies that she ever held a formal position on the work team: *Nie Yuanzi's Memoirs*, p. 145.

34. Detailed descriptions of the accused and the charges are in *Dazibao xuan (ershi)* (*Selected Wall Posters, 20*), Beijing daxue wenhua geming weiyuanhui (chouweihui), bangongshi, 14 August 1966.

35. *Beijing University Chronology*, pp. 647–48.

36. *Ibid.* p. 645.

The leaders of the work team tried to limit the violence. At a mass meeting of political activists on 13 June, Zhang Chengxian called for restraint.[37] Violent struggle sessions nevertheless broke out across the campus on 18 June. Around 70 cadres and teachers were dragged on to platforms, faces smeared with black ink, and were beaten and kicked while accusations were screamed at them. Six were members of the Party standing committee, and 41 were Party committee members, general branch secretaries or general branch committee members.[38] The work team fanned out across campus, shut down the struggle sessions, rescued the victims and treated their wounds.[39]

Zhang Chengxian broadcast a speech that evening blaming the day's violence on four "bad elements" who had used students' revolutionary enthusiasm to lead them astray, and he promised further investigations.[40] The next day the work team submitted a report about the "18 June incident," condemning the "counter-revolutionary conspiratorial behaviour of such bad people." On 20 June the report was transmitted to Party committees nationwide as a central Party document, with the Secretariat's comment that the work team's actions were "correct and timely."[41] Some CCRG members urged a harsher line. Cao Yi'ou transmitted a second report on 21 June that blamed the incident on a conspiracy of enemies inside and outside the school.[42] Chen Boda (陈伯达), head of the CCRG, pushed this conspiracy theory during late June visits to Beida, leading to further investigations that implicated another 24 students.[43]

The 18 June incident took on new meaning after Mao returned to the capital on 18 July, immediately after his famous swim on the Yangtze River, and expressed anger at the work teams.[44] Mao offered a new view diametrically opposed to Chen Boda's: the work team had

37. *Ibid.* p. 645, and "Chronicle of major events of Beijing University's Cultural Revolution," p. 46.

38. *Dazibao xuan (shisan)* (*Selected Wall Posters, 13*), Beijing daxue wenhua geming weiyuanhui (chouwei hui) bangongshi bian, 18 July 1966, pp. 1–64. See also *Dazibao xuan (ershi)* (*Selected Wall Posters, 20*), Beijing daxue wenhua geming weiyuanhui (chouwei hui) bangongshi bian, 14 August 1966, pp. 8–15.

39. Zhang Chengxian, "Beijing University's work team," pp. 28–30, *Beijing University Chronology*, pp. 645–46, "Chronicle of major events of Beijing University's Cultural Revolution," pp. 46–47, and Chen Huanren, *Hongweibing riji* (*Red Guard Diary*)(Hong Kong: Zhongwen daxue chubanshe, 2005), pp. 29–32. Chen Huanren was a student in Beida's philosophy department and his book is based on the detailed diary he kept at the time.

40. Only two of the four were students. One of them had torn the clothes off female Party secretaries and humiliated them by fondling their breasts and forcing his hand into their pants to grope their genitals. *Beijing University Chronology*, pp. 645–46, Zhang Chengxian, "Beijing University's work team," pp. 28–30.

41. "Zhongyang zhuanfa Beijing daxue wenhua geming jianbao (di jiu hao)" ("Party centre transmits bulletin on the Beijing University Cultural Revolution, no. 9"), 20 June 1966.

42. Zhang Chengxian had not seen the report, but Cao signed it with words of praise: *Beijing University Chronology*, p. 636. Zhang Chengxian, "Beijing University's work team," p. 31 assumed that Cao directly expressed Kang Sheng's views.

43. *Ibid.* p. 31, and *Beijing University Chronology*, p. 646.

44. *Mao Zedong zhuan, 1949–1976 (xia)* (*Biography of Mao Zedong, 1949–1976, Vol. 2*) (Beijing: Zhongyang wenxian chubanshe, 2004), pp. 1421–22.

over-reacted in suppressing the students. Mao held a series of meetings over the next few days, explaining his views and ordering the work teams' withdrawal on 21 July.[45] News of this reversal reached Beida immediately, and Zhang Chengxian broadcast a self-criticism to the school on 18 July. It was too late: the next day Nie Yuanzi, using the school's loudspeaker system, denounced Zhang Chengxian for "severe errors of orientation and line."[46] Only afterwards did large numbers of wall posters critical of the work team appear.[47]

Within days, the CCRG intervened publicly. Jiang Qing (江青) and Chen Boda visited Beida on 22 and 23 July, meeting Nie and her supporters and praising their stand. Jiang Qing declared that the work team should stand aside. Chen Boda (reversing his earlier position), declared that "in his personal opinion," the 18 June incident was not counter-revolutionary, and that the work team's verdict was mistaken.[48] Jiang and Chen returned on 25 July with Kang Sheng and other members of the CCRG for a mass meeting to criticize the work team.[49] An even larger delegation returned the next evening for a struggle session against Zhang Chengxian.[50] Chen Boda called for the withdrawal of the work team, and Jiang Qing suggested that a committee headed by Nie Yuanzi should replace it.[51] Two days later a Cultural Revolution preparatory committee was elected with Nie as chair.[52]

45. Mu Xin, "Guanyu gongzuozu cun fei wenti" ("On the question of whether to withdraw the work teams"), *Dangdai Zhongguo shi yanjiu*, No. 2 (1997), p. 59. Mao Zedong, "Mao Zhuxi tong zhongyangju he zhongyang wenge xiaozu chengyuan de jianghua" ("Chairman Mao's talk with members of the Politburo and Central Cultural Revolution Group"), 21 July 1966, *Dazibao xuan (di er ji) (Collected Wall Posters, No. 2)*, Yiyuan dazibao xuanbian xiaozu, December 1966, pp. 20–21.

46. *Beijing University Chronology*, p. 649; Chen Huanren, *Red Guard Diary*, pp. 60–61. Nie did not openly dissent from the work team's course prior to 19 July: "Chronicle of major events of Beijing University's Cultural Revolution," p. 50. The first wall poster critical of the work team appeared on 13 July and attracted widespread attention, but at department meetings Nie chaired she made no comment on it. After her 19 June speech Nie assured students in her department that the CCRG backed her; Chen Huanren, *Red Guard Diary*, pp. 54–57, 63.

47. *Ibid.* pp. 60–61; *Beijing University Chronology*, pp. 648–49, Zhang Chengxian, "Beijing University's work team," pp. 33–34, "Chronicle of major events of Beijing University's Cultural Revolution," pp. 49–50, and *Dazibao xuan (zengkan er) (Selected Wall Posters, Supplement 2)*, Beijing daxue wenhua geming weiyuan hui (chouweihui) bangongshi, 1 August 1966, and *Dazibao xuan (zengkan san) (Selected Wall Posters, Supplement 3)*, Beijing daxue wenhua geming weiyuan hui (chouweihui) bangongshi, 28 July 1966.

48. *Wuchan jieji wenhua geming zhong zhongyang fuze tongzhi jianghua chaolu (di yi ji) (Speeches by Central Leaders during the Cultural Revolution, Vol. 1)*, n.p., October 1966; Chen Huanren, *Red Guard Diary*, pp. 64–67.

49. *Beijing University Chronology*, p. 649, Zhang Chengxian, "Beijing University's work team," p. 37, and *Speeches by Central Leaders, Vol. 1*.

50. *Beijing University Chronology*, p. 650, Zhang Chengxian, "Beijing University's work team," pp. 39–42, "Chronicle of major events of Beijing University's Cultural Revolution," pp. 51–52, Chen Huanren, *Red Guard Diary*, pp. 69–75.

51. *Wuchan jieji wenhua da geming cankao ziliao 1 (Reference Materials on the Great Proletarian Cultural Revolution, 1)*, Beijing jingji xueyuan wuchan jieji geming zaofantuan, 1966.

52. See *Xin Beida*, 22 August 1966, p. 2.

Nie Yuanzi's Cultural Revolution Committee

With strong elite backing, Nie consolidated her position at Beida. She organized mass struggle sessions on three consecutive days against Zhang Chengxian. Kang Sheng and Jiang Qing attended the 4 August session at which he was dragged onto the stage, wearing a tall hat, bent at the waist with arms extended in the "jet plane" position, and beaten with leather belts by students from Beida's attached high school.[53] During August, Nie frequently met Cao Yi'ou, Jiang Qing and especially Wang Renzhong (王任重), the CCRG vice-chairman who was assigned to oversee the movement at Beida, and Kang Sheng sent her written instructions.[54] During this period she also had an audience with Mao, after which he provided his calligraphy for the masthead of the school newspaper, *Xin Beida* (新北大).[55] House searches intensified at Beida, and suicides were more frequent.[56] After considerable delay, a Red Guard organization was finally established at a mass rally on 19 August at which Nie presided.[57] Like most of the original Red Guards, it was to be formed from descendants of revolutionaries.[58]

On 9 September 42 people were elected to Beida's Cultural Revolution committee. Nie and her philosophy department comrades took six of the seats. Nie became chair and Kong Fan the first-ranking vice-chair.[59] Administrative posts were dominated by philosophy department stalwarts: Yang Keming was head of propaganda and editor of *Xin Beida*, which put out its first issue on 22 August.[60]

As Nie consolidated power she found herself in an awkward position. At other universities in Beijing, a rebel movement grew out of the minority of students who had led a rebellion against their campus work teams. From August to October 1966 they fought to overthrow "majority" factions that had co-operated with work

---

53. *Speeches by Central Leaders, Vol. 1*; Zhang Chengxian, "Beijing University's work team," pp. 42–43; *Beijing University Chronology*, p. 650, Chen Huanren, *Red Guard Diary*, pp. 83–88.

54. *Beijing University Chronology*, p. 650; *Nie Yuanzi's Memoirs*, pp. 154–58.

55. Chen Huanren, *Red Guard Diary*, pp. 95–96.

56. Five deaths were reported between 25 August and 6 October; *ibid.* pp. 651–52.

57. Note that this was after the 18 August Red Guard rally in Tiananmen Square, where Mao greeted Red Guards who had formed their groups weeks before. *Beijing University Chronology*, p. 651.

58. *Selected Wall Posters, 1*, pp. 40–41. On a visit to the Beida campus on 24 August, Chen Boda was asked whether Red Guards should be "primarily" or "exclusively" made up of students from "red" family origin, and Chen was non-committal: "you talk it over" (*nimen taolun taolun*), *Reference Materials 1*, p. 8–75.

59. Among the other philosophy department delegates were Yang Keming, Sun Pengyi and Zhao Zhengyi, veterans of the earlier battles. *Xin Beida*, 13 September 1966, p. 2.

60. Out of 44 committee members, 12 were work team members, 18 were appointed department head by the work team and 29 were certified as reliable by the work team. Ten of the 14 Standing Committee members had actively supported the work team; *Xin Beida bao*, 5 November 1967, p. 3.

teams.[61] At Beida, by contrast, there was no significant opposition to the work team until days before its withdrawal, and Nie Yuanzi and her comrades had worked closely with the work team. Nie never led a rebel movement: the CCRG simply came to the campus, removed the work team and put her in charge. During the long fight by the rebel "minority" on other Beijing campuses, Nie and her comrades stood awkwardly on the sidelines.

The Rebellion against Nie Yuanzi

Two separate developments converged into an anti-Nie movement in October. The first was resistance to her attempt to control the Red Guards. The second was a split among the veteran Beida leftists. Disaffected Red Guards joined with old leftists who split with Nie to challenge her control of the school. Here the paradox of Nie's position became fully apparent. She criticized Zhang Chengxian's work team for suppressing the student movement, yet as she moved to consolidate power she faced the same charge. After Nie established the Beida Red Guards in mid-August, rival organizations proliferated. By mid-October there were three large Red Guard organizations on campus, and some 3,000 Beida students had formed a total of 92 separate Red Guard groups large and small.[62] By this time they had conducted 536 house searches and untold numbers of interrogations and struggle sessions.[63] To assert authority, Nie created a hierarchy of departmental Cultural Revolution committees and a unified Red Guard command. She appointed Sun Pengyi, a cadre and political instructor in her own department, to lead the Red Guards.[64] All groups were ordered to unify under Sun's leadership; new leaders would be chosen and political activities across department lines must cease.[65]

This attempt to control the Red Guards was immediately challenged by two of the larger groups. They objected to unity that was forced from above and refused to join.[66] This was the first sign of a gathering wave of opposition. In early October a wall poster by two physics students criticized Nie's leadership and called for her to resign. They charged that the elections had been worthless, the candidate lists had been manipulated, more than 3,000 people were off campus and

61. See Andrew G. Walder, "Beijing Red Guard factionalism: social interpretations reconsidered," *Journal of Asian Studies*, Vol. 61 (2002), pp. 437–471.

62. *Beijing University Chronology*, p. 652; see also *Xin Beida*, 13 September 1966, p. 3.

63. Over half the homes of professors and 80% of the homes of cadres at middle rank and above had been searched by Red Guards. *Beijing University Chronology*, pp. 652–53.

64. Sun was a Korean War veteran from a poor peasant/revolutionary martyr household who had been criticized along with Nie after the SEM. *Xin Beida*, 26 March 1968, p. 4; *Nie Yuanzi's Memoirs*, pp. 88 and 169; Chen Huanren, *Red Guard Diary*, p. 309.

65. *Xin Beida*, 27 September 1966, p. 1.

66. *Ibid.* p. 1.

unable to vote, and the leaders unrepresentative. They accused Nie of using the school's propaganda apparatus to pump up her own reputation by celebrating the famous wall poster.[67] They belittled her "rebellion," pointing out that the wall poster appeared ten days after the 16 May circular, when it was already clear that Peng Zhen was purged and the SEM verdict had changed. Finally, they accused Nie of ignoring dissenting views and suppressing criticism.[68] A "great debate" ensued in the following weeks, with one side supporting Nie's Cultural Revolution committee, and the other accusing her of "suppressing the masses," behaving like the work team, and carrying out a "covert bourgeois reactionary line."[69]

A long critical essay by Yang Xun (杨勋), an instructor in economics, expressed the frustrations with Nie Yuanzi of many in the school.[70] Yang Xun was a pre-liberation Party member who had served with the Eighth Route Army. She was familiar with Nie Yuanzi from her earlier stint in economics. Moreover, Yang had been an SEM activist on the same side as Nie, taking a critical stand against Lu Ping, and was elected to the earlier Cultural Revolution preparatory committee.[71] Yang charged that Nie's leadership group had engaged in self-worship, ignored criticism, attacked those who express dissenting views and bureaucratized the movement. Yang pointed out that Nie had fully co-operated with the work team's "right-wing opportunist line," and had been one of its primary architects, yet she acted as if she bore no responsibility for this and saw no need to examine her own errors.

The publication of such criticism in *Xin Beida* showed that the opposition had sympathizers on the Cultural Revolution committee – in particular Kong Fan, first-ranking deputy chairman, and Yang Keming, editor of *Xin Beida*, both of whom were involved in the 25 May wall poster. A final split occurred on 24 October, when Nie convened the standing committee in the absence of several opponents, adding new supporters to the group and putting Sun Pengyi in charge of all Cultural Revolution activities.[72] The next week Yang Keming was fired as editor of *Xin Beida*, and the "great debate" about Nie's leadership ended. Yang Xun was denounced as an "opportunist" in the 5 November issue, leading Nie's opponents to invade the editorial offices and shut down the paper for more than a week.[73]

This split among these "old leftists" crystallized factional alignments: Kong Fan and Yang Keming joined the dissident Red Guards, while pro-Nie forces assembled under the Cultural Revolution

67. The last of these charges was accurate. See *Selected Wall Posters, 1*.
68. *Xin Beida*, 18 October 1966, p. 2.
69. *Beijing University Chronology*, p. 652, Chen Huanren, *Red Guard Diary*, pp. 151–55. The debate began in *Xin Beida*, 8 October 1966, p. 1, and continued in the next two issues. Wall posters arguing both sides were published in *Selected Wall Posters, 3*.
70. *Xin Beida*, 8 October 1966, p. 3.
71. See Yang Xun, *Tolerance*, introduction and p. 134.
72. *Beijing University Chronology*, p. 653.
73. *Xin Beida*, 21 November 1966, p. 2.

committee and Sun Pengyi's Red Guards. Several opposition groups were founded, and a loyalist organization was formed to defend Nie.[74] Opponents accused her of carrying out the work team's "bourgeois reactionary line" – suppressing mass organizations, punishing critics, and seeking to control and restrict the mass movement. Loyalists, in turn, accused the *opposition* of following the "bourgeois reactionary line": Nie was a "genuine revolutionary leftist" and "to oppose Nie Yuanzi is to oppose the CCRG."[75]

Just as Nie faced a mounting rebellion at Beida, her ties with the CCRG strengthened. In mid-November, at Mao's request, she led a Beida delegation to Shanghai to support the growing rebellion against the Shanghai municipal Party committee, and instigate attacks on Chang Xiping, Party secretary of East China Normal University, an adversary on the SEM work team.[76] Nie remained in Shanghai for almost a month, returning to Beijing in mid-December and reporting on her activities to members of the CCRG.[77]

Upon her return, Nie moved to crush her opponents. On 12 December her supporters seized Yang Xun, her younger brother Yang Bingzhang (杨炳章) and Qiao Jianwu (乔兼武), a student in the eastern languages department, as "counter-revolutionaries."[78] Nie linked her opponents with a wave of criticism against the CCRG – the "December black wind" – and had the leaders of the opposition captured and subjected to mass struggle sessions; within days the offices of her opponents were forcibly closed.[79]

Nie's close ties to the CCRG ultimately permitted her to fend off those who opposed her as a "conservative." On 29 December 1966 her Cultural Revolution committee organized a mass struggle meeting at the Beijing workers' stadium against the entire leadership of the old Beijing municipal Party committee.[80] During this period she met Jiang Qing and Kang Sheng several times, and they restated their support

74. *Beijing University Chronology*, pp. 652–53.

75. *Xin Beida* 12 December 1966. pp. 5–7.

76. During this period Li Na, the daughter of Mao and Jiang Qing and a 1965 graduate of Beida, served as Mao's confidential liaison with Nie. *Nie Yuanzi's Memoirs*, pp. 172–190; Wang Li, *Wang Li fansilu* (*Wang Li's Reflections*) (Hong Kong: Xianggang beixing chubanshe, 2001), pp. 758–64.

77. *Beijing University Chronology*, pp. 654–55.

78. *Xin Beida* 24 December 1966, p. 2. Qiao Jianwu put up a wall poster critical of Lin Biao; *Xin Beida*, 12 December 1966, p. 7, *Xin Beida*, 23 May 1968, p. 4. Yang Bingzhang penned a wall poster in December describing Nie Yuanzi as a "political whore," and wrote a series of private letters to Mao, many criticizing Jiang Qing's behaviour. Yang Bingzhang, *Cong Beida dao Hafo* (*From Beida to Harvard*) (Beijing: Zuojia chubanshe, 1998), pp. 136–152. Publicly, Yang was labelled an "active counter-revolutionary" for saying that the Cultural Revolution was simply a factional struggle stirred up by members of the CCRG: *Xin Beida*, 1 January 1967, p. 3.

79. *Beijing University Chronology*, p. 655.

80. Nie could not have staged this rally without the co-operation of the Central Case Examination Group, which controlled access to these political suspects. See Michael Schoenhals, "The Central Case Examination Group, 1966–79," *The China Quarterly*, No. 145 (1996), pp. 88–111.

and affirmed that her opponents were counter-revolutionaries.[81] On 24 December Nie spoke to a mass meeting at Beida, labelled a series of opponents as counter-revolutionaries, and called for "exercising proletarian dictatorship."[82] Yang Xun, Yang Bingzhang and Qiao Jianwu were arrested and sent to prison.[83] On 10 January *Xin Beida* charged that Nie's two former allies, Kong Fan and Yang Keming, were "representatives of the bourgeois reactionary line."[84] Jiang Qing declared them followers of the "Liu–Deng reactionary line and called for "smashing their social base."[85] On 17 January, her critics now crushed, Nie formed a committee formally to "seize power" at Beida.[86]

Heaven and Earth: City-wide Opposition to Nie

Despite these interventions, opposition to Nie soon revived. Other members of the CCRG grew impatient with her unwillingness to compromise, and as 1967 wore on, her relations with key leaders began to fray.[87] Student rebels at other universities also found Nie objectionable. Jiang rallied support for her at meetings with leaders of rebel groups in late January; she warned Qinghua's Kuai Dafu (蒯大富) about his sympathy for Nie's Beida opponents, and stated that Nie retained their support. Jiang acknowledged Nie's shortcomings and errors, but stressed that in the overall struggle they were really on the same side.[88]

Jiang Qing's support for Nie had a broader strategic purpose: Nie was to help seize power in Beijing in imitation of Shanghai's January

81. *Beijing University Chronology*, p. 655. On 3 January Jiang and Kang named several critics and personally branded them as counter-revolutionaries, including Yang Xun and her younger brother Yang Bingzhang. See *Zhongyang shouzhang jianghua 1* (*Central Leaders' Speeches, 1*), Beijing boli zongchang hongweibing lianluozhan bian, March 1967, pp. 17–20. When Kang Sheng heard the criticisms of Nie, he reportedly called her Beida colleagues together and said, "This Nie Yuanzi person isn't so great. I already knew this in Yan'an. But now, even if she's a bastard and an s.o.b. (*huaidan, wangbadan*), we still have to support her." Beida Party history group, "Kang Sheng, Cao Yi'ou, " p. 36. During the Yan'an rectification movement in 1942, Kang Sheng charged that that Nie was a member of an underground traitor group with strong ties to Wang Shiwei; the charges did not stick; *Nie Yuanzi's Memoirs*, pp. 54–55, 109. In his memoirs, CCRG member Wang Li reports that both Kang Sheng and Cao Yi'ou strongly disliked Nie and preferred Yang Keming, the primary wall poster author, over her: *Wang Li's Reflections*, pp. 603, 721–22.
82. *Xin Beida*, 1 January 1967, p. 2.
83. *Beijing University Chronology*, p. 656, Yang Xun, *Tolerance*, pp. 159–167, and Yang Bingzhang, *From Beida to Harvard*, pp. 166–170.
84. *Xin Beida*, 10 January 1967, pp. 5–7.
85. Jiang made this statement on 3 January. *Central Leaders' Speeches, 1*, pp. 17–18.
86. *Beijing University Chronology*, p. 655.
87. Wang Renzhong was particularly critical of Nie's attempts to monopolize power, and expressed openness to dialogue with Kong Fan and Yang Keming. *Central Leaders' Speeches, 1*, p. 18. Wang was dropped from the CCRG in January. See *Beijing University Chronology*, pp. 656, *Central Leaders' Speeches, 1*, p. 140, *Xin Beida*, 24 January 1967, p. 1.
88. *Central Leaders' Speeches, 1*, pp. 236–240.

power seizure. The effort began on 18 January when Nie met leaders from other universities to prepare for power seizures in central ministries and the municipal government by establishing an organization known as Beijing Commune.[89] As part of this effort, Beida groups that supported Nie were merged into a new organization, New Beida Commune.[90] Instead of a unified effort, however, the various Red Guard leaders simply rushed off to seize power at defenceless government offices, and confusion reigned.[91] Clearly unworkable, the Beijing Commune initiative was dropped in February in favour of a revolutionary committee that combined students with military officers and "revolutionary" cadres.[92] The first step was to create the Capital Red Guard Congress on 22 February, with Nie as head.[93] Now the Red Guard movement was to be unified under new organs of power in schools that united students, teachers and cadres.[94]

The effort to unite rebel factions under a single command faced a fundamental contradiction. An effort to build an alliance structure *across* schools inevitably ran foul of factional conflicts *within* schools. From the beginning, Nie and New Beida Commune were drawn into conflicts with rebel groups when they seized power in other units. In January her forces seized power at the ministry of higher education, but another rebel group, headed by Tan Houlan (谭厚兰) of Beijing Normal University, arrived to seize power and an argument ensued over which ministry faction to support. Tan supported a ministry cadre who led a rebel group, but Nie's group charged that the cadre had serious historical problems. Unfortunately for Nie, Tan Houlan was expressing the viewpoints of her *Red Flag* and CCRG sponsors, Lin Jie (林杰), Wang Li (王力), Guan Feng (关锋) and Qi Benyu (戚本禹), who had encouraged this cadre all along. Nie soon was pressured by aggressive phone calls from these figures, but she refused to back down. She eventually yielded only after the intervention of Chen Boda.[95] A similar clash occurred with the same figures over the 15 January seizure of secret Party archives at the CCPs United Front

89. *Beijing University Chronology*, pp. 657. See the founding proclamation in *Xin Beida*, 28 January 1967, signed by rebel groups from 21 large state enterprises and nine universities.

90. On 15 February. See *Xin Beida*, 17 February 1967, pp. 1–2; Chen Huanren, *Red Guard Diary*, pp. 270–272.

91. "At the time, seizing power was a matter of who ran the fastest; power went to whoever got there first and captured the official seal. So Kuai Dafu's people all ran off without telling us." *Nie Yuanzi's Memoirs*, p. 196.

92. See the instructions relayed by Qi Benyu and Xie Fuzhi on 13 and 15 February in *Zhongyang shouzhang jianghua 2* (*Central Leaders' Speeches, 2*), Beijing boli zongchang hongweibing lianluozhan fanyin, March 1967, pp. 104 and 109–110.

93. *Xin Beida*, 1 March 1967, p. 1. Nie's speech at the organization's founding was broadcast nationwide. *Xin Beida*, 4 March 1967, p. 1.

94. "Zhonggong zhongyang guanyu dazhuan yuanxiao dangqian wuchan jiejie wenhua da geming de guiding (cao'an)" ("Decision of the CCP on the Great Proletarian Cultural Revolution in the Universities [draft]"), 7 March 1967, *Xin Beida*, 14 March 1967, p. 1.

95. *Nie Yuanzi's Memoirs*, pp. 199–202.

Work Department.[96] These clashes, and the rivalries they expressed, would eventually be crystallized in the conflict between two wings of the Beijing rebel movement – "heaven" and "earth."[97]

These cleavages had been forming since the abortive efforts to create the Beijing Commune, and they continued after the formation of the Capital Red Guard Congress in late February.[98] Shortly after establishing the Capital Red Guard Congress, national officials were already worrying that the organization was an empty shell and its leading group deeply divided.[99] These tangled alliances led to an open breach after a battle that erupted at the Central Nationalities Museum on 8 April. One of the factions called on the support of their allies from the Geology Institute East is Red, a large rebel faction. The other side was reinforced by their allies from New Beida Commune, and there were casualties on both sides.[100] That evening, Nie Yuanzi and Kuai Dafu issued an order in the name of the Capital Red Guard Congress, calling for an end to hostilities and the withdrawal of all outside organizations.[101]

The battle brought to a head simmering resentment against Nie in the city's rebel ranks. Geology Institute East is Red immediately denounced the Red Guard Congress order because it had not been discussed in the organization's leading body.[102] On 11 April, along with allies from Beijing Normal Jinggangshan and other rebel organizations, they sent contingents to Beida for two days of demonstrations against Nie, calling for her expulsion from the Capital Red Guard Congress. New Beida Commune called in reinforcements from their allies at nearby Qinghua and skirmishes erupted.[103] On the evening of 12 April the minister of public security, Xie Fuzhi (谢富治), issued an urgent announcement in the name of the CCRG ordering all outsiders to leave campus.[104] The skirmish

---

96. *Ibid.* pp. 202–204.

97. The "heaven faction" (*tian pai*) included Nie Yuanzi, Kuai Dafu's Qinghua Jinggangshan, and Han Aijing's Aeronautics Institute Red Flag, and its name was a reference to the latter institute. The "earth faction" (*di pai*) included Tan Houlan's Beijing Normal Jinggangshan and Wang Dabin's Geology Institute East is Red, and its name derived from the latter institute. See Bu Weihua, "Guanyu 'wenge' zhong Beijing de 'tianpai' he 'dipai'," ("The 'heaven' and 'earth' factions in Beijing's Cultural Revolution"), *Zhonggong dangshi ziliao*, No. 73 (2000), pp. 100–126.

98. Rebel groups from the Ministry of Education, the United Front Work Committee, the Naval Academy and several other military academies demonstrated against Nie Yuanzi on the Beida campus every day from 23 to 26 January. See *Xin Beida*, 31 January 1967, p. 2.

99. See the talks by Xie Fuzhi and Qi Benyu on 4 March in *Zhongyang shouzhang jianghua 3* (*Central Leaders' Speeches, 3*), Beijing boli zongchang hongweibing lianluozhan bian, April 1967, pp. 42–44.

100. Bu Weihua, "Heaven and earth," pp. 107–108; *Nie Yuanzi's Memoirs*, pp. 206–208.

101. *Xin Beida*, 13 April 1967, p. 6.

102. *Ibid.* p. 7.

103. Bu Weihua, "Heaven and earth," pp. 109–111, Chen Huanren, *Red Guard Diary*, pp. 304–306. A detailed account of the clashes is in *Xin Beida*, 13 April 1967, pp. 6–8.

104. *Ibid.* 13 April 1967, p. 2.

was over, but the fissures in the Red Guard movement had hardened. The Red Guard Congress was now openly split.

Nie nevertheless continued her activities on behalf of the CCRG. In mid-April, Kang Sheng had her lead investigations of purged officials from the old municipal Party committee, and she staged several large public struggle sessions against them.[105] She was named vice-head of the Beijing municipal revolutionary committee (under its head Xie Fuzhi) when it was formed on 20 April. Anticipating her assumption of permanent political power, she had already begun to rebuild Beida's administrative structure. In early March, she held meetings where "cadres who had made errors" were asked to declare their support for the revolution by pledging loyalty to Nie's Cultural Revolution committee. At the end of March two prominent members of the former Beida Party standing committee, Cui Xiongkun and vice-president Zhou Peiyuan (周培源), pledged their support.[106]

Despite her political ascent, Nie was unable to quell organized opposition. The split between "heaven" and "earth" rekindled the Beida opposition by providing it with strong allies outside the school. There was plenty of fuel for the opposition. On 3 March, during a campaign to reinforce allegiances to Nie, new splits appeared in the Cultural Revolution committee. Philosophy department instructor Guo Luoji (郭罗基) put up a wall poster criticizing Nie for her dictatorial behaviour since assuming power, and demanded that any rectification of leading organs begin with her.[107] Two figures promoted to the standing committee a few weeks earlier – Hou Hanqing (侯汉清) and vice-chairman Xu Yunpu (徐运朴) – sided with Guo.[108] In late May and early June four new anti-Nie alliances appeared.[109]

The new anti-Nie wave was encouraged by signs that CCRG support for Nie was wavering. After the new splits on the school standing committee in late March, Chen Boda and Qi Benyu went to Beida and told students that it was mistaken to say that "to bombard so-and-so is to bombard the proletarian headquarters." Chen said "you cannot just casually say that to oppose you is counter-revolution."[110] After Chen and Qi left Beida, Nie challenged them in a handbill that duplicated Chen's talk (ineptly ensuring that opponents would be encouraged by it), and held meetings to criticize this "new black line."[111] After the armed battles on the Beida campus

105. *Beijing University Chronology*, p. 659.

106. Chen Huanren, *Red Guard Diary*, pp. 296–99. Zhou earned a PhD in theoretical physics after studying at the University of Chicago and California Institute of Technology before 1949, and later become Beida's president.

107. Chen Huanren, *Red Guard Diary*, pp. 280–85. Guo had stood with Nie since the SEM; *Nie Yuanzi's Memoirs*, p. 88.

108. *Beijing University Chronology*, p. 658. Both figures had been promoted in February to replace Kong Fan and Yang Keming.

109. *Ibid.* pp. 660–61.

110. *Central Leaders' Speeches, 3*, p. 272.

111. *Beijing University Chronology*, p. 658.

in April, Jiang Qing called for Nie Yuanzi to make a self-criticism for her role in the conflict and for her resistance to Xie Fuzhi's attempts to mediate, which had incurred Xie's anger.[112] Nie's clashes behind the scenes with Xie Fuzhi would continue into the next year, because she was convinced that he was part of a cabal – along with Qi Benyu, Wang Li and Guan Feng, who supported Tan Houlan and the "earth" faction – who were behind the aggressive attacks against her by Red Guards city-wide and at Beida.[113] As Nie's position deteriorated, Chen Boda returned to Beida on 5 June to qualify his criticisms of Nie, and several days later he phoned her to explain that he was not offended by her attacks on him.[114] Xie Fuzhi urged Nie to exercise diplomacy: the present task was to unite rebel organizations, not crush rivals. In response, *Xin Beida* called for a rectification campaign to correct errors of line that had recently been committed by certain leaders on the Cultural Revolution committee.[115] The paper published a criticism of Nie's recent actions by a group from the philosophy department: she had used the organization to pursue factional struggles and had created deep splits among leftists.[116] Subsequent issues of *Xin Beida* welcomed criticisms from fellow leftists – but they denied that a "second revolution" was needed.[117]

Instead of accepting this olive branch, the opposition stepped up their attacks. On 3 July anti-Nie organizations formed an alliance and soon published the first issue of their newspaper, *Xin Beida bao* (新北大报).[118] It carried news of a major defection of "revolutionary cadres": an open letter signed by Zhou Peiyuan and 134 others, who charged that the Cultural Revolution Committee had committed errors of line since March 1967, and praised the opposition groups.[119] Too late to undo the damage, Chen Boda issued a statement on 10 July

---

112. *Zhongyang shouzhang jianghua 4* (*Central Leaders' Speeches, 4*), Beijing boli zongchang hongweibing lianluo zhan bian, May 1967, pp. 116–122. Sun Pengyi had led a mass meeting at Beida on 12 April that had challenged Xie Fuzhi's leftist credentials and called him a "double-dealer" who took political credit for others contributions, Chen Huanren, *Red Guard Diary*, p. 306.

113. *Nie Yuanzi's Memoirs*, pp. 206–210; 216–224. Nie apparently never considered the possibility that these figures were simply losing confidence in her ability to unify the rebel forces at Beida, which made her a serious political liability and an increasingly quarrelsome one at that. Her memoirs make clear that she felt that her back was against the wall – the earth faction repeatedly attacked her on her home turf, and she was convinced that they were acting on behalf of Qi Benyu and with the acquiescence of Xie Fuzhi.

114. Chen Huanren, *Red Guard Diary*, pp. 344–47. Nie's insecurity was reflected in the pages of *Xin Beida*, 24 May, which devoted an entire issue to glorifying the first anniversary of the 25 May wall poster. The front page carried a large photograph of Nie's meeting one year before with Mao, Kang Sheng and Cao Yi'ou. The 30 May issue was devoted entirely to praise for Jiang Qing's inspiring contributions to the arts.

115. *Xin Beida*, 10 June 1967, p. 1.

116. *Xin Beida*, 14 June 1967, p. 2.

117. *Xin Beida*, 17, 21 and 24 June 1967. Sun Pengyi made a self-criticism in a mass meeting on 29 June but it was openly ridiculed by opposition members in attendance; Nie gave her self criticism on 4 July; Chen Huanren, *Red Guard Diary*, pp. 363–65.

118. *Xin Beida bao*, 12 July 1967.

119. *Ibid.* p. 3.

explaining that his criticisms of Nie did not mean that he no longer supported her. Stung by the losses, Nie dropped her conciliatory line in mid-July, and accused the opposition of "creating public opinion for a plot to seize power" from the "proletarian headquarters."[120]

Stalemate

Instead of fostering compromise, elite interventions had hardened factional divisions. At the end of July, 39 rebel organizations created a new anti-Nie alliance and set up offices at seven other campuses. On 17 August five large anti-Nie groups formed the New Beida Jinggangshan Corps, and the next day it was admitted to the Capital Red Guard Congress.[121] At a mass rally to celebrate its founding, a proclamation of support was read out from 45 organizations in the Red Guard Congress, the Capital Workers Congress and the Capital High School Red Guard Congress. Li Xingchen (李醒尘), a co-author of the 25 May wall poster, spoke at the rally.[122] Nie's two most important allies in the "heaven" faction – Kuai Dafu of Qinghua Jinggangshan and Aeronautics Institute Red Flag – also sent letters of congratulation.[123] None of this would have happened if Nie were not seriously out of favour with key figures on the CCRG.

Against mounting odds, Nie fought back, and survived only with the support of Jiang Qing. Jiang spoke to the Beijing revolutionary committee on 1 September and criticized Nie's accumulating errors, but affirmed that Nie should keep her posts, and she labelled Nie's opponents "bad elements." On 16 September she went further, and charged that Nie's opponents were "old conservatives" who were trying to "overturn verdicts."[124] *Xin Beida bao* countered that Nie was a reactionary who had suppressed the revolutionary masses.[125] This view received validation from rebels elsewhere in the city: a proclamation issued by old Third Headquarters rebels stated that Nie's opponents were revolutionary, not counter-revolutionary, as Nie had charged.[126] Jingangshan threw the accusation of harbouring "old conservatives" back at Nie, reminding everyone of her role on the work team and the questionable political backgrounds of the many cadres who had aligned with her.[127]

120. *Beijing University Chronology*, p. 662.
121. *Ibid.* p. 663.
122. *Xin Beida bao*, 25 August 1967, pp. 1–2.
123. *Ibid.* p. 1. Kuai reportedly called Beida Jingangshan the true rebel faction. *Beijing University Chronology*, p. 663. At the time, Beida students heard that Kuai was secretly supporting one of the anti-Nie groups, and Nie's supporters openly praised Kuai's factional opponents on several occasions; Chen Huanren, *Red Guard Diary*, pp. 326–27.
124. *Beijing University Chronology*, p. 664.
125. *Xin Beida bao*, 7 September 1967, pp. 5–8.
126. *Xin Beida bao*, 16 September 1967, p. 1.
127. *Xin Beida bao*, 5 November 1967, p. 3, 7 November 1967, p. 4, 22 December 1967, p. 3, 6 January 1968, p. 4 and 15 January 1968, p. 4.

Although Nie charged that her opponents were simply "old conservatives," trying to "reverse verdicts"[128] both sides were in fact actively recruiting former cadres to their side. Nie had started the process in March when she encouraged "revolutionary cadres" to declare their support for her. The opposition took the upper hand with the defection of Zhou Peiyuan and 134 other leading cadres. In the ensuing months each faction would praise their supporters as "revolutionary cadres" and denounced those pledged to the other side as "old conservatives" and "reactionaries."

The similarity of each side's stance is vividly illustrated by Ge Hua and Cui Xiongkun, the two members of the old Beida Party standing committee who sided with Nie Yuanzi over the 25 May wall poster. Cui Xiongkun sided with the Cultural Revolution committee in March 1967 and by the end of November he was vice-head of a small group that was preparing to restore Beida's Party organization.[129] Ge Hua joined the opposition and was now celebrated by them as a "revolutionary cadre," as were Nie's old leftist comrades Kong Fan and Yang Keming.[130] In early October the Nie faction issued a call to "drag out" Ge Hua and demanded his surrender for struggle sessions, denouncing him as the "black hand" behind Jinggangshan.[131] On 3 December they finally captured him for interrogation and struggle sessions.[132] In retaliation, Jinggangshan captured Cui Xiongkun and staged a mass struggle session against him as an architect of Beida's capitalist road.[133]

By late 1967 higher authorities had lost patience with the splits in the rebel movement and pushed the factions to put their differences aside. The Beijing garrison command organized "Mao thought study classes" where factional leaders were to be re-educated and their differences reconciled.[134] At Beida, however, the two sides tangled over the terms of participation. Nie demanded that her opponents first recognize her Cultural Revolution committee as Beida's official organ of power.[135] The opposition countered that the Cultural Revolution committee must first be re-organized to represent both factions.[136] The municipal revolutionary committee tried to break the

128. *Xin Beida*, 10 September 1967, p. 7.

129. *Xin Beida*, 2 December 1967, p. 1. Nie Yuanzi was the head, and Sun Pengyi was the other vice-head.

130. On 28 November the latter two were added to Jinggangshan's core leadership group. *Beijing University Chronology*, p. 665, and *Xin Beida bao*, 30 November 1967, pp. 1–2.

131. *Beijing University Chronology*, p. 664, *Xin Beida*, 7 October 1967, pp. 5–8, and 15 October 1967, pp. 3–4.

132. *Beijing University Chronology*, p. 666. *Xin Beida*, 9 December 1967, pp. 2–3, 14 December 1967, p. 4.

133. *Beijing University Chronology*, p. 667. *Xin Beida bao*, 6 January 1968, pp. 3–4, and 15 January 1968, pp. 1–3.

134. Bu Weihua, "Heaven and earth," pp. 118–19.

135. *Xin Beida*, 23 September 1967, pp. 1–2, 19 October 1967, p. 1, and 22 October 1967, p. 2.

136. *Xin Beida bao*, 23 October 1967, pp. 1–4.

impasse on 23 November by ruling that the Beida Cultural Revolution committee was the official organ of power and that New Beida Commune had the permission to absorb Jinggangshan into its ranks.[137] Shortly thereafter *Xin Beida* announced plans to restore the Beida Party organization.[138]

These interventions had no visible impact. The two sides escalated their mutual accusations into February 1968, when the Beijing garrison command sent in a propaganda team to mediate. They insisted that Nie drop her charges of counter-revolution against her former comrades and recognize the legitimacy of their complaints. Li Zhongqi (李钟奇), vice-commander of the Beijing garrison, dictated the terms of compromise: Jinggangshan must accept Nie's Cultural Revolution committee as the official organ of power; the Cultural Revolution committee must acknowledge Jinggangshan as revolutionary; a Beida revolutionary committee would be formed through consultations between the two sides; and the army supports neither faction.[139]

Jinggangshan accepted these principles, which finally gave them a share of power enforced by the army. Nie, however, complained to the Party centre about Li Zhongqi's proposal, questioning whether it represented central policy.[140] She insisted that disunity was created by the counter-revolutionary schemes of her opponents.[141] Nie's stance was encouraged by Jiang Qing and Kang Sheng, who continued to undermine efforts at compromise. In talks with Red Guards in mid-March, Kang Sheng stated that the factional conflict was a continuation of the struggle between the Nationalists and Communists. Jiang Qing called for the "heaven" faction to "drag out" the "bad elements" behind the "earth" faction.[142] The impasse remained.

Warfare: The Escalation of 1968

The stalemate exploded on 20 March 1968. Late that evening members of the "earth" faction marched on to campus, denouncing Nie Yuanzi as a counter-revolutionary and Sun Pengyi as a "climbing insect," and Beida Jinggangshan joined in. In response, Nie organized a militia to "defend with force." Three days later over 1,000 members of Agricultural University East is Red demonstrated against Nie and Sun at Beida. They were joined the next day by some 10,000 from other campuses. Battles erupted across the campus. Xie Fuzhi and

137. *Beijing University Chronology*, p. 665.
138. *Xin Beida*, 2 December 1967, p. 1.
139. *Beijing University Chronology*, p. 668.
140. *Ibid.* p. 668. Transcripts of the two reports, dated 6 March, were printed in *Xin Beida bao*, 22 March 1968, p. 4. Other articles in that issue praise the decisions of Xie Fuzhi and the Beijing garrison command, and attack Sun Pengyi as a traitor and spy for opposing them.
141. *Xin Beida*, 7 March 1968, p. 2.
142. *Xin Beida*, 23 March 1968, p. 1.

Wu De (吴德) arrived to broadcast demands for the withdrawal of outsiders and for the two Beida factions to unite under Nie. Several hundred members of Geology East is Red, armed with clubs, nevertheless arrived the next morning and further violence followed.[143]

On 28 March another armed battle between the two Beida factions erupted just after midnight and continued until dawn, when vice-commander Li Zhongqi of the Beijing garrison broadcast a demand for an immediate truce and negotiations. When Li accompanied Nie to the Jingangshan headquarters to barter a truce, they were attacked – Li was clubbed over the head and Nie bled profusely from a scalp wound.[144] The attack apparently changed the authorities' attitude toward Nie's opponents. When the two sides finally sat down for negotiations late the next morning, Xie Fuzhi demanded an immediate halt to all hostilities, and he criticized Jinggangshan for their stubborn opposition to Nie.[145]

This finally turned the tide in Nie's favour. On 8 April *Xin Beida* denounced Jinggangshan for violating CCRG directives, and on 11 April the charge was repeated in a joint declaration with the Beijing revolutionary committee and ministry of public security.[146] Finally enjoying the unequivocal backing of the authorities, Nie gave a keynote speech at a city-wide rally on campus on 24 April; the two top commanders of the Beijing garrison and rebel leaders from across the city spoke in support. Kuai Dafu, whose support for Nie had wavered repeatedly in the past, praised her and declared that New Beida Commune represented the proletarian revolutionary left.[147]

Jinggangshan held out behind its defence works, but they were no longer able to publish *Xin Beida bao*, whose last issue appeared on 22 March. Nie's forces began to seize and interrogate members of Jinggangshan,[148] and public struggle sessions were held against captured Jinggangshan leaders.[149] Near the end of April, Nie and Sun formed special case groups to prosecute them. They detained teachers and students from the other side and tortured them to confess their crimes, and established a prison where inmates were regularly beaten. Ordinary members of Jinggangshan were told they would be treated leniently if they turned over their leaders for the severe punishment their counter-revolutionary crimes demanded.[150]

---

143. *Beijing University Chronology*, pp. 668–69, Chen Huanren, *Red Guard Diary*, p. 514; *Xin Beida*, 26 March 1968, pp. 1–2.

144. *Nie Yuanzi's Memoirs*, p. 270; Chen Huanren, *Red Guard Diary*, pp. 517–18.

145. *Beijing University Chronology*, p. 669, and *Xin Beida*, 30 March 1968, p. 1.

146. *Xin Beida*, 8 April 1968, p. 4 and 18 April 1968, p. 3; Chen Huanren, *Red Guard Diary*, pp. 518–520.

147. The entire issue of *Xin Beida*, 29 April 1968, was devoted to the rally.

148. See the confessions published in *Xin Beida*, 17 July 1968.

149. Three students were beaten to death during this period, and in late May Deng Xiaoping's son, Deng Pufang, a student in applied physics, was put in detention and then forced to jump from the upper storey of a campus building, causing the injuries that made him a paraplegic; *Beijing University Chronology*, pp. 670–71.

150. *Ibid.* pp. 671–72, and *Xin Beida*, 13 May 1968, p. 1.

By the end of June, Nie's forces claimed that a total of 1,200 members of Jinggangshan had defected; Nie welcomed them in a long speech.[151] On 18 July Nie held the first of a planned series of public trials of captured Jinggangshan leaders, at which the accused read out lengthy confessions.[152]

On 22 July Nie's forces prepared for the final battle. They cut off water and electricity to buildings occupied by the opposition, touching off a battle fought with roof tiles, spears and bricks that spread onto adjacent streets. Similar battles were under way at nearby Qinghua University, where Kuai Dafu was about to crush his opponents. A propaganda team composed of soldiers and workers was dispatched to Qinghua to separate the two sides and enforce a truce. Kuai's forces attacked them, killing five and seriously wounding 149.[153] Nie called an urgent meeting to co-ordinate defences and prevent a propaganda team from entering Beida. They stockpiled Molotov cocktails and other weapons and posted lookouts.[154] Instead, Nie was summoned to an urgent meeting at 3 am on 28 July with four other Red Guard leaders. An angry Mao criticized his guests for refusing to halt factional warfare, said that they had all committed serious errors, and told them that he had personally sent the propaganda team and they were not to be challenged. He told them that the Red Guard movement was over, and they should return to campus to welcome PLA propaganda teams.[155]

Suppression

Things changed drastically after the propaganda team arrived on 19 August. Two hundred of its 492 members were soldiers from the 63rd field army. *Xin Beida* was immediately closed. All prisoners were released, and both sides turned in their arms and were disbanded. The leaders of both sides were treated as if they had committed serious errors, and submitted to re-education in "Mao thought study classes." Nie was charged with responsibility for the violence because she supported the armed suppression of her opponents.[156] She was subjected to mass denunciation meetings on several occasions. Her opponents fared even worse: seven student leaders from the opposition were declared "active counter-revolutionaries."[157]

Beida's Cultural Revolution was not yet over. In late September the "cleansing of the class ranks campaign" began. Ignoring all that had

---

151. *Xin Beida*, 20 June 1966, pp. 1–2.
152. *Xin Beida*, 23 July 1968, pp. 3–4.
153. Tang Shaojie, *Yiye zhichun: Qinghua Daxue 1968 nian "Bairi da wudou"* (*An Episode in the Cultural Revolution: The 1968 100-day War at Qinghua University*) (Hong Kong: Zhongwen daxue chubanshe, 2003), p. 31.
154. *Beijing University Chronology*, p. 672.
155. *Ibid.* p. 673, and *Xin Beida*, 28 July 1968 and 30 July 1968, p. 1.
156. *Beijing University Chronology*, pp. 674–75; Chen Huanren, *Red Guard Diary*, pp. 556–561.
157. *Beijing University Chronology*, pp. 675–76.

transpired over the previous two years, more than 900 cadres and faculty – regardless of factional affiliation – were detained on campus. After a month of grueling interrogations, the propaganda team declared 542 of the inmates "enemies of the people." By the end of the year, 18 of them had committed suicide, including Cui Xiongkun, found floating in the university's swimming pool in mid-October.[158] Nie Yuanzi was isolated for re-education for over a year, and was paroled only for a token appearance as a delegate to the Ninth Party Congress in April 1969 at which, despite her political difficulties, she was elected an alternate member of the Central Committee. In November 1969 she was sent to a state farm for labour reform, a punishment that continued after her 1972 transfer to factories in Beijing until she was tried and imprisoned in April 1978. Suffering from medical problems, she was finally released in 1986.[159]

Conclusion: The Nature of Factionalism at Beida

Factional conflict at Beida expressed competition between rival wings of a movement against the old Party leadership that originated within the Party apparatus itself. "Old leftists" who had been comrades from the days of the SEM, worked together to write the famous 25 May wall poster, co-operated actively in the work team's extensive purges and initially shared power after the work team's disgrace, split into opposed factions. They did not offer rival programmes, articulate different political doctrines or exhibit different orientations towards the status quo ante. They disagreed vehemently about a series of actions taken by Nie Yuanzi as she sought to consolidate her control over the Red Guards and the Cultural Revolution committee in the early autumn of 1966, disagreements that hardened into unalterable opposition after Nie condemned her critics as counter-revolutionaries. Nie based her claim to power on the famous wall poster and the support of Jiang Qing and other figures on the CCRG. The opposition charged that Nie suppressed mass activism and crushed dissenting views – actions more characteristic of "old conservatives" on the Party establishment and the reviled work teams, than of the rebel movement that won victory in Beijing in the autumn of 1966. The issues of tactics and personality served to split the old Party leftists, the Beida Party apparatus, cadres, teachers and the student body.

Because of the way the factional split developed, neither faction could be identified as "conservative" or "radical." Usually these differences were expressed in a faction's stance towards the political status quo ante or "the cadre question": how harshly the alleged errors of cadres should be judged and whether the majority of them

158. *Ibid.* p. 675.
159. *Nie Yuanzi's Memoirs*, pp. 319–369.

should resume their former positions.[160] This issue plausibly resonated with individuals' pre-Cultural Revolution statuses, depending on how close they were to the former authorities. In early 1967 Nie moved to restore the Beida administration, offering "revolutionary cadres" an opportunity to pledge support and join her side. The rekindled anti-Nie opposition, however, did not adopt a different stance; instead, they competed to recruit cadres to Jinggangshan. Each side attacked cadres pledged to the other as "reactionaries" and celebrated those pledged to their own as "revolutionary." The two sides adopted similarly mirrored positions on the restoration of the Party organization. When Nie moved to re-establish the Party organization, Jinggangshan did not object in principle. They only complained that in excluding the prominent Party members in the opposition, Nie had "usurped the Beida Party organization."[161] In the absence of substantive political differences between the two factions it is hard to imagine how students could choose sides according to their vested interests or political values. Tellingly, although the official Beida Red Guards initially placed strong emphasis on family heritage as a criterion for membership, the debate about student "bloodline" that was so important in elite high schools and on some college campuses never divided the Beida factions.[162]

Was the nature of factional conflict at Beida typical of the struggles in other organizations and localities? In some obvious ways it was far from typical. Nie occupied a special position in the official hagiography of the Cultural Revolution. She achieved power without leading an opposition movement and had to defend that power during a period when the "rebel" movement in other schools was in the opposition. She enjoyed a special relationship with Jiang Qing and Kang Sheng, who intervened consistently over two years to rescue her from political blunders, albeit with increasing reluctance and an obvious sense of exasperation.

While Nie's role in Cultural Revolution politics was unique, other features of the Beida story are universal. The most important is the conflict generated in the abrupt shift from open rebellion to a power seizure and re-assertion of authority. This turning point occurred in every unit and locality during the Cultural Revolution, and similar splits among former allies were observed throughout China. Another universal feature is the way that the city-wide alliances drew rebel leaders into conflicts at the organizational level that led to splits in an initially unified city-wide rebel camp. The "heaven" and "earth"

160. This was clearly the case at Qinghua after April 1967. See Xiaowei Zheng, "Passion, reflection, and survival: the political choices of Red Guards at Qinghua University, June 1966–July 1968," in Esherick, Pickowicz and Walder, *The Chinese Cultural Revolution as History*, pp. 29–63.

161. *Xin Beida bao*, 22 December 1967, p. 2.

162. In sharp contrast to Beijing Industrial University, where it was a major – if misinterpreted – issue well into the autumn of 1966: See Andrew G. Walder, "Tan Lifu: a 'reactionary' Red Guard in historical perspective," *The China* Quarterly, No. 180 (2004), pp. 965–988.

factions grew from entangling alliances across organizations that could have occurred anywhere. These features help us to understand how factional struggles could be prolonged and violent without articulating different stances towards the status quo ante, and without adopting stances that resonated with the interests of different status groups.

Zheng Junli, Complicity and the Cultural History of Socialist China, 1949–1976

Paul G. Pickowicz

ABSTRACT   This article explores cultural production during the Mao era (1949–76) by focusing on the evolving relationship between artists and the party-state. The emphasis is on state direction of art in the all-important film industry. From 1949, well-known bourgeois Republican-era artists willingly began the complicated, painful and sometimes deadly process of adjusting to Communist Party state building, nation building and political domination. The career of influential film director Zheng Junli is examined as a case study of creative and strategic accommodation to new circumstances on the one hand, and of complicity on the other. Zheng is seen in his dual and contradictory roles as both trusted, ever loyal insider and unreliable, even degenerate, outsider. His Mao-era films, especially the spectacular Great Leap Forward production of *Lin Zexu*, are analysed in terms of their political thrust and reception in the difficult-to-predict world of the People's Republic.

The most powerful sequence in *East Palace, West Palace* (*Dong gong, xi gong* 东宫西宫), Zhang Yuan's (张元) provocative 1996 underground film, involves a tense confrontation between a young transvestite and a Beijing policeman. Moments before receiving a vicious beating at the hands of this obvious symbol of Party and state power (an authority figure who is nevertheless terrified by his own conflicting emotions of attraction and revulsion), the transvestite calmly, almost seductively, says: "In this desperate situation, the thief falls in love with her executioner. The love she feels is a kind of perversion. … She can already feel the blade against her neck. At that very moment, she throws herself into his arms and gives herself completely to her executioner." "The convict," the transvestite insists, "loves her executioner. The thief loves her jail keeper. We love you. *We have no other choice*. I love you. Why don't you love me?"[1]

This episode offers useful ways of thinking about the fate of run-of-the-mill film director Zheng Junli (郑君里) and thousands of other cultural workers who enthusiastically engaged in creative accommodation with the Communist Party during the Mao years. Zheng did not survive all the way to 1976. He died in prison in 1969 at the age of 58.[2] The abuse he suffered amounted to a slow and painful execution.

---

1. Italics added. For a discussion of power relations in Zhang's film see Paul G. Pickowicz, "Filme und die Legitimation des Staates im Heutigen China," in Kai Vockler and Dirk Luckows (eds.), *Peking, Shanghai, Shenzhen: Stadte des 21. Jahrhunderts* (Frankfurt: Campus Verlag GmbH, 2000), pp. 402–411.

2. "Zheng Junli shengping yu nianbiao" ("Zheng Junli's biography and filmography"), *Dangdai dianying* (*Contemporary Cinema*), No. 125 (2005), p. 63.

© The China Quarterly, 2006   doi: 10.1017/S0305741006000543

Zheng's situation was indeed desperate, and he had experienced desperation on more than one occasion. His status constantly shifted back and forth from privileged insider to distrusted outsider. The evidence suggests, however, that from beginning to end Zheng loved the Party and never questioned the legitimacy of his tormentors. Perhaps he felt he had no other choice. But he could not understand why the Party did not love him in return. Zheng believed he did everything the Party wanted him to do. Still, he failed to fathom why it did not acknowledge his devotion. Since, in Zheng's view, the Party was always right, his many problems must have been the result of his own failings. It is impossible to know what Zheng thought privately about his awful plight. But his masochistic public utterances are quite clear: he deserved what he got every step of the way.

Zheng Junli, like many other little-known and similarly abused cultural workers, was posthumously "rehabilitated" in the late 1970s, long after both he and Mao were dead. The glowing, one-dimensional and always uncritical accounts of his life that suddenly appeared were as distorted and ultimately as dishonest as the harsh attacks on his character circulated in the 1950s and 1960s. During the Mao years the Party had on occasion cast Zheng as a disgusting bourgeois degenerate. In the post-Mao years it preferred to think of him as a progressive and enlightened saint. He was neither.

The truth is that Zheng Junli, like most of the artists who populated the state-controlled cultural world of China after 1949, had a very interesting, though highly untidy, background. For example, in the late 1920s and early 1930s, Zheng faced the challenge of accommodating himself in political and cultural terms to Nationalist Party rule and the brave new world of the Nanjing decade. He did extremely well in those days, moving freely between the foreign-controlled international settlement in Shanghai and the "national" space controlled by the new government. In 1932, a time when the film world was expanding rapidly, Zheng made the transition from stage to screen by joining the famous Lianhua Film Studio. He was not a big star in the mid-1930s, but his contacts in the stage and film worlds were extensive.[3]

Zheng's immediate post-Mao biographers stress his connections to Xia Yan (夏衍), Chen Baichen (陈白尘) and others loosely described as "leftists." Standard accounts of his 1930s film career dwell exclusively on roles he played in such vaguely defined "progressive" films as *Big Road* (大路, d. Sun Yu 孙瑜, 1934).[4] They never mention

3. Zheng's visibility in the 1930s is captured in articles that appeared in the popular film press: Zheng Junli, "Ying mi yu 'mingxing zhidu'" ("Film fans and the 'star system'"), *Ying mi zhoubao* (*Film Fan Weekly*), Vol. 1, No. 1 (1934), p. 12, and Liu Baoxing, "Mingxing beiwanglu" ("Crib notes on film stars"), *Dianying hua bao* (*Film Pictorial*), No. 39, 1 March 1937.

4. Zhongguo dianyingjia xie hui, Dianying shi yanjiu bu (eds.), *Zhongguo dianyingjia lie zhuan* (*Biographies of Chinese Filmmakers*) (*ZDLZ*) (Beijing: Zhongguo dianying chubanshe, 1982), Vol. 2, pp. 287–290.

that there was much in "progressive" films, including portrayals of gender and class relations, that was not progressive. Emphasizing the "white terror" environment that supposedly prevailed during the Nanjing decade, biographers fail to point out that Zheng and "progressives" like him had cordial relations with artists who, in the Mao and early post-Mao periods, were seen as pro-Nationalist and even reactionary. For instance, in 1935, the year after he acted in *Big Road*, Zheng played a prominent part in *The Spirit of the Nation* (*Guo feng* 国风, d. Luo Mingyou 罗明佑), a film produced for Chiang Kai-shek's neo-conservative New Life Movement. In 1935 he also played an important role in *Filial Piety* (*Tian lun* 天伦), a Confucian-oriented film by Fei Mu (费穆) also made expressly for the New Life Movement. Fei Mu's co-director, Luo Mingyou, expressed open support for the Nationalist regime.[5] Although these types of Republican-era contacts were left out of post-1949 sketches of people like Zheng, cultural bureaucrats and senior Party leaders never forgot.

Zheng Junli and many in his circle who later rose to prominence in Mao's China also adjusted remarkably well to the new circumstances created by the Japanese invasion in 1937. For instance, before and after the Japanese attack on Shanghai, Zheng and numerous other Nanjing-era actors formed theatre troupes devoted to the Nationalist-led resistance cause. Zheng led the third brigade of the Shanghai Salvation Drama Troupe which included the famous actor Zhao Dan (赵丹) whose life would intertwine with Zheng's in many fascinating ways after 1949.[6]

With the Japanese takeover, Zheng Junli left Shanghai, arriving in Chongqing in 1938. There, he and many others with multifaceted backgrounds went to work for Chiang Kai-shek's Nationalist government. Although there was nothing unusual about this type of activity, early post-Mao biographers did not mention it, referring instead to vague "resistance" activities in the interior. In fact, Zheng functioned as the director of the government's Children's Theatre Troupe (Haizi jutuan 孩子剧团) and then in 1940–42 worked on documentary film projects for the state-run China Film Studio, including one entitled *Long Live the Nation* (*Minzu wan sui* 民族万岁, 1942).[7]

Zheng and many of his associates of the Nanjing decade and resistance war eras, including those who had worked for the government, grew increasingly disillusioned with the Nationalists during the 1945–49 civil war. There is no convincing evidence that Zheng was attracted to the Communist Party, but, as a film director in Shanghai's privately owned Kunlun Film Studio, he made films that reflected poorly on the government. The best of these was an

5. See Paul G. Pickowicz, "The theme of spiritual pollution in Chinese films of the 1930s," *Modern China*, Vol. 17, No. 1 (1991), pp. 38–75.
6. "Zheng Junli's biography and filmography," p. 63.
7. *ZDLZ*, Vol. 2, pp. 290–91.

astonishingly popular melodrama entitled *A Spring River Flows East* (*Yi jiang chun shui xiang dong liu* 江春水向东流, 1947). His treatment of the demoralization that was sweeping post-war China was bold because it was by no means clear when the film was released which side would emerge victorious in the civil war.[8] His second film, *Crows and Sparrows* (*Wuya yu maque* 乌鸦与麻雀, 1949), is frequently referred to as a classic "progressive" work, but in reality it was made at the tail end of the civil war when the outcome of the conflict was obvious to all, and when cultural workers who were disinclined to flee Shanghai with the Nationalists were already positioning themselves for favourable treatment in the post-revolutionary era.

Zheng Junli's civil war activities were later acclaimed by the Communist Party, but *A Spring River Flows East* posed problems for Party cultural bureaucrats. For one thing, the film's success complicated the notion that cultural production in the late Nationalist era was subjected to ruthless, state-sanctioned, "white terror" repression. If there was "white terror," how could such a critical and destabilizing film be openly produced and widely distributed? And how could it win a Chiang Kai-shek Prize (*Zhongzheng jiang* 中正奖) after its release in 1947?[9]

Zheng Junli was typical of the middle-level cultural personalities with complex and even politically embarrassing Republican-era backgrounds who remained in place after the Communist takeover and looked forward to working with the new regime. Zheng, like many others, was a survivor who grew up in a world that was adjusting to the shift from monarchy to republic, and who, as a young adult, adjusted in rapid succession to the advent of Nationalist rule in Nanjing, the "golden age" of foreign domination of Shanghai's international settlement, life in Chongqing during the resistance war, and the agonies of the civil war. Zheng was only 37 years old in spring 1949 when Communist forces occupied Shanghai. He and most of his associates had every intention of accommodating themselves to and even playing a leading role in the new cultural order, even though they knew almost nothing about the Party, its policies and its plans for China. They were eager to serve a powerful state and looked forward to surviving and even prospering by learning the new rules of the game and working to strengthen pre-existing networks that bound like-minded friends. The Party, based for so many years in the rural sector, actively courted the support of urban cultural personalities

---

8. For a discussion of *Spring River* see Paul G. Pickowicz, "Victory as defeat: postwar visualizations of China's war of resistance," in Wen-hsin Yeh (ed.), *Becoming Chinese: Passages to Modernity and Beyond* (Berkeley: University of California Press, 2000), pp. 365–398.

9. See "Zheng Junli's biography and filmography," p. 63, and *Dianying xiju sishi nian liang tiao luxian douzheng jishi* (*A 40-Year Record of the Two-Line Struggle in the Film and Theatre Worlds*) (Shanghai: Shanghai hongqi dianying zhipianchang hongqi geming zaofan bingtuan, Shanghai tushuguan hongse geming zaofan pai, 1967), p. 82.

whose skills and notoriety were badly needed during the transition. Messy personal histories could be ignored.

On 18 June 1949 the Shanghai Theatre and Film Association was set up by the Party. An election was then held among stage and screen professionals to select its leaders. Zheng Junli was undoubtedly happy with the results. Of the top 27 vote-getters, veteran Communist Party members Yu Ling (于伶) and Xia Yan got 586 and 554 votes. The rest of the list consisted mainly of well-known non-Party personalities, including virtually all of Zheng's best Republican-era friends: writer and director Shen Fu (沈浮) with 547 votes, writer Chen Baichen with 459, actor Zhao Dan with 356, actress Wu Yin (吴茵) with 224 and actress Huang Zongying (黄宗英) with 180. Zheng himself was 14th with 235 votes, finishing ahead of such gifted actors as Shi Hui (石挥), Zhang Fa (张伐) and Shi Yu (石羽).[10] Zheng was also pleased that his two civil war-era films continued to be shown. *A Spring River Flows East* was screened 137 times in Shanghai in 1949 and 135 times in 1950. *Crows and Sparrows*, which Zheng reworked in the months following the Communist takeover of Shanghai, was screened 577 times in Shanghai in 1950 to an audience of 287,000.[11] It was all very exhilarating and promising. Zheng and his old friends must have felt like insiders.

Zheng Junli continued to work for the privately run Kunlun Film Studio in the early years of transition. The new state allowed private sector cultural activity. His first screen-writing and directorial project was a low-budget political film entitled *Husband and Wife* (*Women fu fu zhi jian* 我们夫妇之间), based on a propaganda novel by Xiao Yemu (肖也牧). It became a common practice in socialist China to base films on theatrical scripts or works of fiction that had already passed by censors. The production was initiated in late 1950 at about the time of China's entry into the Korean War, and was released in spring 1951.

Husband and Wife starred Zheng's old friend Zhao Dan, who had just finished playing the title role in Kunlun's much more expensive production of *The Life of Wu Xun* (*Wu Xun zhuan* 武训传, d. Sun Yu), a film about a legendary Qing dynasty education reformer who tried to help rural people. *Husband and Wife*, a far more modest work, concerns a Shanghai intellectual, Li Ke, who serves the revolution in rural Shandong during the civil war. He meets and marries an illiterate peasant woman, Zhang Ying, who has been cited as a "labour hero." They have a son, and things go well until the couple is assigned to Shanghai after the revolution. He is thrilled to return to the urban environment; she feels awkward and out of place. In fact, issues of this sort were not uncommon in the early 1950s years of transition.

10. *Qingqing dianying* (*Qingqing Film Magazine*), Vol. 17, No. 15, 1 August 1949.
11. Shanghai shi dang'anguan (SMA), B-172-1-35.

Various stresses and strains soon drive a wedge between the two revolutionaries. Often confrontational and shrill, she complains that he has changed. Enjoying the good life in the city, it seems he has forgotten the peasants. He responds that she is inflexible, mired in the ways of the past and unable to appreciate China's modern future. Naturally, the film ends on a happy note. Thanks to Party intervention, the two reconcile, with each admitting shortcomings and a need to make ideological progress. The film was fairly harmless. Movie fans liked it. In the first five months of 1951 it was screened in Shanghai 236 times to an audience of 106,500. *Platoon Commander Guan* (*Guan lianzhang* 关连长, d. Shi Hui), a somewhat similar, though more polished, film released at about the same time by Wenhua, another private film studio, was shown 347 times to an audience of 199,000.[12]

Initial reviews of the film, which appeared in mid-April 1951, were encouraging. *Popular Cinema* (*Dazhong dianying* 大众电影), the leading film fan magazine, ran a nicely illustrated and friendly report that contained no hint of problems. *Xin min bao* (新民报), a Shanghai news daily, published three reviews, all praising it.[13]

Then Zheng Junli got the first political shock of his post-1949 career when the apparently politically correct film was criticized harshly in the press beginning in late April and continuing into July. Zheng and Zhao Dan were quite upset. Hard-line critics like Zhao Han (赵涵), writing first in *Popular Cinema* and then in *Wen hui bao* (文汇报), claimed that Zheng's portrait of Li Ke, the revolutionary urban intellectual, was much too sympathetic.[14] Li's petty bourgeois essence was inadequately denounced. The depiction of Zhang Ying, the peasant woman, was, by contrast, unflattering and harsh. The peasants shown in the first part of the film seemed excessively backward and buffoon-like. When the conflict between husband and wife is resolved, it seems to be mainly on his terms. Another critic worried about the negative impact the movie would have on the film audience in places that had only recently been taken over by the Communists. Party cadres – indeed the Party itself – looked bad in it. Li Ke, a Party official with eight years experience, seemed like a condescending and self-centred petty bourgeois element; Zhang Ying, a labour hero, looked ignorant and petty.[15] Zheng Junli, the critics

---

12. See SMA, B-172-35 for the screening statistics.

13. "Fu fu zhi jian de xiao fengbao" ("A little storm between husband and wife"), *Dazhong dianying* (*Popular Cinema*), No. 20, 10 April 1951, pp. 10–14; "Ping *Women fu fu zhi jian*" ("A review of *Husband and Wife*"), *Xin min bao* (*New People Daily*), 21 April 1951; Wang Qian, "*Fu fu zhi jian* guan hou" ("After viewing *Husband and Wife*"), *Xin min bao*, 24 April 1951; Ying Wei, *Women fu fu zhi jian* jiao ren ruhe gao hao fu fu guanxi" ("*Husband and Wife* teaches us how to maintain good spousal relations"), *Xinmin bao*, 25 April 1951.

14. Zhao Han, "Ping *Women fu fu zhi jian*" ("A critique of *Husband and Wife*"), *Dazhong dianying*, No. 21, 25 April 1951, reprinted with minor changes in *Wen hui bao* (*Wen hui Daily*), 15 May 1951.

15. Fang Renshou, "Fandui waiqu geming ganbu" ("Oppose distortions of revolutionary cadres"), *Dazhong dianying*, No. 24, 5 July 1951, pp. 26–27.

implied, suffered from the same petty bourgeois afflictions that plagued the protagonist, Li Ke. How else to explain his glorification of the bourgeois urban intellectual?

The problem was not primarily the film, but very bad timing; the intellectual-bashing so characteristic of the Mao era had already begun. The main focus of attention was not Zheng's film but *The Life of Wu Xun*, the movie Kunlun had released just before *Husband and Wife*. Indeed, in the context of the Cold War, the Korean War and the new movement to suppress counter-revolutionaries launched in early 1951, Mao Zedong personally intervened by writing a militant critique of *The Life of Wu Xun*. The result was the "first major campaign of criticism in literature and art after 1949."[16] Both *Husband and Wife* and Shi Hui's *Platoon Commander Guan* were ensnared in Mao's initial assault on "bourgeois" intellectuals. In case anyone failed to get the message, the 5 May 1951 *Wen hui bao* attack on *Husband and Wife* was published right beside an article entitled "*The Life of Wu Xun*: a film that should never have been made." Zheng Junli and Republican-era cultural activists had to be wondering what the connection was between counter-revolutionaries who deserved to be shot and well-connected, loyal intellectuals who exhibited some bourgeois tendencies in the early transition to the "new society."

Zheng scrambled to save himself. First, despite his initial unhappiness, he quickly surrendered unconditionally to the Party by writing a ritualistic and humiliating confession entitled "With deep remorse I must reform myself" (*Wo bixu tongqie gaizao ziji* 我必须痛切改造自己).[17] Without such self-flagellating confessions, he and many others quickly learned, there was no hope of salvation. After writing his self-criticism, Zheng disappeared from sight for quite a while. In part, this was punishment for him and the others targeted. The Party used the 1951 campaign to frighten and terrorize friendly people like Zheng, and to gain much tighter control of the cultural world.

In the post-Mao period sympathetic biographers continued to assert that Zheng had bourgeois tendencies, and that the "censure and criticism" he received in 1951 was appropriate.[18] Zheng was idle for the rest of 1951 and 1952, and then in 1953 he was allowed to remould his thinking by immersing himself in the lives of the "workers, peasants and soldiers." He is credited with making two propaganda documentaries during this time of study and reflection: *The People's New Hangzhou* and a work about a factory in Shanghai entitled *Glorious Creativity*.

Despite his sincere efforts to reform himself, Zheng was not allowed to direct another feature until 1954 when he made *The Rebels* (*Song*

16. Paul Clark, *Chinese Cinema: Culture and Politics since 1949* (Cambridge: Cambridge University Press, 1987), pp. 45–50.
17. *ZDLZ*, Vol. 2, p. 293.
18. *Ibid.*

Jingshi 宋景诗), a story about an early 19th-century peasant rebel, at the state-run Shanghai Film Studio. The project was a test for Zheng and others recently suspected of bourgeois maladies. Zheng co-directed the picture with Sun Yu, the director of the disastrous film about Wu Xun. Released in 1955, *The Rebels* was quite forgettable, but Zheng Junli clearly passed the test by mastering the Party's official position on the actual peasant rebellion led by Song Jingshi.[19]

Zheng kept a low profile, professionally speaking, for the next three years. He had learned his lesson, or so he thought, with the *Husband and Wife* débâcle of 1951. He would keep his mouth shut. By contrast, the famous actor and director Shi Hui, who was criticized before and after the Wu Xun campaign, became active in the Hundred Flowers free speech movement of spring 1957. Shi Hui and other cultural workers criticized the Party. Zheng's strategy of maintaining silence seemed at the time to pay big dividends. His outspoken colleagues were denounced, jailed and driven to suicide during the brutal Anti-Rightist Campaign of mid-1957. Zheng and many like him did nothing to support these old friends from Republican days. Indeed, Zheng wanted more than ever to find a way into the Party. He was thrilled when he was included in a small group of Shanghai filmmakers visited by Mao Zedong on 7 July 1957.[20] Though it is not mentioned by his post-Mao biographers, Zheng's political life declined to a shameful low point in August 1957, at the height of the anti-rightist witch hunt, when he published an article that not only referred to the pernicious influence of "rightists" and the brilliance of Mao's ideas about literature and art, but also discredited the contributions of Republican-era filmmakers like himself. "We are opposed to going backward," he asserted, "we want to advance and then advance again" under the leadership of the Party.[21] Many respected non-Party cultural luminaries, including the famous writer Ba Jin (巴金), supported the Anti-Rightist Campaign. They no doubt felt they had no choice.

In 1958 Zheng Junli was rewarded for his loyalty. In fact, he was presented with the greatest opportunity of his life. He was told he might be able to direct the film that was going to be the visual centrepiece of the tenth anniversary celebration of the People's Republic scheduled for October 1959.

Mao Zedong's Great Leap Forward, a spectacular utopian effort to initiate a transition from socialism to communism, was now under way. With both Sino-Western and Sino-Soviet relations in serious disarray, and with China quite isolated in the international arena, the

19. See Yingjin Zhang and Zhiwei Xiao, *Encyclopedia of Chinese Film* (London & New York: Routledge, 1998), p. 393.

20. Chen Jinliang and Zou Jianwen (eds.), *Bai nian Zhongguo dianying jing xuan* (*The Best of Centennial Chinese Cinema*) (Beijing: Zhongguo shehui kexue chubanshe, 2005), Vol. 2, Part 1, p. 357.

21. Zheng Junli, "Tan Zhongguo dianying de chuantong" ("On the Chinese tradition of filmmaking") in *Zhongguo dianying* (*Chinese Cinema*), No. 8 (1957), pp. 13–15.

movement took on an extremely nationalistic, almost chauvinistic, tone. Mass mobilization was on an unprecedented scale and, by almost all accounts, a mood of euphoria swept through Chinese society in mid-1958. It appeared to those who were swept up by the Leap that China could shortly surpass the industrial West in virtually every field of endeavour. Zheng Junli was among those energized by all this.

The Chinese film industry, entirely state-owned by 1958, participated enthusiastically. In keeping with the fantastic production mania of the Leap, the industry was expected to produce "more, better, faster and less costly" films. Output "leaped" from less than 50 titles in 1957 to more than 130 in 1958.[22] In spring and summer 1958, at the apogee of Leap zeal, ambitious plans were being made for film production in 1959, the eagerly awaited tenth anniversary of the People's Republic. Party leaders responsible for cultural affairs decided that the most important film project of 1959 was to be a lavish colour movie on the Opium War entitled *Lin Zexu* (林则徐). In some respects it was a strange choice. During the first decade of Party rule, filmmakers had generally avoided sensitive imperial-era historical topics. Indeed, the 1951 campaign against *The Life of Wu Xun*, a so-called "reactionary" film about Qing history, had sent chills through the film world.[23] Still, there was a strong sense that it was crucial to turn out a glossy film version of the story of Lin Zexu, a film consistent with Mao's view that anti-imperialist and anti-feudal activities associated with the Opium War marked the beginning of "modern Chinese history." Moreover, the old guard that dominated the film establishment, many of them based in Shanghai, was opposed to the idea that all film projects had to deal with life under socialism.[24]

The gala film was based on a draft entitled *Yapian zhanzheng* (鸦片战争), first published by Ye Yuan (叶元) and others in late spring 1956. It was revised following the Anti-Rightist Campaign and republished in late 1957.[25] The movie was to be made at the Haiyan Film Studio in Shanghai, and director Zheng Junli, still very much a favourite of such major cultural bureaucrats as Xia Yan and Chen Baichen, was chosen to lead the project.[26] In fact, ever since the 1954–55 *Song Jingshi* project that brought Zheng into the world of imperial-era peasant rebellions, he had expressed a strong desire to make historical films. In October 1956 Zheng had organized a "small work group" that explored ways to convert Ye Yuan's text into a usable screenplay.[27] After Zheng was chosen as director, Ye Yuan completed

22. *Zhongguo yishu yingpian bianmu* (*A Catalogue of Chinese Art Films*) (Beijing: Wenhua yishu chubanshe, 1981), Vol. 1, pp. 253–447.

23. Zhiwei Xiao, "Chinese cinema," in Yingjin Zhang and Zhiwei Xiao, *Encyclopedia of Chinese Film*, pp. 23–24.

24. *A 40-Year Record of the Two-Line Struggle*, p. 82.

25. *Lin Zexu: cong juben dao yingpian* (*Lin Zexu: From Screenplay to Movie*) (Beijing: Zhongguo dianying chubanshe, 1979), p. 407.

26. *ZDLZ*, Vol. 2, pp. 293–94.

27. Zheng Junli, *Hua waiyin* (*Offscreen Voices*) (Beijing: Zhongguo dianying chubanshe, 1979), p. 64.

yet another revision of the screenplay in January 1958, renaming it *Lin Zexu*.[28] Caught up in the euphoria of the Leap, a jubilant Zheng Junli was finally offered membership in the Communist Party, one year after his dear friend Zhao Dan had been admitted.[29] Zheng's political problems of 1951 could now be forgotten, or so he thought.

Members of the cast recall that expectations were unusually high. Huang Shaofen (黄绍芬), the famous cinematographer whose artistry dominated the Republican-era film world, was put in charge of filming. Zheng Junli's old friend Zhao Dan, who had starred in two ill-fated films (*The Life of Wu Xun* and *Husband and Wife*) was recruited to play the role of Lin Zexu.[30] Foreign actors virtually never appeared in Chinese films, but on this grand occasion Gerald Tannebaum, a leftist American expatriot residing in China, agreed to play the distasteful part of Lancelot Dent, a notorious British opium merchant, on the condition that he be allowed in the future to play the revolutionary role of Dr Norman Bethune. A Czech resident of China played the part of Captain Charles Elliot, the British superintendent of trade.

Qin Yi (秦怡), the actress assigned to the role of A Kuan sao, a fictionalized peasant activist, recalled that "everyone" associated with the production behaved in an "ultra-leftist" (*ji zuo* 极左) manner. Tannebaum, "unusually obedient" during the shooting, rode about on a bicycle and cheerfully ate the ordinary Chinese food served in the staff canteen. Director Zheng constantly reminded the team of the political import of the film. He would not allow filming, much of it scheduled for autumn 1958 on location in Guangdong, Zheng's ancestral home, to get bogged down.[31]

The main political problem facing Zheng was the absolute need to find a way to make not merely a Marxist film about the Opium War, but a distinctively Maoist film. Despite his work on the Song Jingshi story, Zheng was not well suited to the task. Like many other privileged artists, Zheng wanted to prove his loyalty to Chairman Mao and the Leap to communism. But, even more than the Li Ke character in *Husband and Wife*, Zheng was a stereotypical urban intellectual with no practical revolutionary experience and no political links to Mao's rural-based revolution or to the Red Army. He had far more in common with the bourgeois cultural stars of Republican Shanghai than he had with the peasants and soldiers who had swept the Communist Party to power. Although elite cultural workers like Zheng were most comfortable in cosmopolitan cities like Shanghai,

28. Ye Yuan's revised text is in *Lin Zexu*, pp. 1–59. Zheng Junli's shooting script is in *Lin Zexu*, pp. 61–204.

29. Shu Xiaoming, *Zhongguo dianying yishu shi jiaocheng* (*Lectures on the History of Chinese Film Art*) (Beijing: Zhongguo dianying chubanshe, 1996), p. 73

30. See Zhao Dan, *Yinmu xingxiang chuangzao* (*Creating Screen Images*) (Beijing: Zhongguo dianying chubanshe, 1980), pp. 67–104, for one of Zhao's 1960 commentaries on the project.

31. Qin Yi, "Pao long tao" ("Playing a bit part"), *Bi hui wen cong* (*Pen Society Essays*), No. 4, pp. 121–26.

the politics of the Leap were profoundly anti-urban and anti-intellectual.

To qualify as a Maoist film, *Lin Zexu* would have to be militantly anti-imperialist and stridently nationalistic. Those who resisted British imperialism would have to be shown as not merely anti-foreign, but motivated by modern ideas about devotion to nation. The Chinese people would have to be portrayed as broadly united in defiant struggle. But resistance to imperialism and defence of nation could not be described as rooted in a popular attachment to traditional Chinese culture. Class conflict would have to be accounted for, but it would be important to show that it was in the interest of all classes to rid China of imperialist aggressors. It would not be appropriate to suggest that the upper classes as a whole were the mortal enemies of the sacred national struggle. Instead, the film would have to say that only a small percentage of elites had betrayed the nation. Perhaps most important, a proper Maoist treatment of the Opium War would have to end on an optimistic note. It would have to show that China did not really lose the war. A politically acceptable ending would have to focus attention on the spontaneous uprisings of indignant Chinese masses. The unmistakable message of the Leap was that the broad masses, imbued with an unshakeable will, could overcome even the most formidable obstacles and race ahead in the quest for revolutionary transformation.

Zheng Junli understood that the cultural politics of Maoism and the Leap imposed aesthetic standards as well. Although no one associated with the *Lin Zexu* project dared to mention the existence of *Eternal Flame* (*Wan shi liu fang* 万世流芳, d. Bu Wancang 卜万苍, 1943), a politically tainted film about the Opium War made with Japanese approval during the Japanese occupation of Shanghai, artists like Zheng Junli, Huang Shaofen and Zhao Dan had certainly seen the hopelessly discredited film and were keenly aware that among other things it had been criticized for blindly following the unsavoury Hollywood "entertainment" model. But given the tensions in Sino-Soviet relations, it would not be advisable to make the sort of Soviet-type film that had been turned out in such large numbers in China in the mid-1950s. The new project was expected to have "national" aesthetic integrity, which meant that it would have to resonate with *respectable* Chinese cultural standards.[32]

The political stakes were extremely high, but Zheng and the others sincerely believed that they had fashioned a Maoist version of the Opium War. In sharp contrast to the discredited *Eternal Flame*, *Lin Zexu* never loses its almost exclusive focus on the heroic activities of a saintly Commissioner Lin, and never explores Lin's personal life. The film makes extensive use of various conventions associated with traditional Chinese stagecraft to paint a picture of a Chinese universe

32. Lin Niantong, *Zhongguo dianying meixue* (*The Aesthetics of Chinese Film*) (Taibei: Yunchen wenhua, 1991), pp. 67–112.

inhabited by two types of people: proud patriots and detestable traitors. The first type will risk anything to defend the Chinese nation, while the second shamelessly sells out China to foreign aggressors for private gain. Furthermore, the heroes are all Hans (Lin Zexu, Guan Tianpei (关天培), who is the commander in chief of naval forces, and Deng Tingzhen (邓廷桢), who is the governor-general of Guangdong and Guangxi), while the villains are all Manchus or Mongols (Muzhanga (穆彰阿), who is an influential grand councillor and imperial favourite, Qishan (琦善), who is the governor-general of Zhili, and Yukun (豫坤), who is the superintendent of customs in Guangzhou). When the heroes appear on screen, they stand upright and are flooded in bright light, while the villains, including the foreigners, are usually seen stooped over as they conspire in the shadows.

In structural terms, the film treats three specific episodes rather than the complex entirety of the conflict with the British. The first episode begins with the triumphant arrival of Lin Zexu in Guangzhou in March 1839 and ends with the seizure and destruction of foreign opium in June. This portion of the film treats the economic and moral dimensions of the opium trade, but the overriding focus is on the imposing personage of Commissioner Lin. In quick succession, Lin establishes his authority, gathers reliable intelligence, forges unshake-able alliances with such Han patriots as Admiral Guan and Governor-General Deng, and discovers that a small group of corrupt and traitorous officials led by Superintendent Yukun is acting in concert with the odious foreign aggressors. Even more important, during an undercover tour, Lin comes into contact with honest and highly nationalistic local working people with whom he establishes warm relations. The masses are encouraged by the news that the emperor has sent a high commissioner to the region. Lin learns that the father of one of his new allies was shot by a "foreign devil" because he refused to unload opium. Arrogant opium merchants, by contrast, take delight in insulting China. "If this fellow Lin is Chinese," they laugh, "then he can be bribed!"

During this first portion of the film, Lin deals confidently with the foreign menace. Arrangements are made to improve coastal fortifications, isolate the foreign community and confiscate all opium supplies. At one point, the British merchant Dent tries to escape to Macau with the help of corrupt local officials, but A Kuan sao, the militant young working woman, and others intercept his flight. Terrified of ordinary Chinese, Dent tries at first to intimidate them by saying: "I am a foreigner!" To the delight of the film audience, A Kuan sao, a woman, responds by slapping Dent across the face. The subsequent destruc-tion of the confiscated opium in June 1839 is portrayed as a magnificent victory for the coalition of upright officials and patriotic masses led by Commissioner Lin.

The second part of the film covers the period from summer 1840, when British forces initiate the Opium War by attacking China, to

September 1840, when the emperor removes Lin from his position. The political message of the film is quite clear at this juncture. Despite the failure of traitorous local officials to lend their support, Chinese forces are able to defend Guangzhou. The credit is given to Lin, the honest officials who surround him and, above all, the popular masses who are led by a sagely, charismatic fisherman named Kuang Dongshan. Lin is shown consulting Kuang and the others on a regular basis. An organic relationship of mutual respect guides their collective actions. Kuang tells Lin: "If you want to settle accounts with the foreign devils, rely on us!"

But when the British navy heads north in mid-summer 1840 to capture Dinghai (定海) in Zhejiang province, attack Tianjin and threaten Beijing itself, the emperor panics. He blames Lin for causing all the problems, and replaces him with his rival, Qishan, who is sent to Guangzhou to do whatever is necessary to appease the British. The masses, now distraught about this sudden turn of events, come to pay their respects to Lin. Bowing before a disgraced Lin, they cry out "Tell us what to do!" Lin responds emotionally: "Never allow the foreign devils to fight their way into Guangzhou!"

The final segment of the film treats the period from autumn–winter 1840, when Lin is still on hand in Guangzhou trying in vain to assist Qishan, to spring 1841, when he leaves Guangzhou and the peasants stage an anti-British uprising at Sanyuanli (三元里). The emphasis is on how the Manchus, from the emperor in Beijing to Qishan in Guangzhou, betray Lin and the Han masses who are prepared to sacrifice anything to defend China. Qishan asserts that the peace can be won if Elliot's various demands are met. These include dismantling coastal fortifications, disbanding local militia units and reining in the patriotic masses. The film makes it clear, however, that by taking such actions the duplicitous Manchus are also defending against Han threats to Qing rule. Unfortunately for Qishan, however, the British continue to attack.

With the transfer of Lin Zexu to Zhejiang in April 1841, the patriotic masses are on their own. Led by Kuang Dongshan, local people gather in Sanyuanli village in May 1841. The assembled masses swear an oath to bring "death to the invaders," and rush out with primitive weapons in hand to take on a unit of British regulars. When driving rain makes it impossible for the British to use their rifles, the masses go on the offensive and force the frightened invaders to run away like cowards. The film ends with a shot of the proud and victorious throng massed on a lush hillside with weapons and battle standards held aloft.

In sharp contrast to the reception of Zheng Junli's *Husband and Wife* in 1951, *Lin Zexu* generated a veritable avalanche of enthusiasm in state-controlled news dailies in the weeks before and after its release on National Day 1959. Beginning with "Comments on a splendid movie," a glowing article by veteran cultural revolutionary Yang Hansheng (杨翰笙), the popular press lavished praise on Zheng's epic film.[33] The fast-rising Maoist literary critic Li Xifan (李希凡) contributed a piece entitled "An heroic historical image that is authentic and profound."[34] The old proletarian cultural romantic Zheng Boqi (郑伯奇) produced an open letter to director Zheng under the heading, "*Lin Zexu*: an artistic image that excites the heart."[35] Across the land, the headlines repeated the same triumphant message: "A grand and heroic historical poem,"[36] "An image of a resolute and steadfast patriot,"[37] "The first time we took up arms,"[38] "The outstanding film *Lin Zexu* is highly recommended,"[39] "A splendid poem that resists aggression,"[40] "The fury of the race,"[41] and "The heroism of the race is not in decay."[42] *Lin Zexu* was portrayed as the most important film made in the short history of the People's Republic.

These glowing press accounts left the strong, but highly misleading, impression that Zheng Junli had succeeded in making a Maoist film at the peak of Leap euphoria in 1958. The problem was that by the time the film was released in late 1959 the political situation in China had shifted rather significantly. Mao and the Leap were now under attack at the highest levels of power. At the famous Lushan Conference in July 1959 Mao was the target of a stunning criticism by defence minister Peng Dehuai. The Leap had caused the worst famine in history. At least 20 million people died in a holocaust that began unfolding in spring 1959. News of the disaster and of the political battles being waged at the summit of power was not carried in the media. But urban intellectuals heard rumours about starvation in the countryside and middle-level Party members, including those like Zheng Junli who were engaged in cultural work, had access to information about high-level criticisms of Mao and the ultra-communist winds that had blown so hard in the first year of the Leap. Before 1959 ended, veteran cultural bureaucrats like Xia Yan were already mobilizing against the Maoist approach to art and culture.

The popular audience clearly enjoyed the movie. After all, it was beautifully filmed on location in an exotic coastal region, Zhao Dan's performance as Lin Zexu was unforgettable, it featured non-stop action that pitted valiant heroes against cruel villains, and it definitely aroused patriotic passions. But, in the transformed political

33. Yang Hansheng, "Tan youxiu yingpian *Lin Zexu*," *Renmin ribao* (*People's Daily*), 17 September 1959.
34. Li Xifan, "Zhenshi shenke de lishi yingxiong xingxiang," *Dazhong dianying*, No. 18, 1959.
35. Zheng Boqi, "*Lin Zexu*: jidong renxin de yishu xingxiang," *Shaanxi ribao* (*Shaanxi Daily*), 14 October, 1959.
36. *Fujian ribao* (*Fujian Daily*), 25 September 1959.
37. *Shanxi ribao* (*Shanxi Daily*), 24 September 1959.
38. *Gongren ribao* (*Workers Daily*), 24 September 1959.
39. *Liaoning ribao* (*Liaoning Daily*), 27 September 1959.
40. *Xinwen ribao* (*Daily News*), 23 September 1959.
41. *Nanchang ribao* (*Nanchang Daily*), 27 September 1959.
42. *Guangzhou ribao* (*Guangzhou Daily*), 27 September 1959.

environment of late 1959, influential senior intellectuals were starting to position themselves to the right of Mao, and pointing to problems with the film. For example, Professor Zhang Kaiyuan (章开沅), a famous scholar of Qing history, published a commentary on the movie that conflicted with the universally upbeat tone of earlier popular reviews.[43]

Zhang stated that the film properly emphasized the main tendency of historical development, that is, the anti-imperialism of the Chinese people. But, he noted, the leading representatives of the masses, namely Kuang Dongshan, the young woman A Kuan sao and others, were purely fictional. The invention of these characters posed problems about "the question of historical truth." Zhang conceded that it is permissible to invent characters who represent the "spirit of the times." But then he pointed to aspects of the film which he believed were simply inaccurate. The portrait of Yukun was excessively negative and betrayed the film's anti-Manchu bias. Furthermore, the film failed to show that Lin Zexu was open-minded about learning from advanced aspects of Western knowledge.

Even more interesting than Zhang's article was the seminar on *Lin Zexu* convened on 2 September 1959 by the Chinese Film Workers' Association.[44] The participants included such cultural notables as Yang Hansheng, the Manchu novelist Lao She (老舍), leading playwrights Tian Han (田汉) and Li Jianwu (李健吾), film director Jin Shan (金山), veteran actor Lan Ma (蓝马), and film administrator Chen Huangmei (陈荒煤). Here too, praise was heaped on Zheng Junli's film, but a number of intriguing questions were raised about the exaggerated quality of the production and its tendency to omit certain information and to depart from strict realism.

Lao She, an expert on Manchu culture, pointed to errors in the film's depiction of Qing rituals, official attire, modes of transportation and greeting etiquette. He complained that the film should have been more explicit about the harmful effects of opium consumption. Historian Ding Mingnan (丁明楠) expressed the view that the film seriously distorted the historical role of Yukun, the Manchu superintendent of customs. The historic Yukun was not so reactionary and had a good working relationship with Lin Zexu. Ding also pointed out that the dramatic meeting between Lin and Captain Elliot that is portrayed in the film never took place. According to Qing rituals, an official of Lin's rank would not have met face to face with the foreigner.

Qian Hong (钱宏), another seminar participant, agreed that the characterization of Yukun "did not conform to the historical facts." Unfortunately, for the sake of simplicity, he noted, Yukun had been

---

43. Zhang Kaiyuan, "Ao shuanghua yan Lingnan zhi" ("A flower of dignity blooms in Lingnan"), *Renmin ribao*, 15 November 1959.
44. *Lin Zexu* zuotan hui," *Dianying yishu* (*Film Art*), No. 10 (1959), reprinted in *Lin Zexu*, pp. 332–356.

thrown into the broad, but stereotypical, category of corrupt officials. It is one thing to suggest that these people were ineffective in dealing with the British, but quite another to say that people like Yukun were actually colluding with foreigners. Since characters like Kuang Dongshan and A Kuan were invented, Qian quipped, it would have been better to invent some officials who were acting in concert with the British.

The famous playwright Tian Han (Zheng Junli's old mentor in the late 1920s) made perhaps the boldest statement about the Yukun issue. The filmmakers had sacrificed Yukun in order to bolster the image of Lin Zexu. Nevertheless, he observed, "Yukun stood on the side of the Chinese people at that time. We should give him a positive appraisal."

The most authoritative voice heard at the seminar was that of Yang Hansheng, who summed up the general feeling. The film was successful and moving, Yang said, not because all the historical facts were accurate, but because it made the powerful point that during the Opium War a broad spectrum of Chinese people took up arms for the first time to resist foreign imperialism. That theme was more important than the issue of class tensions in China, he seemed to say. It was important to see China united rather than divided in the face of a hostile external world. Thus, instead of offering a nuanced class analysis of Chinese society, the movie focused on the over-whelming mass of patriots and a small group of traitors. Yang regretted that Yukun was described as a negative figure. "The main problem in this movie," he concluded, "is that all the Manchu officials are described as corrupt and tending to compromise."

Furthermore, Yang argued, the need to represent a broad united front in the struggle with foreign enemies required that the masses be shown working in concert with others, rather than acting alone. "Though the struggle of the militia was spontaneous," Yang observed, "we can't say that it had no connection to the activities of Lin Zexu. Lin's policies were popular." Yang then made a comment that would haunt him in later years: "It was correct to describe the confluence of landlord and mass resistance."

Despite these reservations expressed in late 1959, the film continued to be shown throughout China as the massive famine deepened. But press coverage of *Lin Zexu* declined significantly in early 1960. The most interesting articles that appeared in 1960 were written by celebrities associated with the production. Ye Yuan, the author of the original screenplay, wrote several articles,[45] Zhao Dan contributed a couple of essays,[46] and Zheng Junli himself wrote two pieces,

45. Ye Yuan, "Lue tan ruhe biaoxian lishi renwu de juxian xing" ("Comments on how to express the limitations of historical figures") *Shanghai dianying* (*Shanghai Film*), No. 4 (1961); Ye Yuan, "Lin Zexu yu Ping ying tuan de guanxi" ("The relationship between Lin Zexu and the Ping ying tuan"), *Wen hui bao*, 29 April 1961.

46. Zhao Dan, "Yanzhe kangzhuang dadao yongwang zhi qian" ("Advance bravely along the great path"), *Beijing ribao* (*Beijing Daily*), 24 January 1960; Zhao Dan, "Lin Zexu xingxiang de chuangzao" ("Creating an image of Lin Zexu"), *Dianying yishu*, No. 5 (1961).

including one for *People's Daily* entitled "Mao Zedong thought illuminates the creative path of filmmaking."[47] Zheng was still trying hard to present himself as a loyal Maoist. All these works were written to defend the artistic choices made by the production team. Maoism and the Leap were in retreat by late 1959, but even anti-Maoists saw no reason why *Lin Zexu* should not continue to be promoted. Indeed, on 22 September 1959 the Film Bureau selected Zheng Junli to lead a film delegation to North Vietnam to participate in a ten-day "Chinese film festival." *Lin Zexu* was the centrepiece of the Chinese titles screened in Hanoi.[48]

After *Lin Zexu* was finished, Zheng Junli immediately threw himself into yet another directorial effort associated with the tenth anniversary of the People's Republic. But this film, entitled *Nie Er* (聶耳), was a disappointment to both Maoists and anti-Maoists and received far less attention than the visually spectacular and highly emotional *Lin Zexu*. *Nie Er* was made because Xia Yan and other anti-Maoists at the top of the cultural bureaucracy saw Mao as a narrow nativist, while viewing themselves as cosmopolitans whose cultural activities in Shanghai in the 1930s were linked to sophisticated global currents. Consequently, they advocated the production of films that were based on important works of Republican era fiction by Lu Xun, Mao Dun (茅盾), Rou Shi (若石) and others. By glorifying the 1930s, these cultural officials reinforced their own non-Mao lineage, legitimacy and power in the rough-and-tumble cultural politics of China. Celebrating the 1930s also meant making biographical films that paid tribute to cultural heroes of the era, people like Lu Xun and Nie Er.

Born in 1912, Nie Er was a young composer who wrote popular Western-style songs for motion pictures.[49] In 1933 he joined the Communist Party and began work at the Lianhua studio where Zheng Junli was employed as an actor. Nie was connected to many well-known people, including Cai Chusheng (蔡楚生) and Tian Han. Among the tunes written by Nie was "March of the volunteers," a revised version of which became the national anthem of the People's Republic. He drowned in 1935 at the age of 23 during a beach outing in Japan. "Dead in youth and venerated by the Party," Nie was a perfect candidate for film biography.

But the movie was a flop. Jay Leyda, who was living and working in China at the time, wrote in his diary that *Lin Zexu* "had alerted me to some of the dilemmas of Chinese biographical films, but I was quite unprepared for the nonsense and uselessness" of *Nie Er*. People who knew Nie Er, Leyda wrote, "told me that the figure on screen was

47. Zheng Junli, "Mao Zedong sixiang zhaoliangle chuangzuo de daolu," *Renmin ribao*, 22 March 1960.

48. *A 40-Year Record of the Two-Line Struggle*, p. 84.

49. See Richard Kraus, *Pianos and Politics in China: Middle-Class Ambitions and the Struggle over Western Music* (Oxford: Oxford University Press, 1989) for a discussion of Nie Er and Xian Xinghai, another popular leftist musician.

wholly fictional." The scenarists, the cinematographer and Zheng Junli (who Leyda noted was "leaping from one anniversary film to another") knew Nie, but had decided to "make a 'stronger' film story than could be made" from Nie's real life.[50] It must have been extremely painful for Zheng to produce a dishonest film about an old friend from Republican days, unless he had convinced himself that the real Nie Er and the one he had created on screen were one and the same. Zheng's embarrassment was lessened a bit when he learned that *Nie Er* had won a prize in 1959 for biographical films at the Karlovy Vary Film Festival in socialist Czechoslovakia.[51] The Czechs, no doubt, recognized and appreciated the Europeanized quality of Nie's life and work at a time when much of the Soviet bloc was disturbed by the chauvinism of Mao's Great Leap.

What Zheng Junli really wanted, though, was a chance to make the long-awaited film about culture icon Lu Xun. The 80th anniversary of Lu Xun's birth created the perfect opportunity. What Zheng did not fully grasp, however, was that the towering figure of Lu Xun was not at all like the inconsequential Nie Er. Indeed, a film about Lu Xun would be even more difficult to make than a film about Lin Zexu. Various factions in the post-Leap party were struggling for proprietary rights to Lu Xun's legacy. Maoists did not want a film that depicted Lu Xun as a member of the 1930s cosmopolitan camp. Anti-Maoists did not want to see a patently distorted, unrecognizable, Nie Er-like representation of Lu Xun.

While Zheng Junli waited patiently for a decision, his career began a long downward spiral. At first glance, it appears that Zheng was trying in 1961 to replicate, in political terms, what he did in 1951 after the *Husband and Wife* débâcle. That is, he left Shanghai and his dangerously bourgeois cultural contacts and went out once again humbly to learn from the masses. This had become a standard strategy for cultural personalities with Zheng's sort of background. It amounted to a pre-emptive initiative, especially because Mao was in substantial retreat in 1961 and the cultural field was now more open and diverse than at any time since 1949–50 and spring 1957.

On this occasion, Zheng's merge with the masses took the form of a dreadful film entitled *Spring Comes to a Withered Tree* (*Kumu feng chun* 枯木逢春). In this utterly predictable socialist realist tale, a poor peasant woman, Meizi, is afflicted with schistosomiasis. A young man named Dong, Meizi's childhood friend and now a tractor driver in socialist China, loves the rural woman and is determined to take care of her. Two bourgeois urban physicians arrive from Shanghai to work on the epidemic that haunts the region. But they have ideological problems. Progress is made only when the village head returns from a meeting with Mao (!) and reports that the Chairman wants people to

---

50. Jay Leyda, *Dianying: An Account of Films and the Film Audience in China* (Cambridge, MA: MIT Press, 1972), p. 308.
51. "Zheng Junli's biography and filmography," p. 63.

work as a collective. Then, as if by magic, a cure is found, Meizi returns to full health, she marries the tractor driver and gives birth to twins. Dong is so excited he resolves to teach Meizi how to drive a tractor. No one, not even the Czechs, liked this movie. It is hard to imagine that Zheng was proud of the film. But years earlier he had learned that it was impossible to err in a direction too far to the "left." The Party seemed to forgive "leftist" errors, but it never forgave "rightist" errors.

This time, however, Zheng's effort to learn from the masses did him little good. In spring 1962, after multiple stops and starts, the decision was made to kill the Lu Xun film. At a time when the new Socialist Education Movement was under way, there was simply no way to tell the Lu Xun story without deeply offending one power faction or another. Zheng must have been bitterly disappointed. This would have been the most important Chinese film since *Lin Zexu*. But at another level he was probably relieved. It would have been an impossible task, closely scrutinized and dissected by both sympathizers and political opportunists. Naturally, Zhao Dan was scheduled to play the lead role. Cultural insiders knew the project was dead when Zhao appeared for dinner at the Peace Hotel in Shanghai without the bushy Lu Xun-type moustache he had been sporting for several months.[52]

For more than two years after the filming of *Spring Comes to a Withered Tree*, Zheng Junli was denied filmmaking opportunities. He was only 49 years old in mid-1961, hardly a candidate for retirement. Life in socialist China had taught Zheng not to fall into a passive mode in times of change. Thus he made yet another desperate attempt, his final one, to prove his loyalty to Mao and the Party, and to secure his position on the "inside."

At a dance party in Shanghai in summer 1963, Zhou Enlai told Zheng and screenwriter Wang Lian (王炼) that he wanted them to make a film based on a North Korean play entitled *Red Propagandist* (*Hongse xuanchuan yuan* 红色宣传员). The team dropped everything and rushed to Beijing where it met Zhou twice more before travelling to North Korea for two months in September 1963. The screenplay was hurried to completion in early 1964, whereupon Zheng returned to North Korea to film exterior scenes. The picture was ready for release at the end of 1964.[53]

The movie, entitled *Li Shanzi* (李善子), is set in North Korea and involves the never-ending activities of a woman propaganda activist named Li Shanzi to spread the word of Kim Il Song in her rural community. Initially, no one in the village is enthusiastic about collective work and everyone, including the local leaders, is ideologically backward. Morale is low and people are suspicious.

---

52. Leyda, *Dianying*, p. 309.
53. See Wang Lian, "Zheng Junli de yi zuo: *Li Shanzi*" ("Zheng Junli's lost work: *Li Shanzi*"), *Dazhong dianying*, No. 9 (1996), p. 40.

But Li's determined propaganda work is highly effective and the whole community unites and happily sprints ahead under the banner of socialism. Kim Il Song is so pleased he grants Li a personal audience.

In late 1964 word came down that the film had problems. Screenwriter Wang Lian was urged to revise his work. Wang was puzzled, since the film had already been completed. A document entitled "Criticisms by leading comrades at the state centre and relevant units concerning the film *Li Shanzi*" was circulated, and Zheng and the others were summoned to a series of meetings convened in Beijing starting in December 1964. Bombarded by criticisms, Zheng was advised by Zhou Enlai to "reform his world view" and pay a call on Mao's wife Jiang Qing (now active in a movement to "reform" the theatre world) to seek her advice. The meeting with Jiang Qing did not go well. She told Zheng that he "was not standing alongside the proletariat" and that his film gave her "the shivers."

In July 1965 Zhou Enlai presided over one final gathering devoted to *Li Shanzi*. The film was not going to be released. Zhou asked Zheng how he was sleeping. Zheng responded that he was taking sleeping pills. According to a witness, Zhou laughed and said, "You should think hard about these questions."[54] Screenwriter Wang Lian wondered why Zheng had been singled out time and again over the years. Abandoned by Zhou Enlai, Zheng's film career was finished, though the worst was yet to come.

Unfortunately for Zheng Junli and many like him, their agitprop work of the mid-1960s was unappreciated. Worse still, new and even deadlier political winds were beginning to swirl. One suspects, however, that Zheng still had hopes. Given that the thrust of rebel politics during the early stages of the Cultural Revolution was decidedly Maoist and that Zheng had distorted the historical record in 1958 in order to fashion a Maoist interpretation of the Opium War, Zheng might have thought that he and his greatest post-1949 film achievement were beyond criticism from the left, that he would escape the onslaught of the Red Guards just as he had avoided the cruelties of the Anti-Rightist Campaign in 1957. After all, it was only with the 1951 film *Husband and Wife* that he had erred to the "right." In every other case he had been careful to stand to the "left." He still loved the Party and continued to hope that the Party would at long last express its unconditional love for him. He was totally unprepared for the inhumanities that followed.

Red Guard publications attacked every film Zheng Junli made before and after 1949, including the unbearably propagandistic *Li Shanzi*. *Husband and Wife* was no good. *Nie Er* was no good. *Spring Comes to a Withered Tree* was no good. Indeed, Zheng was said to be part of a bourgeois plot led by Xia Yan, Tian Han, Yang Hansheng

54. *Ibid.*

and others who had sneaked into the Party to "oppose the formation of a film industry that served the workers, peasants and soldiers."[55] Not surprisingly, much was made suddenly of Zheng's extensive contacts in the 1930s with film personalities connected to the Nationalist Party and of his work for the Nationalist government in Chongqing during the Second World War.

But the harshest attacks on Zheng were reserved for his most celebrated film, *Lin Zexu*. The 1959 seminar on *Lin Zexu* had revealed that some leading intellectuals thought the movie was excessively "leftist." But the Red Guards who waged war on Chinese culture concluded that it was a shameless right-wing project. It was labelled a "poisonous weed" (du cao 毒草) and a "black model" (*hei yangban* 黑样板), and banned.[56] The problem was that the movie glorified not just one but a number of "feudal" officials. Even the Daoguang emperor was given credit at the outset of the film for pursuing an aggressive anti-British policy. From the Red Guard point of view (a perspective that focused almost entirely on domestic political battles, not the conflicts that pitted China against foreign enemies), the class struggle that raged in the 1840s was totally ignored in the film. Even its treatment of the popular uprising against the British was unacceptable. The masses not only take orders from Lin Zexu, a feudal official, but they express an almost slavish admiration for him. After Lin is removed from his post, the masses bow before him and beg him to issue directives. To make matters worse, before the masses attack the British at Sanyuanli, they are viewed in a Buddhist temple praying: "Lord Buddha, help us destroy the enemy!" Zheng Junli was guilty of defaming the patriotic masses.

Red Guard publications shrilly denounced Zheng and his film as reactionary to the core. A broadside prepared by Cultural Revolution insurgents in the Shanghai film world stated that it was a disgrace that Zheng and his "poisonous weed" *Lin Zexu* had been sent to North Vietnam in 1959.[57] Vicious biographical sketches of Zheng highlighted his appearances as an actor in many "right wing" films of the mid-1930s and his cultural work for the Nationalist Party and government in the interior during the resistance war.[58] Zheng was destroyed by Chairman Mao's rebels. He was arrested in 1967 and died in prison on 23 April 1969 at the age of 58.[59]

In the late 1970s, a decade after Zheng's death, Chinese cultural production began to head in new directions. But if we focus on 1949 to 1976, and take note of the party-state's nearly monopolistic control of the cultural sphere, the problem of the relationship between artists and the state remains the key issue. Denied research access to China until the late 1970s, scholars of Chinese culture working outside China

---

55. *A 40-Year Record of the Two-Line Struggle*, pp. 130–31.
56. *Ibid.* p. 131.
57. *Ibid.* p. 84.
58. *Ibid.* pp. 130–31.
59. *ZDLZ*, Vol. 2, p. 297.

tended to emphasize trends in policy formation, state-directed campaigns and culture struggles at the centre of state and Party power. More recently, scholars have used newly available biographical sources to approach the relationship between artists and the state in different ways. By looking in detail at a rank-and-file artist like Zheng Junli, we are able to learn how socialist cultural production was experienced by artists themselves. This type of research is by definition artist-centred and thus helps to put a human face on an important aspect of state–society relations after 1949.

But highly personalized narratives of this sort inevitably move into sensitive areas. The Communist Party is still in power in China, and, despite leaks, information about former state employees is still closely guarded. Scholars are thus hampered in their ability to address questions about the Party's relationship with the thousands of art and culture workers in its employ during the Mao era. One tries to imagine what sort of research on interactions between artists and the Party from 1949 to 1976 would emerge if the Communist Party lost power. Investigations of this sort were launched in places like East Germany, Hungary and Czechoslovakia following the demise of the ruling Communist Party. It is possible that a new generation of scholars working in a post-communist political environment and making research use of classified materials and oral histories would compare China after 1949 to China during Nationalist Party rule or to China under the Japanese occupation of 1937–45. If one thinks of China as having been under the control of an unaccountable communist party after 1949, then the issue of "creative accommodation" arises. Who made accommodations with the Party? Who did not? To what extent were there degrees of accommodation? Why did artists choose to accommodate themselves to party-state rule? Are accommodation and complicity the same thing? Is it going too far to speak of collaboration? Was resistance an option? Who resisted? Who stood by or benefited when colleagues were scapegoated? Who informed on colleagues or assisted in persecutions? How did artists manoeuvre to make themselves, their families and their friends in the arts less vulnerable politically? How did survival strategies evolve? What privileges and protections were afforded artists who were successful in joining the Communist Party? How did artists prove their loyalty? Did the Party love people like Zheng Junli who engaged in creative accommodation? Did such artists really love the Communist Party? Did they have any choice?

In Search of a Master Narrative for 20th-Century Chinese History*

Susanne Weigelin-Schwiedrzik

ABSTRACT Since the Yan'an Rectification Campaign the Communist Party of China has dominated the interpretation of modern Chinese history. With its 1981 resolution it renewed its claim, but a close look at official and unofficial publications on 20th-century Chinese history reveals its loss of control. There is no longer a CCP-designed master narrative of modern Chinese history. This article uses the case of the Cultural Revolution to show how much post-1949 history is contested in mainland China today. It argues that the CCP is unable to impose its interpretation of the "ten years of chaos" on society. Instead many divergent and highly fragmentized views circulate in society, and there is no overwhelmingly acceptable view on this period of post-1949 history. While this is a positive sign of diversification, it leaves unsatisfied both inside and outside observers who hope that the Chinese people might eventually come to terms with their own troublesome history.

In his paper on official histories published on the occasion of the 50th anniversary of the founding of the People's Republic of China (PRC) William Kirby expressed his surprise at the (curious) absence of a master narrative on 20th-century Chinese history. He reported that there was an enormous number of publications focusing on a myriad of different aspects of "national history," full of historical details and sources, but he was unable to detect a coherent master narrative undergirding this plethora of detail.[1] Left unexplored was the larger question of why PRC historiography was unable to present such a narrative on such an important commemorative occasion. This is particularly surprising, as through such exercises as the Yan'an (延安) Rectification Campaign and the "Resolution on some historical questions"[2] the Chinese Communist Party (CCP) defined a frame for the interpretation of post-Opium War history that has served as the unchallengeable basis for official history writing in the PRC.

* Research for this article was supported by an appointment as Madeleine H. Russell Visiting Professor for Non-Western and Comparative Studies at Brandeis University during the spring term of 2005. Some aspects of the article were presented at the Fairbank Center, Harvard University and at the Academia Sinica Institute for Modern History, Taipei in May and July 2005. Special thanks for valuable commentaries to Merle Goldman, Ralph Thaxton and Peter Zarrow, and for enormous support from Julia Strauss.

1. William C. Kirby, "Reflections on official histories in 20th century China," paper presented to the International Conference on Modern Chinese Historiography and Historical Thinking, Heidelberg, May 2001.

2. "Guanyu ruogan lishi wenti de jueyi" ("Some questions concerning history"), in Mao Zedong, *Xuanji* (*Selected Works*), Vol. 3 (Beijing: Renmin chubanshe, 1953), pp. 975–995.

Textbooks for middle-school and university students are still written according to this resolution, and history examinations are based on what the resolution has to say about the period between 1840 and 1945.

The period since 1945 was brought into the realm of official history with the "Resolution on some questions regarding the history of the Party since the founding of the PRC"[3] of 1981. However, it has so far not been able to claim as much authority as the 1945 Resolution. Indeed, instead of dominating the interpretation of 20th-century Chinese history, the CCP has increasingly been unable to hinder alternative interpretations from entering the discussion. This article analyses the process of writing and re-writing history in the PRC trying to give an answer to why the CCP has lost its ability to define a master narrative for post-1949 Chinese history and why other forces have so far not been strong enough to replace the CCP historiography with an alternative dominant interpretation.

History and Identity

The whole question of whether a master narrative is necessary or desirable is much contested. For post-modern philosophers, the very core of post-modern thought consists of "modernist total 'grand narratives' being continually repudiated by different forms of post-modern scepticism."[4] However, recent discussions stress the multi-plicity of grant-narratives and the necessity to accept divergent ways of writing history in the context of different cultures. The French philosopher Lyotard as one of the major proponents of this idea stresses:

It seems to me that there is now a sort of comprehension of the so-called multiple ways of understanding the meaning of communities in Africa, South America, North America, India, Russia, or Asia, and so to be vigilant against grand narratives is precisely to be prudent and aware of the capacity for human communities to have different ways of narrating their stories. It's not destroying these narratives, and it's not necessarily protecting them; it's just respecting them.[5]

Instead of repudiating the idea of a grand or master narrative, Lyotard seems to stress that the "meaning of communities" is established through narratives that relate to the past and that define the identity of the community. If people do not have an idea of the past that they can share they are unable to develop ideas for the

3. "Guanyu jianguo yilai dang de ruogan lishi wenti de jueyi" ("On some questions concerning the history of the Party since the founding of the PRC"), *Renmin ribao* (*People's Daily*), 1 July 1981, pp. 1–7.
4. Linda Hutcheon, *A Poetics of Postmodernism: History, Theory, Fiction* (New York: Routledge, 1988), p. 44.
5. Gary A. Olson, "Resisting a discourse of mastery: a conversation with Jean-Francois Lyotard," in http://jac.gsu.edu/jac/15.3/Articles/1.htm, last seen 8 February 2006.

future. That is why authors like Arif Dirlik, known for his in-depth research on Chinese historiography, now acknowledge the fact that "master narratives" are not only imposed on communities by states or particular elites, but can also serve to empower social groups in their contest for authority and recognition.[6]

History is contested, and yet societies strive for a shared understanding of history. The German Egyptologist Jan Assman combines the necessity of contestation with the possibility of a common understanding of history.[7] Although far removed from the substance of the historiography of the PRC, Jan Assman's work on ancient Egypt offers insights into how history is produced that are extremely useful in understanding the current state of Chinese historiography and its lack of a master narrative. He distinguishes between two different forms of memory – cultural memory and communicative memory[8] – and defines the former as written into sacred texts which explain to their readers the origin of the society and polity they live in. As life in the present is rooted way back in the past, cultural memory does not have to stand the test of reality. It merely has to give a plausible account of how things came into being, and it has to leave enough room for interpretation so that readers can find answers to their questions raised against the background of changing everyday experiences in the present. Cultural memory in ancient civilizations is based on myth written into narratives by specialists who very often were not trained to explore the past, but to foresee the future. Cultural memory is what people who belong to one community relate to whenever they try to define their identity on the basis of a shared understanding of their history.

Communicative memory, in contrast, is within living memory; it is the memory of the 100 years people in their respective presents can look back on and to which the three generations that live simultaneously can relate with their own experiences. As the writing of history in this time period has to stand the test of divergent personal memories, it is not regarded as producing "sacred texts" and changes with time and perspective. Communicative memory is always contested as different social groups and different individuals not only exchange their views on the recent past, but also voice their interpretations in order to gain acclaim and support.[9]

---

6. Arif Dirlik, *After the Revolution: Waking to Global Capitalism* (Hanover: Wesleyan University Press, 1994), p. 89.
7. Jan Assmann, *Das kulturelle Gedächtnis. Schrift, Erinnerung und politische Identität in frühen Hochkulturen*. München (Beck) 2001. For an English translation of the introductory chapter see: Jan Assmann, "Cultural memory: script, recollection, and political identity in early civilizations," *Historiography East and West*, Vol. 1, No. 2 (2003), pp. 154–177.
8. *Ibid.*
9. Compare Maurice Halbwachs (ed., trans. and intro. Lewis A. Coser), *On Collective Memory* (Chicago and London: University of Chicago Press, 1992).

Chinese historiography since the beginning of the 20th century has been acutely aware of the effect history writing might have on communities.[10] In China, it was most prominently Liang Qichao who vigorously demanded a new way of writing history parallel to his call for a change of the dynastic system. The transition from empire to nation had to be accompanied by a transition from dynastic historiography to national history.[11] The historiography of the early 20th century in China is a radical departure from dynastic history writing in form and style, though not necessarily in content, and it has to fulfil the task – according to Liang Qichao – of uniting the nation and informing the citizens of this new polity on their common identity.[12]

At the time of writing, the end of dynastic rule and the beginning of the Republican era in China do not exceed the 100 years suggested by Assman as the appropriate time frame for communicative memory. During the "century of revolutions," the Chinese nation lived through several beginnings and endings, and historians (particularly official historians) have had to explain the necessity of change and continuity against the test of eyewitness observations and in competition with each other on both sides of the strait. In both mainland China and Taiwan, historians have produced texts that belong to the time span of communicative memory, while claiming authority for these texts as if they belonged to cultural memory. Up until recently, the CCP used its power monopoly to impose its version of Chinese history since the Opium Wars on the nation. And even though recent developments in the context of the magazine *Freezing Point* (*Bingdian* 冰点)[13] show that it still tries to use its power monopoly to suppress open debates on history, this article shows by the example of the Cultural Revolution that the CCP is no longer able to dominate the

10. For an analysis of Chinese historiography from its beginning to the present, see Helwig Schmidt-Glintzer, Achim Mittag and Jörn Rüsen (eds.), *Historical Truth, Historical Criticism, and Ideology. Chinese Historiography and Historical Culture from a New Comparative Perspective* (Leiden: Brill, 2005)

11. See Peter Zarrow, "Old myth into new history. The building blocks of Liang Qichao's new history," paper given on the AAS Conference in Washington DC, 2002. See also Axel Schneider, *Wahrheit und Geschichte. Zwei chinesische Historiker auf der Suche nach einer modernen Identität für China* (Wiesbaden: Harrassowitz, 1997). For the state of the art of scholarly discussions in China on Liang Qichao see Susanne Weigelin-Schwiedrzik, "Chinese historiography and globalization: the case of Liang Qichao," in Martin Jandl and Kurt Greiner (eds.), *Science, Medicine and Culture. Festschrift for Fritz G. Wallner* (Frankfurt/Main: Peter Lang, 2005), pp. 176–198.

12. *Ibid.*

13. "Freezing point" is a supplement to the widely read newspaper *Chinese Youth* (*Zhongguo qingnianbao*). It was closed on the directive of the Propaganda Department of the CCP after publishing an article by Yuan Weishi under the title of "Modernization and history textbooks" (*Xiandaihua yu lishi jiaokeshu*). Yuan, Professor at Sun Yatsen University in Canton, criticized textbooks in the PRC for not basing arguments on facts and for sticking to an outdated and xenophobic way of interpreting post-1840 Chinese history. The editor in chief Li Datong was expelled from office because of allowing this article to appear. See "Zhong qing bao biangdian chushi wenzhang: xiandaihua yu lishi jiaokeshu" ("The article which triggered events at the Chinese Youth supplement 'Freezing point': modernization and history textbooks"), blog.chinesenewsnet.com/?p=7085 (last seen on 27 January 2006).

interpretation of contemporary history. The CCP version of the master narrative of 20th-century Chinese history no longer exists.

Official Historiography in Crisis

In the PRC, the writing of modern and contemporary history has been based on the "sacred texts" edited and published as Mao Zedong's *Selected Works* and framed by the CCP Central Committee's resolution "On some historical questions"[14] passed shortly before the Seventh Party Congress in 1945. Even though the CCP went through several rounds of internal struggle, the textbooks based on these documents have changed less than most people would expect.[15] Up until today, they reiterate the master narrative on how the CCP legitimately took over mainland China as if it were part of the nation's cultural memory.

The 1981 resolution "On some questions regarding the history of the Party since the founding of the PRC"[16] was passed by the Central Committee on the 60th anniversary of the founding of the CCP, only five years after Mao had died. It underlines the importance and validity of the 1945 resolution and frames the interpretation of the time period between 1945 and 1976. However, it has so far not been able to dominate the discussion on post-1949 PRC history. Instead the field of history writing has split into two different spheres: that of official historiography including Party historiography; and unofficial historiography comprising everything from documentary literature and memoirs to eyewitness accounts, historical documentaries and history books written by people from outside the field of academic historiography. The common denominator of official historiography is its compliance with the two above-mentioned resolutions; the common denominator of unofficial historiography is its attempt to escape from the Party resolutions and break through the taboos of history writing related to China's 20th-century and especially post-1949 history.[17]

---

14. "Guanyu ruogan lishi wenti de jueyi" ("Some questions concerning history"), in Mao Zedong, *Selected Works*), Vol. 3 (Beijing: Renmin chubanshe, 1953), pp. 975–995.

15. Susanne Weigelin-Schwiedrzik, *Parteigeschichtsschreibung in der VR China: Typen, Methoden, Themen und Funktionen* (Wiesbaden: Harrassowitz, 1984). For an English-language article on the topic see Susanne Weigelin-Schwiedrzik, "Party historiography in the People's Republic of China," *The Australian Journal of Chinese Affairs*, No.17 (January 1987), pp. 77–95.

16. On some questions concerning the history of the Party since the founding of the PRC," pp. 1–7.

17. On the difference between official and unofficial historiography see Susanne Weigelin-Schwiedrzik,"Die chinesische Historiographie in den 90ger Jahren: Zwischen Erkenntnistheorie und Marktwirtschaft," in Hartmut Kaelble and Dietmar Rothermund (eds.), *Comparativ. Leipziger Beiträge zur Universalgeschichte und vergleichenden Geschichtsforschung, 11.Jahrgang, Heft 4, 2001: Nichtwestliche Geschichtswissenschaften seit 1945*, pp. 53–79. For an early analysis of unofficial historiography see: Geremie Barmé, "Using the past to save the present: Dai Qing's historiographical dissent," *East Asian History*, No. 1 (1991), pp. 141–181.

The two different spheres of history writing, though very much apart, influence each other. Post-1949 history used to be a field official historiography would not dare to write about. As up until 1981 no Party resolution covered this time period and Mao's post-1949 speeches had not been officially published, textbooks on CCP history had very little to say about this period. Only after unofficial historians such as Ye Yonglie (叶永烈)[18] started writing on issues related to post-1949 history did the period gain more attention. Today the post-1949 period is under heavy contestation, and official historiography is pushed into publishing on events so far left uncovered.

The CCP leadership had already lost control over what people knew about CCP history during the Cultural Revolution (1966–76). With Red Guards storming archives and digging into the histories of leading intellectuals and Party cadres, their understanding of the communist revolution had become more complex and more realistic. Instead of reading textbooks on the Chinese Revolution young people had the chance to read the life stories of individuals. However, after the death of Mao Zedong and the dismissal of the Gang of Four two problems occurred simultaneously. Those who had actively participated in the Cultural Revolution knew too much to be able to submit to the then prevalent interpretation of post-1949 history, and the Party, in order to adjust history to the needs of the present, had to re-write its own history. During the years 1976 to 1981, Party historiography was preoccupied with re-defining the role of Mao Zedong and Mao Zedong Thought. Consequently, the hermetic system of Party historiography in which history was identical with Mao Zedong Thought and Mao Zedong Thought was supposed to be the product of history started to dissolve. While in pre-Cultural Revolution times the only aspects of CCP history which were included in the narrative were those that were able to make the basic assumptions of Mao Zedong Thought plausible, post-Cultural Revolution historiography had to explain how the Party could exist and succeed without Mao Zedong. The master narrative that had evolved from the Yan'an (延安) Rectification Campaign[19] had institutionalized itself during the 1950s and 1960s,[20] supplying the basic concepts and assessments every candidate for a position in post-1949 Chinese bureaucracy had to be able to reproduce. When "de-Maofication" was put on to the agenda, Party historiography did not dare to deconstruct the general principles and basic assessments. Instead it broadened the scope of data to be included in the narrative.

18. See for example: Ye Yonglie, *Chenzhong de 1957* (*The Heavy Year 1957*) (Hong Kong: Mingxing chubanshe, 1988), *Zhonggong milu* (*Secret History of the CCP*) (Hong Kong: Liwen chubanshe, 1993), *Lishi beige: Fan youpai neimu* (*A Tragedy of History: The Inside Story of the Movement against Rightist Elements*) (Hong Kong: Tiandi tushu youxian gongsi, 1995).

19. See David E. Apter, "Discourse as power: Yan'an and the Chinese revolution," in Tony Saich and Hans van de Ven (eds.), *New Perspectives on the Chinese Communist Revolution* (Armonk, M.E. Sharpe, 1995), pp. 193–234.

20. See n. 15.

By allowing their readers to become acquainted with so far unknown details of history, Party historiographers were able to reduce the role of Mao Zedong without deconstructing Mao Zedong Thought. They hence tried to solve two problems at once: they complied with the Party's needs to adapt Party history to the necessity of collective leadership, and they accommodated their readers who were tired of only reading about principles and eager to know more facts. However, the gradual augmentation of facts would sooner or later hit the limits of the hermetic system. Li Honglin's (李洪林) call for breaking through the taboos of Party history[21] made clear to everybody that in the many books and textbooks published not even half the story had been told. The more the details leaked out, the more the system stumbled into crisis.

While re-writing pre-1949 history, Party historiographers still shied away from writing about the post-1949 period. Although the fifth volume of Mao Zedong's *Selected Works*[22] covering this period was eventually published by a group of editors under the then Party chairman Hua Guofeng (华国锋), internal struggles among the leadership did not allow it to gain uncontested authority. Just as the strategy of reform and opening initiated by the CCP Central Committee in 1978 lacked a theoretical foundation, so the writing of history on the Maoist period was devoid of "theoretical guidance" and teleological orientation. Party historiography cannot establish truth without theoretical guidance, and the theory cannot claim to be true without victory. The credibility of the master narrative on pre-1949 history was built on the indisputable victory of the revolution; the writing of post-1949 history lacked this credibility by the absence of success.

As soon as the Party declared the dismissal of the Gang of Four and allowed criticism of the Cultural Revolution under the disguise of criticizing the Gang of Four, reality started working against historiography. The hermetic system of Party historiography gradually lost its authority as the CCP leadership admitted past mistakes in order to gain support for the future. Consequently, Party historiographers had to cope with a new paradox: when writing about the Maoist era they inevitably ran the risk of creating a counter-narrative subversive to the post-1978 system. If they radically criticized the Maoist era they separated the CCP from its historical and ideological roots. But if they applauded what Mao had designed as his path to socialism they inevitably contradicted the policy of reform and opening. When the Party finally took control of the situation in 1981 the only solution it found to the dilemma was the 70:30 assessment: Mao Zedong's contributions to the Chinese revolution were 70 per cent good and only 30 per cent mistaken.

21. Li Honglin, "Dapo danshi jinqu" ("Break through the taboos of Party history"), *Lishi yanjiu*, No. 1 (1979), p. 20.
22. Mao Zedong, *Selected Works*, Vol. 5 (Beijing: Foreign Language Press, 1977).

The Cultural Revolution was among many other things a form of re-enacted memory. Through Party history textbooks and films the Red Guard generation had learnt to admire the heroism of the "generation of old proletarian revolutionaries" (*lao yi bei wuchanjieji gemingjia* 老一辈无产阶级革命家). However, with Mao putting the question of successors for the revolutionary cause on the table, the sons and daughters of the old revolutionaries had to answer some difficult questions. How could they prove their merit as successors to the revolutionary cause without going through the same kind of dangers and hardships as the older generation? How should they prove their willingness to sacrifice everything, including their own lives, as members of a privileged elite sheltered against any kind of danger and hardship? Only by re-enacting the revolution could they show that they were revolutionaries and qualify as successors to the revolutionary cause.

Soon the younger generation had to realize that they had learned the wrong lesson. Even the bravest among them were sent to the countryside with no hope of their dreams coming true. Some were even imprisoned as their revolutionary enthusiasm was regarded as dangerous. The revolution had turned against its protagonists while it was still going on, and by doing so it switched from one storybook to the other: access to elite positions did not have a front door designed for revolutionary spirit and sacrifice; it only had a back door defined by network access to the educational system. The farewell from revolution took place long before the Cultural Revolution was officially declared to have come to an end. No wonder students turned their backs on Party historiography after the end of the Cultural Revolution and the obligatory programme on Party history for university students was cancelled during the 1980s.

Unofficial historiography started flourishing under these conditions. Writers from the Red Guard generation, in most cases not professional historians, circumvented official control in search for answers to the many historical questions the CCP and Party historians had so far left unanswered. As they were denied access to the archives, their investigative methods had to be unconventional. They successfully broke through the taboos of Party history and gained credibility by penetrating into the realm of communicative memory. Some years before oral history was discussed[23] and finally accepted by official historians,[24] Ye Yonglie (叶永烈) and Dai Qing (戴晴) had already started interviewing old cadres and expelled former Party members to

---

23. Shen Guchao, "Yu renmin gongxie lishi – xifang koushushi de fazhan tedian jiqi dui women de qifa" ("To write history with the people – the particularity of the development of oral history in the West and lessons it contains for us"), *Shixue lilun yanjiu*, No. 2 (1995), pp. 98–107.

24. See Liu Xiaomeng: *Zhongguo zhiqing koushushi* (*Oral History of Sent-Down Chinese Youths*) (Beijing: Zhongguo shehuikexue chubanshe, 2004), pp. 10–14.

collect material.[25] Through their books and articles, they showed that the problem of the lack of teleological orientation and theoretical guidance could be solved by writing history into a story with a convincing plot structure. As a result, even though the 1981 resolution is still respected by official historiography, Party historiography engages in a dialogue with the many publications spreading news about what the Party has passed over in silence. Today, official historiography is trying to catch up with unofficial historiography. This is especially true for the case of the Cultural Revolution.

Framing the Memory of the Cultural Revolution

There is a widespread belief both in and outside China that the CCP has imposed total silence on questions related to the Cultural Revolution. The well-known slogan about looking for money (*xiang qian kan* 向钱看) and looking at the future (*xiang qian kan* 向前看) reflects a mood which seems to attest to the CCP relying on a lack of interest in the past on the part of the people. A close look at the Chinese book market, however, reveals that this assumption is not matched by facts. The Cultural Revolution is everywhere, in films, in novels and poems, but also in official and unofficial accounts, in memoirs and in many articles published in conventional journals as well as on the internet.[26] A 1999 survey on the ten most important events of 20th-century Chinese history reportedly showed that intellectuals overwhelmingly ranked the Cultural Revolution as the most important.[27]

On the occasion of the 40th anniversary of the Cultural Revolution in May 2006, the Propaganda Department of the CCP Central Committee tried to ban public discussions on the Cultural Revolution but was apparently unable to prevent a debate on the necessity to remember and re-assess it. In March 2006, an "underground" symposium was held near Beijing, the report on which states that the focus of research on the Cultural Revolution is no longer from outside the PRC. Major inputs and research results now originate

25. See n.17. For Dai Qing see Dai Qing (David E. Apter and Timothy Cheek (eds.)), *Wang Shiwei and the "Wild Lilies." Rectification and Purges in the Chinese Communist Party* (Armonk: M.E. Sharpe, 1993); also *Liang Shuming. Wang Shiwei, Zhu Anping* (Nanjing: Jiangsu wenyi chubanshe, 1989).

26. For a more detailed discussion on published memory of the Cultural Revolution see Gao Mobo, "Debating the Cultural Revolution. Do we only know what we believe?" *Critical Asian Studies*, Vol. 34, No. 3 (2002), pp. 419–434; and Gao Mobo, "Memoirs and interpretations of the Cultural Revolution," *Bulletin of Concerned Asian Scholars*, Vol. 27, No. 1, pp. 49–57; Susanne Weigelin-Schwiedrzik, "Coping with the trauma. Official and unofficial histories of the Cultural Revolution," paper given at the Conference "Rethinking 20th-century Chinese history," Institute of Modern History, Academia Sinica, July 2005, soon to be published in *Jindaishi yanjiusuo jikan*.

27. Luo Bing, "Guanfang minyi diaocha xiahuai le Zhongnanhai" ("An official survey of popular opinions horrifies Zhongnanhai"), *Zhengming* , No. 1 (2000), pp. 8–9.

from scholars working and living in China.[28] At the same time, the Propaganda Department invited a group of cadres from the older generation to discuss the Cultural Revolution. During this meeting, it was confronted with strong demands to build a museum of the Cultural Revolution (a wish Ba Jin had voiced several times, first in 1986[29]) and to grant compensation to the families of those killed or injured.[30]

In fact, even before the Cultural Revolution was officially declared to have come to an end in 1976, discussion on its assessment had already begun,[31] reaching its first climax at the end of 1976 after Mao's demise and the fall of the Gang of Four. This phase of the debate was closely related to the denunciation of the Gang of Four and the rehabilitations on all levels of Chinese society. Newspapers and magazines were full of articles on the individual fates of victims among CCP cadres and intellectuals. As long as the debate on the Cultural Revolution could be linked to criticizing the Gang of Four, hardly anything was taboo and just about everything possible. Because the new leadership under Hua Guofeng was longing for popular support, it allowed a comparatively open debate of the Cultural Revolution and defined the "guiding principle" of this debate to be the idea of universal victimhood. The Gang of Four was held responsible for misinterpreting and misusing Mao Zedong's ideas with the aim of seizing power. People who had participated in the Cultural Revolution with good intentions had been instrumentalized by the Gang of Four and unknowingly misled so they could not be held responsible for the bad results of their actions.

In 1981, the Party leadership re-defined the memory frame with its rough assessment of the Cultural Revolution given in the "Resolution on some questions of Party history since the founding of the PRC."[32] The resolution is full of direct and indirect criticisms of CCP policies since 1949, although it does not match the well-known "secret speech" Krushchev gave repudiating the terror of the Stalinist era in the Soviet Union.[33] Later commentators complained that because of internal

28. Zeng Huiyan, "Renmin bu hui wangji – Yi ge gaoya xia zai Beijing juxing de wenge yantaohui" ("The people will not forget – a symposium on the Cultural Revolution that was held under high pressure in Beijing"), http://www.ncn.org/asp/zwginfo/da.asp?ID=68736&ad=5/24/2006 (last seen 17 June 2006).

29. Li Hui, "'Wenge bowuguan': Ba Jin wan nian de tong yu meng" ("'The Cultural Revolution Museum': pain and hope of old aged Ba Jin"), http://www.sina.com.cn (last seen 16 May 2005).

30. "Zhengming: Wan Li shang shu hu chongping Mao Zedong" ("[A report from] Zhengming: Wan Li writes a letter to the leadership asking for a re-assessment of Mao Zedong"), www.epochtimes.com/gb /6/6/15/n1352522.htm (last seen 17 June 2006).

31. Compare Wang Xizhe's recent article which shows how the meaning of the Cultural Revolution had already been contested while it was still going on. Wang Xizhe, "Wenhua da geming shi pipanshu" ("An article on the ten forms of criticism of the Cultural Revolution"), http://www4.bbsland.com/forums/politics/messages/1503434.html (last seen 17 June 2006).

32. See n. 3.

33. For an English language internet version see http://www.fordham.edu/halsall/mod/1956krutshchev_secret1.html (last seen 18 September 2005).

struggles between the then Party leader Hua Guofeng (华国锋) and his opponent Deng Xiaoping (邓小平), the resolution did not "totally negate" (*quanpan fouding* 全盘否定) the Cultural Revolution.[34] Instead it is ambiguous by avoiding clear answers to questions like: who are the culprits and who are the victims; what was right and what was wrong behaviour; and what are the reasons for a mass movement like the Cultural Revolution developing into a civil war lasting for ten years?

The 1981 resolution defines three levels of responsibility. Mao is held responsible for developing the idea of the Cultural Revolution as a logical consequence of the theoretical considerations he had been pursuing since the late 1950s. The Party is held responsible for being unable to prevent Mao's theories from being put into practice although "the majority of members of the Eighth Central Committee of the Party and the members it elected to its Political Bureau, Standing Committee, and Secretariat" are all assessed as good comrades standing on the right side of the struggle. Last but not least, the Gang of Four is held responsible for the negative consequences of "rigging up two counter-revolutionary cliques in an attempt to seize supreme power, taking advantage of Comrade Mao Zedong's errors."[35]

By defining these three levels of responsibility, the CCP deviated from the model of Krushchev's "secret speech." Krushchev had drawn a clear line between Stalin as the culprit and the party as the victim, making the cult of the supreme leader responsible for the party's inability to inhibit Stalin's terror from spreading throughout the party and the country. In contrast, the 1981 resolution claims universal complicity. Without giving any details, it builds on a widespread feeling of culpability uniting elite and masses. Leading Party cadres had complied with Mao's Zedong's idea of launching the Cultural Revolution in its initial phase, and even when they were targeted by Mao and his supporters they were unable to escape from the Cultural Revolution discourse, trying to defend themselves or admit to their errors in terms defined by their persecutors. Their compliance, reinterpreted as an act of complicity, was well known to the public and therefore hardly deniable. Even after the ordeal was over, they had no way to escape from it.

How about the masses? Did they show more wisdom than the leaders in dealing with Mao Zedong and the Cultural Revolution? According to the 1981 resolution, people believed in Mao, then began "to adopt a sceptical or wait-and-see attitude towards the Cultural Revolution, or even resisted and opposed it." Only very few exploited

34. See Lowell Dittmer, "Rethinking China's Cultural Revolution," in Woei Lien Chong (ed.), *China's Great Proletarian Cultural Revolution. Master Narratives and Post-Mao Counternarratives* (London: Rowman & Littlefield, 2002), pp. 3–26.
35. All quotations from the translation in Michael Schoenhals (ed.), *China's Cultural Revolution, 1966–1969. Not a Dinner Party* (Armonk: M.E. Sharpe, 1996), pp. 297–310.

the situation and "were escalated to high or even key positions."[36] This is all that can be read about the "masses" in the resolution. No word on the Red Guard movement, no word on violence and terror, no word about the many victims, people who were killed or sent to prison, people who lost their property and their health. Instead the "masses" are included in the system of complicity. They "supported" the idea of the Cultural Revolution and only later became sceptical. Did the young people not respond enthusiastically to Mao's appeal? Their involvement was not compliance but an active form of support. Again, the resolution refrains from giving any details; it neither condemns nor applauds the participation of the young generation in the Cultural Revolution. The Red Guards and the "rebels" are neither heroes nor victims. They are accomplices.

One plausible explanation for the curious silence on what many would regard as one of the most important aspects of the Cultural Revolution might be derived from looking at the "family system" still dominating recruitment to the political elite in China. As part of this system, the Party leaders in power during the late 1970s wanted their offspring to take over as soon as the biological factor made this necessary. The Beijing Red Guard movement of the early Cultural Revolution was initiated by the group of young people the CCP needed as future leaders of the country. If the older generation had condemned them for their participation and violent excesses, they would have put the whole system of "revolutionary families" at risk. At present the leadership of the CCP is dominated by the so-called Red Guard generation. Hu Jintao (胡锦涛) and Wen Jiabao (温家宝) are both members of it, with Hu Jintao participating in the so-called "414" faction at Qinghua University (清华大学), one of those places in Cultural Revolution China where armed fighting was extremely fierce. Other members of the leadership who are said to have been actively involved in factional fighting were gradually reintegrated into the political elite without having gone through any investigations related to their Cultural Revolution activities.[37] Also, the early Red Guards had been violent in fighting against intellectuals, not in criticizing Party cadres. Why did the resolution not spare them the official condemnation and instead criticize the "rebels" who had turned against the "capitalist roaders" inside the Party? The truth is that the Party leadership could only condemn both or spare both, or run the risk of continued factionalism. It was forced to leave the assessment of Red Guard and rebel involvement ambiguous in order to prevent Cultural Revolution factionalism from dominating the competition for access to elite positions. Nowadays, insiders clearly remember who among the national, regional and local leadership

36. *Ibid.*
37. "*Pingguo ribao*: wenge shiqi de Hu Jintai, Wen Jiabao" ("*Apple Daily*: Hu Jintao and Wen Jiaobao during the Cultural Revolution"), published 11 May 2006; see also www.ncn.org/asp/zwginfo /da.asp?ID=68706&ad=5/22/2006 (last seen 17 June 2006).

belonged to which faction, but refrain from making a public issue out of it.

For the older generation of intellectuals and especially leading Party cadres, refraining from articulating a clear judgement of Red Guard and rebel factionalism, while solving one problem, generated another. If the members of the younger generation were not denounced as the "real" culprits, even the victims among the leadership of the Party, not to mention those among the rank and file, could not be acknowledged victim status. Up until today, the Party cannot allow mourning its victims in public. Neither the victims from the elite nor those from the grassroots are honoured in commemorative activities.[38]

Deng Xiaoping had hoped for the debate on the Cultural Revolution to end with the 1981 resolution.[39] However, his hopes were not realized. The ambiguity emerging from the idea of overall complicity impeded public debate of the Cultural Revolution and yet incited new rounds of discussion. According to recent accounts, Deng Xiaoping had already asked for a future revision of the 1981 resolution in 1982. He criticized that the resolution "compromised on important issues ..., in some cases argued against its own convictions and was to a certain degree selfish [in its assessment]."[40] In 1985, he again spoke in favour of a revision because he felt that too much blame had been put on the Gang of Four.[41] On the occasion of the tenth anniversary of the Cultural Revolution, for a very short time during the summer of 1986, public debate re-emerged demanding the "total negation" of the Cultural Revolution and stressing that without this there could be no guarantee against a re-emergence of the "ten years of chaos." Only fundamental change and a reform of the political system could protect the Chinese people from having to go through this kind of turmoil again.[42]

Today, the 1981 resolution is officially regarded as totally negating the Cultural Revolution[43] stressing that there is no need for revision or further discussion. Much in line with this official interpretation,

38. See Mary G. Mazur, "Public space for memory in contemporary civil society: freedom to learn from the mirror of the past?" *The China Quarterly*, No. 160 (1999), pp. 1019–35; Zhou Ziren, "Guanyu ling yi lei shounanzhe de sikao" ("Reflecting on another sort of victim"), *Huaxia wenzhai zengkan*, No. 276 (2001), see http://scenery.cnd.org/CR/ZK01/cr115.hz8.html#1 (last seen 16 June 2006).
39. See Deng Xiaoping in Jin Chunming, *"Wenhua da geming" shigao (Outline of the History of the Cultural Revolution)* (Chengdu: Sichuan renmin chubanshe, 1995), p. 503.
40. See n. 30.
41. *Ibid.*
42. See Dittmer, "Rethinking China's Cultural Revolution," n. 34; "Guanyu 'Wenhua da geming' de zai renshi zuotanhui fayan (zhaideng)" ("Extracts from the roundtable discussion regarding a new assessment of the Cultural Revolution"), *Qingnian luntan*, No. 7 (1986), pp. 1–10.
43. Wen Yanshan, "Chongwen Deng Xiaoping deng gemingjia lunshu: jianchi tuanjie yizhi xiang qian kan" ("Let's appreciate Deng Xiaoping's and other revolutionaries' assessment: stick to solidarity and to looking into the future"), http://politics.people.com.cn/GB/1026/4376050.html (last seen 17 June 2006).

Wang Xizhe regards the idea of totally negating the Cultural Revolution as the programme of those who took over the leadership after Mao's death hoping to reinstall a regime similar to that before 1966. He therefore clearly argues against the CCP totally negating the Cultural Revolution. He wants to rescue the Cultural Revolution by looking at it as a form of popular resistance against a dictatorial regime. That is why totally negating the Cultural Revolution in his view serves the aim of stabilizing the communist regime in China and is therefore in the interest of today's leading elite.

Anita Chan who analysed the debate in 1986 sees it in a different light. The then leadership of the Party tried to stop the discussion for fear of factionalism rather than for fear of debates on the future democratization of the political system.[44] If her assessment is true, it helps to explain why the CCP decided to turn away from the idea of universal victimhood and instead define complicity as the basis for assessing the Cultural Revolution. As long as the idea of victimhood dominated the discussion, survivors who were undeniably maltreated during the Cultural Revolution could speak up openly about their experiences and demand recognition for their suffering, if not compensation for their losses, and this idea included the rehabilitation of persecuted cadres and intellectuals. To a certain extent, it even helped making rehabilitations possible as – *pars pro toto* – they stood for the rehabilitation of all and thus underlined the idea of universal victimhood. Those who had victimized others, however, had not been relieved although they were officially pardoned and included into universal victimhood. As long as the victims were publicly acknowledged as such, the victimizers had to fear that the rehabilitated cadres or intellectuals who had regained their standing in society would demand revenge. The 1981 resolution with its idea of universal complicity tried to avoid revenge. When the discussion came back to the surface in 1986, it showed that factionalism and revenge were two sides of the same coin and both were a major threat to the idea of a peaceful society trying to catch up with the world's most advanced nations.

The Party's two attempts at framing the memory of the Cultural Revolution were not successful. Neither the idea of universal victimhood nor the idea of universal complicity had been able to reconcile Chinese society to a point where revenge was no longer a feasible option. The fear of continual factionalism and the inability to achieve reconciliation put the CCP into a position where it could no longer act as the focus in Chinese society producing the ideas and texts that would eventually form the basis of the master narrative. No wonder the Party tried to impose silence on society for the years to come.

44. Anita Chan, "Editor's introduction," in Liu Guokai, "A brief analysis of the Cultural Revolution," *Chinese Sociology and Anthropology* (Winter 1986–87), pp. 3–13.

Communicative Memory as Fragmentized Memory

Some years went by without many publications on the Cultural Revolution. It seemed as if the Party had been successful in imposing amnesia on society.[45] However, this only attests to the lack of public debate on the Cultural Revolution. In fact, the discussion went on especially among those who had actively participated in the event or had otherwise been involved more than the average population. Liu Xiaomeng (刘小萌) describes in his book how groups of sent-down youths who had been together in the same village tended to keep in touch and help each other re-integrate into urban society.[46] However, groups who share common experiences, whether positive or negative, are rarely able to overcome their own limitations and need support in accessing the public. Mary Mazur reports survivor groups coming together and mourning the deaths of their siblings, friends or colleagues, even though their activities are looked upon as subversive by the Party leadership.[47] The families of Wu Han (吴晗) and Liao Mosha (廖沫沙) she writes about belong to the survivor group of intellectuals and cadres who voice their opinions in public through the well-known journal *Yanhuang chunqiu* (炎黄春秋).[48]

But even if survivor groups have access to the public and spokespersons informing the public, the realm of communicative memory dealing with a contested past does not necessarily generate a view that is more than one narrative among others. Looking through the many publications on the Cultural Revolution I have so far been unable to find a single one that surpasses the perspective of its author and the respective constituency he or she is writing for. Whether in memoirs or in essays trying to explain the Cultural Revolution in more theoretical terms, the fragmentation of Chinese society that surfaced during that period is reproduced by the fragmentation of communicative memory today. Authors from the rebel factions still give explanations for their own behaviour rather then trying to understand the other side of the struggle[49]; memoirs of old cadres

45. On imposing silence and amnesia see Luisa Passerini, "Memories between silence and oblivion," in Katharine Hodgkin and Susannah Radstone (eds.), *The Politics of Memory* (London: Routledge, 2003), pp. 238–254; and as a discussion in the context of PRC history, Susanne Weigelin-Schwiedrzik, "Trauma and memory: the case of the great famine in the People's Republic of China (1959–1961)," *Historiography East and West*, Vol. 1, No.1 (2003), pp. 39–67.

46. Liu Xiaomeng, *Oral History of Sent-Down Chinese Youths*, pp. 15–21.

47. See n. 38.

48. For a recent example of public mourning and remembering see *Yanhuang chunqiu*, No. 11 (2005) with a choice of articles on Hu Yaobang.

49. As examples see Fang Su, "Wenge – yi chang honghong lieliede da geming" ("The Cultural Revolution: a grand and spectacular great revolution"), *Huaxia wenzhai zengkan*, No. 84 (1996), http://www.cnd.org/CR/ZK96/zk84.hz8.html#1 (last seen 17 June 2006); Zheng Yi, "Jin yi ci wen jinian wenhua da geming zhong suoyou junanzhe" ("Only to commemorate with this text all those who were in fear of trouble during the Great Cultural Revolution"), *Huaxia wenzhai zengkan*, No. 83 (1996), http://www.cnd.org/CR/ZK96/zk83.hz8.html#2 (last seen 17 June 2006). For a new development in this field combined with the explicit hope to overcome fragmentation see Wang Xizhe, "The ten forms of criticism of the Cultural Revolution."

targeted during the Cultural Revolution, even though more inclined toward reconciliation, still reflect the enormous generation gap that had become apparent[50]; prominent intellectuals often refrain from voicing their remembrances and leave it to their sons, daughters or disciples to write their stories of disillusionment, anger and despair.[51] The more individual the account, the more it reveals how the complicity complex makes coping with the experience of the Cultural Revolution so difficult.

The only solution all authors come up with (and which surpasses the fragmentation) is to focus on the role of Mao Zedong and implicitly repel the CCP leadership's idea of continuity with the Maoist era.[52] No matter what the Party resolution says, recent discussions reveal how complicity is re-interpreted into victimization. By now, everybody is Mao's victim, no matter whether beaten, thrown into prison, criticized or re-educated, no matter whether once an ardent supporter, a fellow-traveller or an observer.[53] Everybody is assumed to have gone through an initial phase of admiring Mao and his idea of launching a Cultural Revolution followed by disillusionment as a common experience related to the second phase. Through the experience of disillusionment even those who were not victimized in the literal sense can be regarded as deceived, if not trapped, by Mao Zedong. They are victims of their own idealism and hope that would never have arisen if not ignited by Mao Zedong. This pattern of hope and disillusion can be found in all the different genres of publications on the Cultural Revolution. Feng Jicai's (冯骥才) *Ten Years in the Lives of 100 People*[54] abounds with this kind of narrative. Even official Party history accounts cannot do without it, and internet publications which speak in favour of a more positive assessment of

50. For examples see Wu Guang, *Bu shi meng – dui "wenge" niandai de huiyi* (*This was Not a Dream – Memories of the Times of the "Cultural Revolution"*) (Beijing: Zhonggong dangshi chubanshe, 2000); Ma Shitu, *Cangsang shinian* (*Ten years of Vicissitudes*) (Beijing: Zhonggong dangshi chubanshe, 1999).

51. For a most prominent example, see Zhou Ming, "Lishi zai zheli chensi, 1966–1976 nian jishi" ("This is where history is reflecting upon, a report on the years 1966–1976"), Vols. 1–6 (Beijing: Huaxia chubanshe, 1986).

52. This is true for all the publications mentioned in nn. 49 and 50, and especially clear in Xi Dong, "'Liangge wenge' haishi yi ge wenge?" ("'Two Cultural Revolutions' or one Cultural Revolution?") *Huaxia wenzhai zengkan*, No. 83 (1996), http://www.cwrank.com/NewRank/show.php?id=49 (last seen 22 January 2005); as examples of official Party historiography see also Jin Chunming, "*Wenhua da geming*" *shigao* (*Outline of the History of the "Great Cultural Revolution"*) (Chengdu: Sichuan renmin chubanshe, 1995); on the question of victimization see Edward Friedman, "Modernity's bourgeoisie: victim or victimizer?" *China Information*, Vol. 11, Nos. 2–3 (1996), pp. 89–98. For a recent intervention see the report on Wang Li's letter to the Central Committee as cited in n. 30.

53. On the question of empathy for those who died during the Cultural Revolution, see Wang Youqin, *Wenge shounanzhe* (*The Victims of the Cultural Revolution*) (Hong Kong: Kaifang zazhi chubanshe, 2004); Susanne Weigelin-Schwiedrzik (Wei Gelin), "Ruhe miandui wenhua geming de lishi" ("How to face the history of the Cultural Revolution"), *Ershiyi shiji*, No. 93 (2006), pp. 12–18.

54. Feng Jicai , *Yi bai ge ren de shi nian* (*Ten Years in the Life of 100 People*) (Changchun: Shidai wenyi chubanshe, 2001).

the Cultural Revolution reiterate the idea that it was Mao who destroyed it when he turned against his own intentions and all those who had supported him.[55] Arif Dirlik speaks of Mao's turnaround as the trauma of the Cultural Revolution.[56] Is this form of looking at Chinese society as the victim of Mao Zedong's policies and theories the guiding principle which a future master narrative of 20th-century Chinese history could build on?

The Memory of the Cultural Revolution in Comparative Perspective

Alexander and Margarete Mitscherlich who analysed the situation in post-war Germany observed that fragmentation and self-victimization were common traits of memory after the Second World War.[57] They explained this phenomenon by the experience of having lost the supreme leader in a situation of defeat and chaos. While admiration of the supreme leader had bestowed people with a level of self esteem they could never have reached by relying on their own strength, the loss of this figure caused a sudden loss of self esteem for every individual involved. Communicating memories in such a situation serves the purpose of re-establishing self esteem which means that the aspects of the past selected for public communication are those that have the potential to gain respect from relevant peer groups. The peer groups that form under these circumstances are survivor groups with membership based on a common experience: soldiers of the same army unit, refugees from the same place, people from the same city. As long as communicative memory is confined to exchanging memories among insiders it cannot overcome fragmentation and generate a narrative that is accepted beyond the limits of the peer group.

Self-victimization is explained by the Mitscherlichs as an emergency measure to avoid melancholia. In a situation where the state is in chaos, people have to rely on their own strength for their survival. If they focus on trying to find an explanation for their behaviour in the past they will be impeded in developing the necessary survival strategies. The tendency to shy away from personal responsibility is morally unacceptable, yet it is socially legitimated when it comes to matters of life and death. However, as people live in a situation of depravation, they look upon themselves as victims of the present. And the more they are victims of the present, the more they project this experience on to the past and thus solve the problem of personal responsibility and guilt. In the German context of post-war chaos, the defeat and the loss of the supreme leader served as legitimation for

55. See n. 52.
56. Arif Dirlik, "The politics of the Cultural Revolution in historical perspective," in Kam-yee Law (ed.), *The Chinese Cultural Revolution Reconsidered. Beyond Purge and Holocaust* (Basingstoke: Palgrave Macmillan, 2003), pp. 158–183.
57. Alexander Mitscherlich and Margarete Mitscherlich, *The Inability to Mourn. Principals of Collective Behaviour* (New York: Grove Press, 1975).

universal self-victimization. Whoever ran against this tide was met with disgust and isolation.

The third characteristic the Mitscherlichs spotted when analysing Germany's post-war situation is the enormous drive people developed in building their own future. While often criticized as a materialistic denial of moral standards, it seems to be a much more complicated phenomenon. It is not only a form of getting rid of memories related to the incriminating past, but also an indirect form of "practical self criticism." By rebuilding their country with as much success as possible people admitted that the illusions which had driven the whole country into a devastating war had to be replaced by a reality of which everyone could be proud. The disillusionment people went through opened the door for a matter-of-fact attitude towards themselves which, in combination with their striving for excellence, triggered the enormous creativity which has been the basis of the post-war economic boom in Germany.

As noted above, nearly all accounts of the Cultural Revolution written in mainland China – both official and unofficial histories – are structured by initial adoration of and confidence in the supreme leader and a second phase of deep disappointment and disillusionment. Even when it comes to evaluating the Cultural Revolution strategy with its advantages and disadvantages for China, dissidents and official Party historians alike stress that the initial hope was not only disappointed by the development of events, but especially by the unexpected and to this day unexplainable turns Mao took in the course of the events.[58] The loss of the supreme leader had already taken place before Mao died when he turned against his ardent supporters: no wonder that all three characteristics of the German post-war situation can be traced in China as well. There is the tendency to shy away from publicly reflecting on the past, the fragmentation of memories in survivor groups, and the orientation towards the present and the future including a turn away from illusions or visions towards the reality of present-day life and economic success.

The main differences relate to the important fact that intellectuals were among the major targets of the Cultural Revolution, that survivors among the victims had to live side by side with their persecutors after the nightmare was over, and that the post-Cultural Revolution generation has so far not demanded to establish a master narrative surpassing fragmentized memories. All these factors can help in the search for an explanation of why the master narrative on

---

58. See nn. 49 and 52. For a most astonishing assessment of the Red Guard movement which is also shaped by this pattern, see as a publication from the realm of official historiography, Yin Hongbiao, "Hongweibing yundong pingshu" ("An evaluation of the Red Guard movement"), in Zhang Hua and Su Caiqing (eds.), *Huishou "wenge"* (*A Look Back on the "Cultural Revolution"*), 2 vols. (Beijing: Zhonggong dangshi chubanshe 1999), pp. 694–730.

the Cultural Revolution has not yet evolved from public or semi-public debate.

For memories to be communicated publicly, survivor groups need the attention of intellectuals who take over the task of articulating memories on behalf of those who do not have access to the public sphere.[59] Only those survivor groups which attract intellectuals enter the contest of interpretations as carrier groups. They access the public sphere with their view on the past claiming that their interpretation be accepted not only by the majority of survivors, but especially by those generations that were born after the event. This is how fragmentation can eventually be overcome. In Germany, the allied forces were not able to impose their interpretation of Nazi Germany on to the public. The post-war generation of intellectuals was needed to make this interpretation acceptable as the master narrative evolving from the debate of the 1960s.[60]

The fact that intellectuals were among the main targets of the Cultural Revolution explains that compared to other events in 20th-century Chinese history the Cultural Revolution attracts a lot of attention. However, this does not mean that interpretations surpassing the perspective of the survivor groups generate more easily. The memories of the intellectuals are themselves fragmentized according to their different experiences during the Cultural Revolution.[61] They form survivor groups according to the Red Guard faction they belonged to, or according to the city in which they lived during the Cultural Revolution. If their memories of the early phase are not vivid enough, they go back to their experience as sent-down youth (*zhishi qingnian* 知识青年) and form survivor groups along the lines of the villages they were sent to.[62] As intellectuals, they have direct access to the public sphere and do not need support from outside to communicate their memories publicly. Thus fragmentation and contestation are not as clearly separated as seems to have been the case in Germany. The survivor group is a carrier group *per se*, and communicating memories is not only related to recovering self esteem but also to gaining social status as a group.

---

59. See Passerini, "Memories between silence and oblivion." For the idea of carrier group see Ron Eyerman, *Cultural Trauma. Slavery, and the Formation of African American Identity* (Cambridge: Cambridge University Press, 2001).

60. For an overview over the debate see Peter Jürgen, *Der Historikerstreit und die Suche nach einer nationalen Identität der achtziger Jahre* (Frankfurt/Main:Lang, 1995).

61. A very interesting example in this context is the reaction in the internet to Wang Youqin's publication on teachers who were beaten to death during the Cultural Revolution (*The Victims of the Cultural Revolution*); for a reaction that falls into the pattern of fragmentation see Liu Guokai, "Ping Hong Zhisheng 85% lun bing zai zhi Wang Youqin, Hu Ping ji, Da Hanzi, Ban Suni" ("Commenting on Hong Zhisheng's theory of 85% and addressing again Wang Youqin, Hu Ping, Da Hanzi and Ban Suni"), www.haichuan.net/BBS_Data/1/600/1000/400/500385.asp (last seen 28 March 2005), and Wang Xizhe, "Huo gai! Shui yao ni ba xuesheng peiyangcheng lang. Wo dui Wang Youqin de yanjiu cunzai gaodu de baoliu" ("Well served! Who asked you to teach students to become wolves? I have my reserves about Wang Youqin's research"), www.haichuan.net/BBS_Data/1/600/1000/400/500385.asp, (last seen 28 March 2005).

62. Liu Xiaomeng, *Oral History of Sent-Down Youths.*

Intellectuals occupy such a prominent position in the debate on the Cultural Revolution that survivor groups of other social backgrounds hardly have any chance to communicate their memories in public. Thus quite a lot is known about intellectuals, Party cadres and students during the Cultural Revolution. A lot less is known about the so-called workers, peasants and soldiers. Their memories of the 1966 to 1976 period have not yet surfaced to the level of publicly communicated memory. They are restricted to internal exchange within survivor groups and have a hard time in finding intellectuals who support them in accessing the public sphere.

Fragmentized memory is a product of historical events that cannot be easily integrated into existing narratives of the past. However, it is also a survival strategy and in the Chinese case one of the means that made life after the event possible with people from different factions sitting side by side in one office. Fragmentation allows for memories to be exchanged without attracting public attention. Thus the realm of communicative memory established by survivor groups opens a window for voicing memories without political aims. These memories do not necessarily challenge the Party's interpretation or define an alternative frame for the explanation of the Cultural Revolution that could eventually be overwhelmingly accepted. They simply need to be articulated.

As long as memories are fragmentized and exchanged within survivor groups, they cannot transgress generational boundaries. The post-Cultural Revolution generation was kept uninformed about what had happened during the years 1966 to 1976, and Xu Youyu (徐友渔) as a member of the Red Guard generation blames not only the Party but also his friends and colleagues for this.[63] Only recently have there been signs of growing interest in finding out about what the older generation does not talk about in public. The 2006 "underground" symposium on the Cultural Revolution included young writers and intellectuals who were born in the 1970s and 1980s who voiced their criticism regarding the tendency towards universal victimhood combined with a lack of interest in public debate on the Cultural Revolution.[64] In comparison to the German situation, the post-Cultural Revolution generation lacks the outside support and incentive to demand their parents to face the past and bear witness to their share of the responsibility. China's post-1976 generation is interested in the present and the future, and in the outside world. Deng Xiaoping's appeal to look for money and head for the future is as welcome in Chinese society as it was in Germany in the aftermath of the Second World War. Student demonstrations in 1989 and 2005, however, show that consumerism can distract attention but not fill the

63. Xu Youyu, "Women gan bu gan zhimian lishi" ("Do we dare to face history?"), first published in *Qingnian baokan shijie* No. 4 (1995), see http://www.cnd.org/CR/ZK02 /cr131.hz8.html#3 (last seen 17 June 2006).
64. See n. 28.

void that the survivors of the Cultural Revolution transfer to the next generation by excluding them from their exchange of memories.

The master narrative on the Cultural Revolution cannot generate from society under these circumstances. Neither is the CCP capable of dominating the discourse with its version, nor has the public contest of different interpretations yet generated a dominant position. The fact that this situation has been pending for so long is the consequence of a communist party too weak to act as the generator of the master narrative and a society not strong enough (and perhaps also unused) to establish alternatives by itself.

Do We Need a Master Narrative on Post-1949 Chinese History?

To go back to Lyotard's idea of deconstructing the "master narrative of emancipation" and replacing it by multiple master narratives, the situation of historiography in the PRC as described above complies very much with what one would expect it to be like in a pluralistic society. Different interest groups compete with each other for resources in terms of symbolic and economic capital. The realm of communicative memory is active in the PRC, and divergent views of the past compete with each other with no view strong enough to exclude others. Compared to the years before 1976, China is going through a period of normalization and therefore has no master narrative authoritative enough to be imposed on or accepted by the people.

However, if the Cultural Revolution is focused on as one major event of post-1949 Chinese history, the question of whether or not a master narrative is necessary or welcome might find a different answer. As in the case of Germany trying to come to terms with its past, outside observers expect Chinese society to work through the trauma of the Cultural Revolution collectively. Recently, in the context of discussing Japan and the Second World War in China, the discussion on this question has become even more heated as Chinese intellectuals reminded the Chinese public of its inability to face the many unfortunate events of recent history, especially the Cultural Revolution. "Doing research on the Cultural Revolution is of enormous importance," says Xu Youyu, author of a book on the Red Guard movement[65] and professor at the Academy for Social Science in Beijing:

Compared to what the Germans did after the end of the Second World War in terms of self-questioning and repent, nearly all Chinese feel angry about the attitude of the Japanese because they refuse to take over responsibility and to seriously question themselves with regard to the violent occupation of the past. However we should ask ourselves: how hard have we been self-questioning what

---

65. Xu Youyu, *Xingxing sese de zaofan – Hongweibing jingshen sushi de xingcheng yanbian* (*All Kinds of Rebels – The Emergence and Development of the Spirit of Red Guards*) (Hong Kong, 1999).

we did during what we call the catastrophic Cultural Revolution? Most of the victims of the Cultural Revolution are still alive; the generation of enthusiastic participants and fanatical followers is now the backbone of Chinese society. But how many are able to explain what the Cultural Revolution was really about?[66]

If we compare the situation in the PRC today with the situation in Germany 60 years after the end of the Second World War, we tend to stress the differences. Many applaud the success Germany has achieved in coming to terms with its own past while criticizing China for keeping silent about the Cultural Revolution. However, if we compare the German situation 20 to 30 years after the Second World War with what we can observe in China today, there is a striking amount of similarity. Both societies have gone through a phase of turning away from public debate during which they concentrate on building a new future. Simultaneously, intellectuals start demanding a process of self-questioning and repentance. In Germany they were eventually supported, if not surpassed, by the post-war young generation asking for a collective act of taking over responsibility for what happened during the Third Reich. The outcome of this debate is Germany's official stand today. Germany has a master narrative on its past that is public and official, taught in schools and accepted by people and governments outside the country. It is supposed to prevent national-socialism from re-emerging in Germany.

If people ask for a master narrative of post-1949 Chinese history, that is what they want. Societies in South America and South Africa decided to go through an institutionalized process of reconciliation after experiencing extreme political turmoil, oppression and exclusion. The PRC government and the CCP decided not to organize a process of reconciliation after the end of the Cultural Revolution. That is why the survivors of the Cultural Revolution continue battling in their memories over the conflicts that had come to the surface during that period. By trying to oblige society into accepting the idea of universal complicity, the CCP hoped to avoid factionalism and revenge and to let time heal the wounds. But ongoing discussions show that the struggle over whose memory of the Cultural Revolution can dominate the overall assessment is gaining momentum. This struggle is not about respect, it is about power.

66. See Xu Youyu in Zhang Min, "Hong ba yue" de huiyi yu fansi (er zhi er)" ("Remembering and reassessing the 'Red August,' two out of two"), *Huaxia wenzhai zengkan*, No. 227 (2000), http://museums.cnd.org/CR/ZK00/zk227.hz8.html#1 (last seen 17 June 2006).

The China Quarterly and the History of the PRC

Roderick MacFarquhar

When I was appointed editor of the *CQ* in 1959, my vision was that it should focus primarily on all aspects of the People's Republic of China (PRC) and on Chinese Communist Party (CCP) history, but that there should also be occasional articles on contemporary Taiwan and the overseas Chinese. That autumn, I did a quick tour of a few American campuses to try to drum up contributors; basically I needed social scientists. But even those universities with significant China programmes were peopled mainly by historians who were not doing research on the PRC. Benjamin Schwartz at Harvard, who had already published *Chinese Communism and the Rise of Mao*, did write articles from time to time on the current scene; at MIT, Lucian Pye was ensuring that political scientists should incorporate East Asia into analyses of comparative politics; at Berkeley, Franz Schurmann (a Yuan historian in an earlier incarnation) was engaged in what became *Ideology and Organization in Communist China*, S.H. Chen was interested in contemporary mainland literature, and Choh-ming Li (like Alexander Eckstein at Michigan) was studying the economy; at Columbia, C. Martin Wilbur was working on the documents captured when the Soviet embassy in Beijing was raided in the 1920s, but Doak Barnett would not get there till the end of 1960; the only real nest of social scientists examining Chinese behaviour on a daily basis that I found on that trip was located at RAND: Allen Whiting, A.M. Halpern and Alice Langley Hsieh, all working on Chinese foreign relations. The shock of the launch of the first sputnik in 1957 had already led the US government to allocate massive funds to academia for the training of specialists on Russia and China, but the first beneficiaries of that largesse did not start coming out of the pipeline until the late 1960s. With so few potential contributors available, I stopped reviewing China books in case I offended any of them! But the scarcity of talent was also an advantage, for Western and Asian China watchers – diplomats in Beijing, journalists in Hong Kong, businessmen travelling in and out – all subscribed, making the *CQ* the house magazine of a growing community.

I exploited that community, perforce, and so the *CQ* had a much wider range of authors back then, coming not just from academia but also from journalism, think tanks, government, business and even the intelligence community. Donald Zagoria left the CIA to write his famous analysis of the Sino-Soviet dispute, but later the CIA allowed Philip Bridgham to publish under his own name his series of perceptive *CQ* articles on the Cultural Revolution. Partly because most authors could not get into China, the *CQ* published several articles about the PRC in relation to the outside world. And since the mildness or fervour of China's foreign policy tended to mirror the domestic scene, it was not a bad perspective. Considering the lack of information in the 1960s, I think that it was creditable that our authors, watching from afar, were broadly right in their analyses of what was going on in China. The *CQ* did not have the information to plumb the depths of the Great Leap famine though we did have a debate about it. Nor did it predict the coming of the Cultural Revolution, but then neither did Liu Shaoqi. Mao kept his cards close to his chest, not revealing skullduggery, probably to preserve his image for posterity.

There was one advantage of being able only to see the wood and not to get in among the trees. As contemporaries living through the events, *CQ* authors, day by day and as a matter of course, read in their newspapers what was going on in the world outside China. One had an immediate perception of the external environment within which Mao and his colleagues were operating. It was thus easier to understand Chinese actions and reactions, especially as one knew from a *CQ* article that, in addition to their own sources, the Chinese leadership had those same Western news reports translated for them in internal publications. One important example of the advantage of the contemporary perspective, though it occurred before the *CQ* was inaugurated, was the 1958 Taiwan Straits crisis. At the time, it seemed plain that China's shelling of Quemoy (Jinmen) and Matsu was a reaction to the Middle East crisis and the stationing of US and UK troops in the Lebanon and Jordan, but looked at from a later perspective it could be seen as part of an effort to arouse militancy in connection with the formation of the communes. After 40 years, the role of the Middle East crisis was finally confirmed in Wu Lengxi's *Shinian lunzhan* (1, p. 175). Today, when access to China is so much easier, and scholars can bury themselves for long periods in among the trees, in town or country, it may sometimes be more difficult to grasp any overall relationship between domestic and foreign developments. And yet with China so open to the outside world, there must be thousands of daily interactions, some of importance. This problem is mitigated, however, by the existence of China internet chat rooms through which scholars can derive differing perspectives and observations from all over the China-watching world.

Looking back over PRC history, one can see that the *CQ* first appeared on the cusp of a new leftist era, though it was not clear to me at the time. The first issue provided some of the older grandees of our field a chance to look back over the decade since "liberation." A common theme was the power and discipline of the Chinese party-state that had been set up. And even though the united front policies of the "hundred flowers" period had been abandoned in the Anti-Rightist Campaign, a united China at peace with the outside world looked a lot better than what had preceded it. Only Richard Walker, in *Chinese Communism: The First Five Years*, had chronicled in detail the harsh campaigns and purges which the CCP had used to assert its power. Mao turned left again in the summer of 1957, and crossed the Rubicon with his colleagues by purging Marshal Peng Dehuai and other Long March comrades in 1959 (the subject of a famous *CQ* article a few years later). After a breather to recover from the famine, Mao adjured his comrades-in-arms never to forget class struggle, and in 1963 launched the Socialist Education Movement. For the Chairman at least, it was then but a hop, skip and a jump to the Cultural Revolution, the triumph and the downfall of his utopianism, the alpha and omega of Maoism, the chasm between the old dream of a socialist China and the new hope of a modern China. All Mao's worst fears have come to pass. Fortunately today the *CQ* can call on dozens of scholars world-wide to chronicle and analyse the stunning transformations.

What has been lost in the reform era is an authoritative master narrative. The original communist master narrative is most easily accessible in the work of Hu Qiaomu, who, on Mao's instructions, laid it out in his brief *Thirty Years of the Communist Party of China: An Outline History*. The Chinese revolution had two origins: the need to fight against the imperialism which had transformed China into a semi-colony, a "most fundamental task of the Chinese revolution" from the Opium War onwards; and the need to overthrow "feudalism," because before and after the 1911–12 revolution various factions of feudal rulers refused to carry out any real social reforms. Many struggles against imperialism and feudalism had taken place in the 19th century – most significantly the Taiping rebellion – but they all ultimately failed because of the lack of correct leadership, for which a new class, the proletariat, had to emerge.

According to Hu, the proletariat – which had grown in strength as Chinese industry flourished during the First World War – first demonstrated its power in the May Fourth Movement and began to accept the influence of Marxism-Leninism. As a result, China's nationalist revolution became part of the world proletarian socialist revolution, and shortly thereafter the CCP was born. Writing soon after the communist victory in 1949, Hu asserted that the "establishment of the People's Republic of China was a glorious culmination of the struggles of the Chinese people over the past century against imperialism and feudalism and especially of their struggle in the previous 28 years under the leadership of the Chinese Communist Party." The Chinese revolution had now entered "a new stage." An outsider might note, though, that the Chinese had gone back to the future, erecting a state which again had a maximum leader and a loyal bureaucracy, whose right to rule was enshrined in a doctrine that embraced state and society.

While the Chinese under Mao had hitherto made their own revolution, in this "new stage" they were prepared to accept the path followed by the Soviet Union under Stalin as their model. "The Soviet Union's today is our tomorrow" was the watchword as they proceeded with their two major goals: transforming their country economically and socially. After a period of rapid economic recovery, the Chinese geared up for a command economy to be masterminded in a series of Five-Year Plans with the principal aim of establishing heavy industrial bases in various parts of the country. There was a tragic detour when Mao decided to abandon the Five-Year Plan system in favour of a bootstrap development model in the Great Leap Forward, but on the eve of the Cultural Revolution China was ready to restart the system with the new slogan of the "four modernizations."

In social transformation, the CCP outperformed its Soviet model. Within seven years of the revolution, China's peasants were all in collective farms and its industries and commerce were nationalized or under joint state-private ownership. And yet the country had managed to avoid the terrible disruption of agriculture that collectivization had brought about in the Soviet Union. Again, Mao went wrong in the Great Leap by amalgamating collectives into communes, but by 1965 the worst egalitarian excesses had been recouped and the countryside had recovered from the famine. Then came the chasm of the Cultural Revolution and the end of Hu Qiaomu's master narrative. Since 1978, China has been launched on a course which Hu could not have foreseen.

Looking back from the early 21st century over the period covered in Hu's brief history, it is possible to discern a different master narrative whose theme is the modernization of China and its incorporation into the global system. The familiar problems are still there even if one might use different terminology. China needed to be able to get rid of extraterritoriality and other imperialist encroach-ments on its sovereign territory; and in order to do that its traditionalist government had to make some hard decisions, which it failed to do for most of the 19th century. British and French aggression was insufficient to shake the mandarins out of their Confucian complacency. Reforms were necessary, but the slogan was "Chinese learning for the essence, Western learning for practical use."

The moment of truth came with defeat by Japan in 1894–95. The Confucian master narrative had depicted the Chinese as the creators of a civilization that embraced their known world, including Japan, Korea and northern Vietnam. But the Japanese victory revealed that, whatever these "younger brothers" owed to Chinese civilization, they had now transformed themselves into a Western-style nation state. They could no longer be seen as integral part of the Confucian world order. They were an "other." This was rubbed home in 1900 when Japanese troops marched as of right with Western troops to the relief of the Beijing legations during the Boxer uprising. The massive shock dealt by defeat by Japan resulted first in the abortive 100 days reform of 1898, and then, after the march on Beijing, the abandonment of Confucianism in 1905 as the basis of the Chinese education system. Perhaps finally China had begun its march to "wealth and power."

Yuan Shikai's prevention of Sun Yat-sen and his colleagues from establishing a viable democratic system after the 1911–12 revolution, the division of the country under the warlords, the Kuomintang's inability to proceed with nation-building as a result of Japanese aggression, all seemed to underline Hu's point that it was only with the creation of the PRC and the restoration of peace and unity, that the modernization of China could really begin. But Mao prevented it from happening, first with the Great Leap, but finally and decisively with the Cultural Revolution.

To gauge the extent of the shock the 1966–76 decade was to Deng Xiaoping and other leaders who survived it, one has to start by thinking about how the world looked in 1951 when Hu Qiaomu was writing his triumphal 30-year history of the CCP. Japan had received a crushing defeat after the devastation of two atomic bombs and the fire-bombing of its capital, and was only just about to recover its independence after the post-war American occupation. The whole of South Korea was in the process of being even more thoroughly devastated by struggle between the American-led UN armies and the forces of North Korea and the Chinese People's Volunteers. On Taiwan, Chiang Kai-shek was licking his wounds in his rural refuge. Singapore and Hong Kong were sleepy colonial entrepôts. In 1951, China's leaders had to be confident that they would once again show East Asia, perhaps all Asia, the way forward.

As late as the eve of the Cultural Revolution in 1965, Japan was independent, but its "miracle" was only just visible over the horizon; on Taiwan, Chiang Kai-shek had carried out the land reform that he had balked at on the mainland, but not much else seemed to have changed. South Korea was under military rule, Singapore was independent, Hong Kong was still Hong Kong, but there was nothing eye-catching in any of them. By 1978, East Asia was transformed, miracles of economic development everywhere. In 1978, the leaders who survived the Cultural Revolution should surely have felt the humiliation of knowing that they had allowed Mao to throw away the likelihood of China's leadership. And so the reform era began. Japan's achievement in becoming a world economic power was awe-inspiring; South Korea's neo-authoritarian nation-building was envied as was Singapore's social stability. Even the Kuomintang on Taiwan were an example to their mainland enemies of what Chinese could accomplish. China would now learn not lead: it did not matter what colour the cat was as long as it caught the mice. The master narrative of China's modernization thus seems to be that break-throughs are achieved only after massive shocks. The first shock led to the abandonment of the traditional Confucian system, the second to the shelving of Marxism-Leninism-Mao Zedong Thought. This poses a problem. Chinese regimes, traditional and communist, seem to need a doctrine to glue state and society together. Doubtless this is why Hu Jintao has had senior officials lead ideological refresher sessions in their units in the past year. "Marxist-Leninist learning for the essence, Western and East Asian learning for practical use"? This approach will not work any better for communists than it did for Confucians. The CCP leadership is clinging to a doctrine which combines a mid 19th-century analysis of the English industrial revolution with an early 20th-century covert action plan devised to take on a traditional autocracy. If 21st-century Chinese leaders in the information age do find ways to corral the internet it will not be by consulting Marx or Lenin.

The essence of modernity, even in most of East Asia today, is that the only glue that will bind state and society – as Sun Yat-sen grasped – is some form of democracy, which gives citizens the confidence of ownership of their state and gives politicians a mandate to lead it. The master narrative of China's march to modernity suggests that it will require another massive shock before there is a political transformation. Absent Deng Xiaoping, the student movement of 1989 might have been that shock. One can only hope that when the third shock comes it will be administered by equally peaceful demonstrations and not by foreign war or internal convulsion as in the past. It may be that at its 45th anniversary, the *CQ* is again on the cusp of a new era. If so, with the enormous scholarly resources now available in the China field, the Editor should be able to spot it and chronicle it better than I could all these years ago!

Index